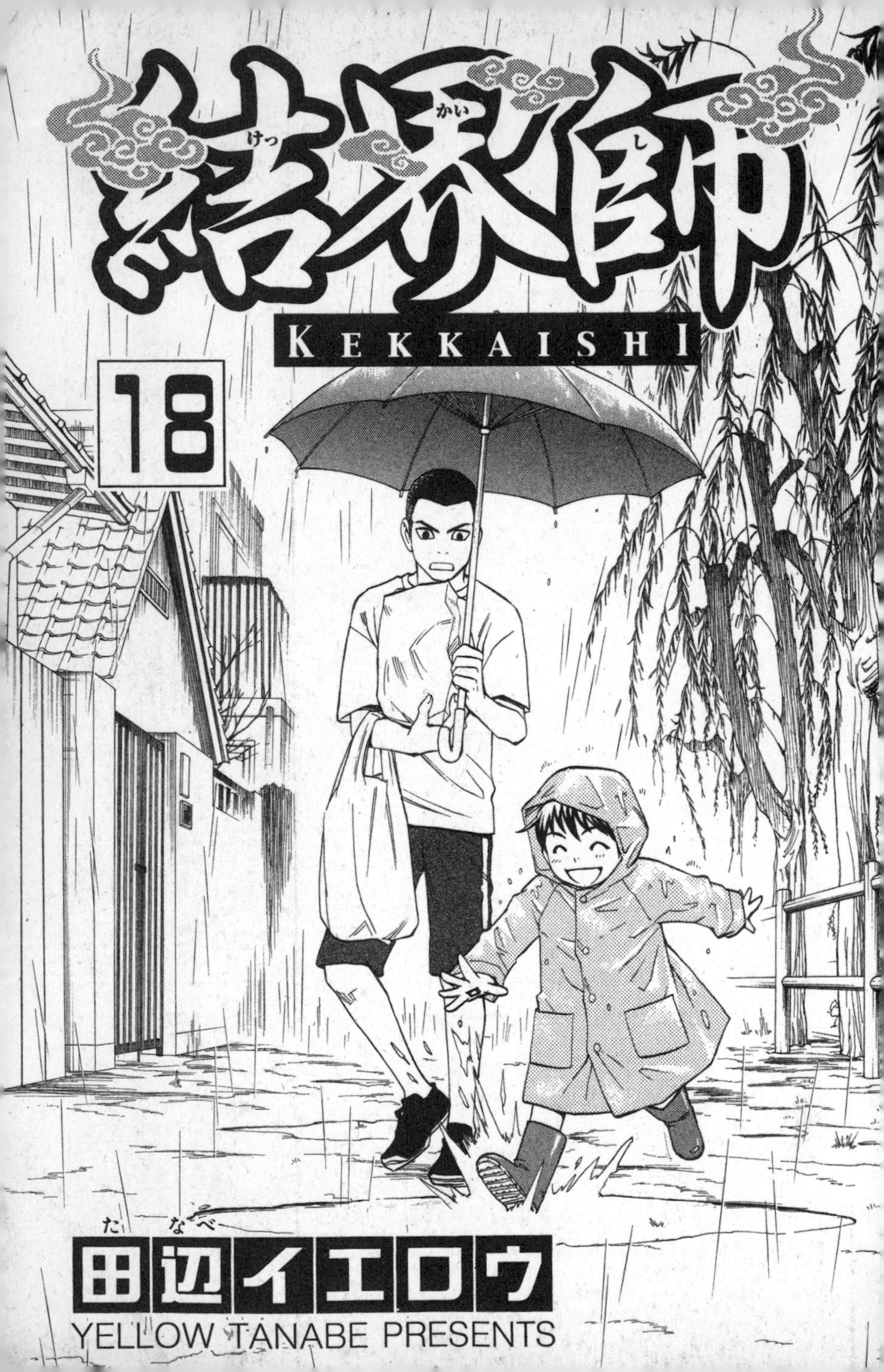
結界師
けっかいし
KEKKAISHI
18
田辺イエロウ
たなべ
YELLOW TANABE PRESENTS

THE STORY THUS FAR

Yoshimori Sumimura and Tokine Yukimura have an ancestral duty to protect the Karasumori Forest from supernatural beings called ayakashi. People with their gift for terminating ayakashi are called kekkaishi, or "barrier masters."

While helping Masamori, Yoshimori is drawn into a holy site where he encounters Mudo, the man Masamori is trying to attack.

Mudo has abandoned his humanity and become an ayakashi. Having absorbed incredible power from the guardian deity of the holy site, Mudo appears to be unbeatable even if Masamori and Yoshimori work together!

As the brothers face almost certain death, the deity Tan-yu marshals his last bit of strength to seal off his holy site and save their lives.

The holy site is sealed off, but Masamori is stranded inside the site alone with Mudo...

KEKKAISHI   VOL. 18
TABLE OF CONTENTS

Chapter 165: A Promise

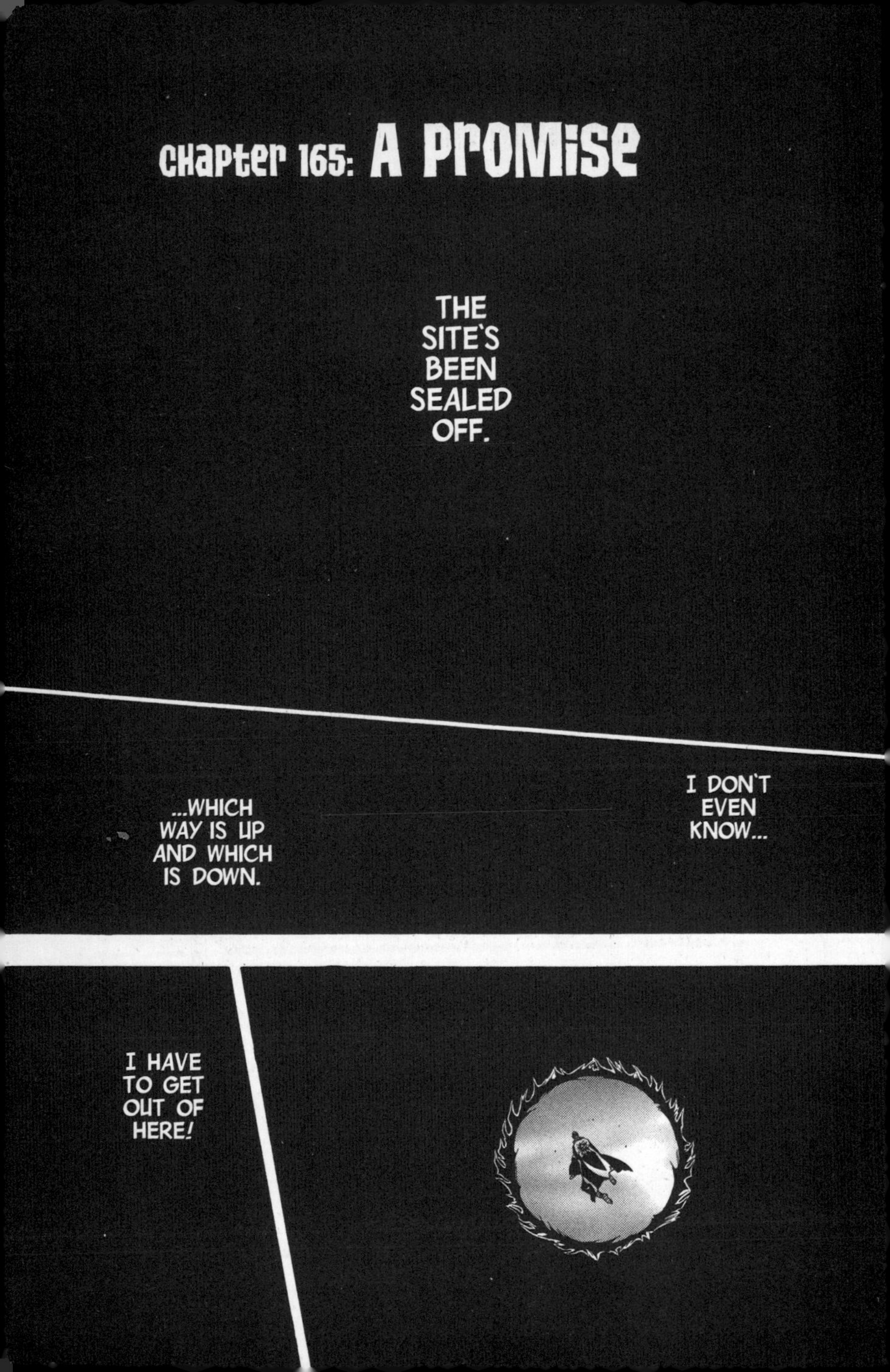
THE SITE'S BEEN SEALED OFF.
I DON'T EVEN KNOW...
...WHICH WAY IS UP AND WHICH IS DOWN.
I HAVE TO GET OUT OF HERE!

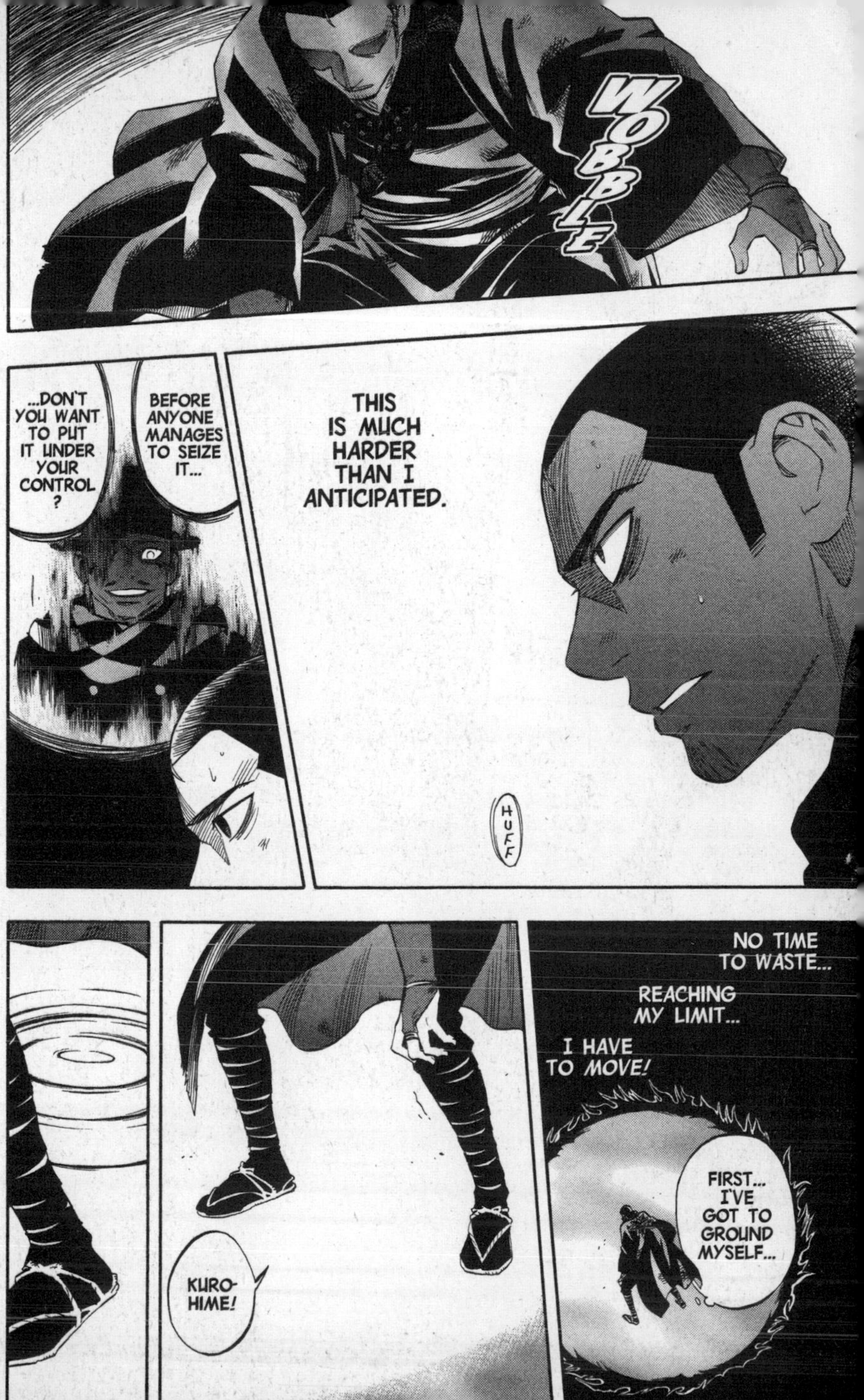
WOBBLE
THIS IS MUCH HARDER THAN I ANTICIPATED.
HUFF
BEFORE ANYONE MANAGES TO SEIZE IT...
...DON'T YOU WANT TO PUT IT UNDER YOUR CONTROL?
NO TIME TO WASTE...
REACHING MY LIMIT...
I HAVE TO *MOVE!*
FIRST... I'VE GOT TO GROUND MYSELF...
KURO-HIME!

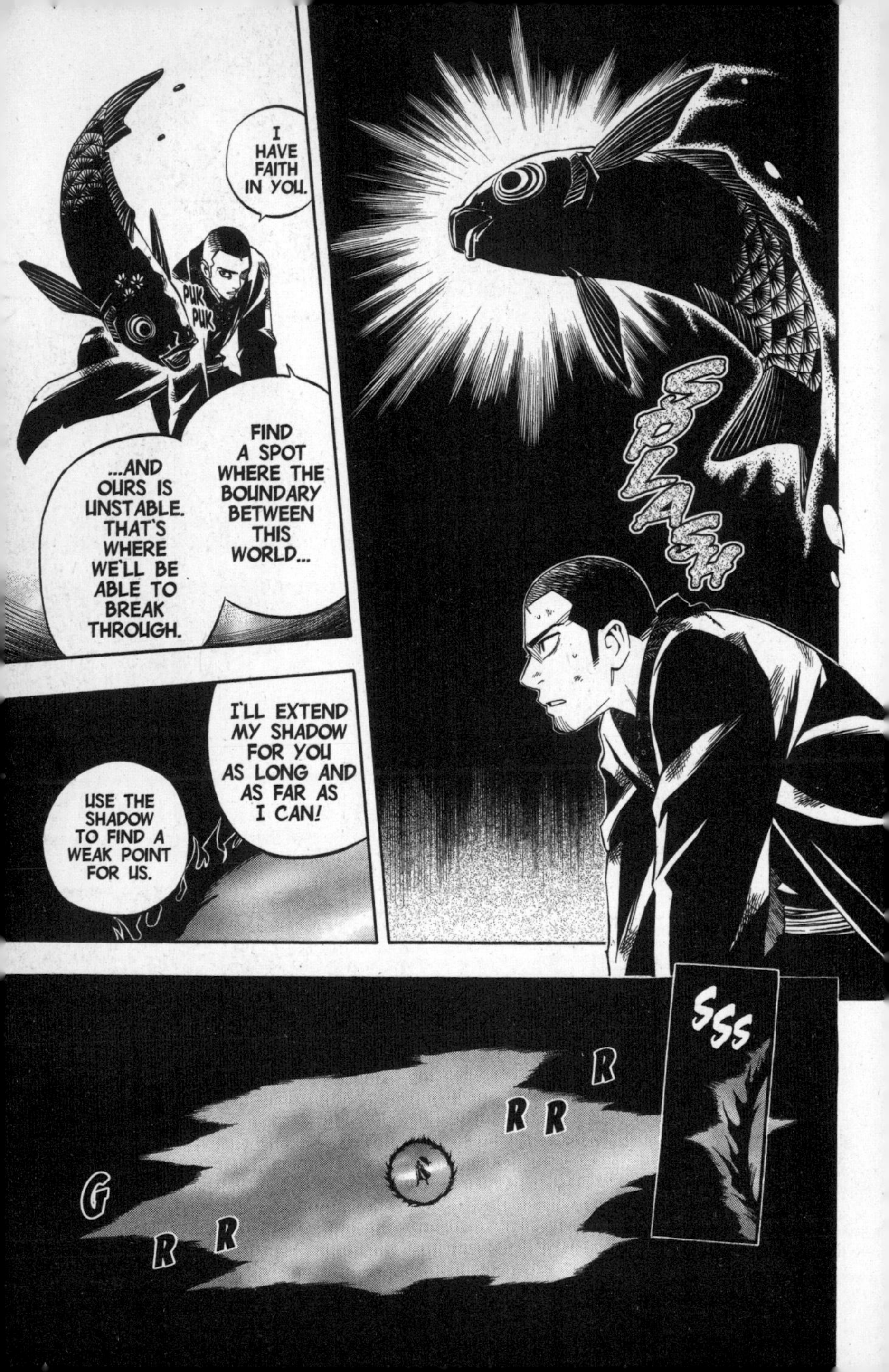
SPLASH
I HAVE FAITH IN YOU.
PUK PUK
FIND A SPOT WHERE THE BOUNDARY BETWEEN THIS WORLD...
...AND OURS IS UNSTABLE. THAT'S WHERE WE'LL BE ABLE TO BREAK THROUGH.
I'LL EXTEND MY SHADOW FOR YOU AS LONG AND AS FAR AS I CAN!
USE THE SHADOW TO FIND A WEAK POINT FOR US.
SSS
R R R
G R R

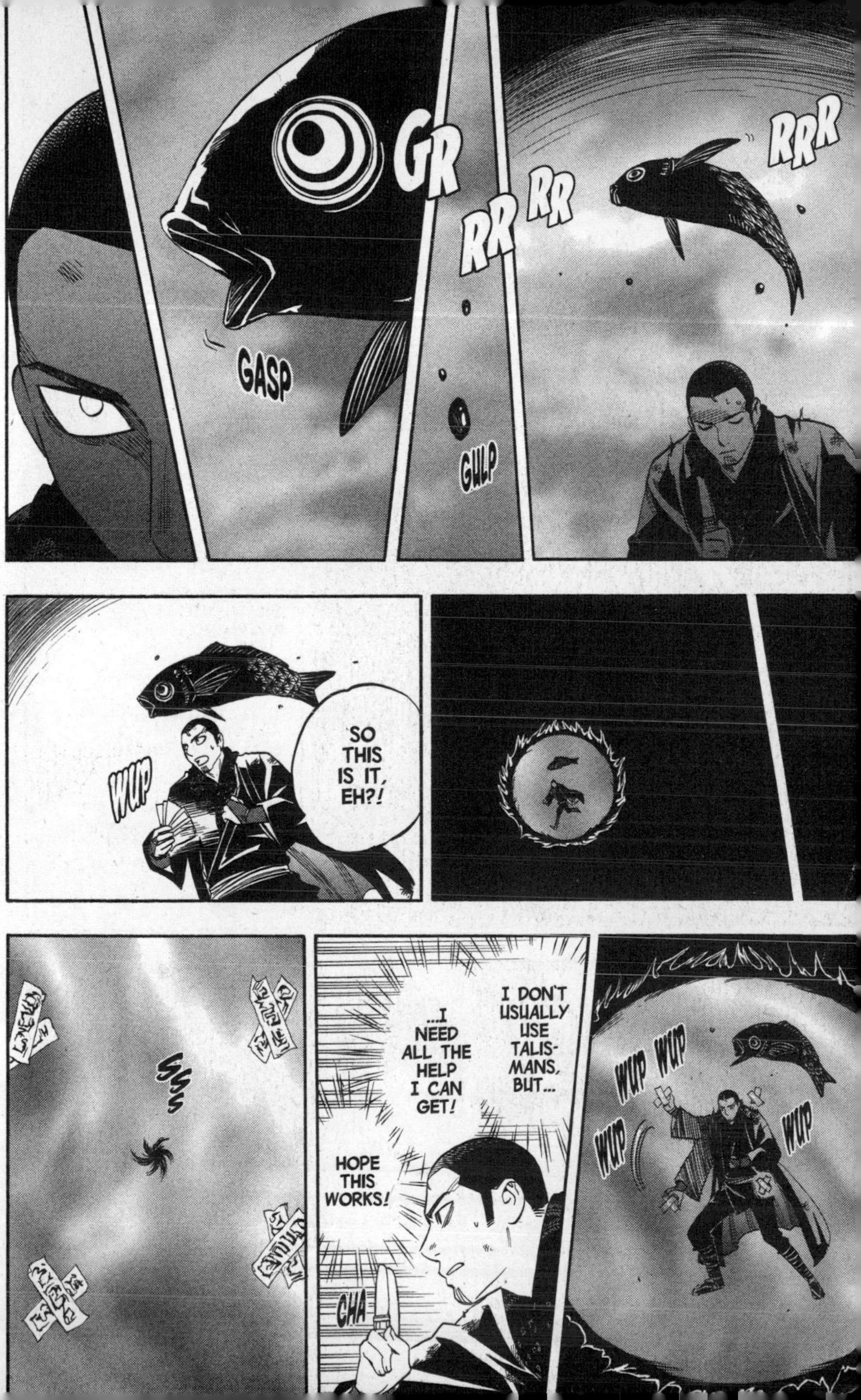
RRR
RR
RR
GULP
GR
GASP
SO THIS IS IT, EH?!
WUP
WUP WUP
WUP
WUP
I DON'T USUALLY USE TALIS-MANS, BUT...
...I NEED ALL THE HELP I CAN GET!
HOPE THIS WORKS!
CHA
SSS

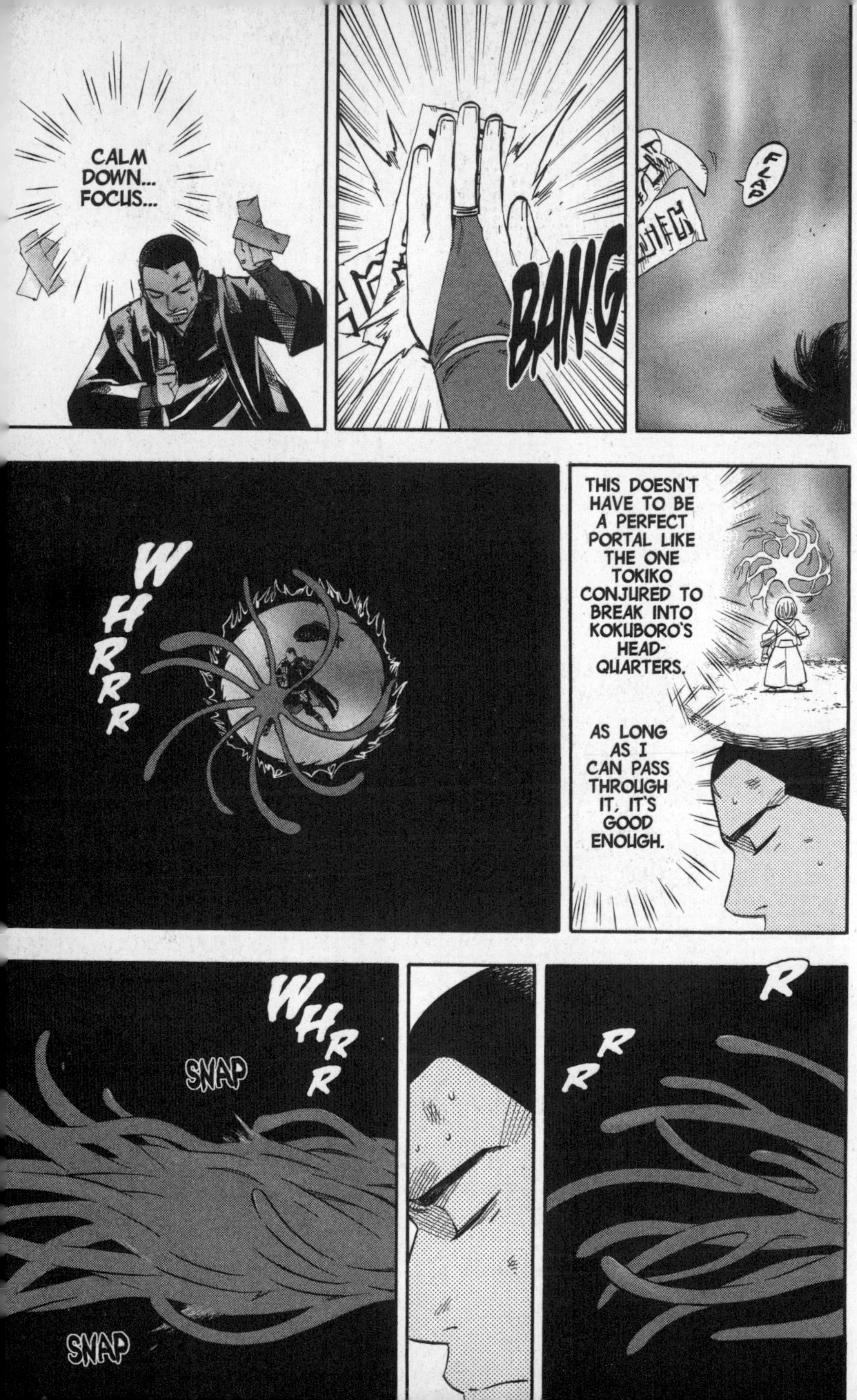
FLAP
BANG
CALM DOWN... FOCUS...
THIS DOESN'T HAVE TO BE A PERFECT PORTAL LIKE THE ONE TOKIKO CONJURED TO BREAK INTO KOKUBORO'S HEAD-QUARTERS.
AS LONG AS I CAN PASS THROUGH IT, IT'S GOOD ENOUGH.
WHRRR
RRR
WHRR
SNAP
SNAP

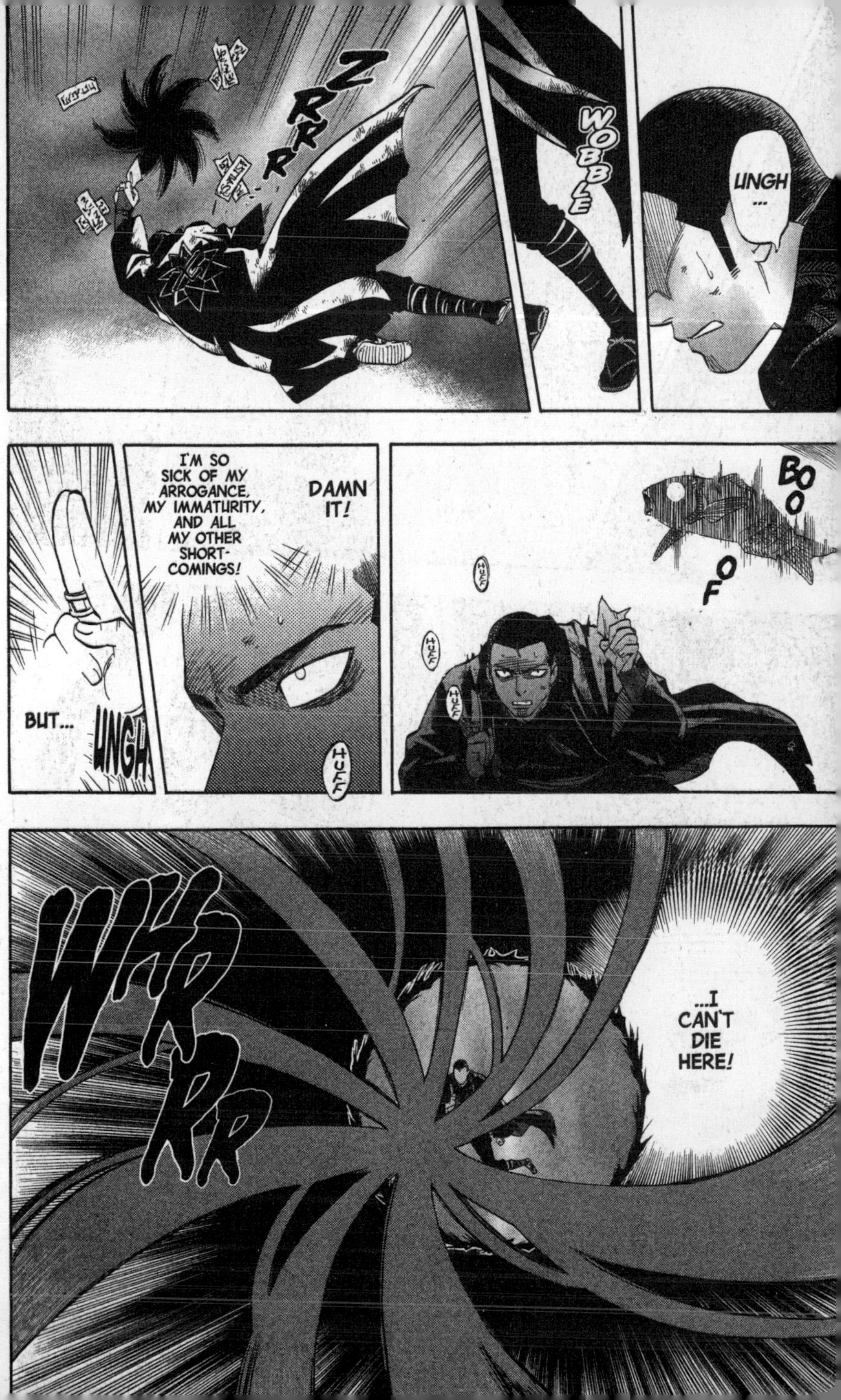
UNGH...
WOBBLE
ZRRR
BOOOOF
HUFF
HUFF
HUFF
DAMN IT!
I'M SO SICK OF MY ARROGANCE, MY IMMATURITY, AND ALL MY OTHER SHORT-COMINGS!
HUFF
UNGH
BUT...
...I CAN'T DIE HERE!
WHRRR

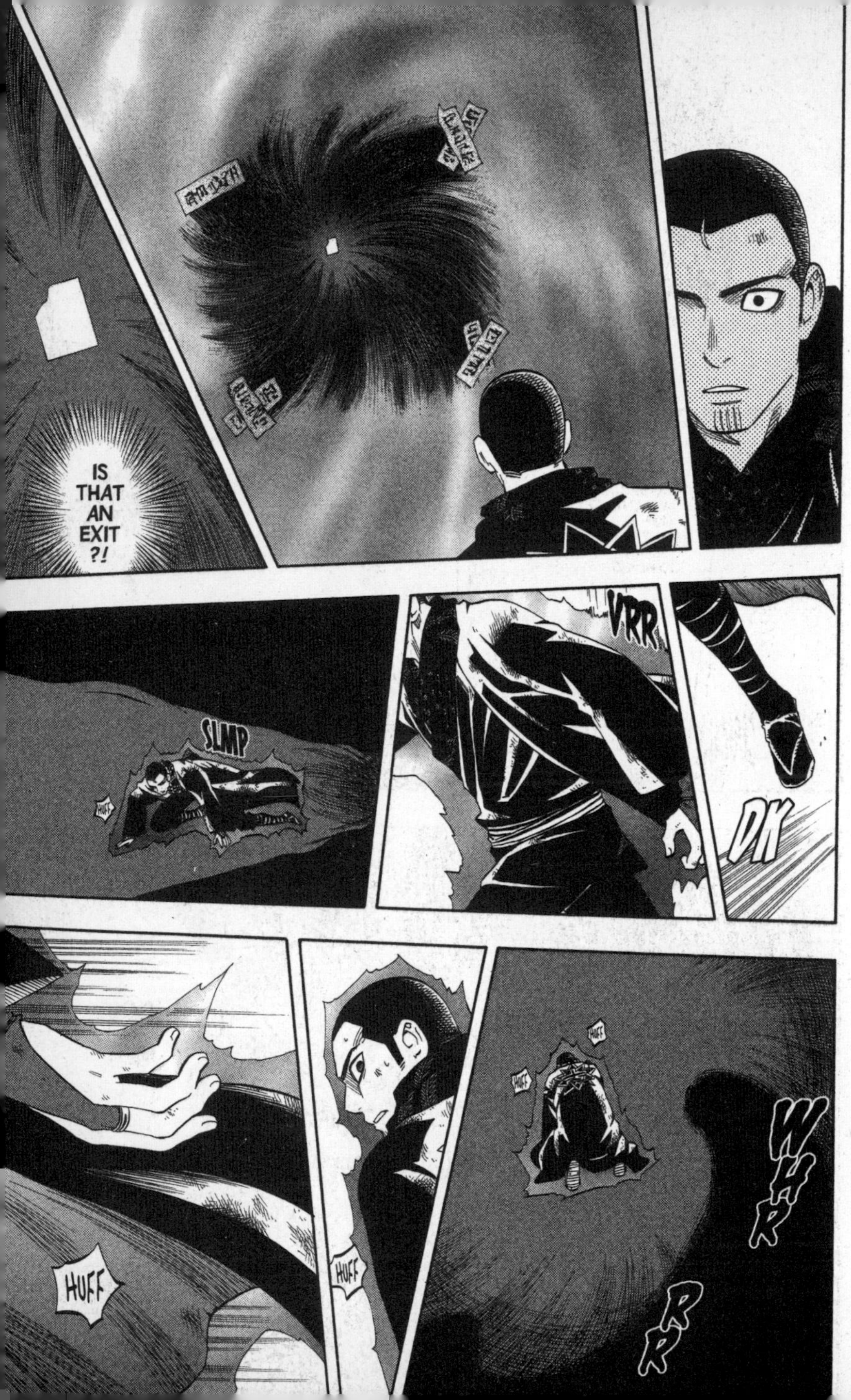
IS THAT AN EXIT ?!
DK
VRR
SLMP
HUFF
WHR
RRR
HUFF
HUFF
HUFF
HUFF

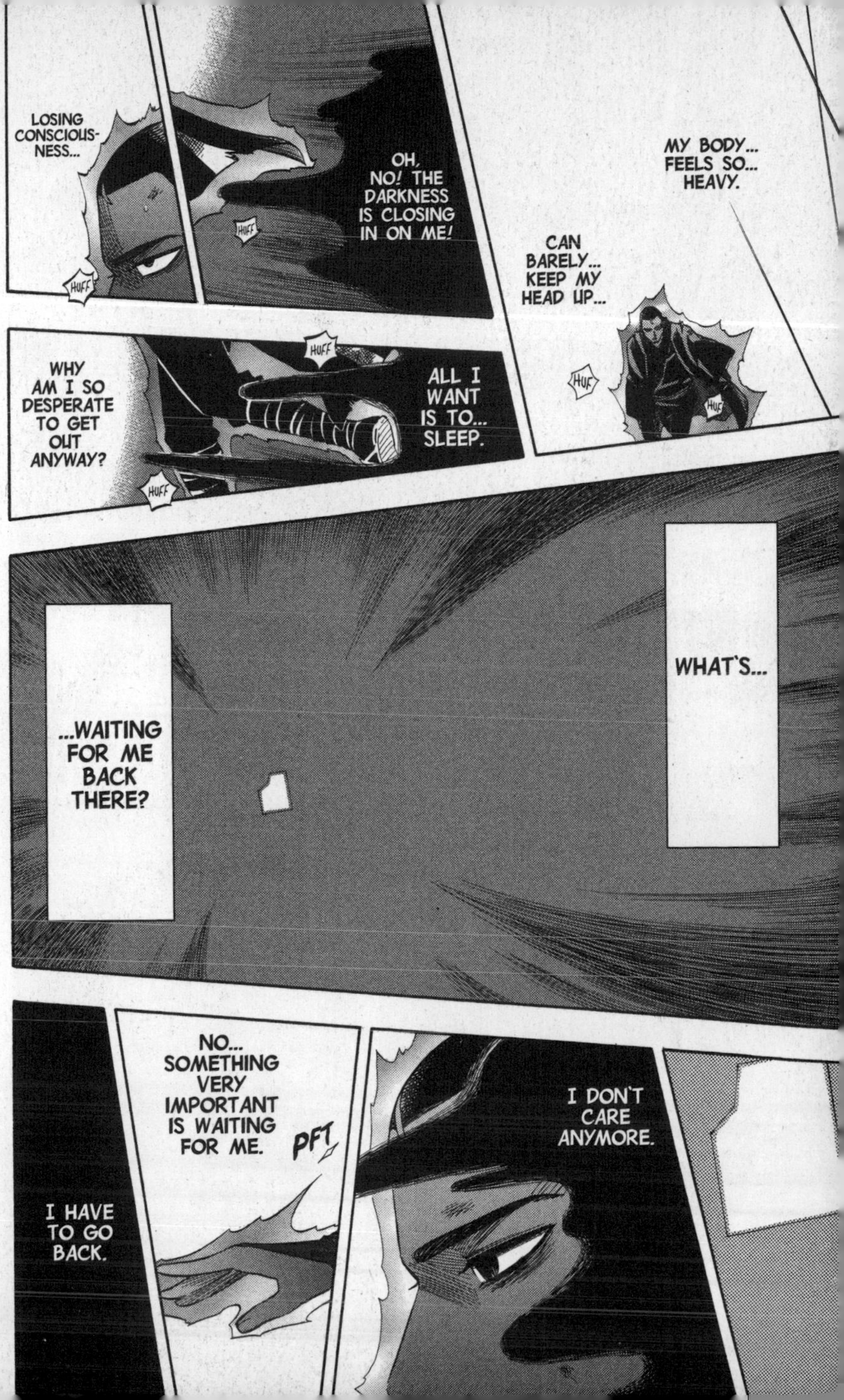
MY BODY... FEELS SO... HEAVY.
CAN BARELY... KEEP MY HEAD UP...
HUF
HUF
OH, NO! THE DARKNESS IS CLOSING IN ON ME!
HUFF
LOSING CONSCIOUS-NESS...
HUFF
HUFF
ALL I WANT IS TO... SLEEP.
WHY AM I SO DESPERATE TO GET OUT ANYWAY?
HUFF
WHAT'S...
...WAITING FOR ME BACK THERE?
I DON'T CARE ANYMORE.
PFT
NO... SOMETHING VERY IMPORTANT IS WAITING FOR ME.
I HAVE TO GO BACK.

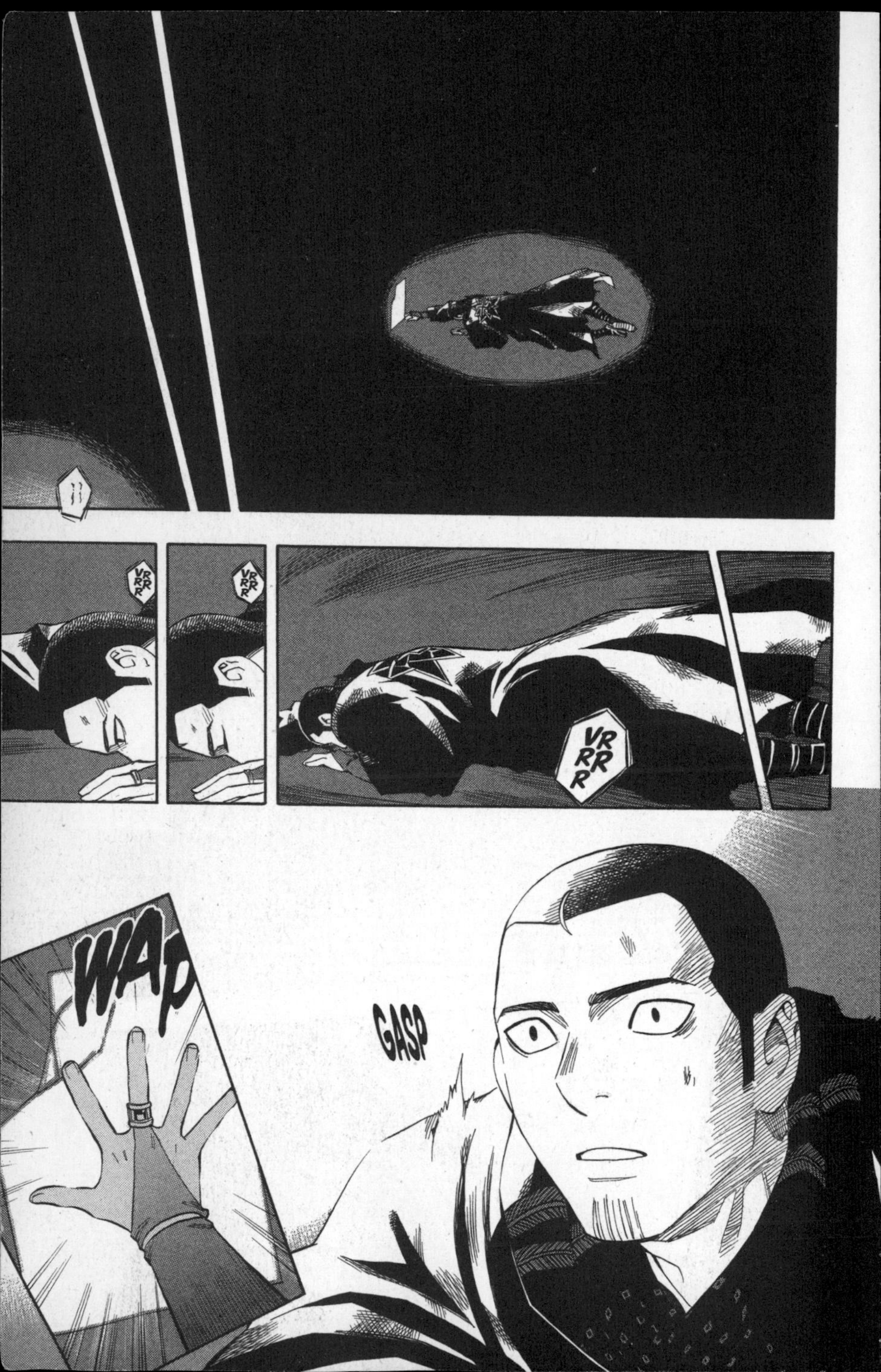
VRRR
VRRR
VRRR
GASP
WAP

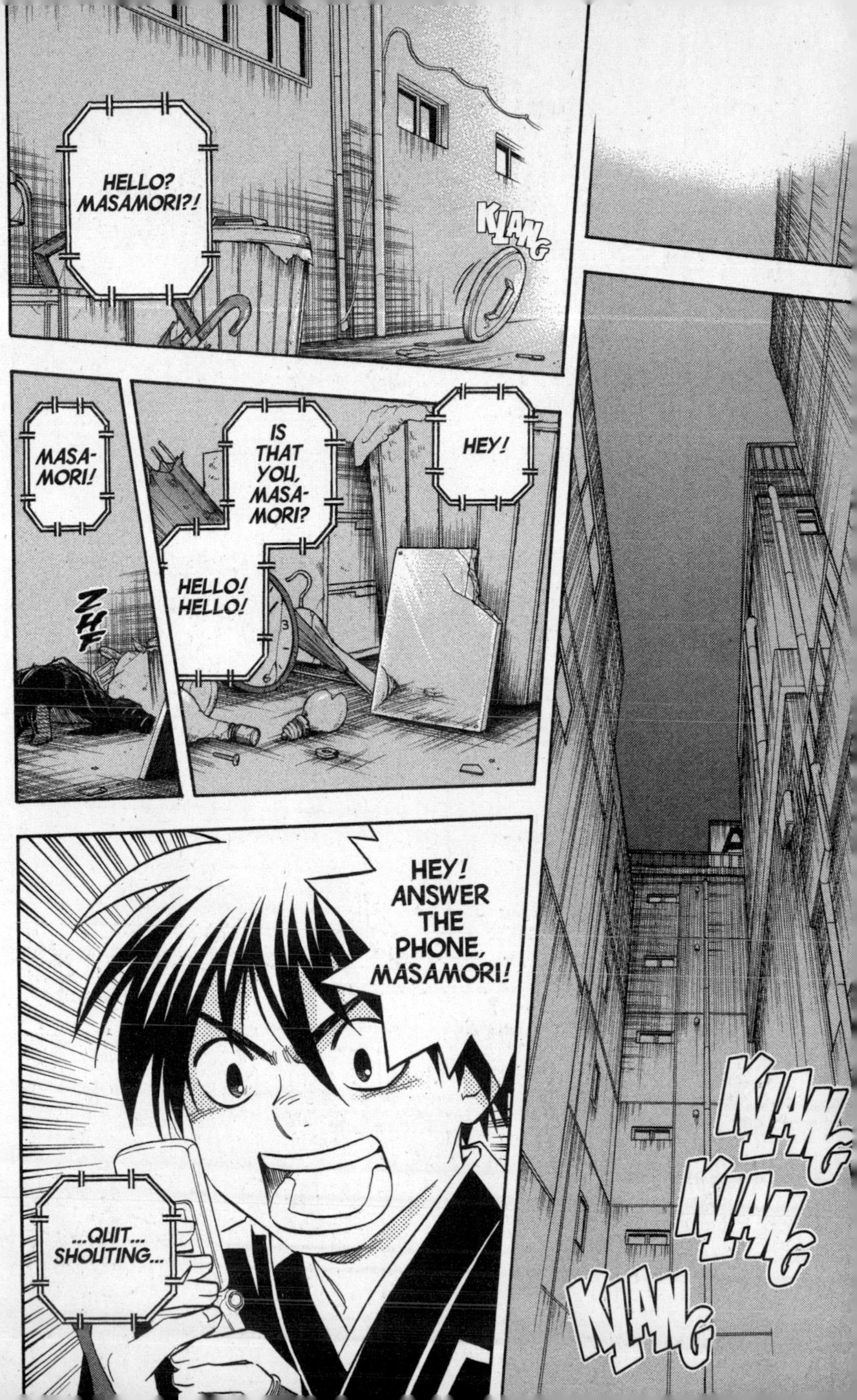
KLANG
HELLO? MASAMORI?!
HEY!
IS THAT YOU, MASA-MORI?
HELLO! HELLO!
MASA-MORI!
ZHF
HEY! ANSWER THE PHONE, MASAMORI!
...QUIT... SHOUTING...
KLANG
KLANG
KLANG

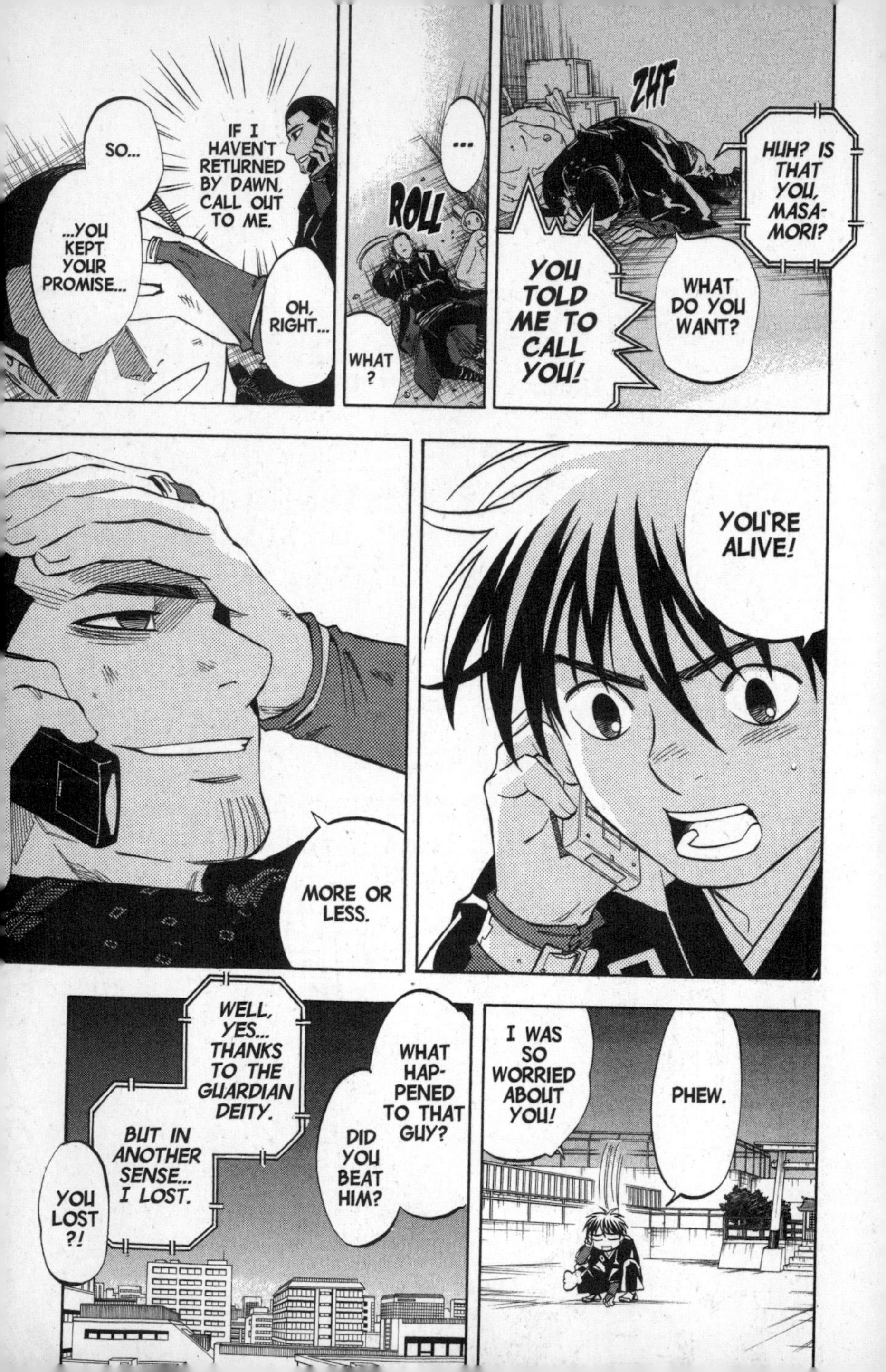
ZHF
HUH? IS THAT YOU, MASAMORI?
WHAT DO YOU WANT?
YOU TOLD ME TO CALL YOU!
...
ROLL
WHAT?
IF I HAVEN'T RETURNED BY DAWN, CALL OUT TO ME.
OH, RIGHT...
SO...
...YOU KEPT YOUR PROMISE...
YOU'RE ALIVE!
MORE OR LESS.
PHEW.
I WAS SO WORRIED ABOUT YOU!
WHAT HAPPENED TO THAT GUY?
DID YOU BEAT HIM?
WELL, YES... THANKS TO THE GUARDIAN DEITY.
BUT IN ANOTHER SENSE... I LOST.
YOU LOST?!

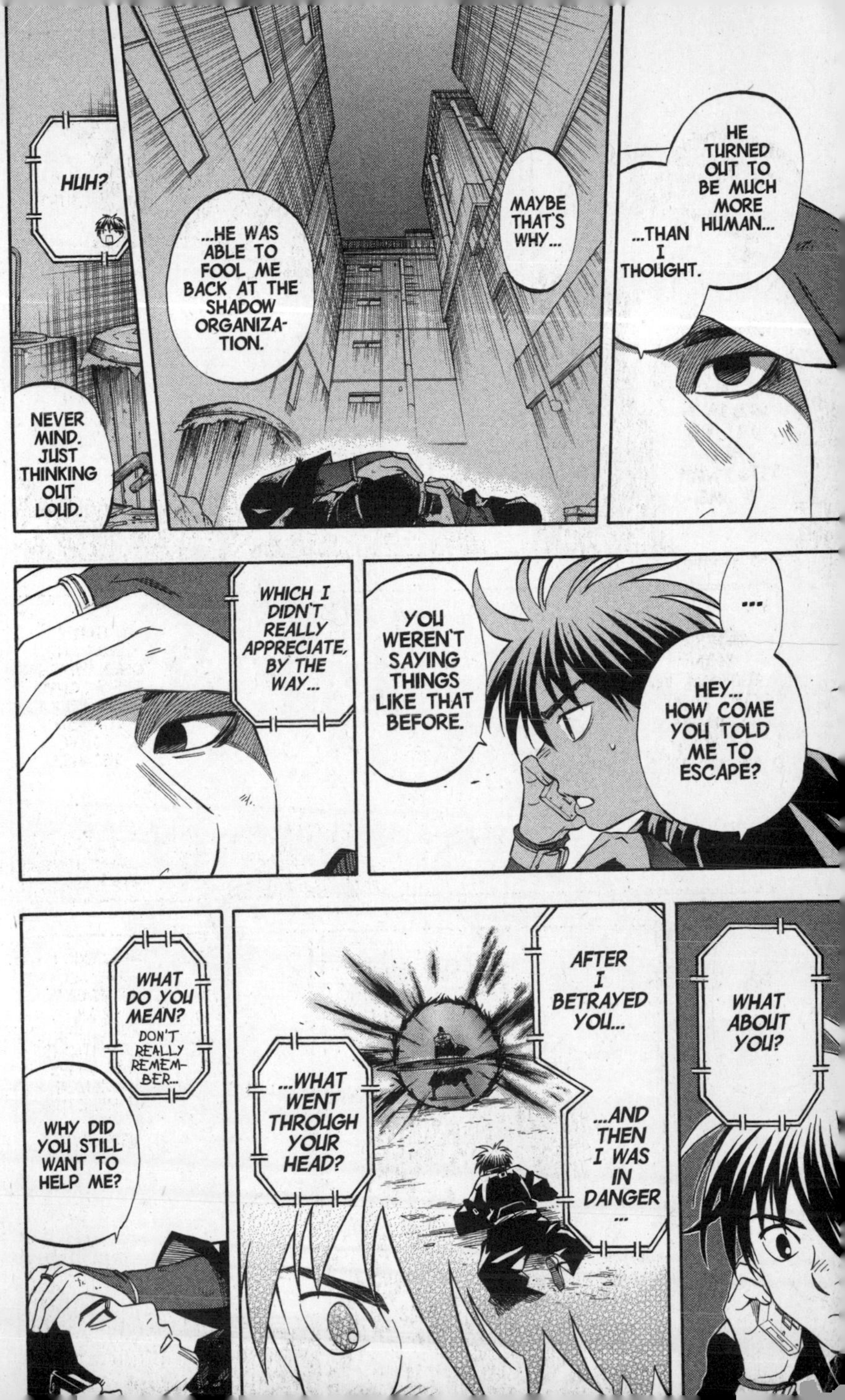
HE TURNED OUT TO BE MUCH MORE HUMAN...
...THAN I THOUGHT.
MAYBE THAT'S WHY...
...HE WAS ABLE TO FOOL ME BACK AT THE SHADOW ORGANIZATION.
HUH?
NEVER MIND. JUST THINKING OUT LOUD.
...
HEY... HOW COME YOU TOLD ME TO ESCAPE?
YOU WEREN'T SAYING THINGS LIKE THAT BEFORE.
WHICH I DIDN'T REALLY APPRECIATE, BY THE WAY...
WHAT ABOUT YOU?
AFTER I BETRAYED YOU...
...AND THEN I WAS IN DANGER...
...WHAT WENT THROUGH YOUR HEAD?
WHAT DO YOU MEAN?
DON'T REALLY REMEMBER...
WHY DID YOU STILL WANT TO HELP ME?

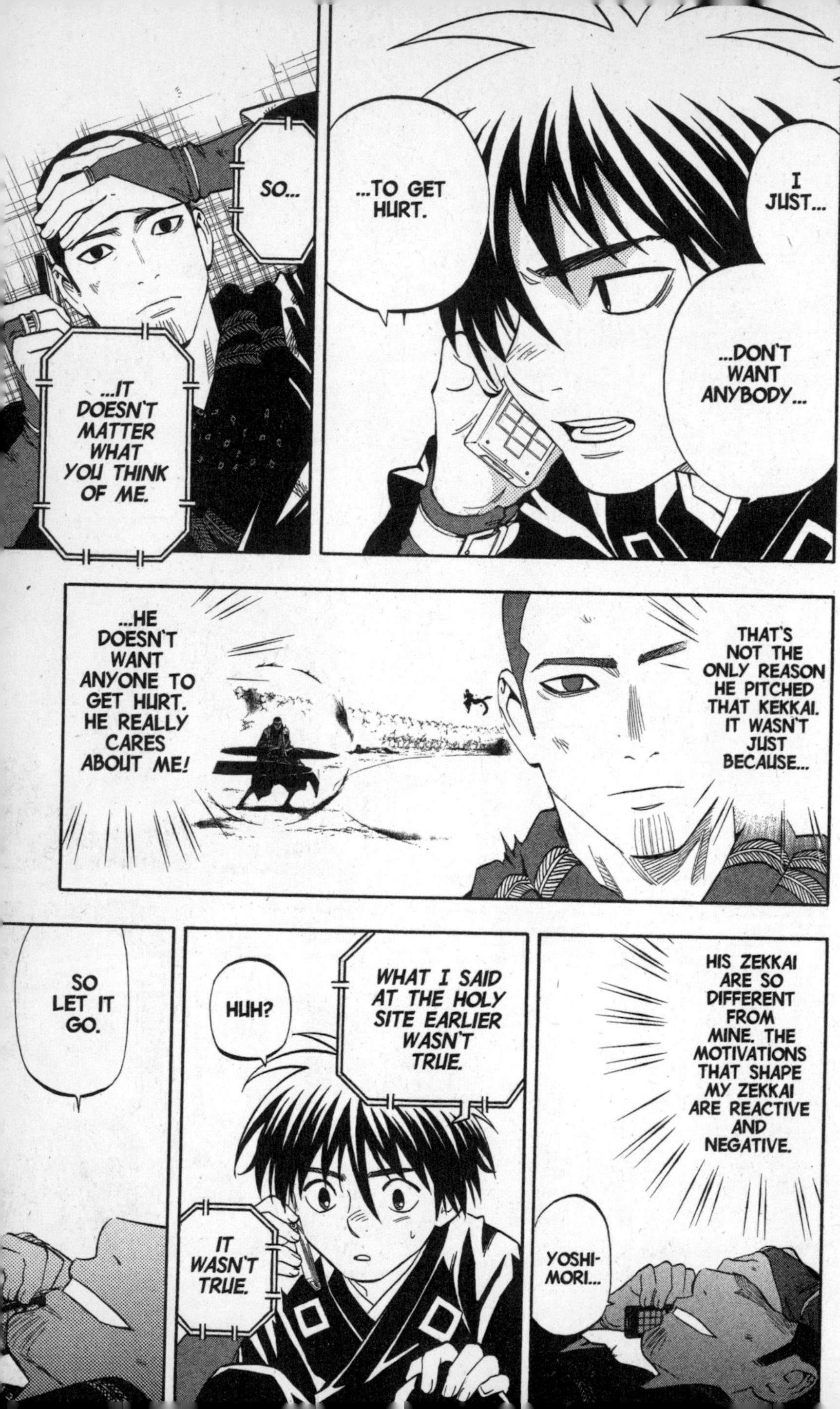
I JUST...
...DON'T WANT ANYBODY...
...TO GET HURT.
SO...
...IT DOESN'T MATTER WHAT YOU THINK OF ME.
THAT'S NOT THE ONLY REASON HE PITCHED THAT KEKKAI. IT WASN'T JUST BECAUSE...
...HE DOESN'T WANT ANYONE TO GET HURT. HE REALLY CARES ABOUT ME!
HIS ZEKKAI ARE SO DIFFERENT FROM MINE. THE MOTIVATIONS THAT SHAPE MY ZEKKAI ARE REACTIVE AND NEGATIVE.
YOSHI-MORI...
WHAT I SAID AT THE HOLY SITE EARLIER WASN'T TRUE.
HUH?
IT WASN'T TRUE.
SO LET IT GO.

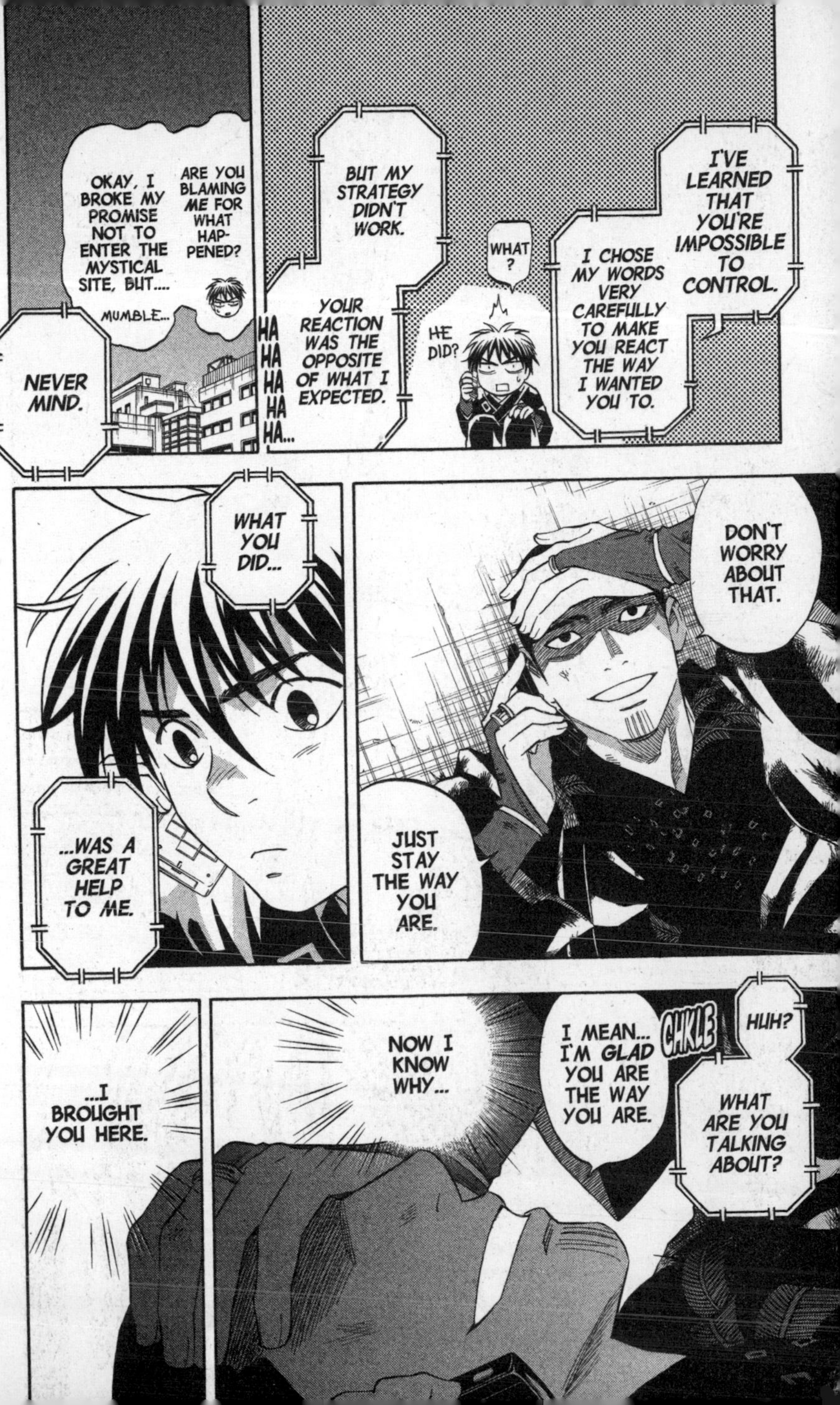
I'VE LEARNED THAT YOU'RE IMPOSSIBLE TO CONTROL.
I CHOSE MY WORDS VERY CAREFULLY TO MAKE YOU REACT THE WAY I WANTED YOU TO.
WHAT?
HE DID?
BUT MY STRATEGY DIDN'T WORK.
YOUR REACTION WAS THE OPPOSITE OF WHAT I EXPECTED.
HA HA HA HA HA HA...
ARE YOU BLAMING ME FOR WHAT HAP-PENED?
OKAY, I BROKE MY PROMISE NOT TO ENTER THE MYSTICAL SITE, BUT....
MUMBLE...
NEVER MIND.
DON'T WORRY ABOUT THAT.
JUST STAY THE WAY YOU ARE.
WHAT YOU DID...
...WAS A GREAT HELP TO ME.
HUH?
WHAT ARE YOU TALKING ABOUT?
CHKLE
I MEAN... I'M GLAD YOU ARE THE WAY YOU ARE.
NOW I KNOW WHY...
...I BROUGHT YOU HERE.

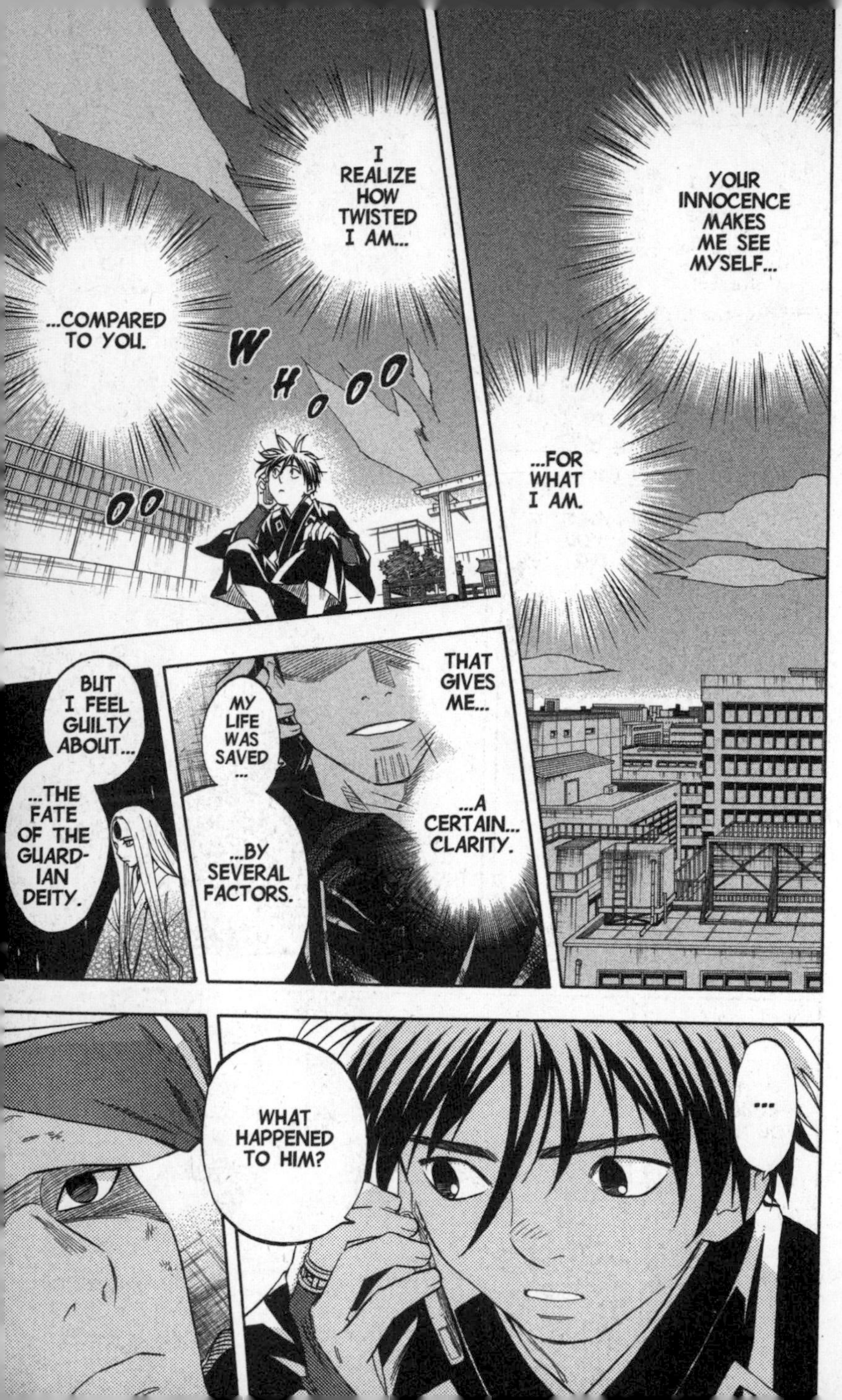
YOUR INNOCENCE MAKES ME SEE MYSELF...
...FOR WHAT I AM.
I REALIZE HOW TWISTED I AM...
...COMPARED TO YOU.
WHOOOOO
MY LIFE WAS SAVED...
...BY SEVERAL FACTORS.
THAT GIVES ME...
...A CERTAIN... CLARITY.
BUT I FEEL GUILTY ABOUT...
...THE FATE OF THE GUARDIAN DEITY.
...
WHAT HAPPENED TO HIM?

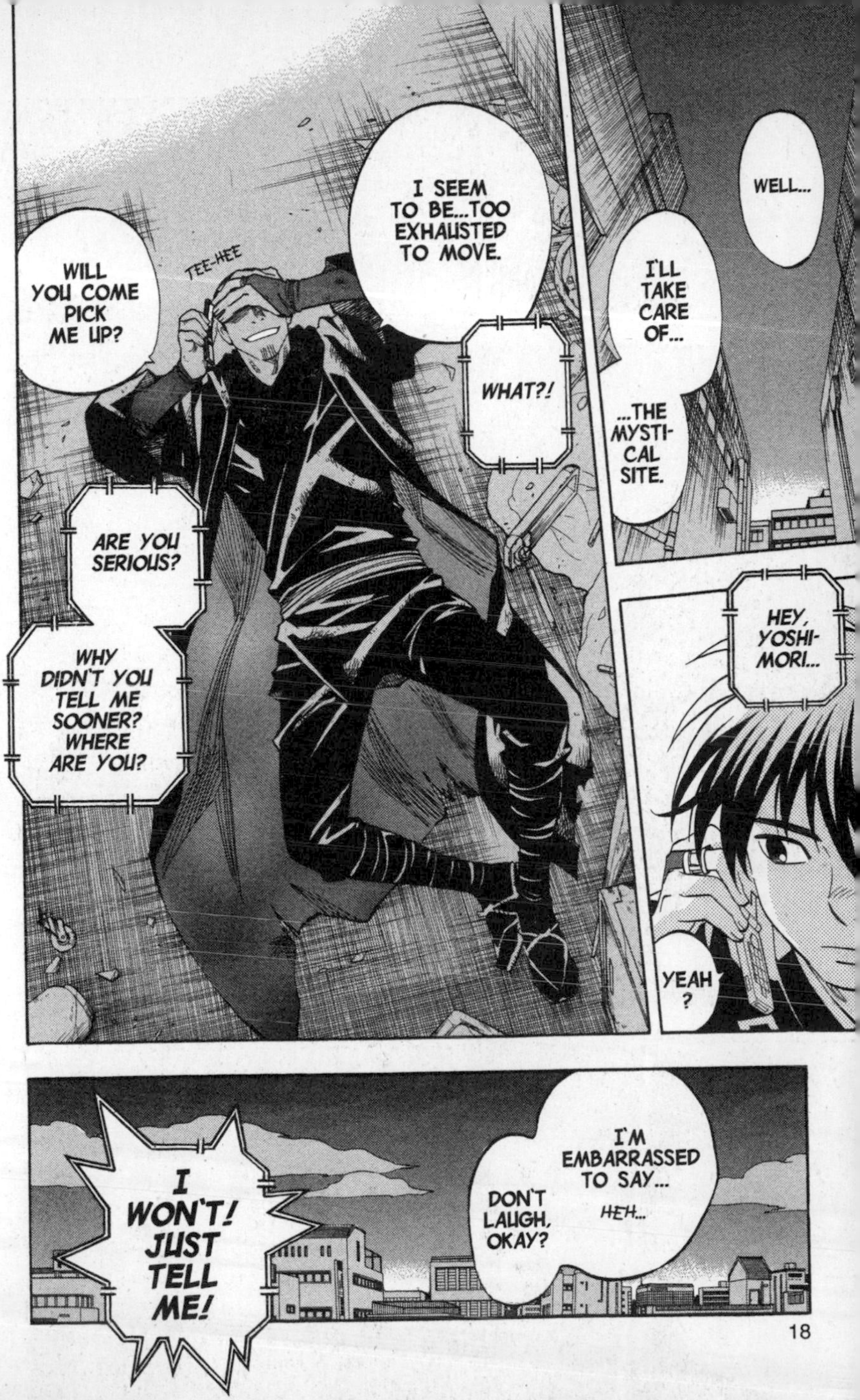
WELL...
I'LL TAKE CARE OF...
...THE MYSTICAL SITE.
HEY, YOSHIMORI...
YEAH?
I SEEM TO BE...TOO EXHAUSTED TO MOVE.
WHAT?!
TEE-HEE
WILL YOU COME PICK ME UP?
ARE YOU SERIOUS?
WHY DIDN'T YOU TELL ME SOONER? WHERE ARE YOU?
I'M EMBARRASSED TO SAY...
HEH...
DON'T LAUGH, OKAY?
I WON'T! JUST TELL ME!

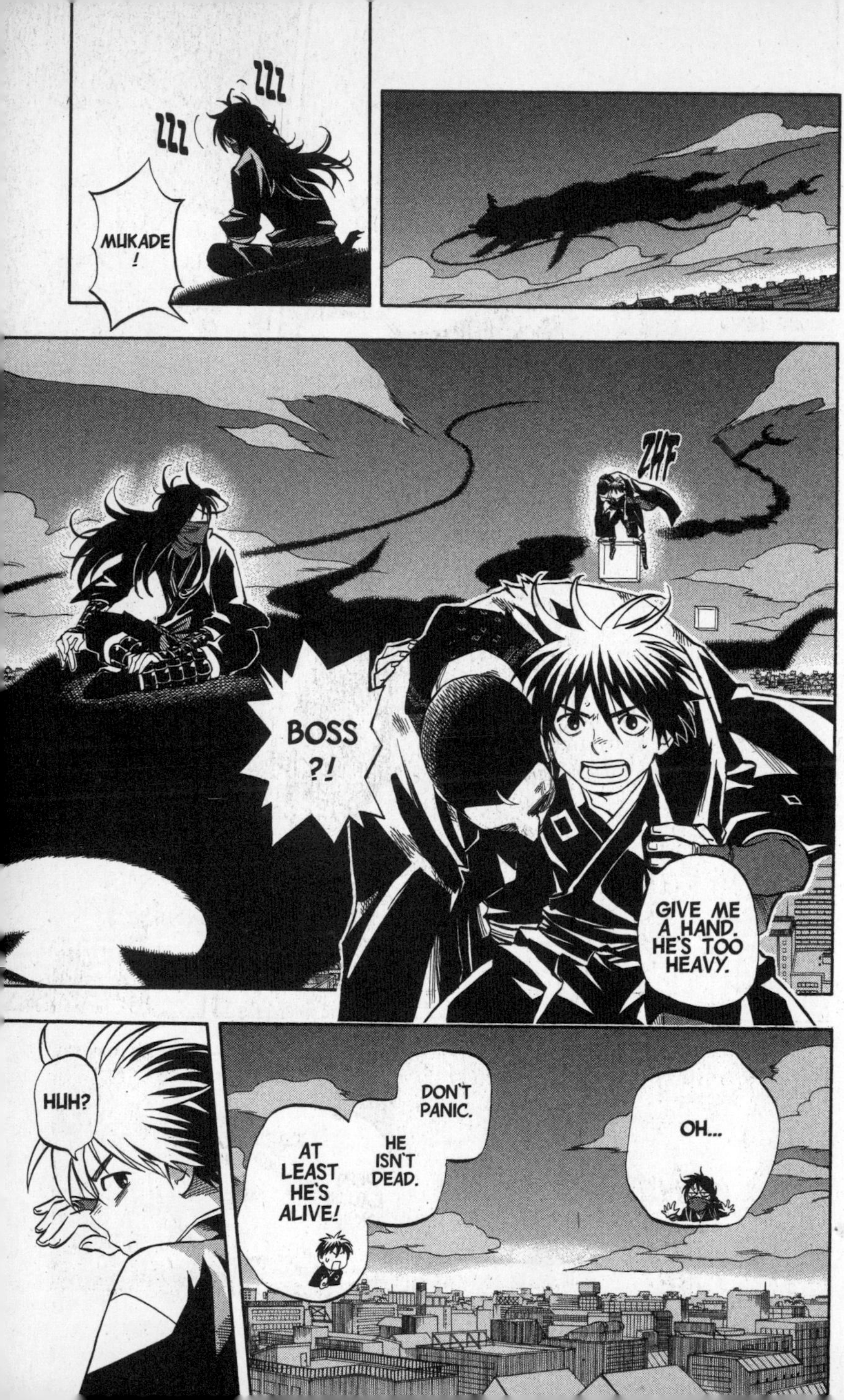
ZZZ
ZZZ
MUKADE!
ZHF
BOSS?!
GIVE ME A HAND. HE'S TOO HEAVY.
OH...
DON'T PANIC.
HE ISN'T DEAD.
AT LEAST HE'S ALIVE!
HUH?

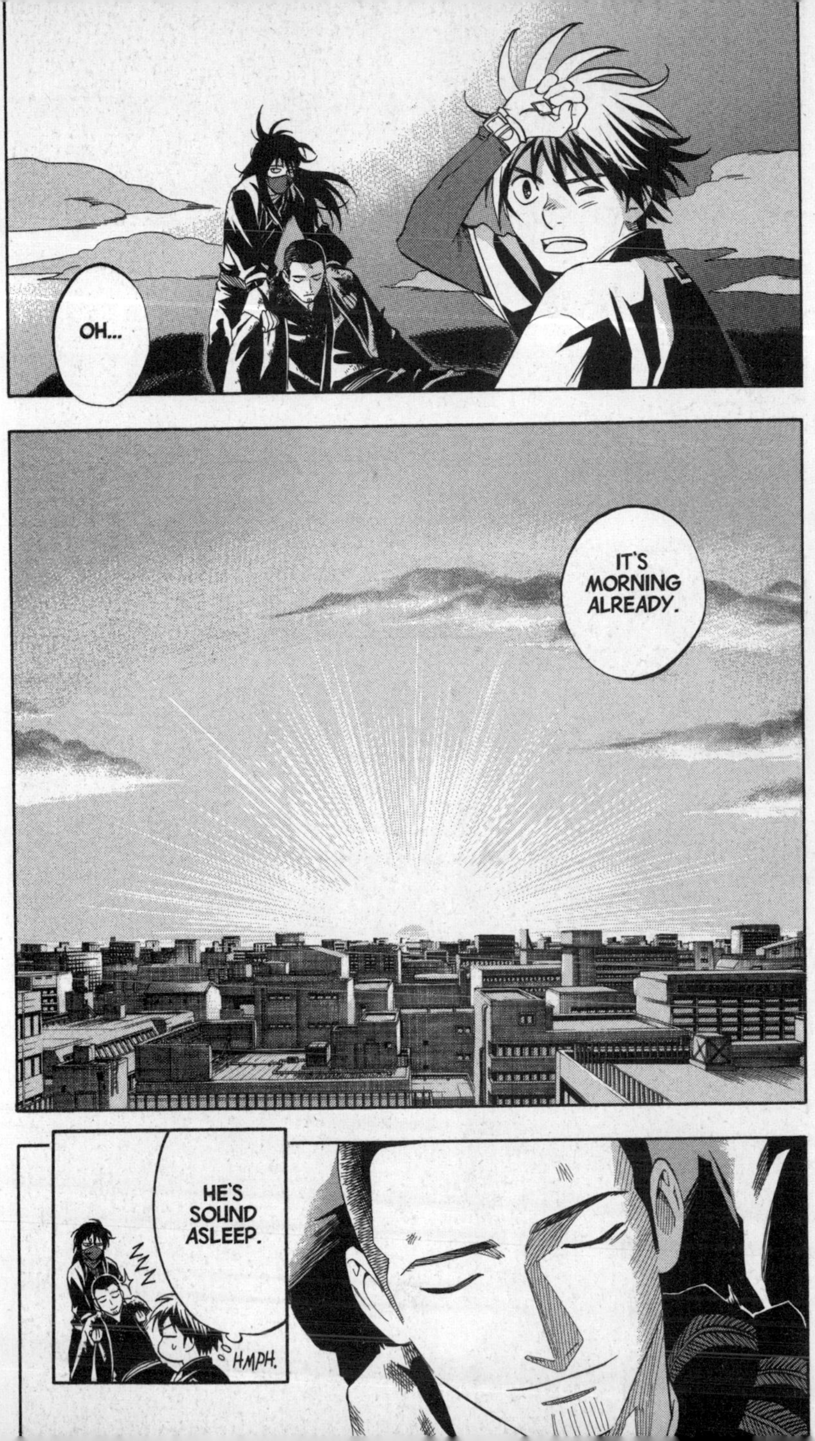
OH...
IT'S MORNING ALREADY.
HE'S SOUND ASLEEP.
ZZZ
HMPH.

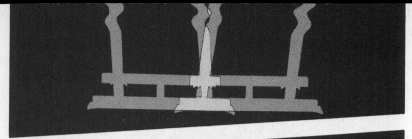

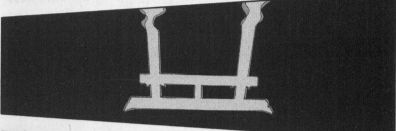

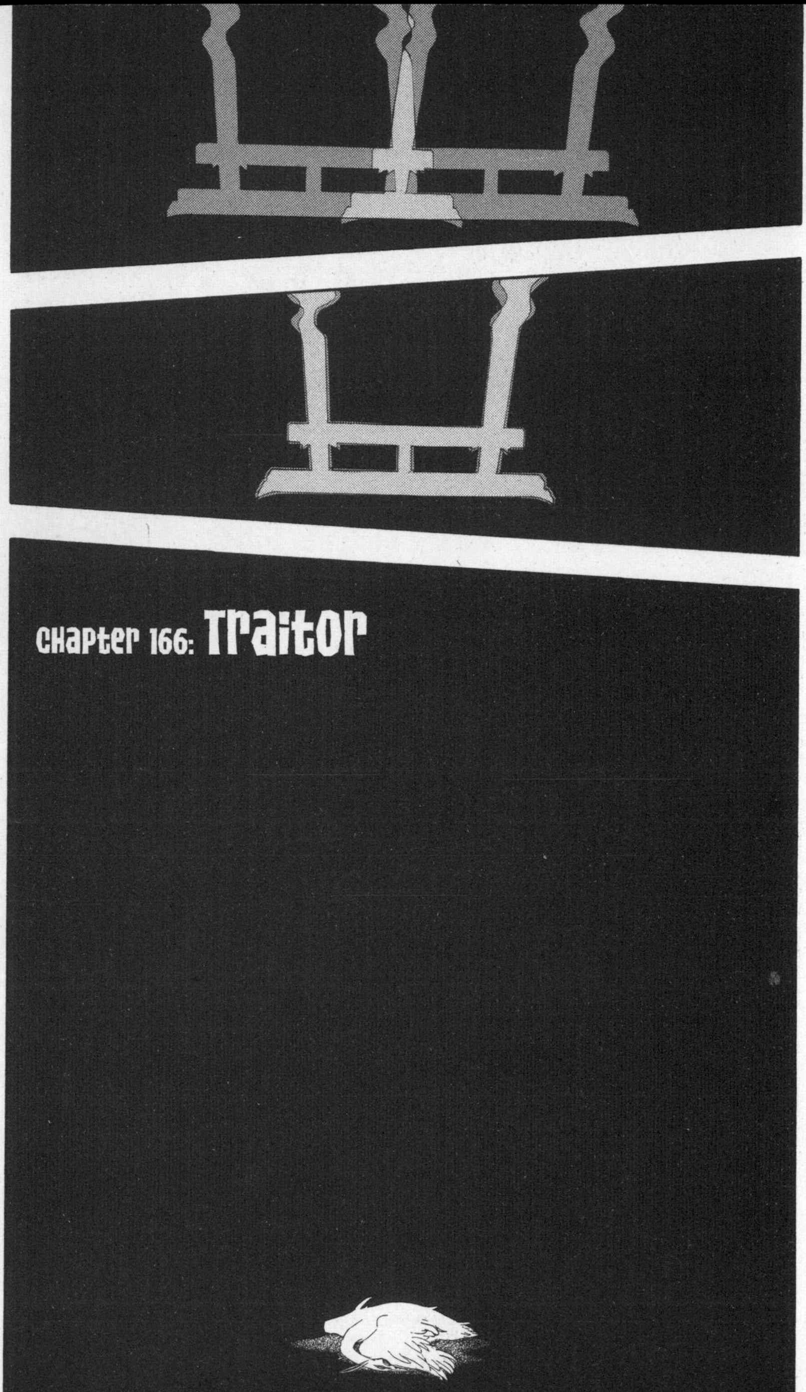

CHAPTER 166: Traitor

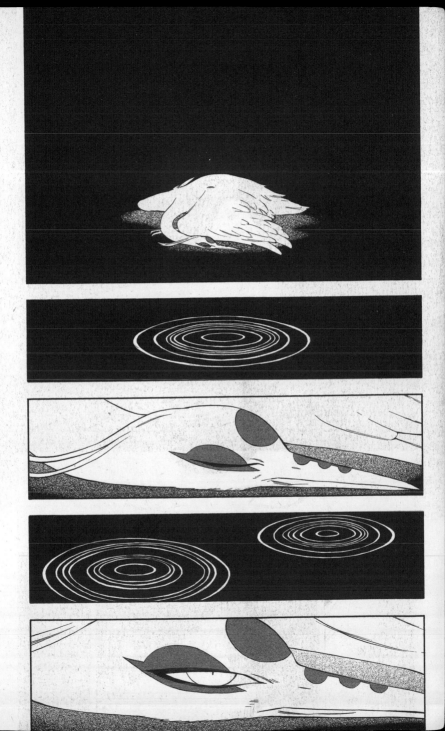

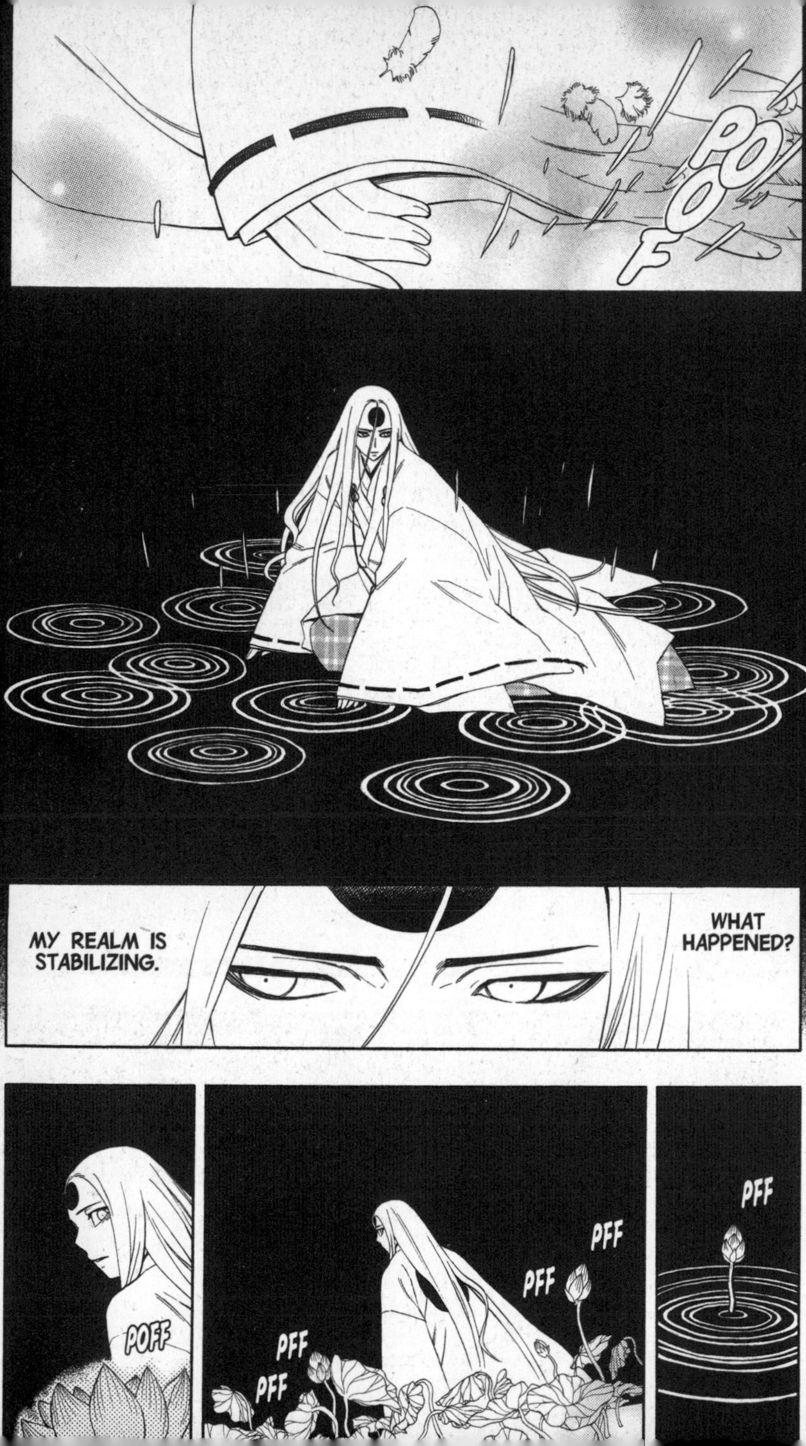
POOF
WHAT HAPPENED?
MY REALM IS STABILIZING.
PFF
PFF
PFF
PFF
PFF
POFF

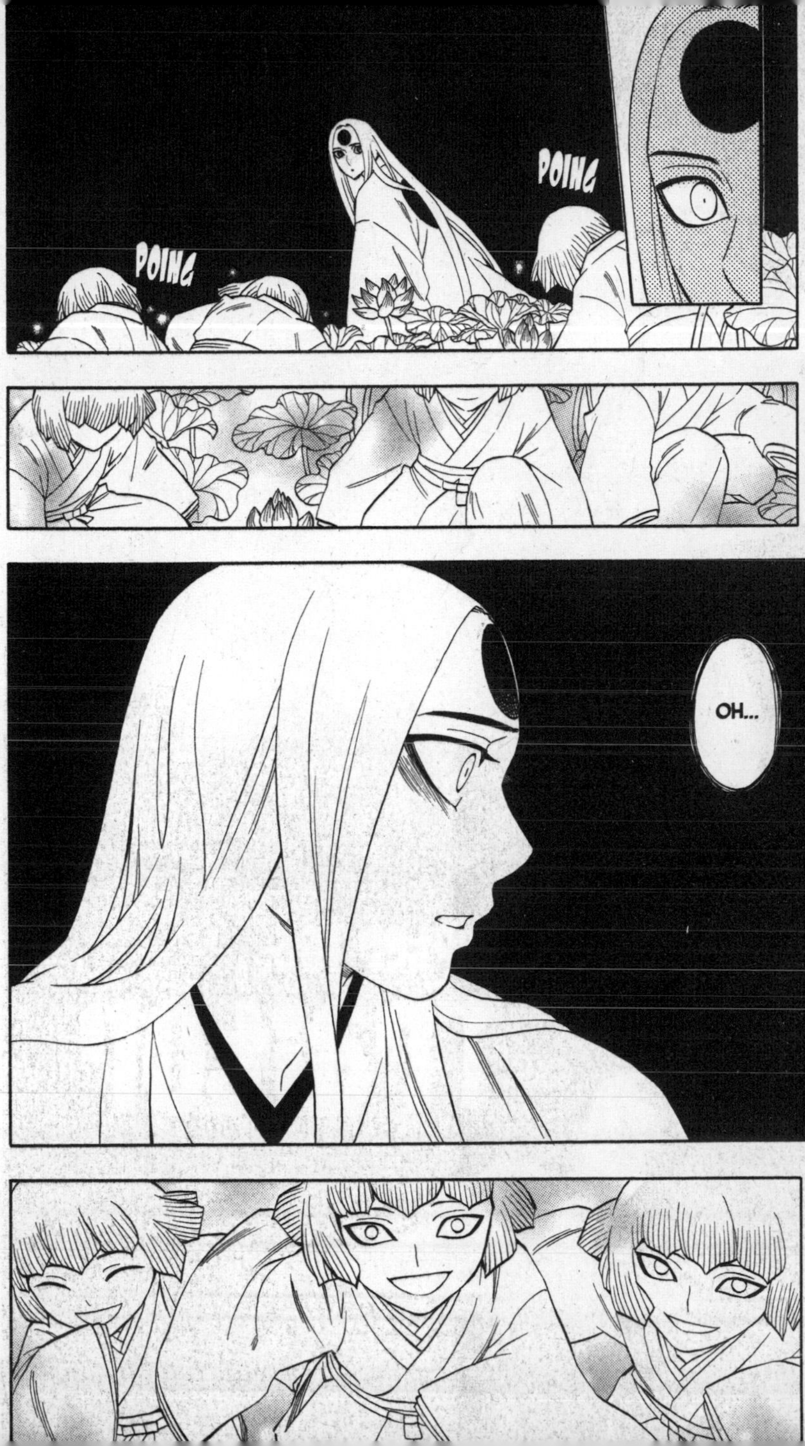
POING
POING
OH...

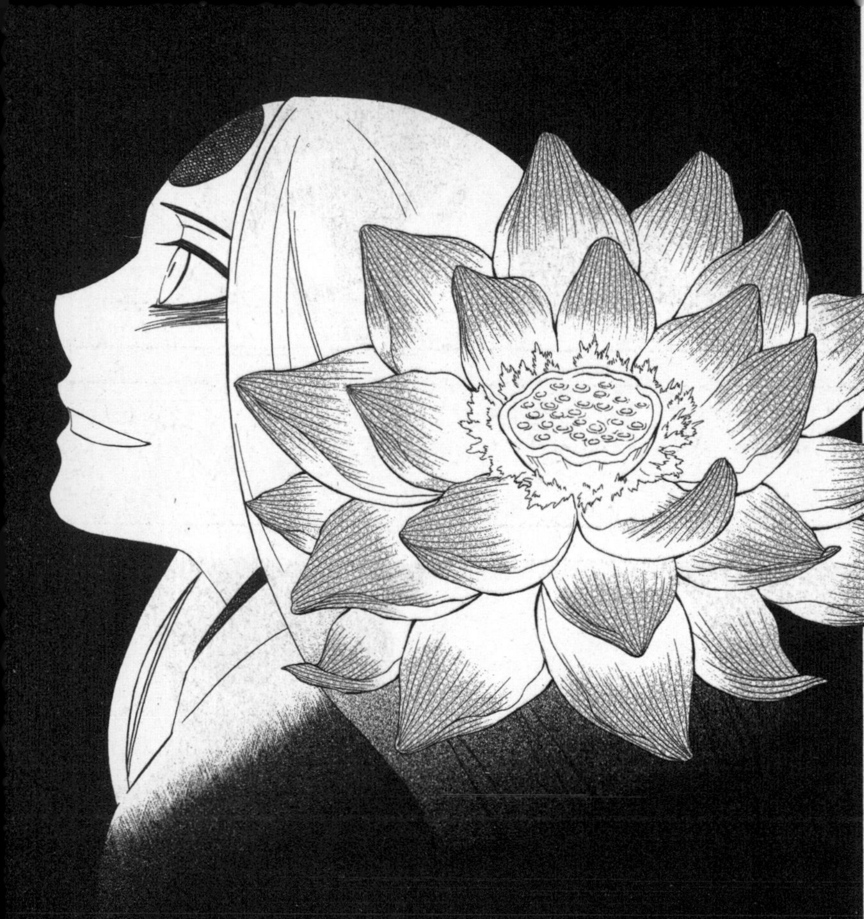

Chapter 166: Traitor

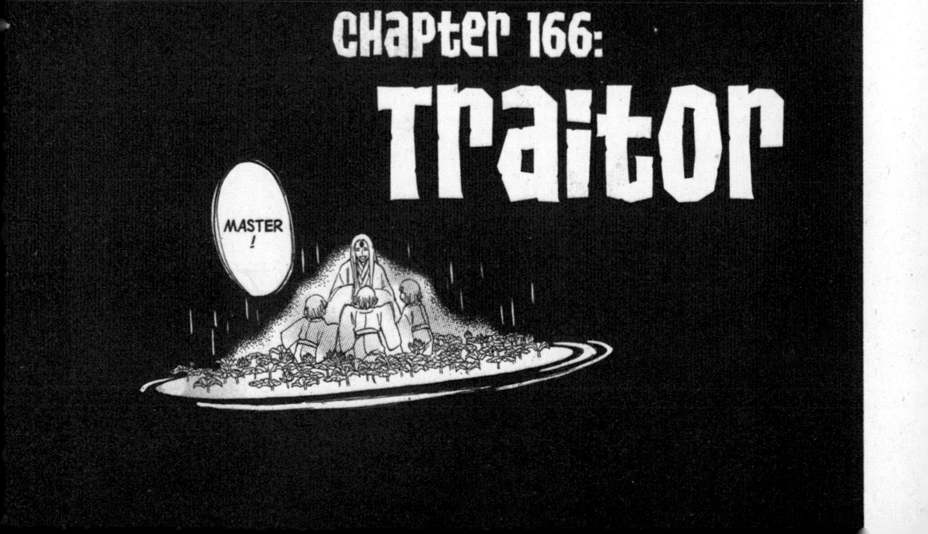
MASTER!

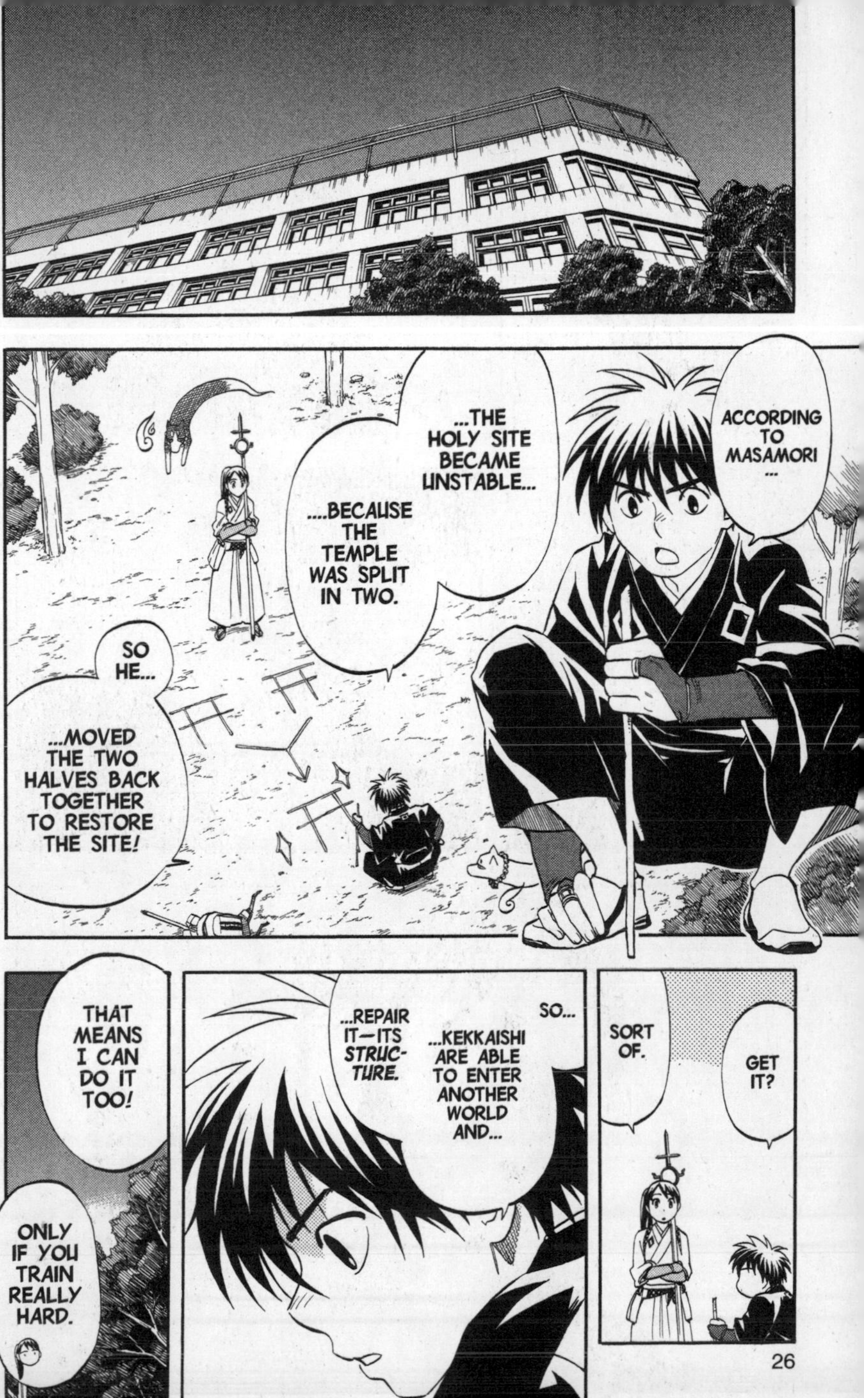
ACCORDING TO MASAMORI...
...THE HOLY SITE BECAME UNSTABLE...
....BECAUSE THE TEMPLE WAS SPLIT IN TWO.
SO HE...
...MOVED THE TWO HALVES BACK TOGETHER TO RESTORE THE SITE!
GET IT?
SORT OF.
SO...
...KEKKAISHI ARE ABLE TO ENTER ANOTHER WORLD AND...
...REPAIR IT—ITS *STRUCTURE.*
THAT MEANS I CAN DO IT TOO!
ONLY IF YOU TRAIN REALLY HARD.

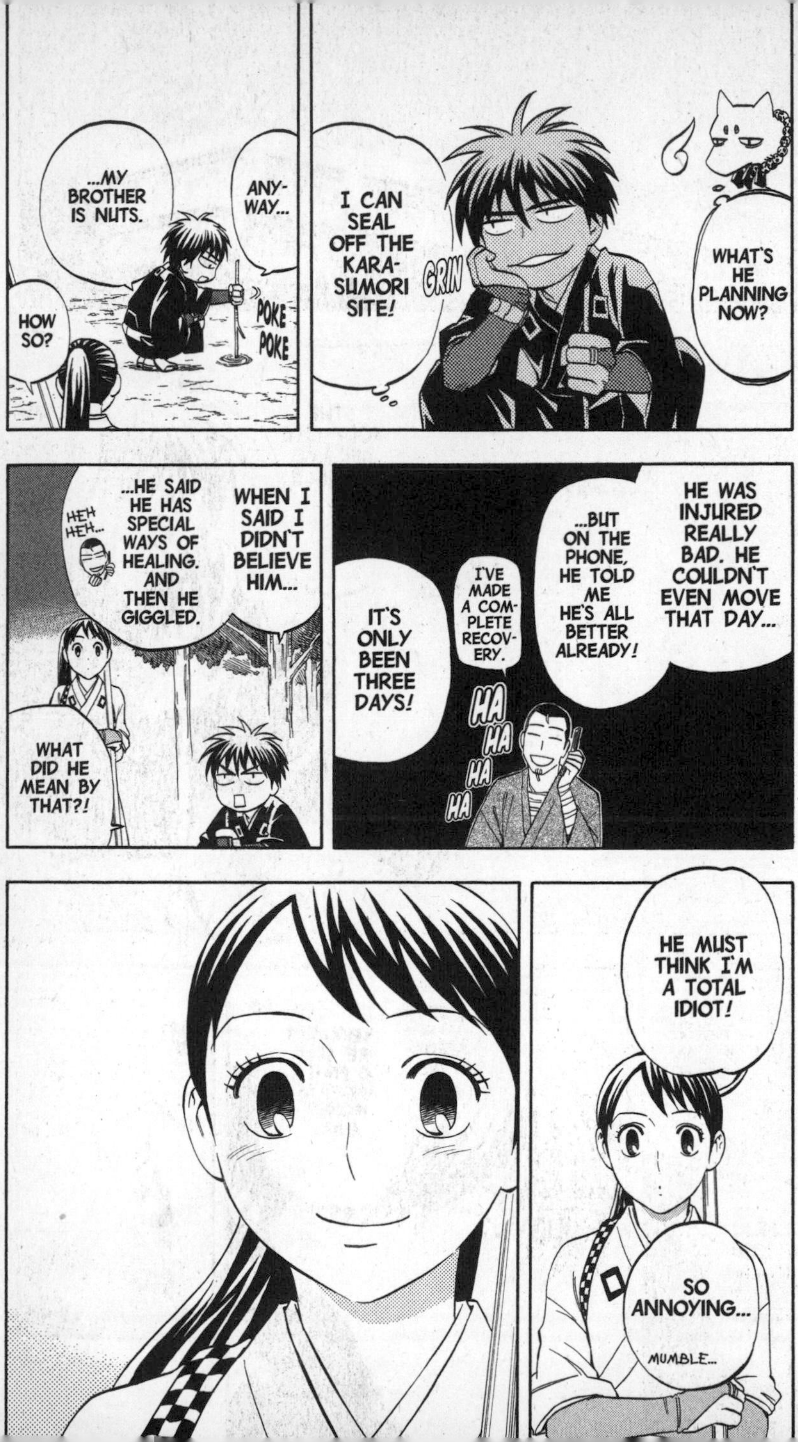
WHAT'S HE PLANNING NOW?
I CAN SEAL OFF THE KARA-SUMORI SITE!
GRIN
ANY-WAY...
...MY BROTHER IS NUTS.
POKE POKE
HOW SO?
HE WAS INJURED REALLY BAD. HE COULDN'T EVEN MOVE THAT DAY...
...BUT ON THE PHONE, HE TOLD ME HE'S ALL BETTER ALREADY!
I'VE MADE A COM-PLETE RECOV-ERY.
IT'S ONLY BEEN THREE DAYS!
HA HA HA HA
WHEN I SAID I DIDN'T BELIEVE HIM...
...HE SAID HE HAS SPECIAL WAYS OF HEALING. AND THEN HE GIGGLED.
HEH HEH...
WHAT DID HE MEAN BY THAT?!
HE MUST THINK I'M A TOTAL IDIOT!
SO ANNOYING...
MUMBLE...

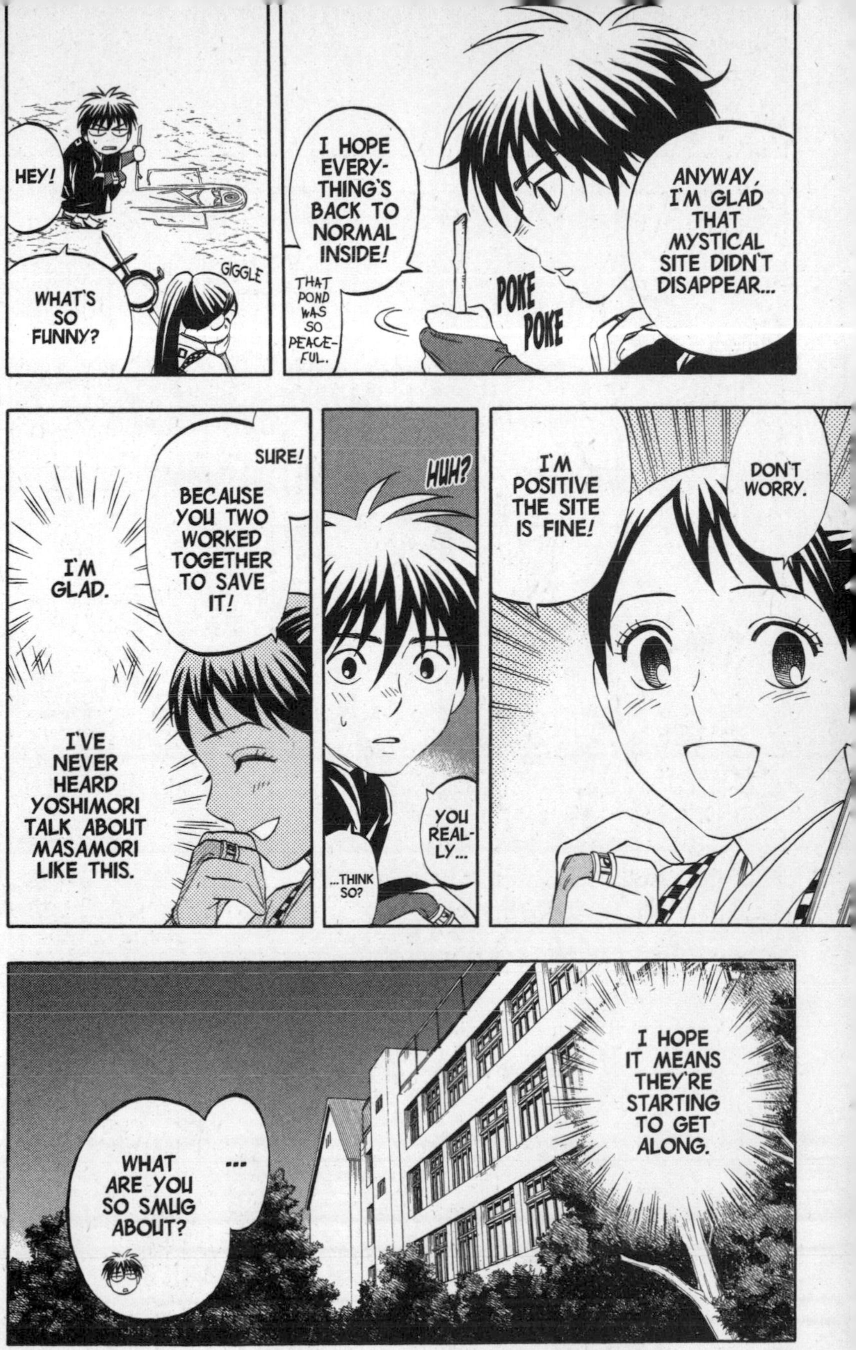
ANYWAY, I'M GLAD THAT MYSTICAL SITE DIDN'T DISAPPEAR...
POKE POKE
I HOPE EVERYTHING'S BACK TO NORMAL INSIDE!
THAT POND WAS SO PEACEFUL.
HEY!
GIGGLE
WHAT'S SO FUNNY?
DON'T WORRY.
I'M POSITIVE THE SITE IS FINE!
HUH?
YOU REALLY...
...THINK SO?
SURE!
BECAUSE YOU TWO WORKED TOGETHER TO SAVE IT!
I'M GLAD.
I'VE NEVER HEARD YOSHIMORI TALK ABOUT MASAMORI LIKE THIS.
I HOPE IT MEANS THEY'RE STARTING TO GET ALONG.
...
WHAT ARE YOU SO SMUG ABOUT?

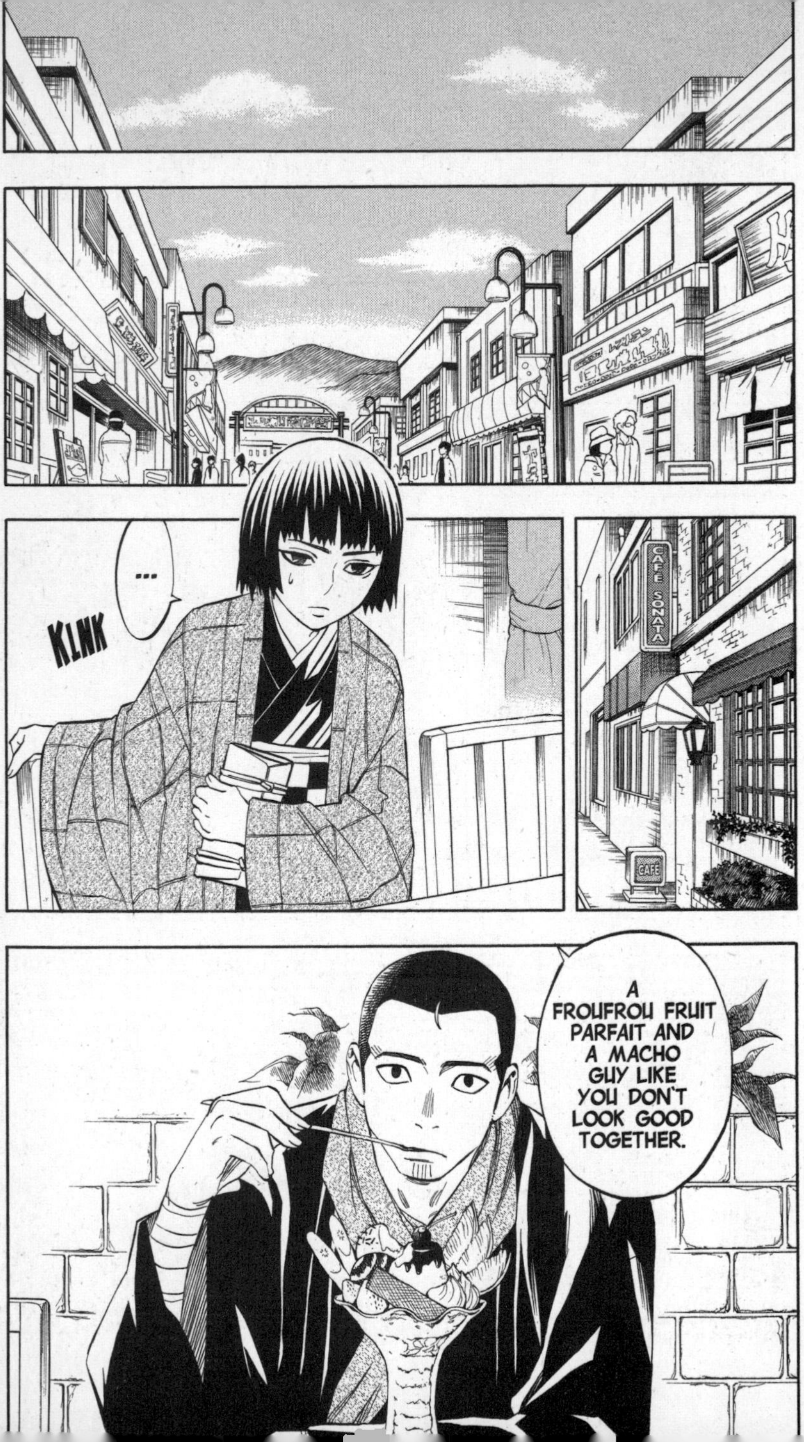
CAFÉ SONATA
CAFÉ
...
KLNK
A FROUFROU FRUIT PARFAIT AND A MACHO GUY LIKE YOU DON'T LOOK GOOD TOGETHER.

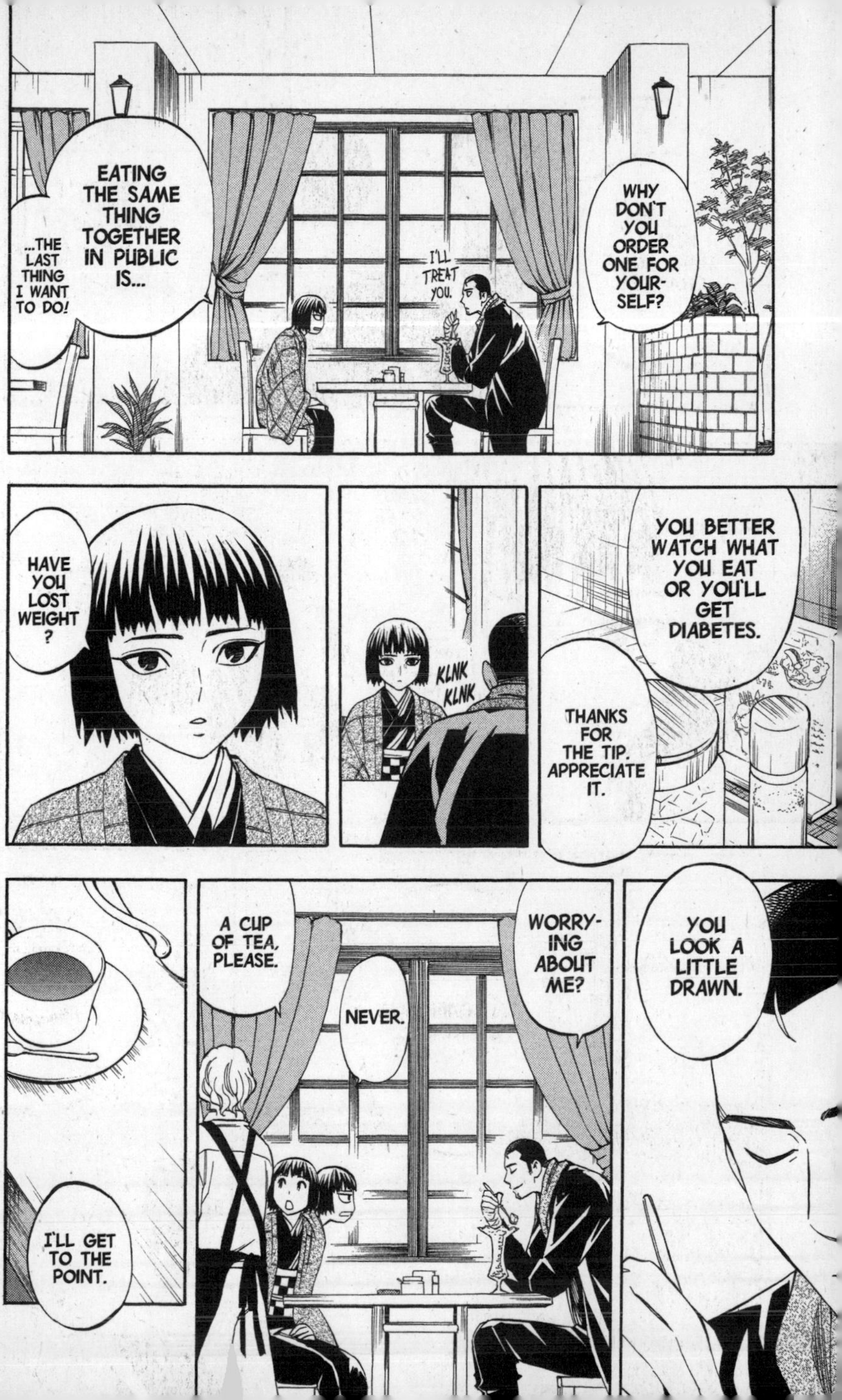
WHY DON'T YOU ORDER ONE FOR YOUR-SELF?
I'LL TREAT YOU.
EATING THE SAME THING TOGETHER IN PUBLIC IS...
...THE LAST THING I WANT TO DO!
YOU BETTER WATCH WHAT YOU EAT OR YOU'LL GET DIABETES.
THANKS FOR THE TIP. APPRECIATE IT.
KLNK KLNK
HAVE YOU LOST WEIGHT?
YOU LOOK A LITTLE DRAWN.
WORRY-ING ABOUT ME?
NEVER.
A CUP OF TEA, PLEASE.
I'LL GET TO THE POINT.

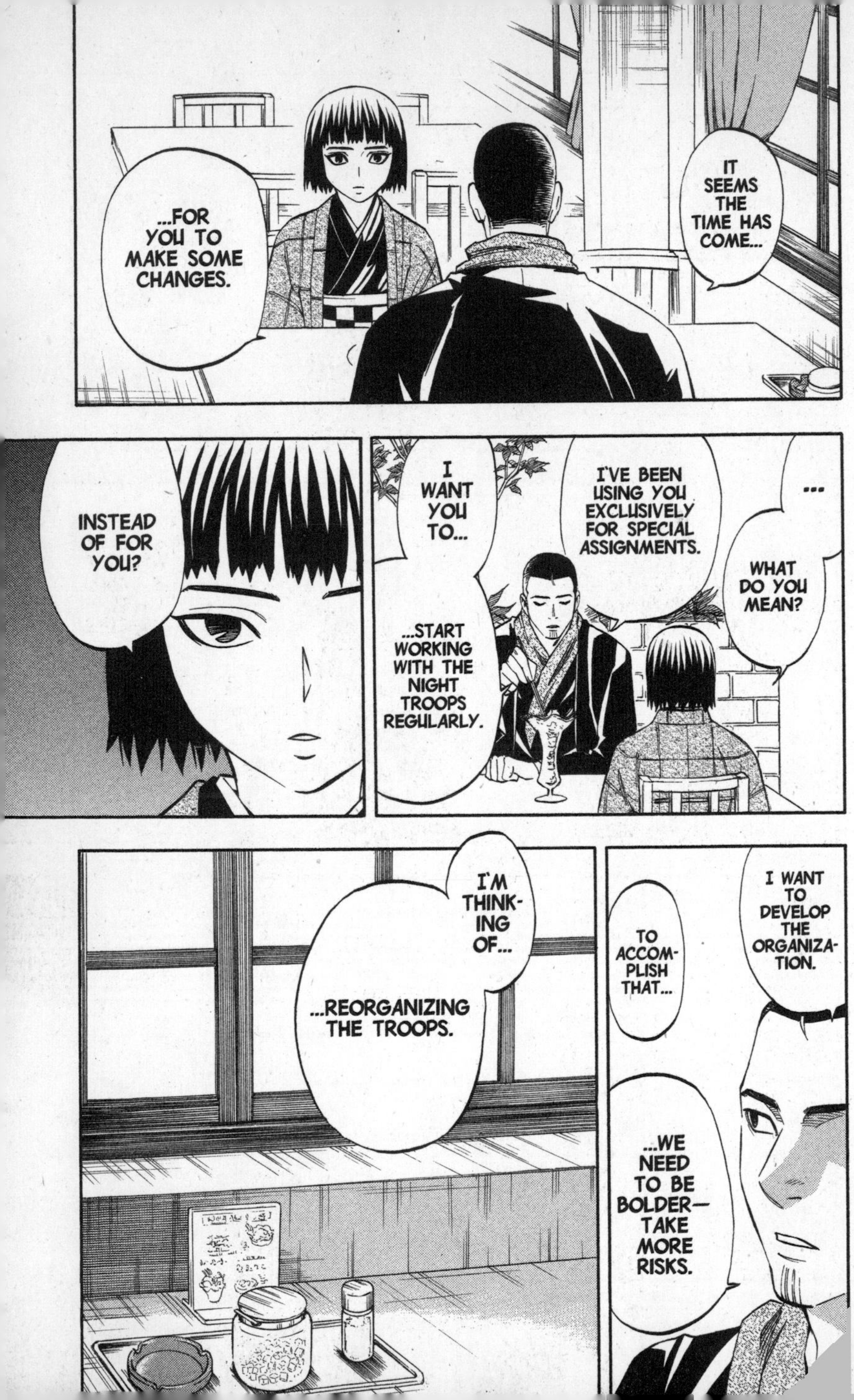
IT SEEMS THE TIME HAS COME...
...FOR YOU TO MAKE SOME CHANGES.
...
WHAT DO YOU MEAN?
I'VE BEEN USING YOU EXCLUSIVELY FOR SPECIAL ASSIGNMENTS.
I WANT YOU TO...
...START WORKING WITH THE NIGHT TROOPS REGULARLY.
INSTEAD OF FOR YOU?
I WANT TO DEVELOP THE ORGANIZATION.
TO ACCOMPLISH THAT...
...WE NEED TO BE BOLDER—TAKE MORE RISKS.
I'M THINKING OF...
...REORGANIZING THE TROOPS.

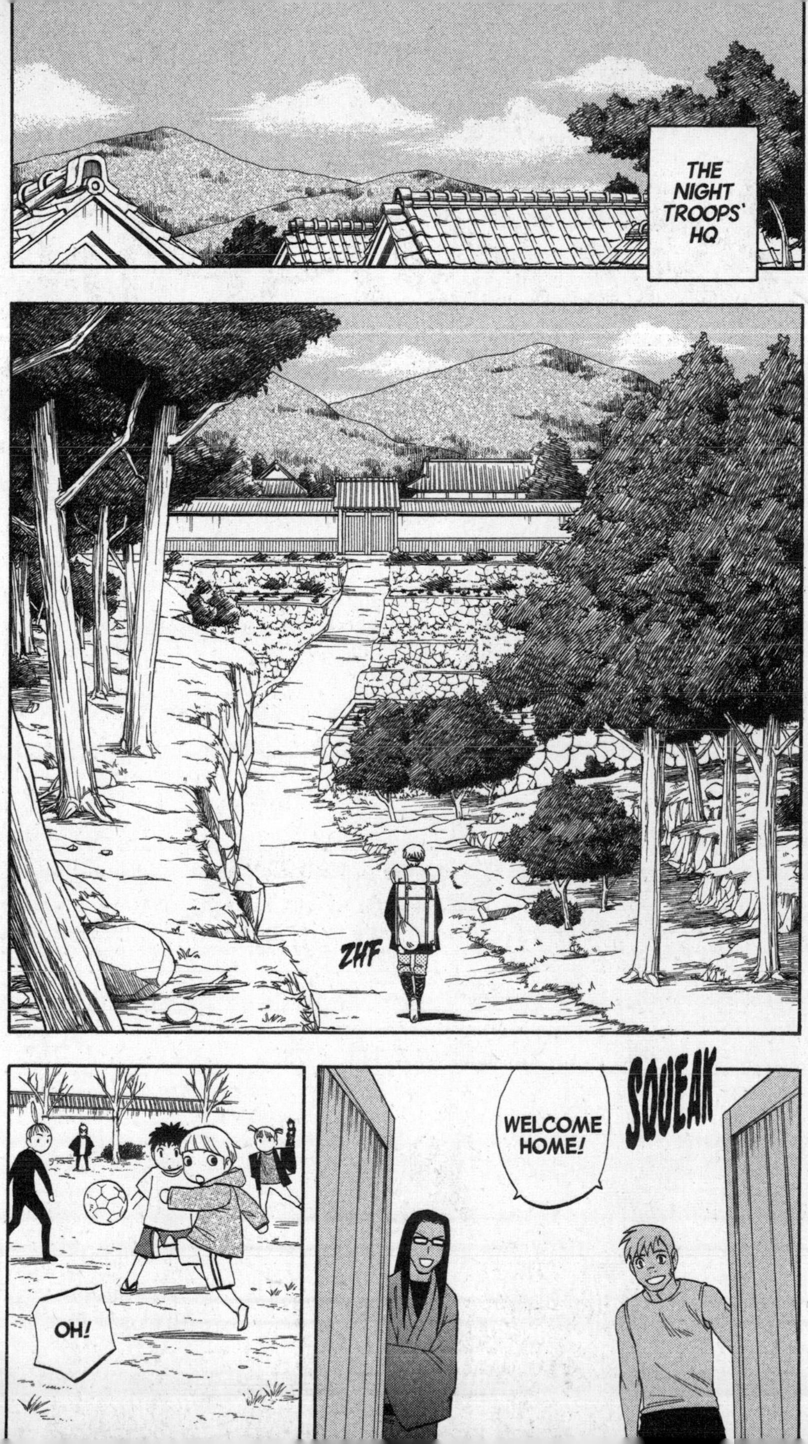
THE NIGHT TROOPS' HQ
ZHF
SQUEAK
WELCOME HOME!
OH!

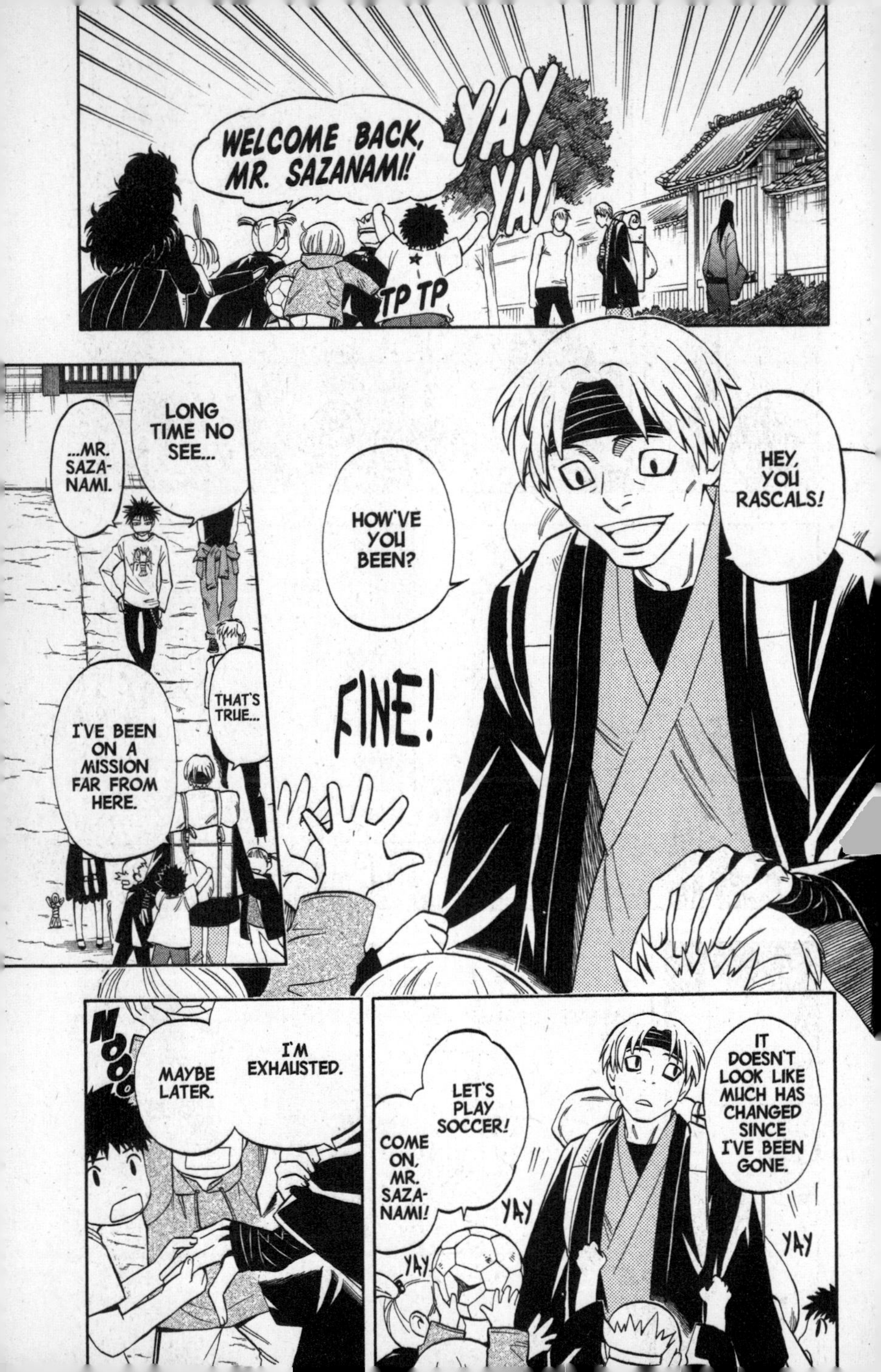
YAY YAY
WELCOME BACK, MR. SAZANAMI!
TP TP
HEY, YOU RASCALS!
HOW'VE YOU BEEN?
FINE!
LONG TIME NO SEE...
...MR. SAZANAMI.
THAT'S TRUE...
I'VE BEEN ON A MISSION FAR FROM HERE.
IT DOESN'T LOOK LIKE MUCH HAS CHANGED SINCE I'VE BEEN GONE.
LET'S PLAY SOCCER!
COME ON, MR. SAZANAMI!
YAY
YAY
YAY
I'M EXHAUSTED.
MAYBE LATER.
NOOO

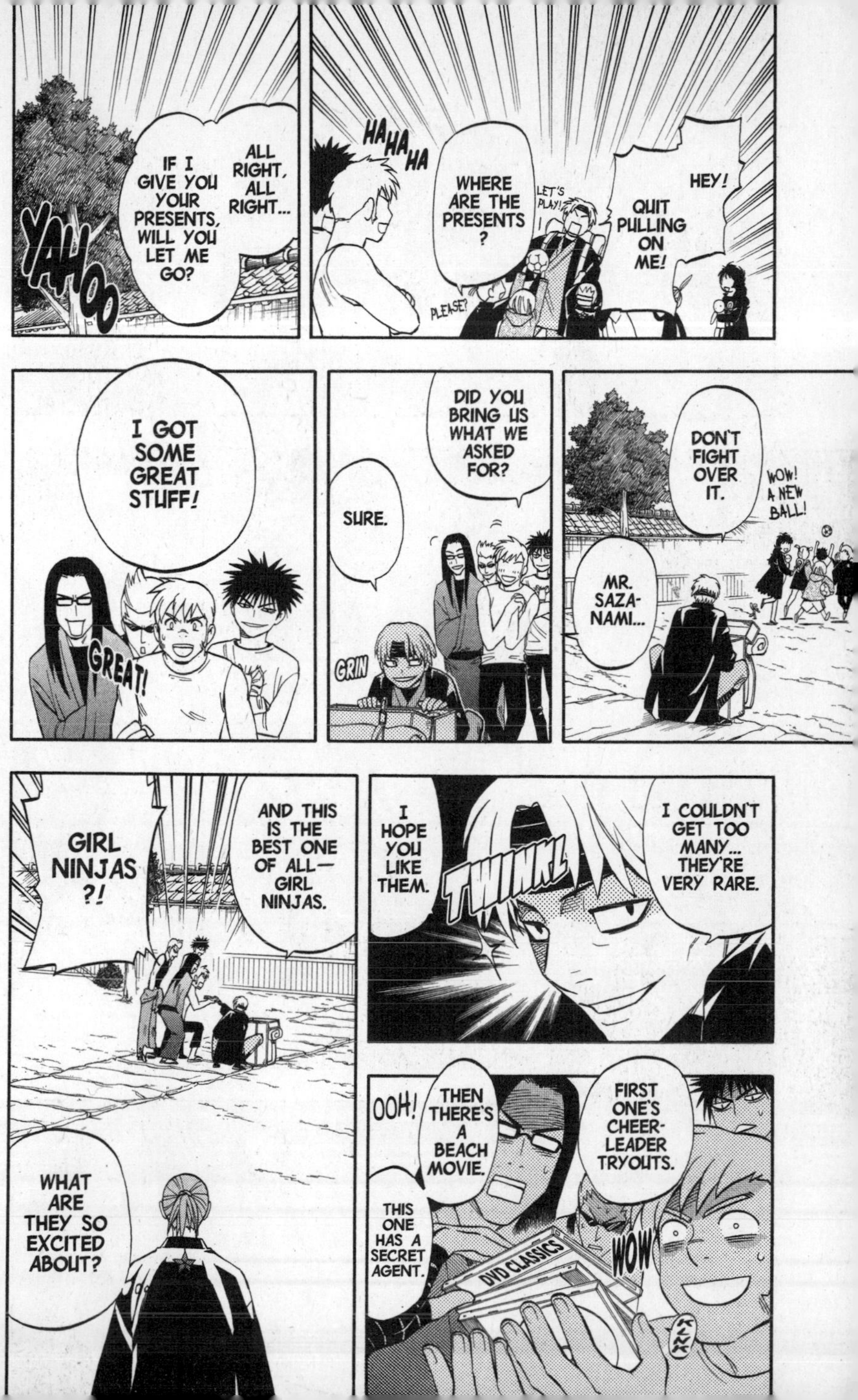
HEY!
QUIT PULLING ON ME!
LET'S PLAY!
WHERE ARE THE PRESENTS?
HA HA HA
PLEASE?
ALL RIGHT, ALL RIGHT...
IF I GIVE YOU YOUR PRESENTS, WILL YOU LET ME GO?
YAHOO
WOW! A NEW BALL!
DON'T FIGHT OVER IT.
MR. SAZA-NAMI...
DID YOU BRING US WHAT WE ASKED FOR?
SURE.
GRIN
I GOT SOME GREAT STUFF!
GREAT!
I COULDN'T GET TOO MANY... THEY'RE VERY RARE.
I HOPE YOU LIKE THEM.
TWINKL
FIRST ONE'S CHEER-LEADER TRYOUTS.
THEN THERE'S A BEACH MOVIE.
OOH!
WOW
THIS ONE HAS A SECRET AGENT.
DVD CLASSICS
AND THIS IS THE BEST ONE OF ALL— GIRL NINJAS.
GIRL NINJAS ?!
WHAT ARE THEY SO EXCITED ABOUT?

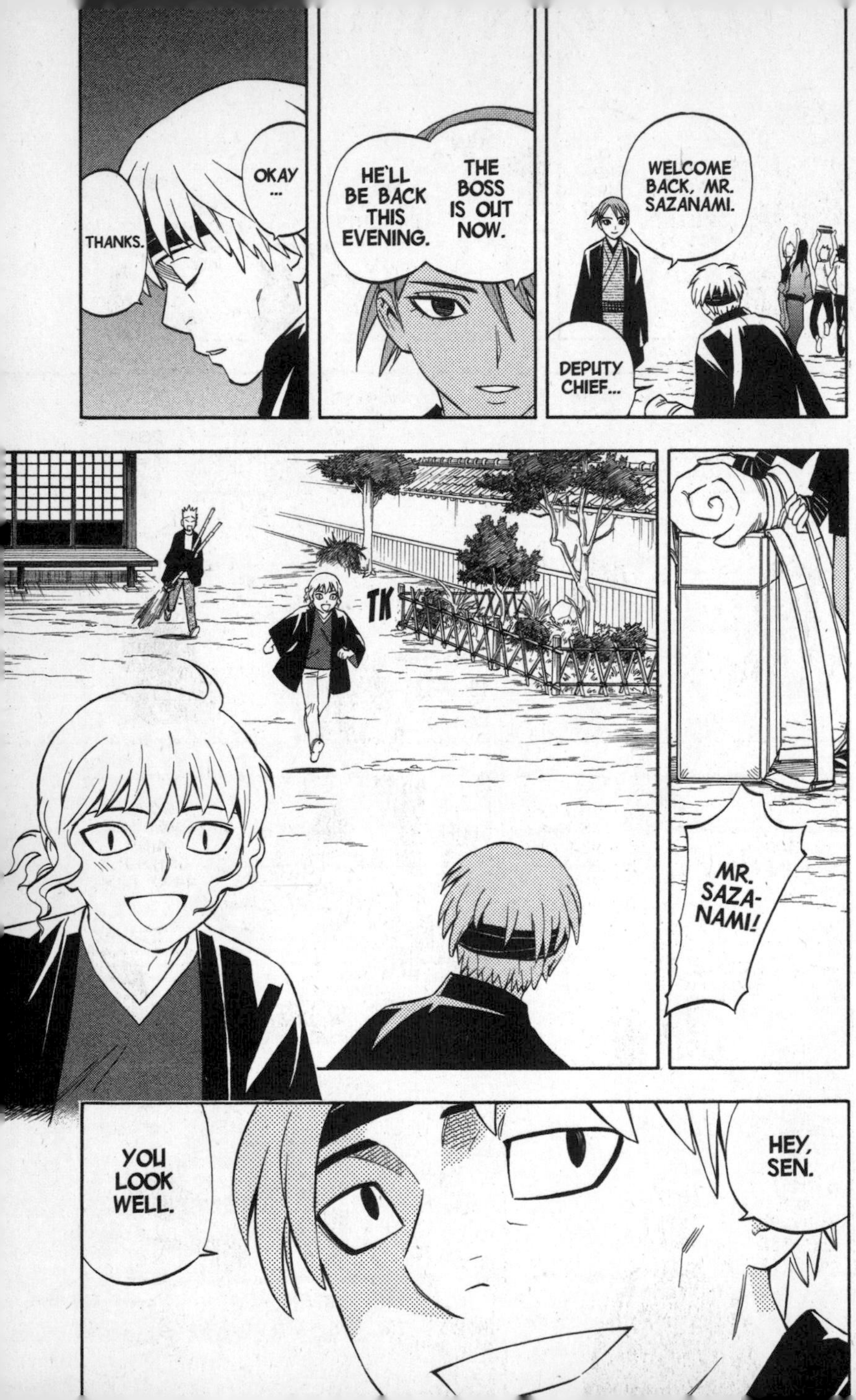
WELCOME BACK, MR. SAZANAMI.
DEPUTY CHIEF...
THE BOSS IS OUT NOW.
HE'LL BE BACK THIS EVENING.
OKAY ...
THANKS.
MR. SAZA-NAMI!
TK
HEY, SEN.
YOU LOOK WELL.

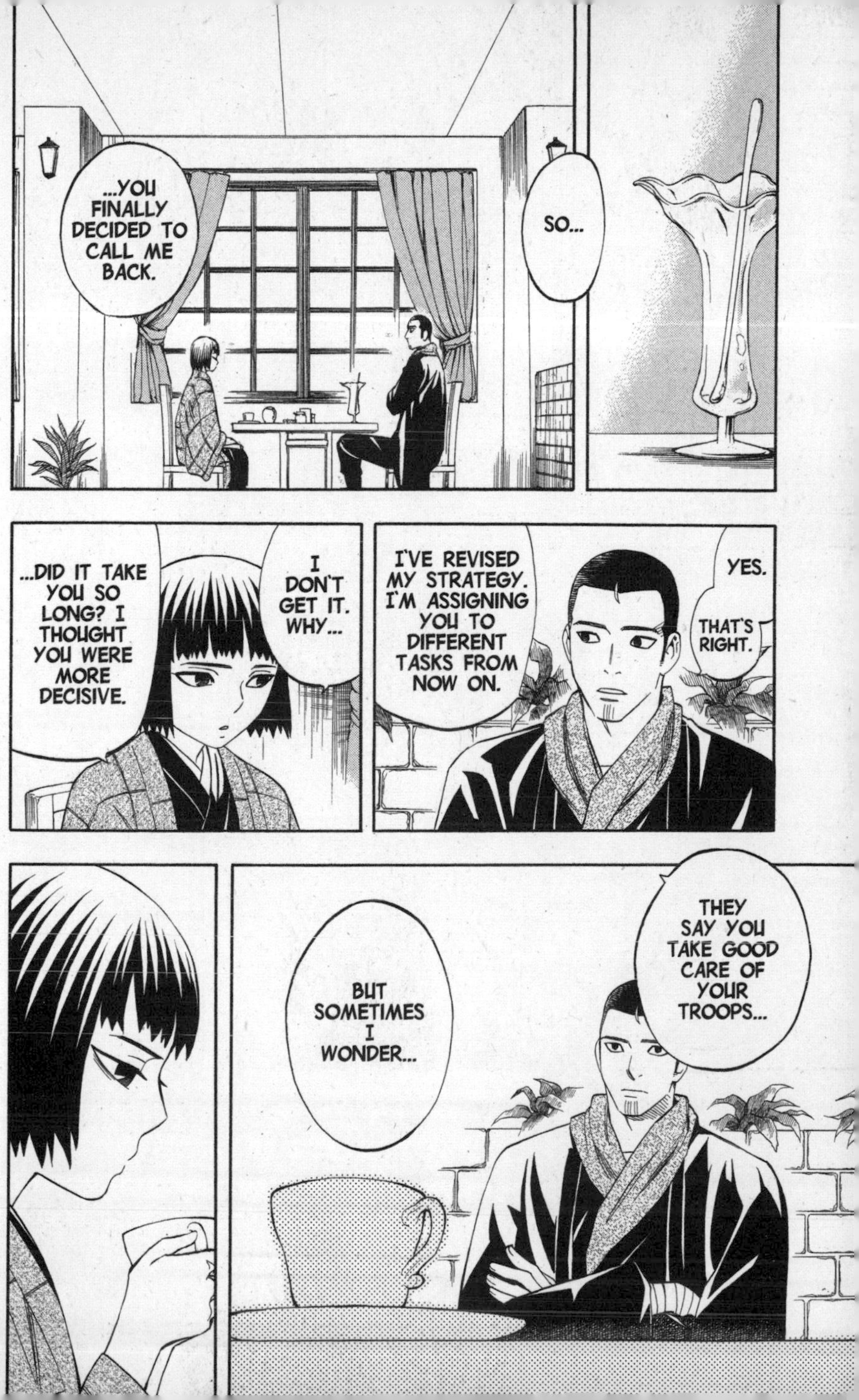
SO...
...YOU FINALLY DECIDED TO CALL ME BACK.
YES.
THAT'S RIGHT.
I'VE REVISED MY STRATEGY. I'M ASSIGNING YOU TO DIFFERENT TASKS FROM NOW ON.
I DON'T GET IT. WHY...
...DID IT TAKE YOU SO LONG? I THOUGHT YOU WERE MORE DECISIVE.
THEY SAY YOU TAKE GOOD CARE OF YOUR TROOPS...
BUT SOMETIMES I WONDER...

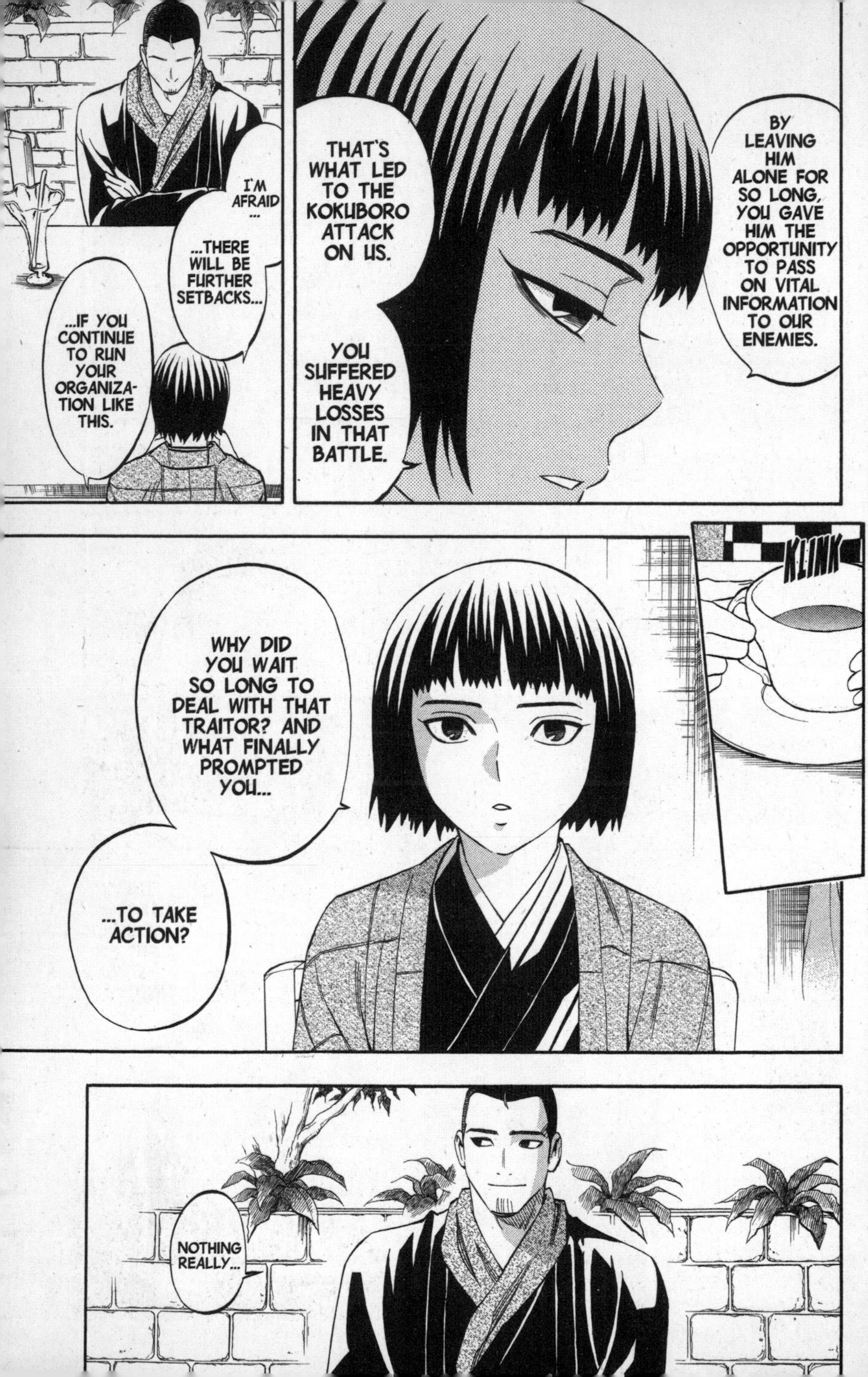
BY LEAVING HIM ALONE FOR SO LONG, YOU GAVE HIM THE OPPORTUNITY TO PASS ON VITAL INFORMATION TO OUR ENEMIES.
THAT'S WHAT LED TO THE KOKUBORO ATTACK ON US.
YOU SUFFERED HEAVY LOSSES IN THAT BATTLE.
I'M AFRAID...
...THERE WILL BE FURTHER SETBACKS...
...IF YOU CONTINUE TO RUN YOUR ORGANIZATION LIKE THIS.
KLINK
WHY DID YOU WAIT SO LONG TO DEAL WITH THAT TRAITOR? AND WHAT FINALLY PROMPTED YOU...
...TO TAKE ACTION?
NOTHING REALLY...

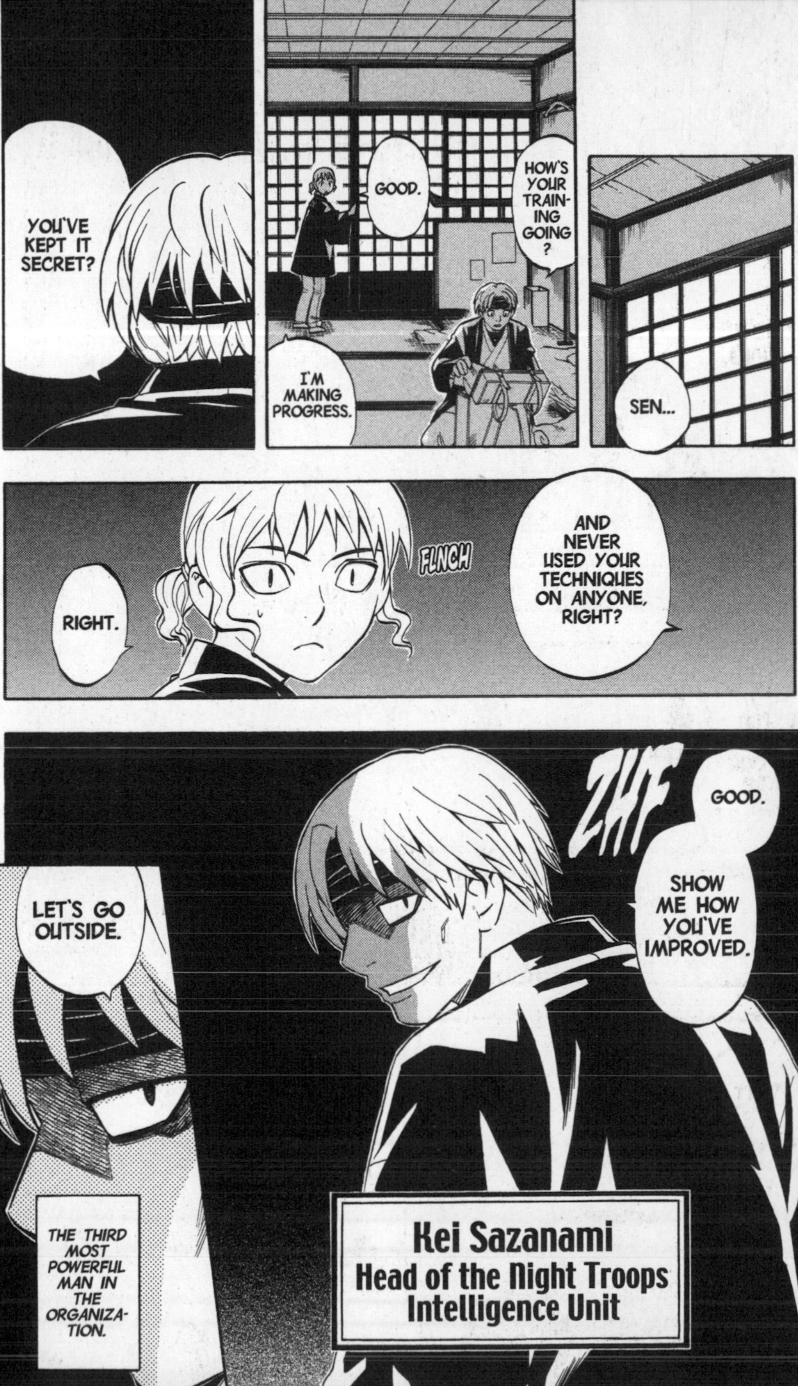
SEN...
HOW'S YOUR TRAINING GOING?
GOOD.
I'M MAKING PROGRESS.
YOU'VE KEPT IT SECRET?
AND NEVER USED YOUR TECHNIQUES ON ANYONE, RIGHT?
FLNCH
RIGHT.
ZHF
GOOD.
SHOW ME HOW YOU'VE IMPROVED.
Kei Sazanami
Head of the Night Troops Intelligence Unit
LET'S GO OUTSIDE.
THE THIRD MOST POWERFUL MAN IN THE ORGANIZATION.

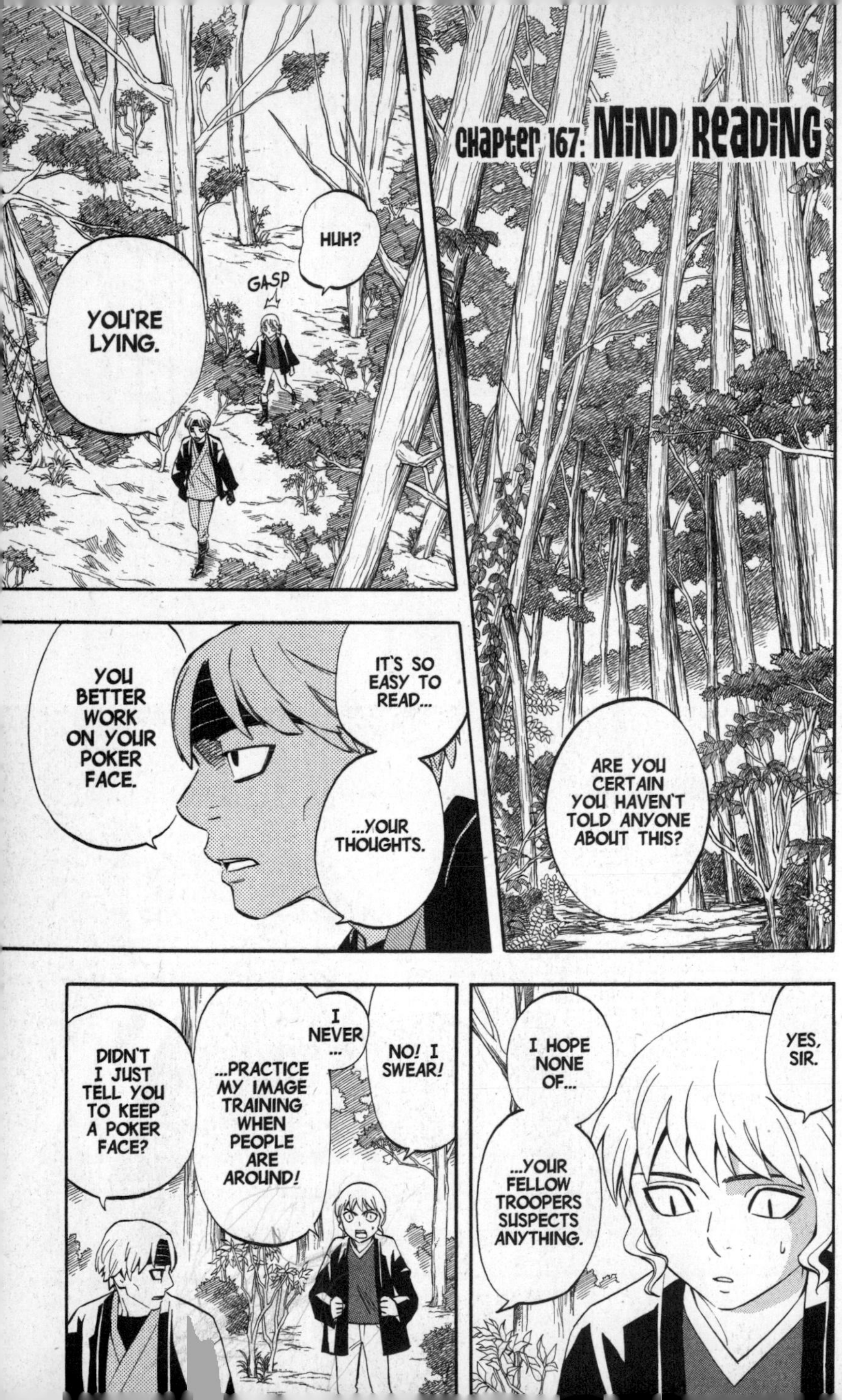
Chapter 167: Mind Reading
ARE YOU CERTAIN YOU HAVEN'T TOLD ANYONE ABOUT THIS?
HUH?
GASP
YOU'RE LYING.
IT'S SO EASY TO READ...
...YOUR THOUGHTS.
YOU BETTER WORK ON YOUR POKER FACE.
YES, SIR.
I HOPE NONE OF...
...YOUR FELLOW TROOPERS SUSPECTS ANYTHING.
NO! I SWEAR!
I NEVER...
...PRACTICE MY IMAGE TRAINING WHEN PEOPLE ARE AROUND!
DIDN'T I JUST TELL YOU TO KEEP A POKER FACE?

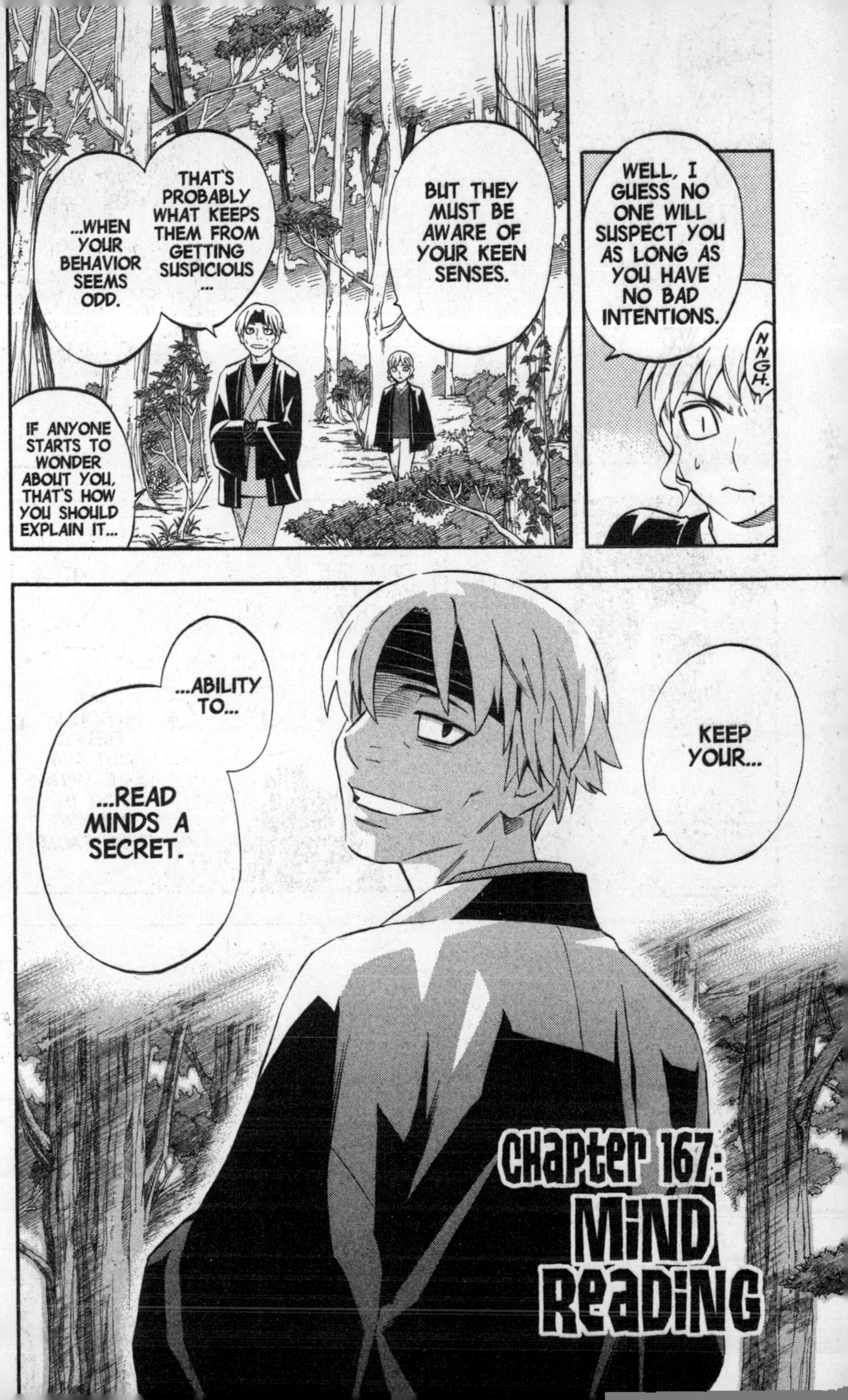
WELL, I GUESS NO ONE WILL SUSPECT YOU AS LONG AS YOU HAVE NO BAD INTENTIONS.
NNGH.
BUT THEY MUST BE AWARE OF YOUR KEEN SENSES.
THAT'S PROBABLY WHAT KEEPS THEM FROM GETTING SUSPICIOUS ...
...WHEN YOUR BEHAVIOR SEEMS ODD.
IF ANYONE STARTS TO WONDER ABOUT YOU, THAT'S HOW YOU SHOULD EXPLAIN IT...
KEEP YOUR...
...ABILITY TO...
...READ MINDS A SECRET.
Chapter 167: Mind Reading

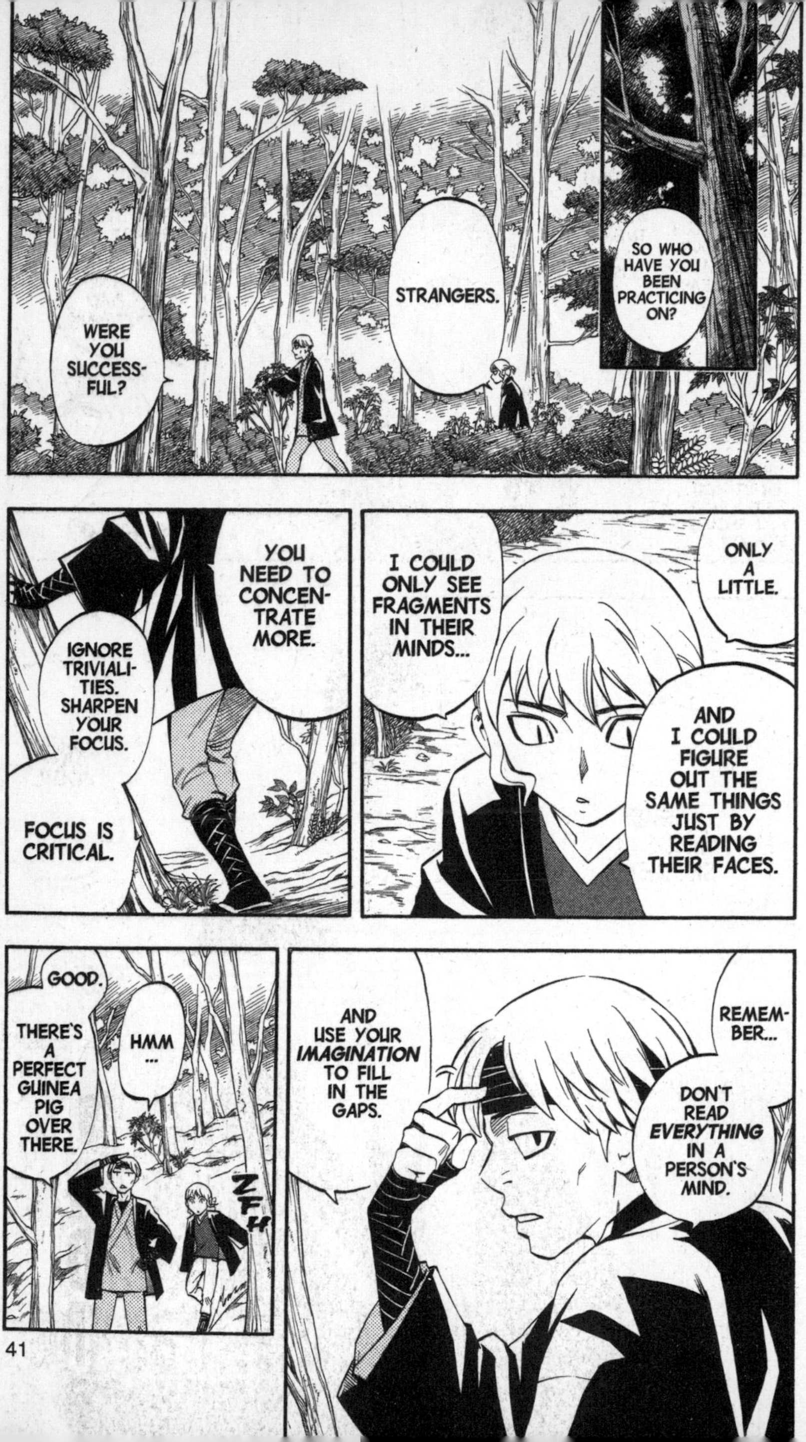
SO WHO HAVE YOU BEEN PRACTICING ON?
STRANGERS.
WERE YOU SUCCESSFUL?
ONLY A LITTLE.
I COULD ONLY SEE FRAGMENTS IN THEIR MINDS...
AND I COULD FIGURE OUT THE SAME THINGS JUST BY READING THEIR FACES.
YOU NEED TO CONCENTRATE MORE.
IGNORE TRIVIALITIES. SHARPEN YOUR FOCUS.
FOCUS IS CRITICAL.
REMEMBER...
DON'T READ *EVERYTHING* IN A PERSON'S MIND.
AND USE YOUR *IMAGINATION* TO FILL IN THE GAPS.
GOOD.
THERE'S A PERFECT GUINEA PIG OVER THERE.
HMM...
ZFH

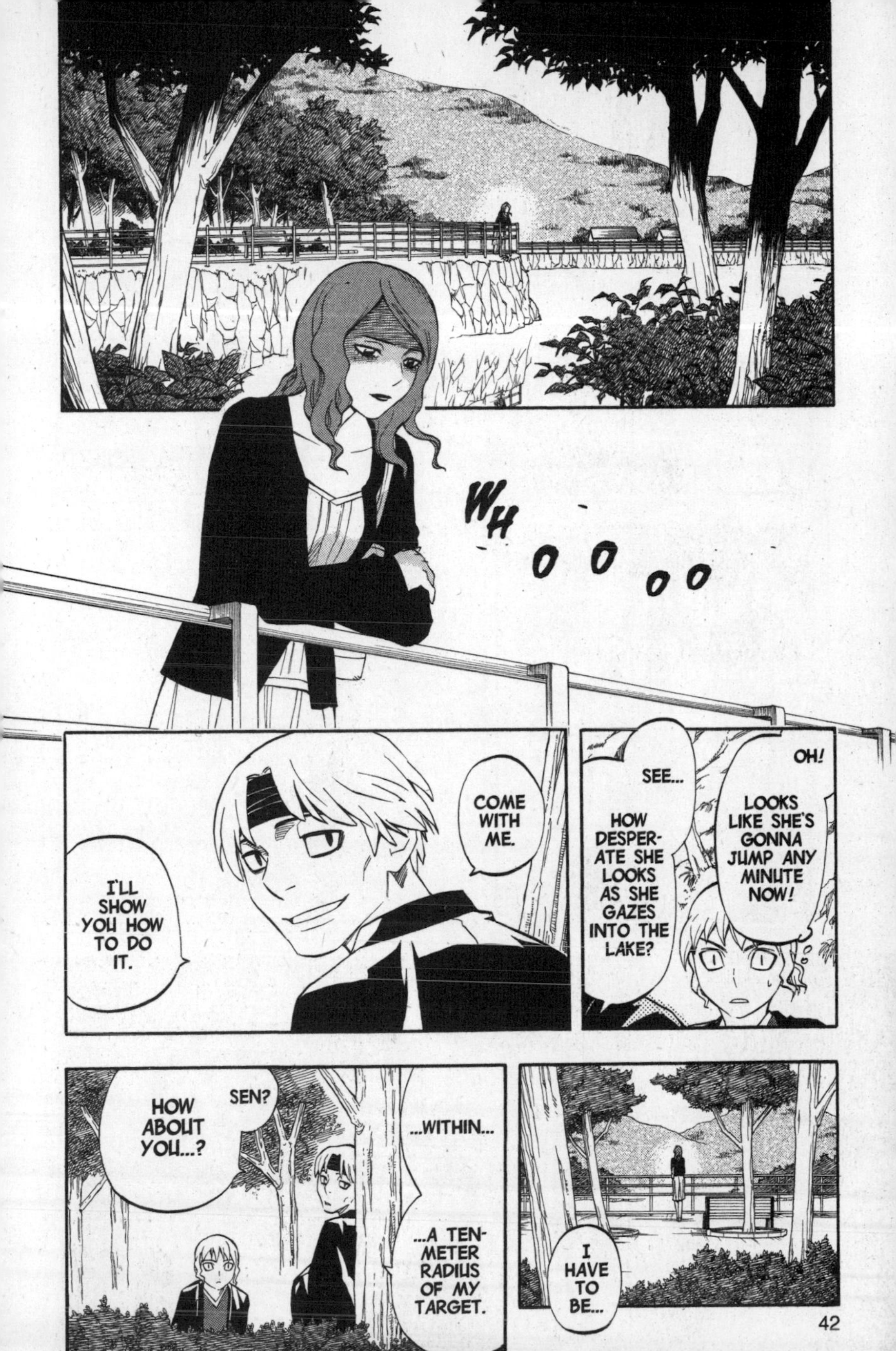
WHOOOOO
OH!
LOOKS LIKE SHE'S GONNA JUMP ANY MINUTE NOW!
SEE...
HOW DESPERATE SHE LOOKS AS SHE GAZES INTO THE LAKE?
COME WITH ME.
I'LL SHOW YOU HOW TO DO IT.
I HAVE TO BE...
...WITHIN...
...A TEN-METER RADIUS OF MY TARGET.
SEN?
HOW ABOUT YOU...?

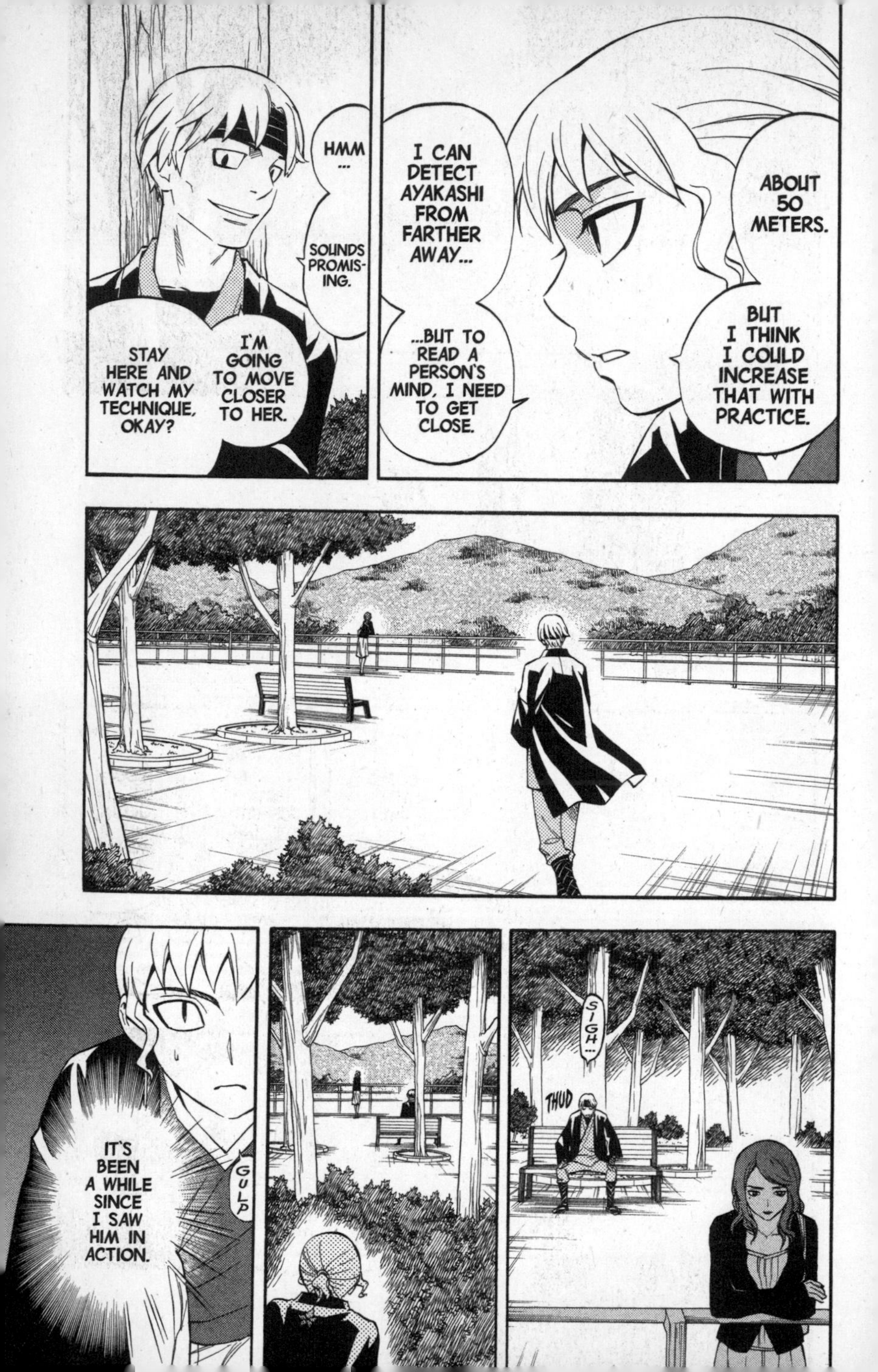
ABOUT 50 METERS.
BUT I THINK I COULD INCREASE THAT WITH PRACTICE.
I CAN DETECT AYAKASHI FROM FARTHER AWAY...
...BUT TO READ A PERSON'S MIND, I NEED TO GET CLOSE.
HMM...
SOUNDS PROMISING.
I'M GOING TO MOVE CLOSER TO HER.
STAY HERE AND WATCH MY TECHNIQUE, OKAY?
SIGH...
THUD
GULP
IT'S BEEN A WHILE SINCE I SAW HIM IN ACTION.

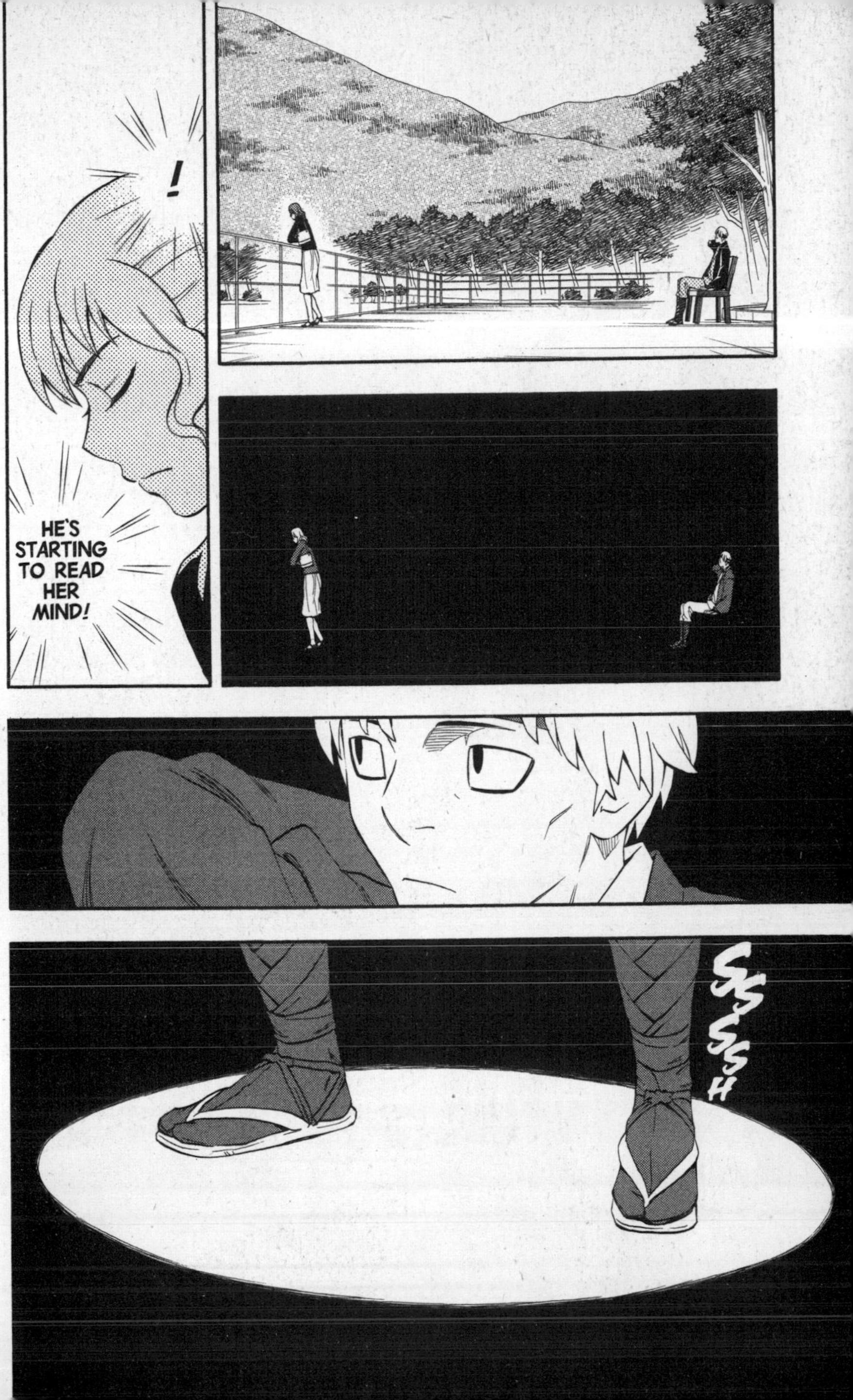
!
HE'S STARTING TO READ HER MIND!
SSSSH

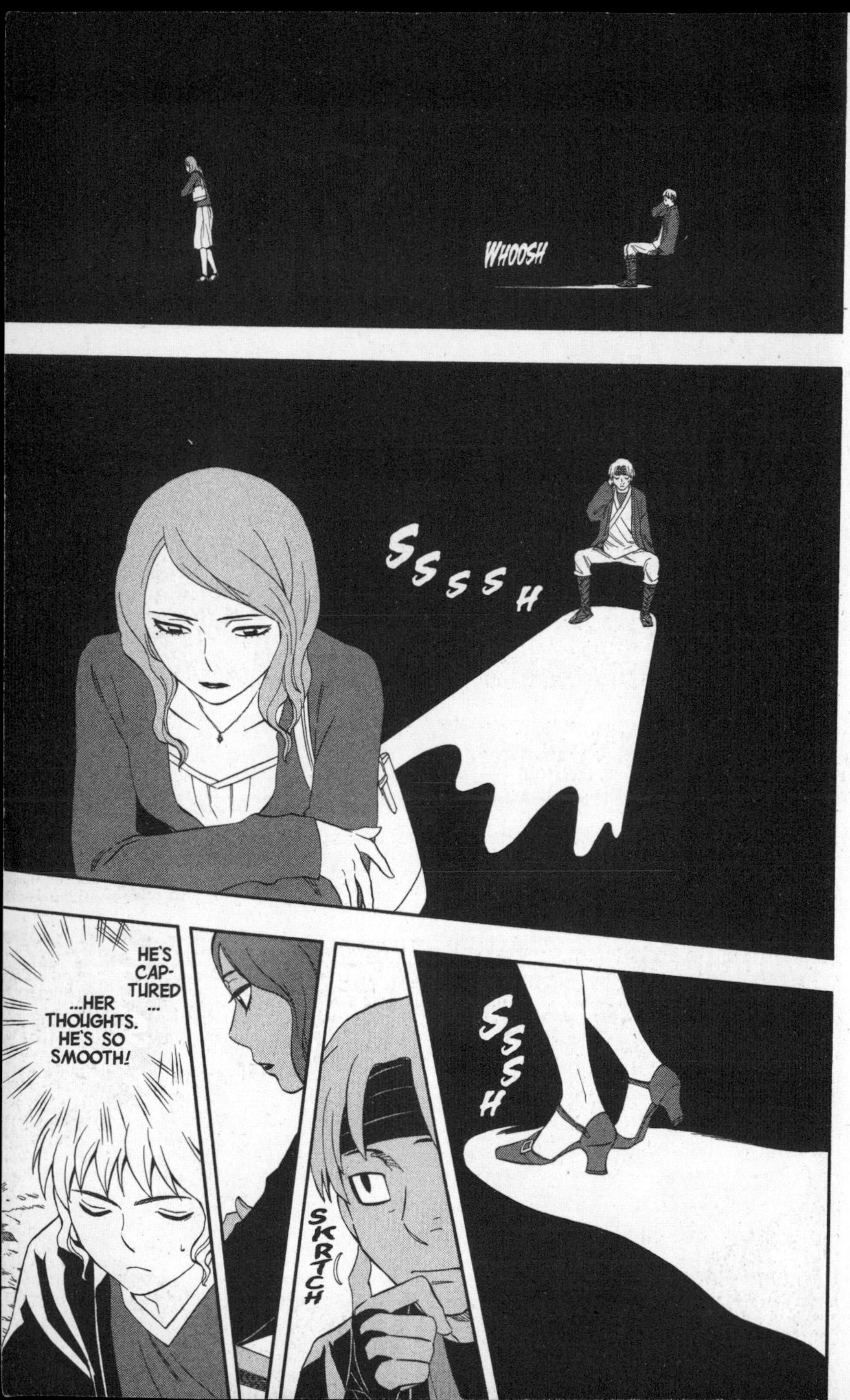
WHOOSH
SSSSH
SSSH
SKRTCH
HE'S CAPTURED...
...HER THOUGHTS. HE'S SO SMOOTH!

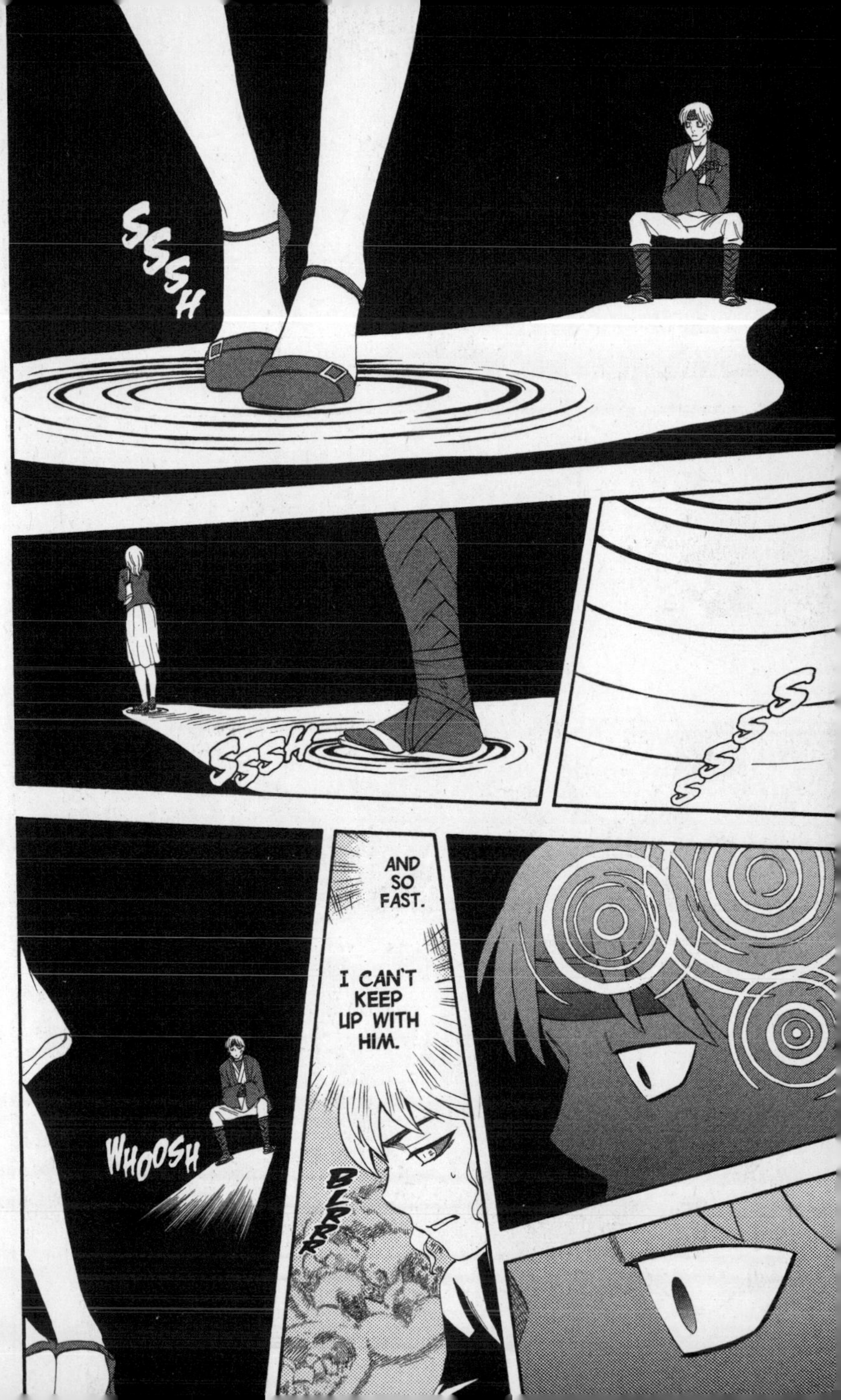
SSSH
SSSSS
SSSH
AND SO FAST.
I CAN'T KEEP UP WITH HIM.
BLRRR
WHOOSH

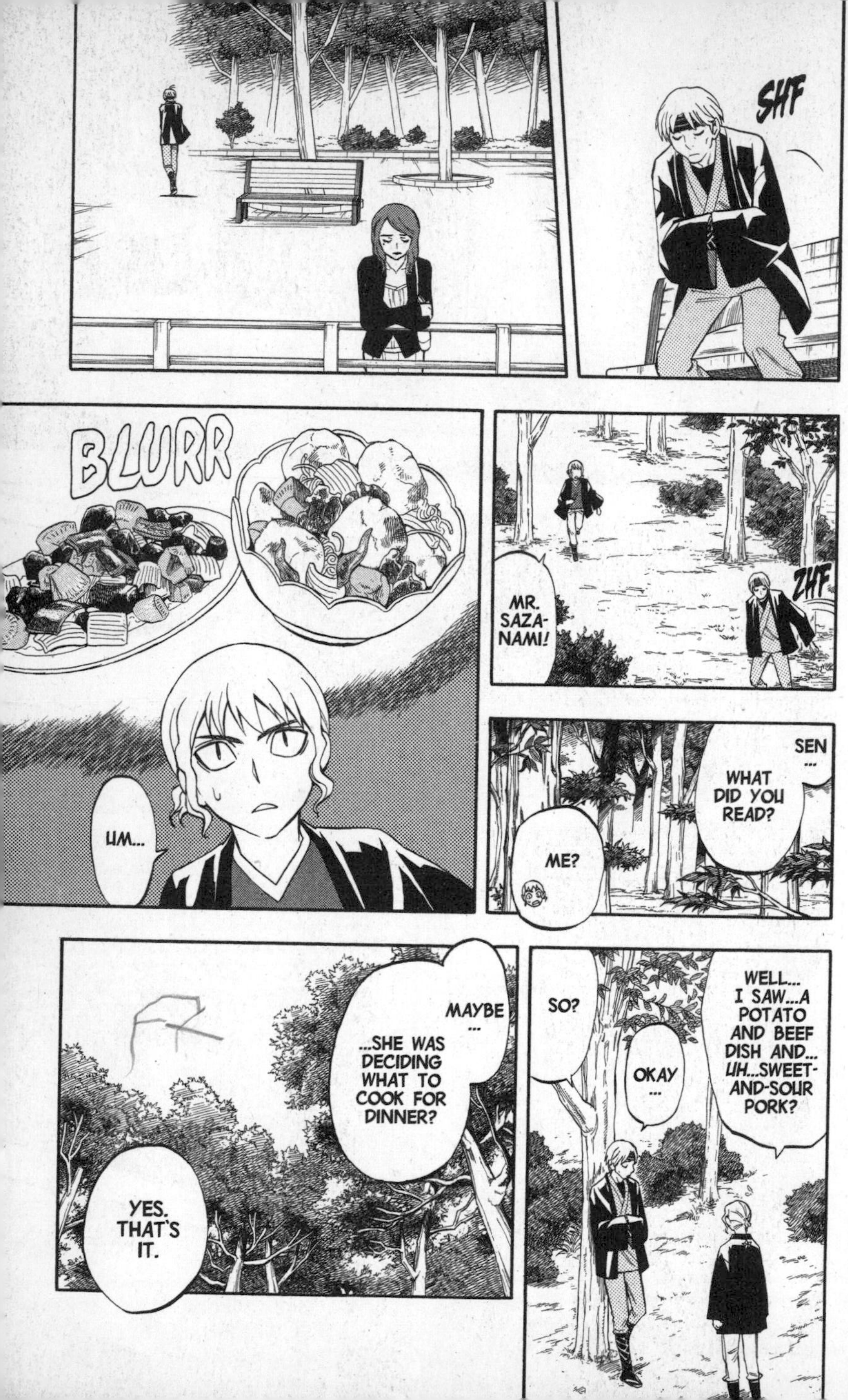
SHF
MR. SAZANAMI!
ZHF
SEN...
WHAT DID YOU READ?
ME?
BLURR
UM...
WELL... I SAW...A POTATO AND BEEF DISH AND... UH...SWEET-AND-SOUR PORK?
SO?
OKAY...
MAYBE...
...SHE WAS DECIDING WHAT TO COOK FOR DINNER?
YES. THAT'S IT.

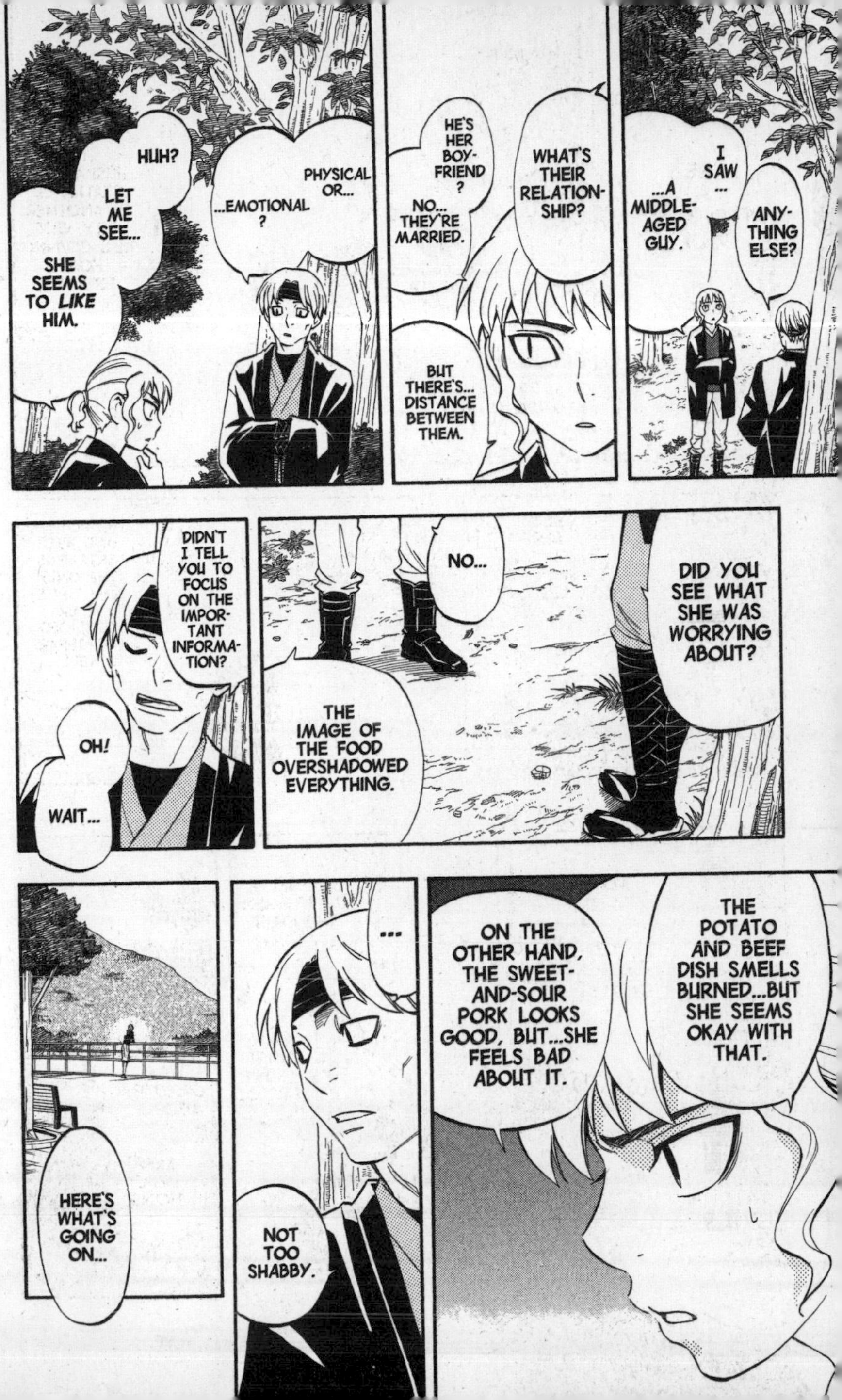
ANYTHING ELSE?
I SAW...
...A MIDDLE-AGED GUY.
WHAT'S THEIR RELATIONSHIP?
HE'S HER BOYFRIEND?
NO... THEY'RE MARRIED.
BUT THERE'S... DISTANCE BETWEEN THEM.
PHYSICAL OR...
...EMOTIONAL?
HUH?
LET ME SEE...
SHE SEEMS TO *LIKE* HIM.
DID YOU SEE WHAT SHE WAS WORRYING ABOUT?
NO...
THE IMAGE OF THE FOOD OVERSHADOWED EVERYTHING.
DIDN'T I TELL YOU TO FOCUS ON THE IMPORTANT INFORMATION?
OH!
WAIT...
THE POTATO AND BEEF DISH SMELLS BURNED...BUT SHE SEEMS OKAY WITH THAT.
ON THE OTHER HAND, THE SWEET-AND-SOUR PORK LOOKS GOOD, BUT...SHE FEELS BAD ABOUT IT.
...
NOT TOO SHABBY.
HERE'S WHAT'S GOING ON...

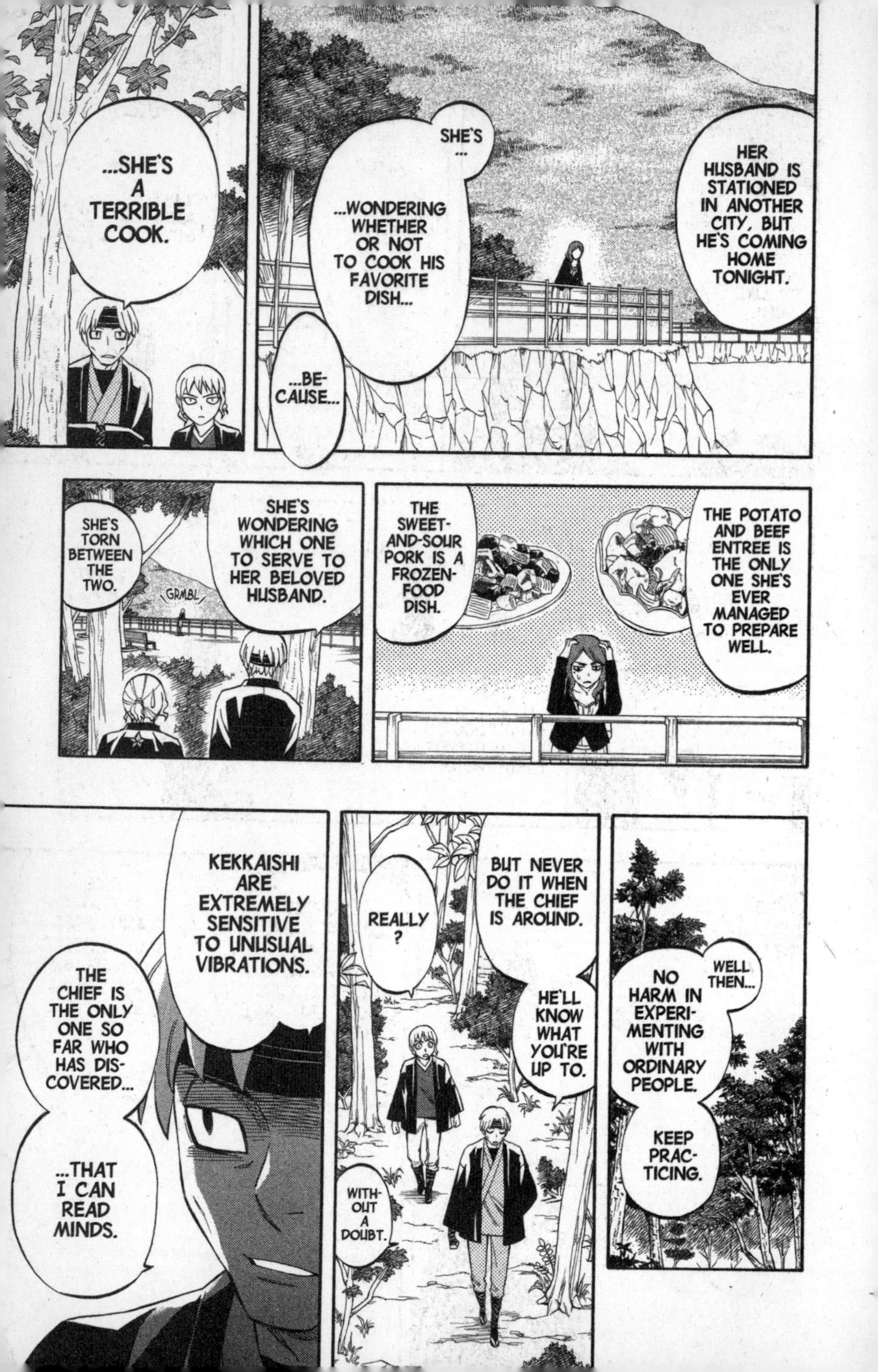
HER HUSBAND IS STATIONED IN ANOTHER CITY, BUT HE'S COMING HOME TONIGHT.
SHE'S...
...WONDERING WHETHER OR NOT TO COOK HIS FAVORITE DISH...
...BECAUSE...
...SHE'S A TERRIBLE COOK.
THE POTATO AND BEEF ENTREE IS THE ONLY ONE SHE'S EVER MANAGED TO PREPARE WELL.
THE SWEET-AND-SOUR PORK IS A FROZEN-FOOD DISH.
SHE'S WONDERING WHICH ONE TO SERVE TO HER BELOVED HUSBAND.
SHE'S TORN BETWEEN THE TWO.
GRMBL
WELL THEN...
NO HARM IN EXPERIMENTING WITH ORDINARY PEOPLE.
KEEP PRACTICING.
BUT NEVER DO IT WHEN THE CHIEF IS AROUND.
REALLY?
HE'LL KNOW WHAT YOU'RE UP TO.
WITHOUT A DOUBT.
KEKKAISHI ARE EXTREMELY SENSITIVE TO UNUSUAL VIBRATIONS.
THE CHIEF IS THE ONLY ONE SO FAR WHO HAS DISCOVERED...
...THAT I CAN READ MINDS.

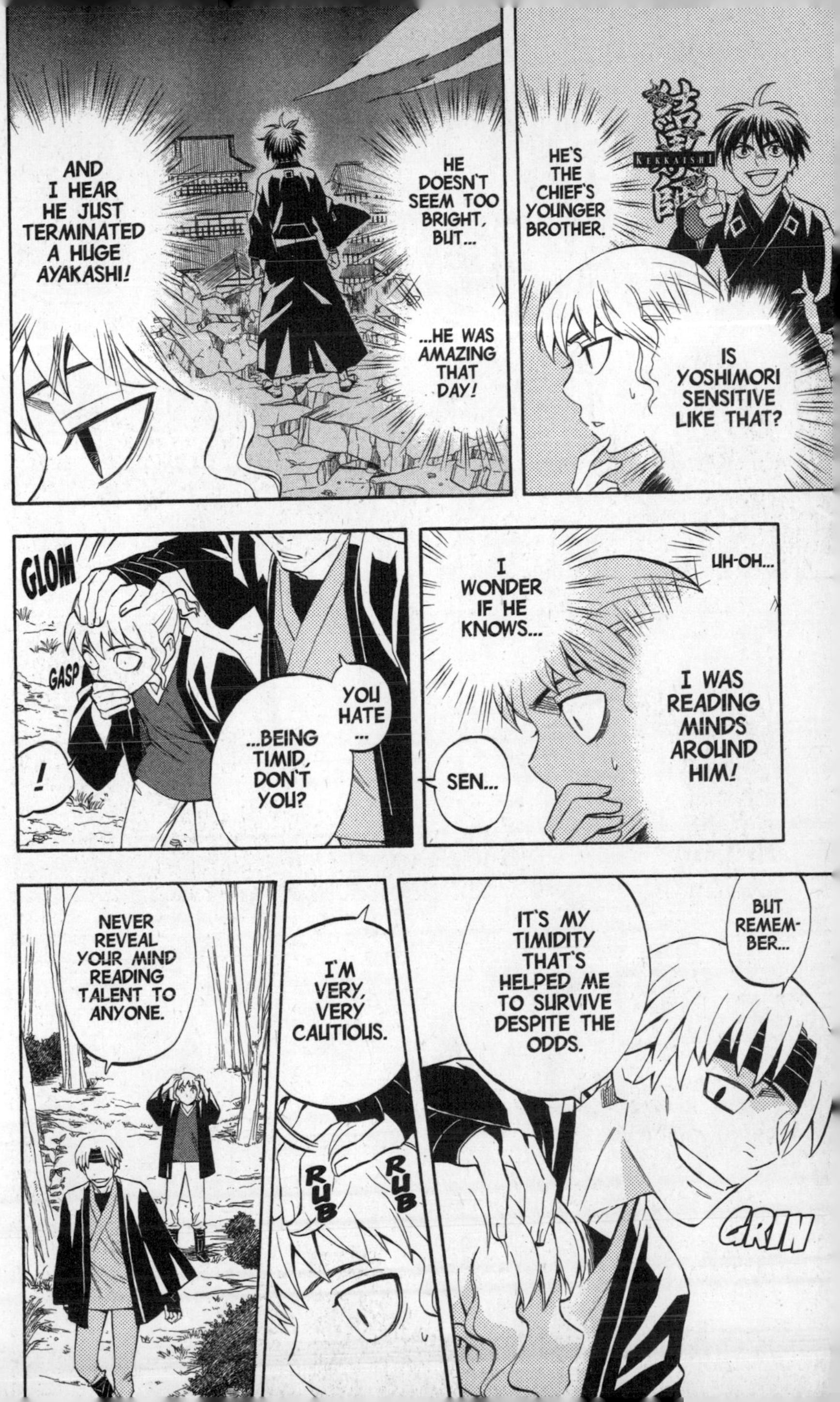

HE'S THE CHIEF'S YOUNGER BROTHER.
IS YOSHIMORI SENSITIVE LIKE THAT?
HE DOESN'T SEEM TOO BRIGHT, BUT...
...HE WAS AMAZING THAT DAY!
AND I HEAR HE JUST TERMINATED A HUGE AYAKASHI!
UH-OH...
I WONDER IF HE KNOWS...
I WAS READING MINDS AROUND HIM!
SEN...
GLOM
YOU HATE...
...BEING TIMID, DON'T YOU?
GASP
!
BUT REMEM-BER...
IT'S MY TIMIDITY THAT'S HELPED ME TO SURVIVE DESPITE THE ODDS.
GRIN
I'M VERY, VERY CAUTIOUS.
RUB
RUB
NEVER REVEAL YOUR MIND READING TALENT TO ANYONE.

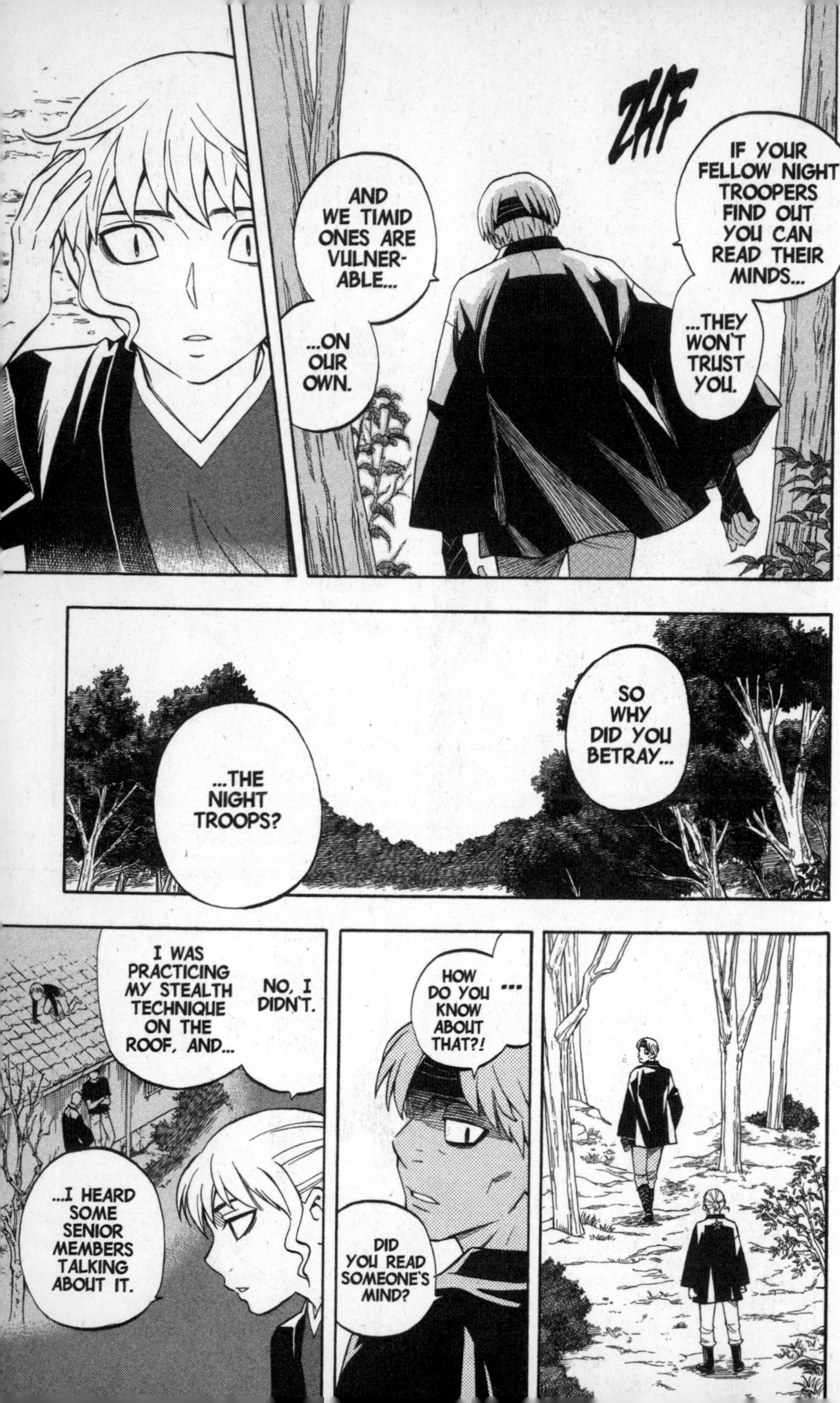
ZHF
IF YOUR FELLOW NIGHT TROOPERS FIND OUT YOU CAN READ THEIR MINDS...
...THEY WON'T TRUST YOU.
AND WE TIMID ONES ARE VULNERABLE...
...ON OUR OWN.
SO WHY DID YOU BETRAY...
...THE NIGHT TROOPS?
...
HOW DO YOU KNOW ABOUT THAT?!
DID YOU READ SOMEONE'S MIND?
NO, I DIDN'T.
I WAS PRACTICING MY STEALTH TECHNIQUE ON THE ROOF, AND...
...I HEARD SOME SENIOR MEMBERS TALKING ABOUT IT.

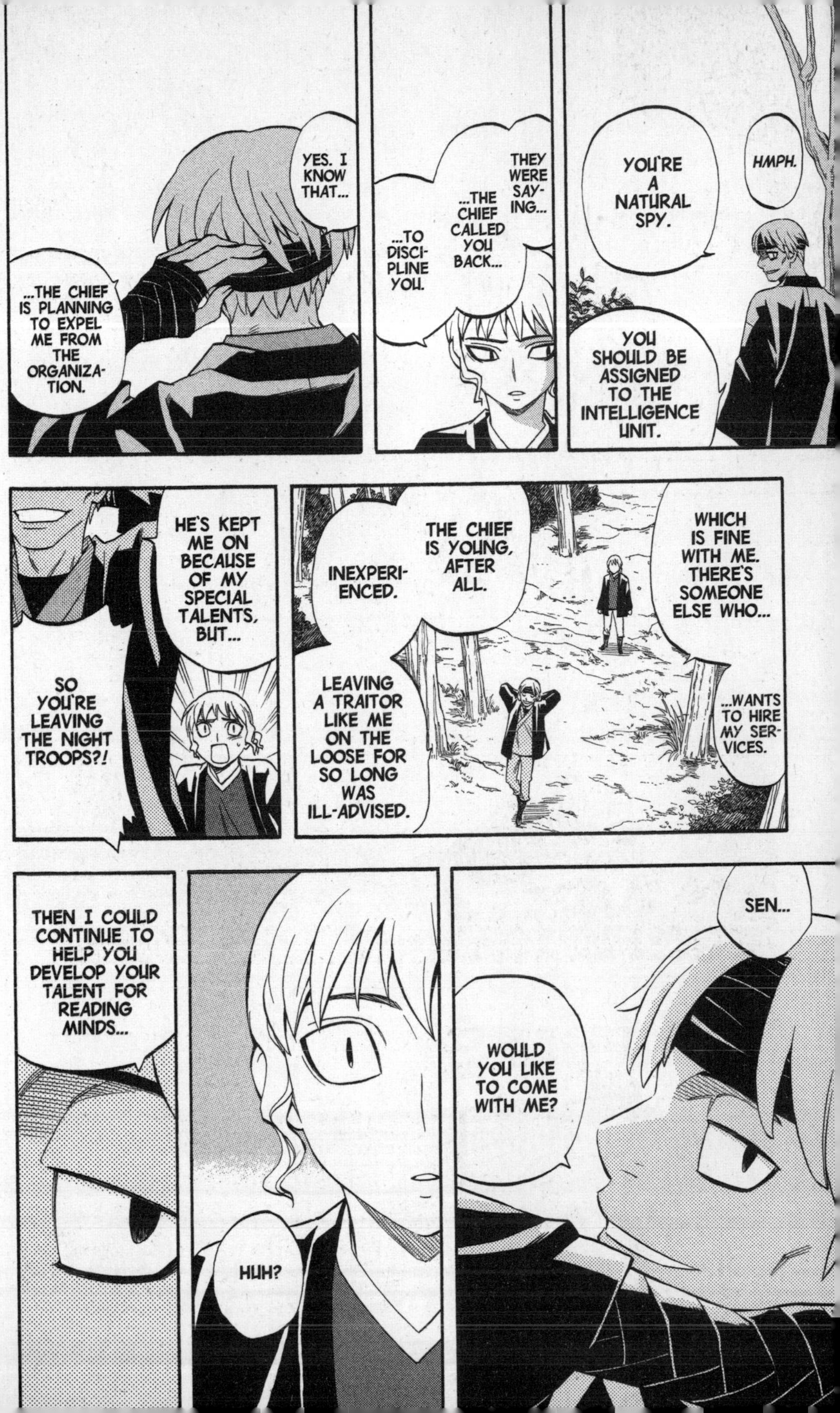
HMPH.
YOU'RE A NATURAL SPY.
YOU SHOULD BE ASSIGNED TO THE INTELLIGENCE UNIT.
THEY WERE SAYING...
...THE CHIEF CALLED YOU BACK...
...TO DISCIPLINE YOU.
YES. I KNOW THAT...
...THE CHIEF IS PLANNING TO EXPEL ME FROM THE ORGANIZATION.
WHICH IS FINE WITH ME. THERE'S SOMEONE ELSE WHO...
...WANTS TO HIRE MY SERVICES.
THE CHIEF IS YOUNG, AFTER ALL.
INEXPERIENCED.
LEAVING A TRAITOR LIKE ME ON THE LOOSE FOR SO LONG WAS ILL-ADVISED.
HE'S KEPT ME ON BECAUSE OF MY SPECIAL TALENTS, BUT...
SO YOU'RE LEAVING THE NIGHT TROOPS?!
SEN...
WOULD YOU LIKE TO COME WITH ME?
HUH?
THEN I COULD CONTINUE TO HELP YOU DEVELOP YOUR TALENT FOR READING MINDS...

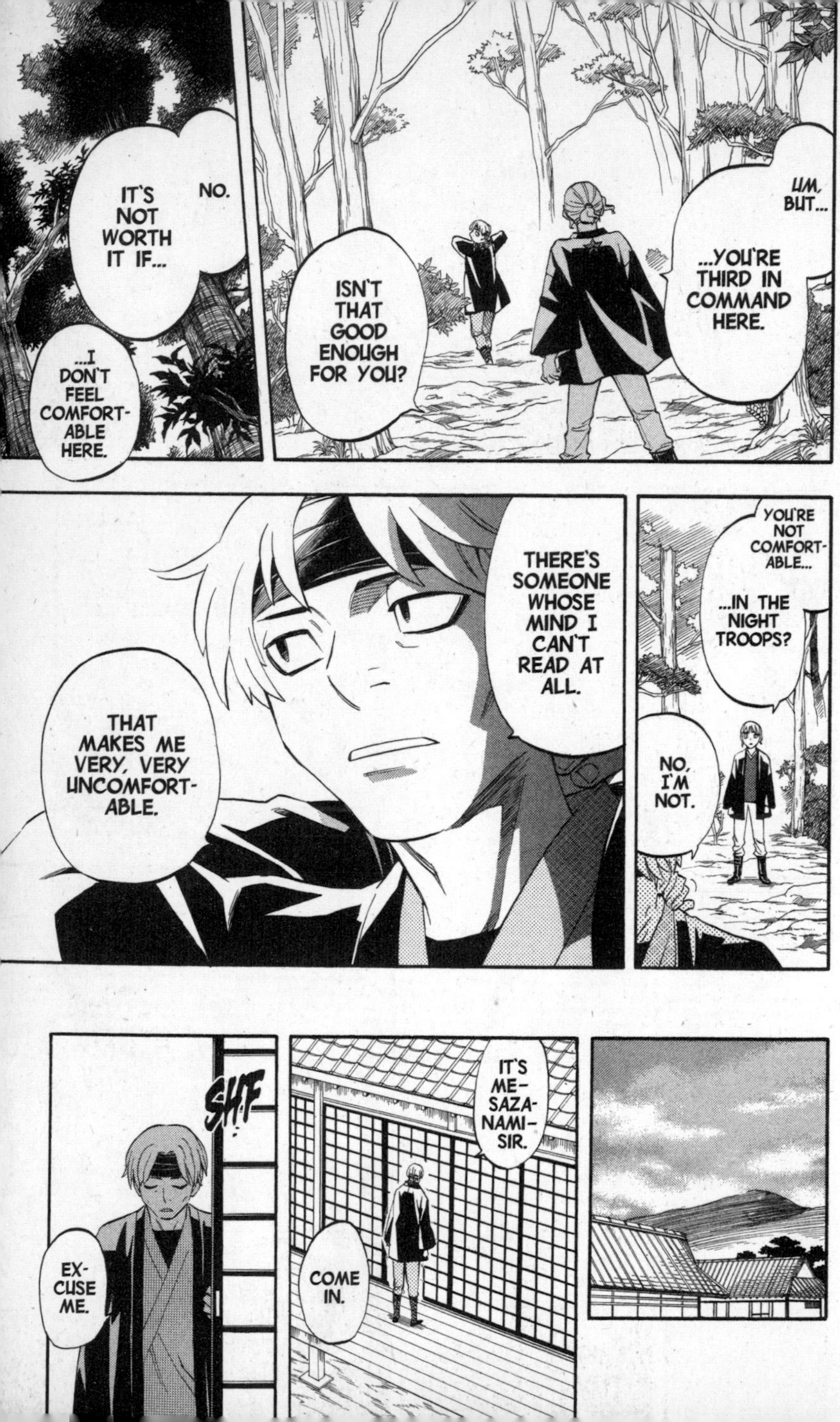
UM, BUT...
...YOU'RE THIRD IN COMMAND HERE.
ISN'T THAT GOOD ENOUGH FOR YOU?
NO.
IT'S NOT WORTH IT IF...
...I DON'T FEEL COMFORTABLE HERE.
YOU'RE NOT COMFORTABLE...
...IN THE NIGHT TROOPS?
NO, I'M NOT.
THERE'S SOMEONE WHOSE MIND I CAN'T READ AT ALL.
THAT MAKES ME VERY, VERY UNCOMFORTABLE.
IT'S ME—SAZANAMI—SIR.
COME IN.
SHF
EXCUSE ME.

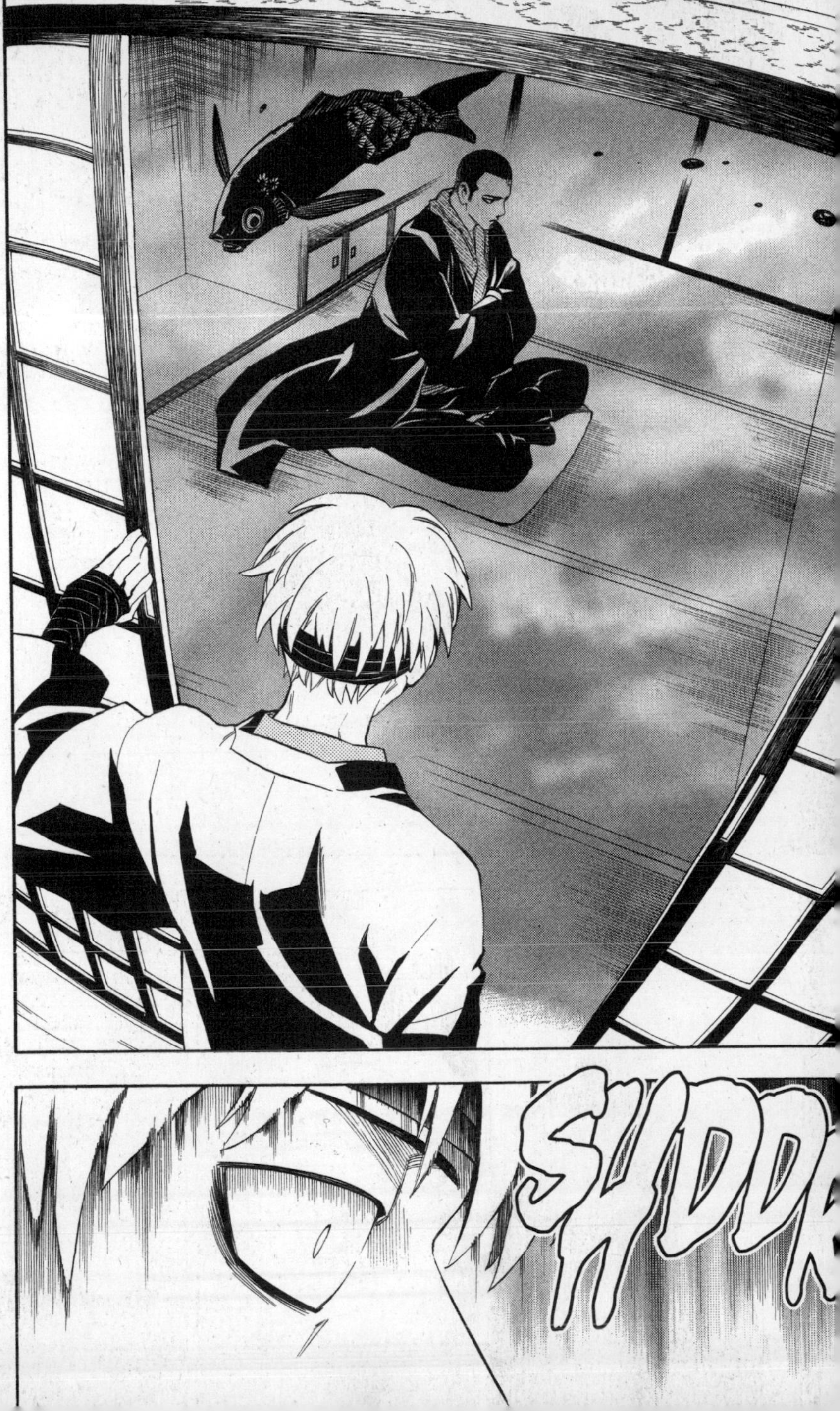
SHDD

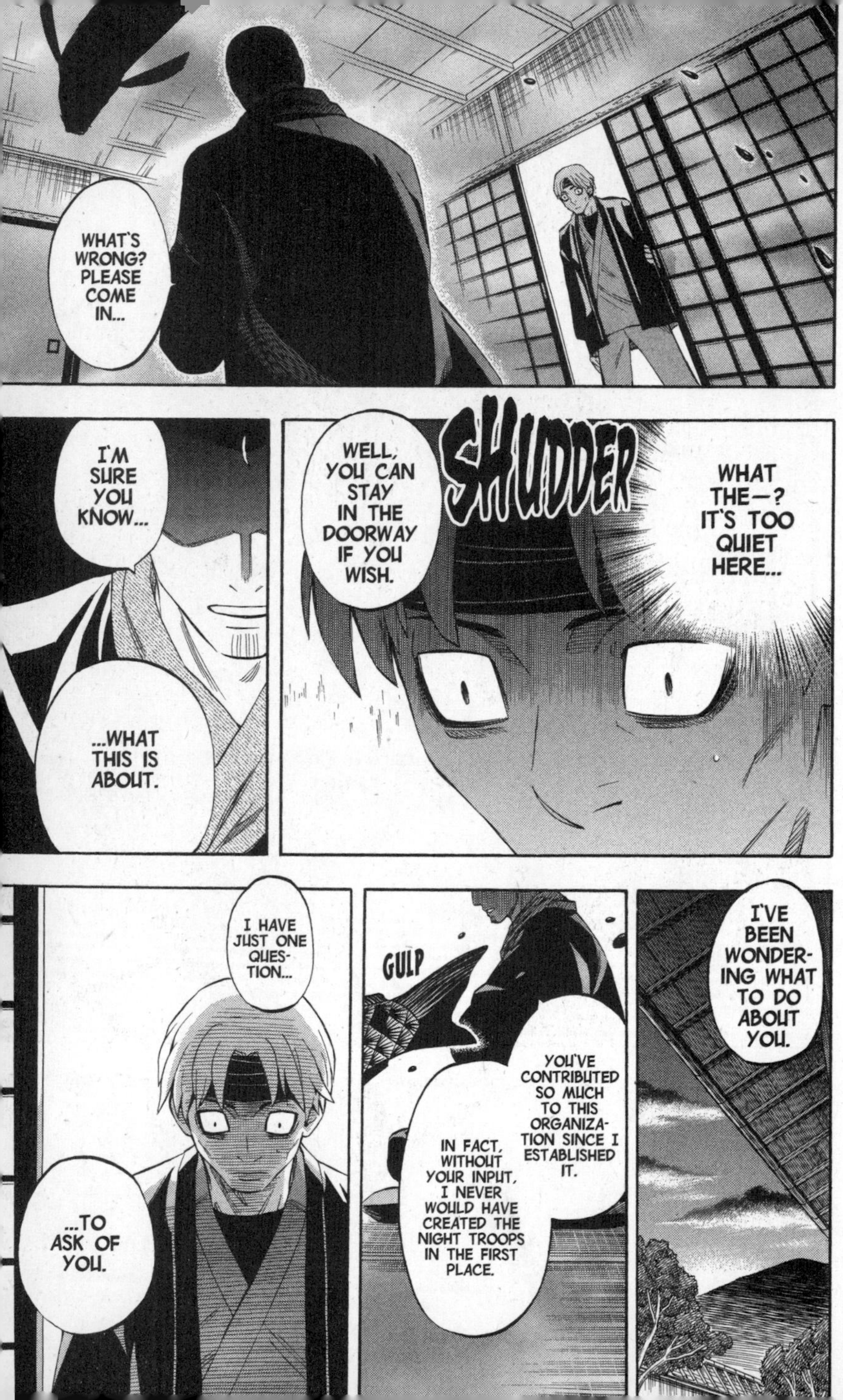
WHAT'S WRONG? PLEASE COME IN...
SHUDDER
WHAT THE—? IT'S TOO QUIET HERE...
WELL, YOU CAN STAY IN THE DOORWAY IF YOU WISH.
I'M SURE YOU KNOW...
...WHAT THIS IS ABOUT.
I'VE BEEN WONDERING WHAT TO DO ABOUT YOU.
GULP
YOU'VE CONTRIBUTED SO MUCH TO THIS ORGANIZATION SINCE I ESTABLISHED IT.
IN FACT, WITHOUT YOUR INPUT, I NEVER WOULD HAVE CREATED THE NIGHT TROOPS IN THE FIRST PLACE.
I HAVE JUST ONE QUESTION...
...TO ASK OF YOU.

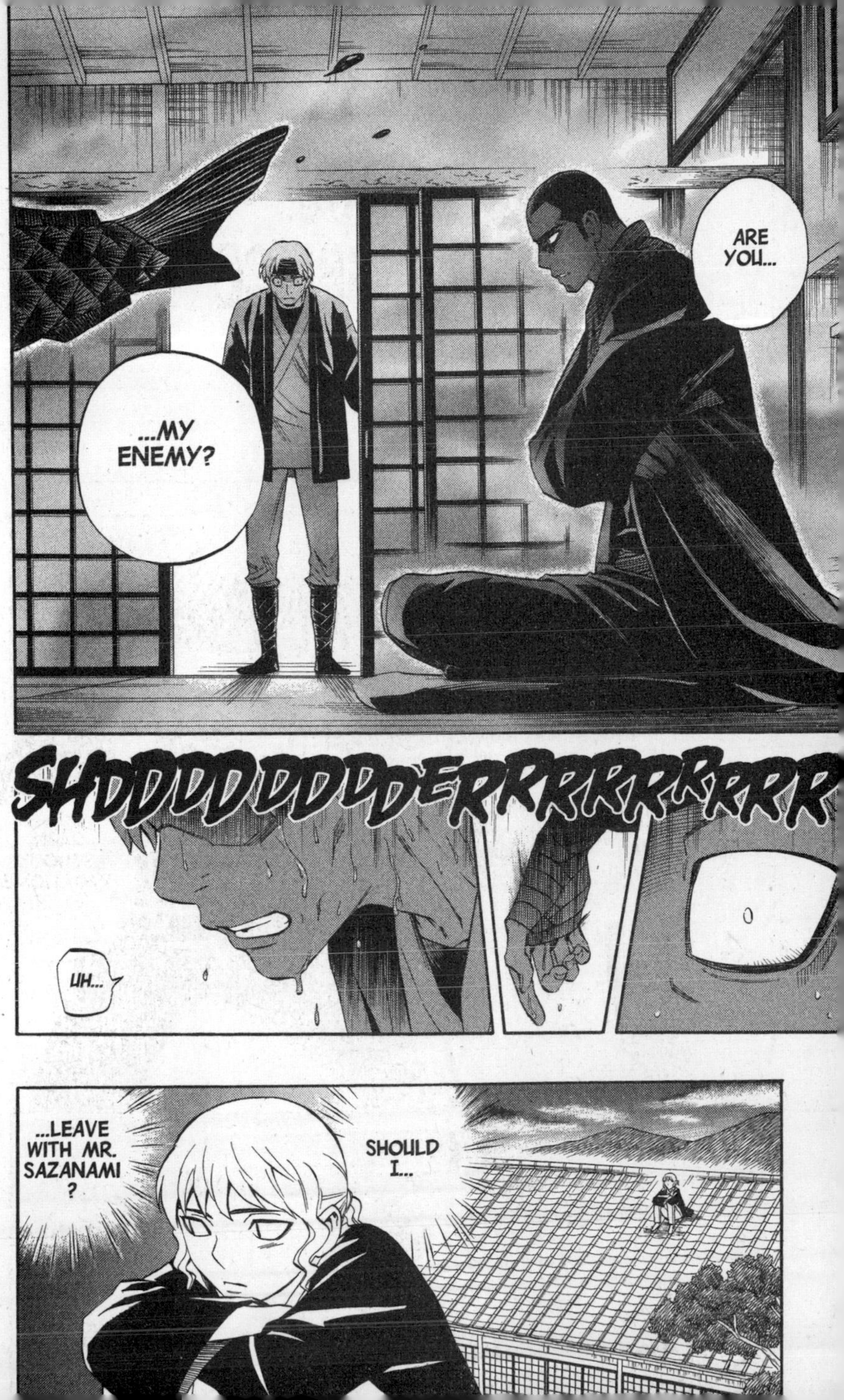
ARE YOU...
...MY ENEMY?
SHDDDDDDDDERRRRRRRRR
UH...
SHOULD I...
...LEAVE WITH MR. SAZANAMI?

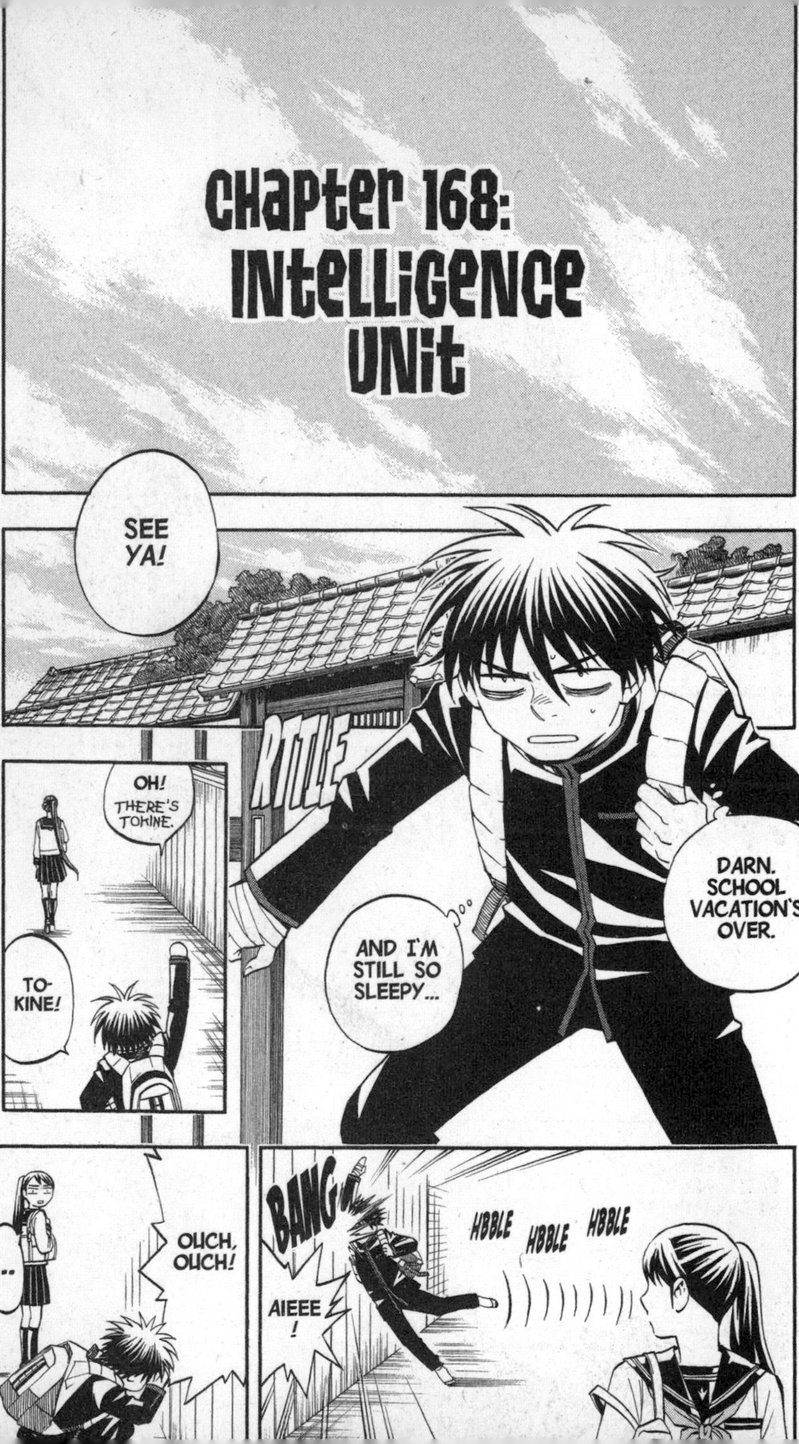
Chapter 168: Intelligence Unit
SEE YA!
RTTLE
DARN. SCHOOL VACATION'S OVER.
AND I'M STILL SO SLEEPY...
OH! THERE'S TOKINE.
TO-KINE!
BANG
AIEEE!
HBBLE HBBLE HBBLE
OUCH, OUCH!
...

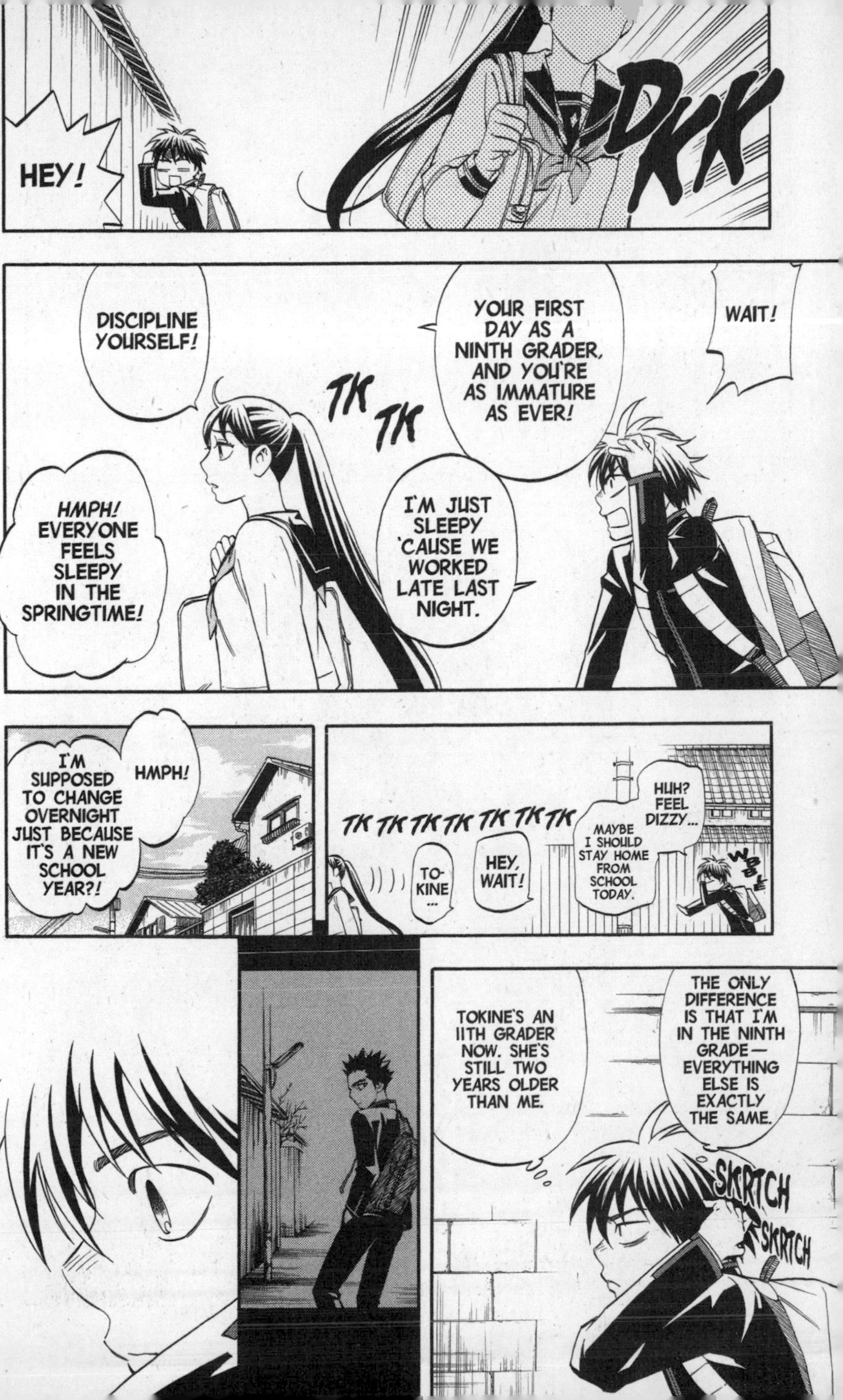
DKK
HEY!
WAIT!
YOUR FIRST DAY AS A NINTH GRADER, AND YOU'RE AS IMMATURE AS EVER!
TK TK
I'M JUST SLEEPY 'CAUSE WE WORKED LATE LAST NIGHT.
DISCIPLINE YOURSELF!
HMPH! EVERYONE FEELS SLEEPY IN THE SPRINGTIME!
HUH? FEEL DIZZY...
MAYBE I SHOULD STAY HOME FROM SCHOOL TODAY.
HEY, WAIT!
TK TK TK TK TK TK TK
TO-KINE...
HMPH!
I'M SUPPOSED TO CHANGE OVERNIGHT JUST BECAUSE IT'S A NEW SCHOOL YEAR?!
THE ONLY DIFFERENCE IS THAT I'M IN THE NINTH GRADE—EVERYTHING ELSE IS EXACTLY THE SAME.
TOKINE'S AN 11TH GRADER NOW. SHE'S STILL TWO YEARS OLDER THAN ME.
SKRTCH
SKRTCH

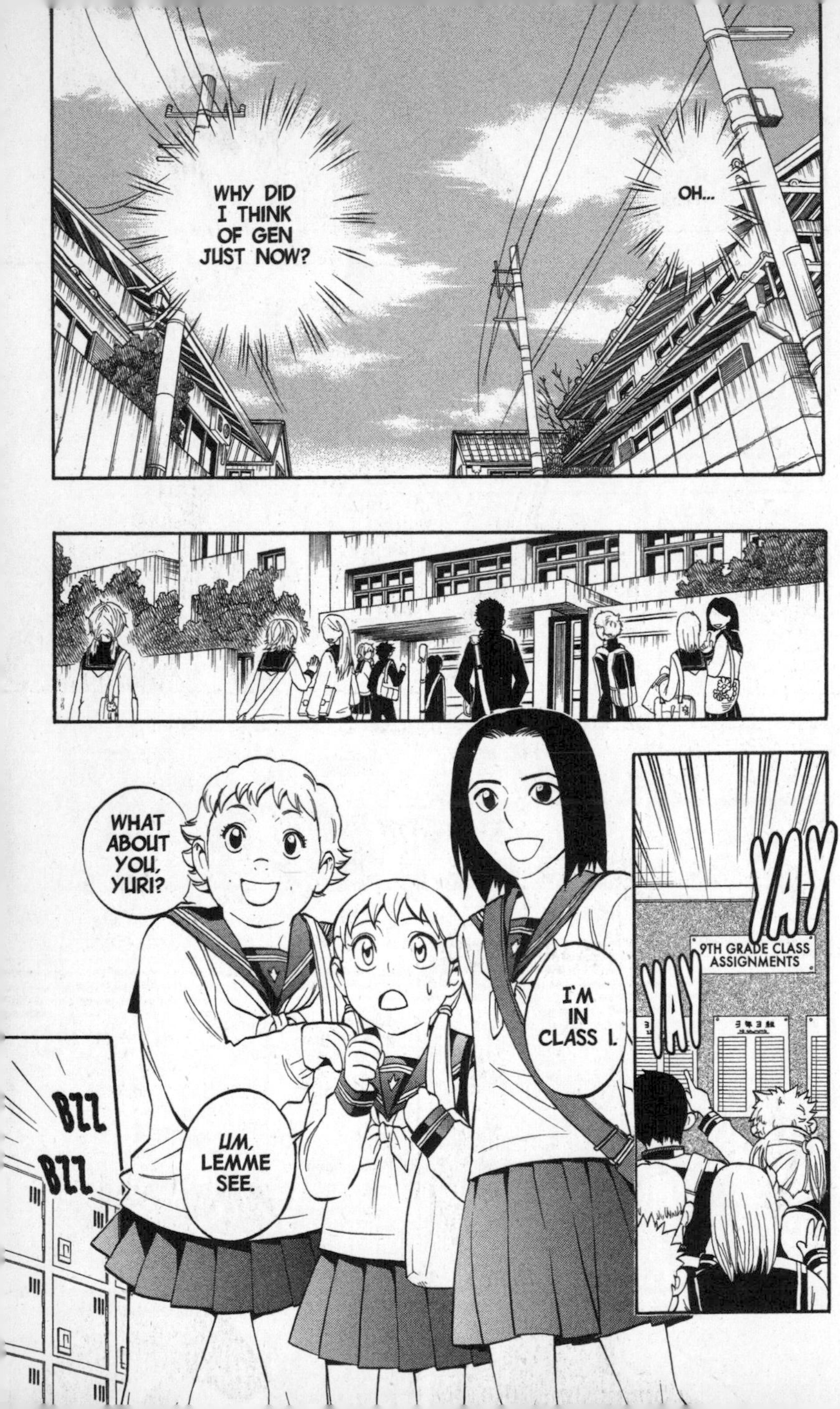
OH...
WHY DID I THINK OF GEN JUST NOW?
YAY
9TH GRADE CLASS ASSIGNMENTS
YAY
I'M IN CLASS 1.
WHAT ABOUT YOU, YURI?
UM, LEMME SEE.
BZZ
BZZ

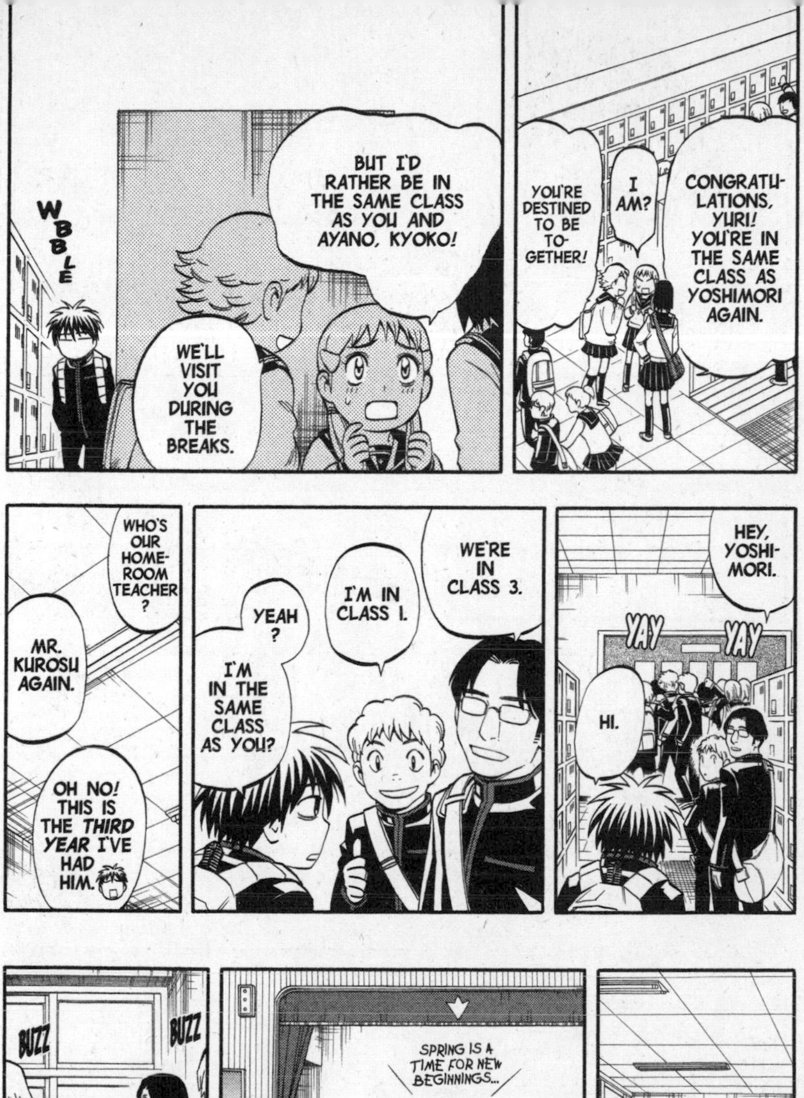
CONGRATU-LATIONS, YURI! YOU'RE IN THE SAME CLASS AS YOSHIMORI AGAIN.
I AM?
YOU'RE DESTINED TO BE TO-GETHER!
BUT I'D RATHER BE IN THE SAME CLASS AS YOU AND AYANO, KYOKO!
WE'LL VISIT YOU DURING THE BREAKS.
WBBLE
HEY, YOSHI-MORI.
YAY
YAY
HI.
WE'RE IN CLASS 3.
I'M IN CLASS 1.
YEAH?
I'M IN THE SAME CLASS AS YOU?
WHO'S OUR HOME-ROOM TEACHER?
MR. KUROSU AGAIN.
OH NO! THIS IS THE *THIRD YEAR* I'VE HAD HIM.
PFF
PFF
SPRING IS A TIME FOR NEW BEGINNINGS...
ZZZZ
BUZZ
BUZZ

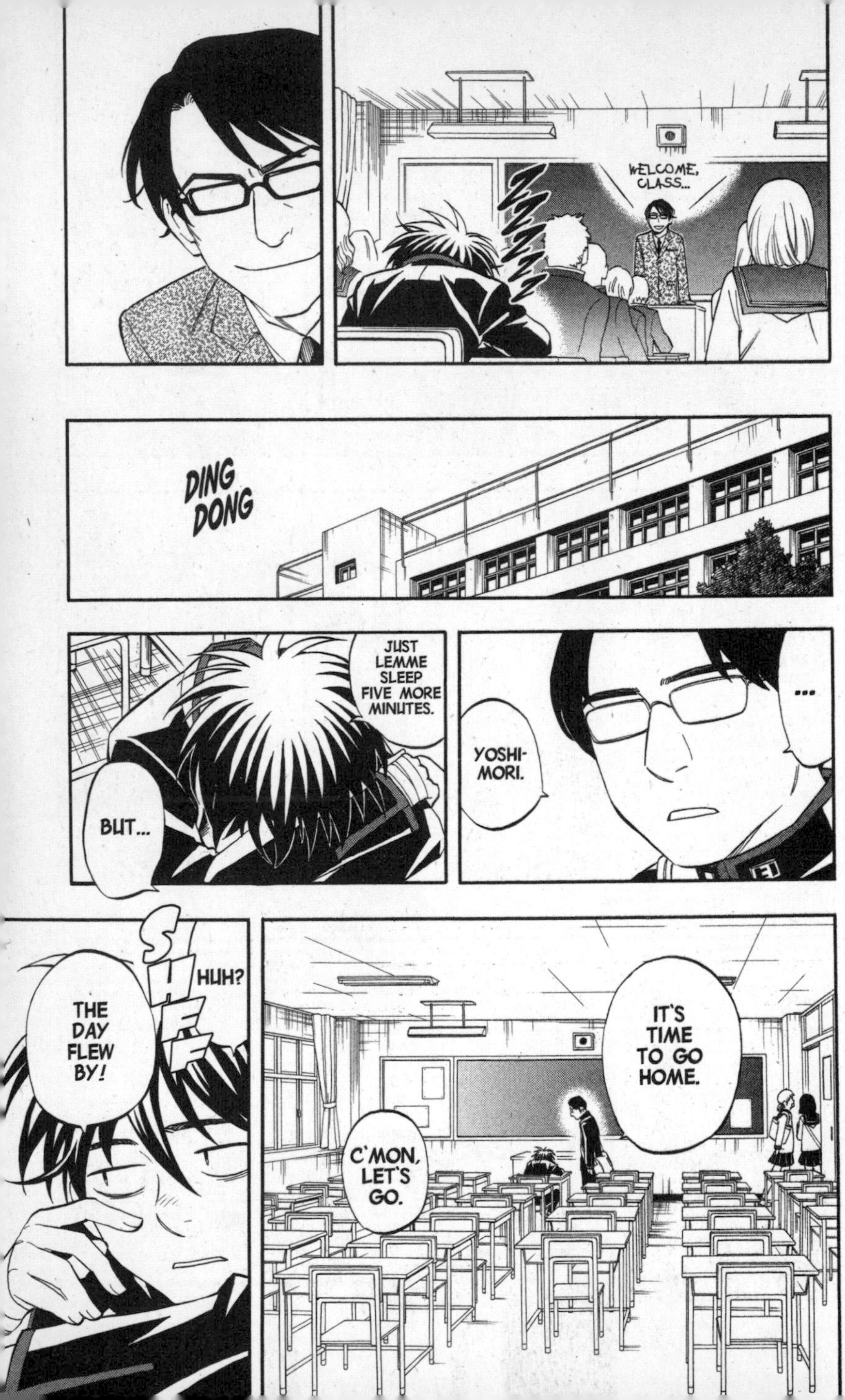
WELCOME, CLASS...
DING DONG
...
YOSHIMORI.
JUST LEMME SLEEP FIVE MORE MINUTES.
BUT...
IT'S TIME TO GO HOME.
C'MON, LET'S GO.
HUH?
THE DAY FLEW BY!

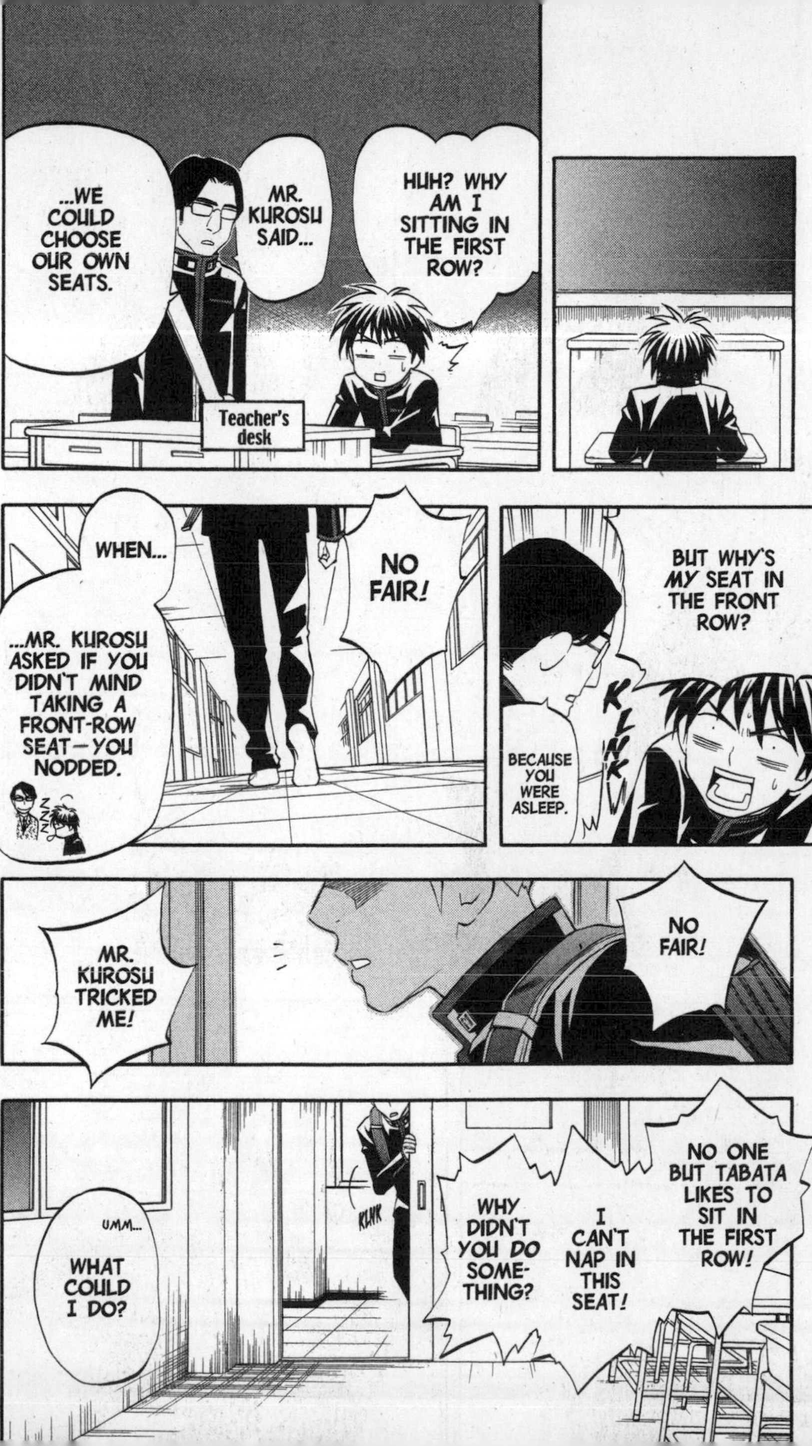
HUH? WHY AM I SITTING IN THE FIRST ROW?
MR. KUROSU SAID...
...WE COULD CHOOSE OUR OWN SEATS.
Teacher's desk
BUT WHY'S *MY* SEAT IN THE FRONT ROW?
KLINK
BECAUSE YOU WERE ASLEEP.
NO FAIR!
WHEN...
...MR. KUROSU ASKED IF YOU DIDN'T MIND TAKING A FRONT-ROW SEAT—YOU NODDED.
ZZZ
NO FAIR!
MR. KUROSU TRICKED ME!
NO ONE BUT TABATA LIKES TO SIT IN THE FIRST ROW!
I CAN'T NAP IN THIS SEAT!
WHY DIDN'T YOU *DO* SOME-THING?
KLNK
UMM...
WHAT COULD I DO?

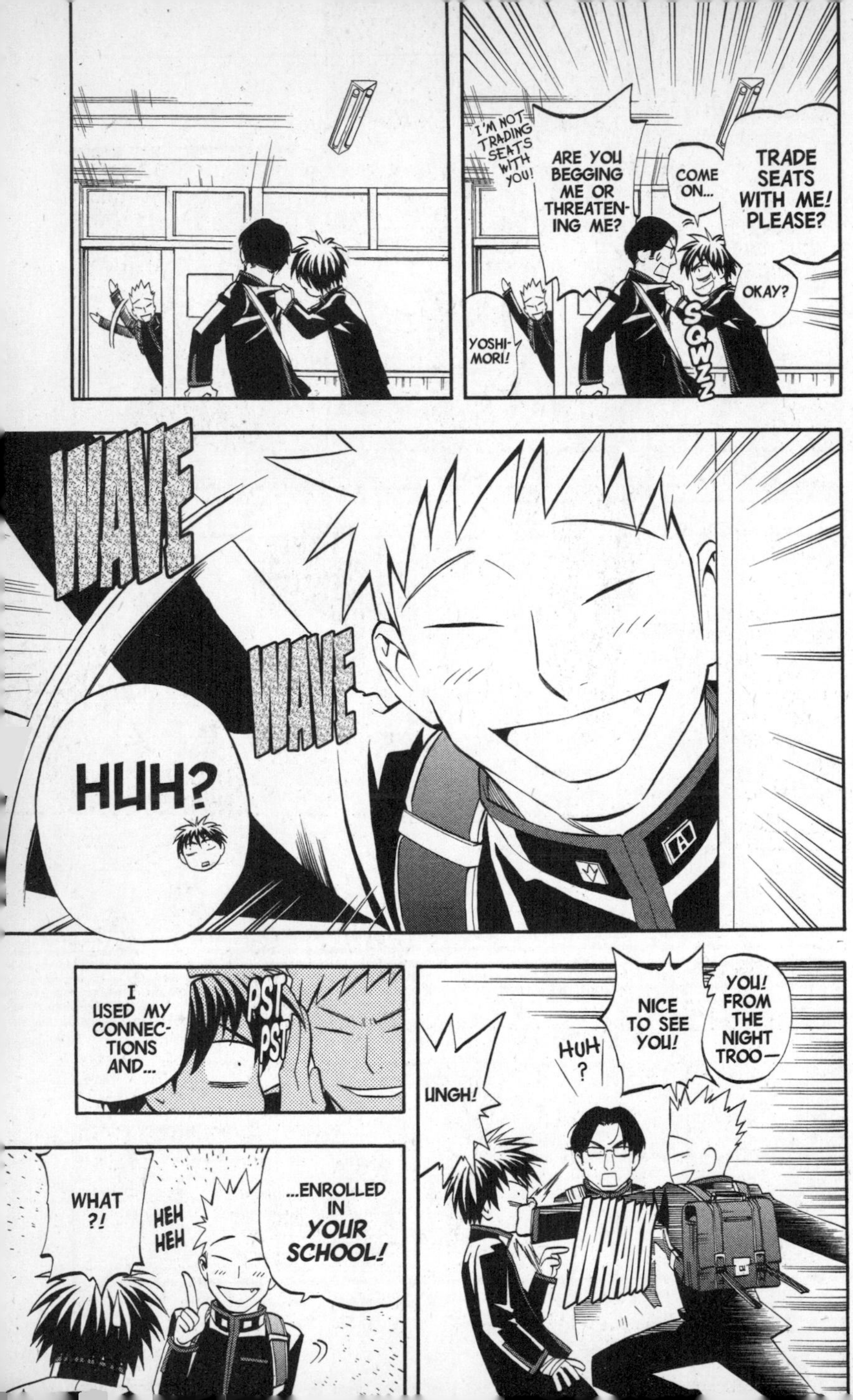
TRADE SEATS WITH ME! PLEASE?
COME ON...
OKAY?
ARE YOU BEGGING ME OR THREATENING ME?
I'M NOT TRADING SEATS WITH YOU!
SQWZZ
YOSHIMORI!
WAVE
WAVE
HUH?
YOU! FROM THE NIGHT TROO—
NICE TO SEE YOU!
HUH?
UNGH!
I USED MY CONNECTIONS AND...
PST PST
...ENROLLED IN YOUR SCHOOL!
HEH HEH
WHAT?!

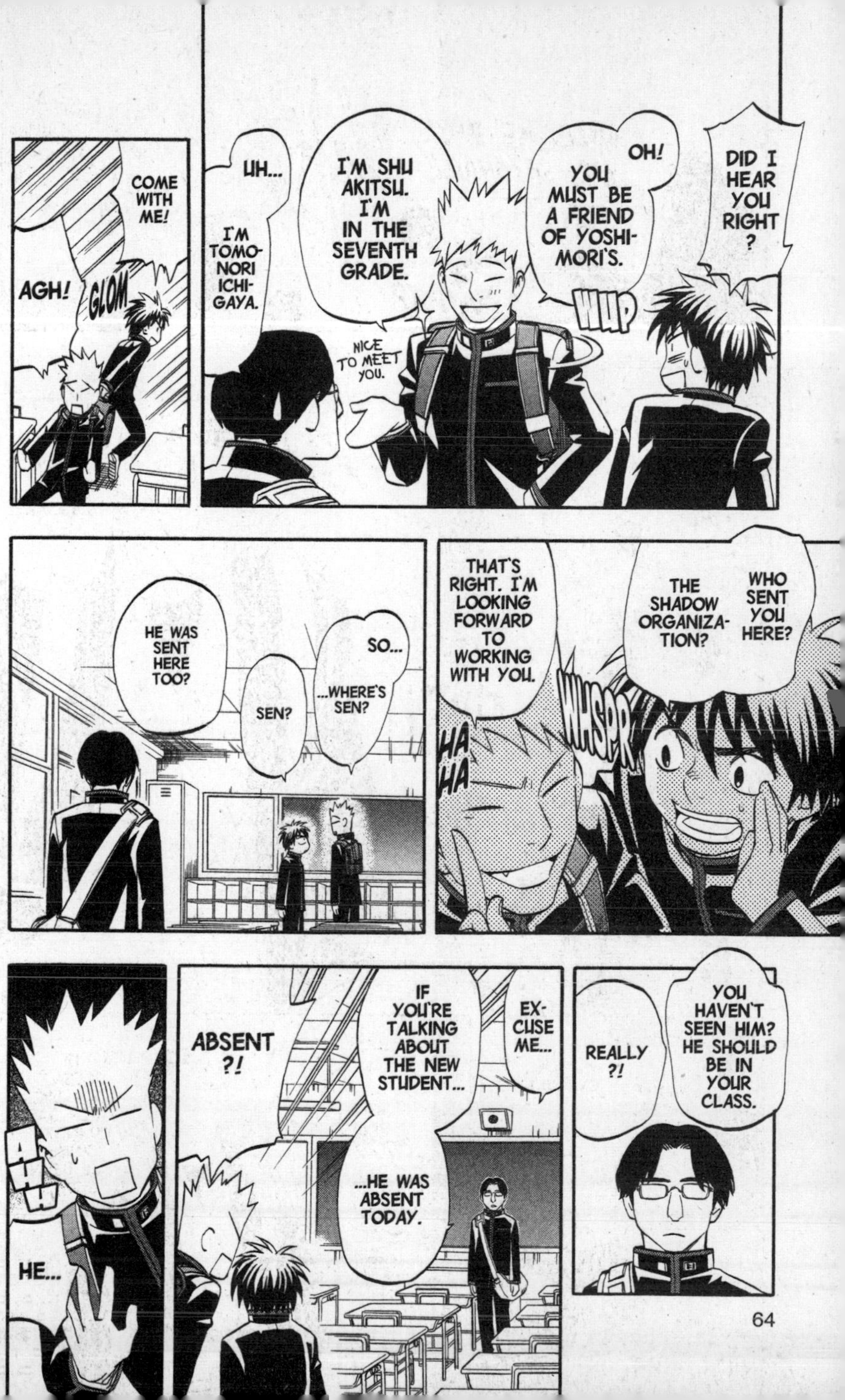
DID I HEAR YOU RIGHT?
OH!
YOU MUST BE A FRIEND OF YOSHI-MORI'S.
WUP
I'M SHU AKITSU. I'M IN THE SEVENTH GRADE.
NICE TO MEET YOU.
UH...
I'M TOMO-NORI ICHI-GAYA.
COME WITH ME!
GLOM
AGH!
WHO SENT YOU HERE?
THE SHADOW ORGANIZA-TION?
WHSPR
THAT'S RIGHT. I'M LOOKING FORWARD TO WORKING WITH YOU.
HA HA
SO...
...WHERE'S SEN?
SEN?
HE WAS SENT HERE TOO?
YOU HAVEN'T SEEN HIM? HE SHOULD BE IN YOUR CLASS.
REALLY ?!
EX-CUSE ME...
IF YOU'RE TALKING ABOUT THE NEW STUDENT...
...HE WAS ABSENT TODAY.
ABSENT ?!
AHH
HE...

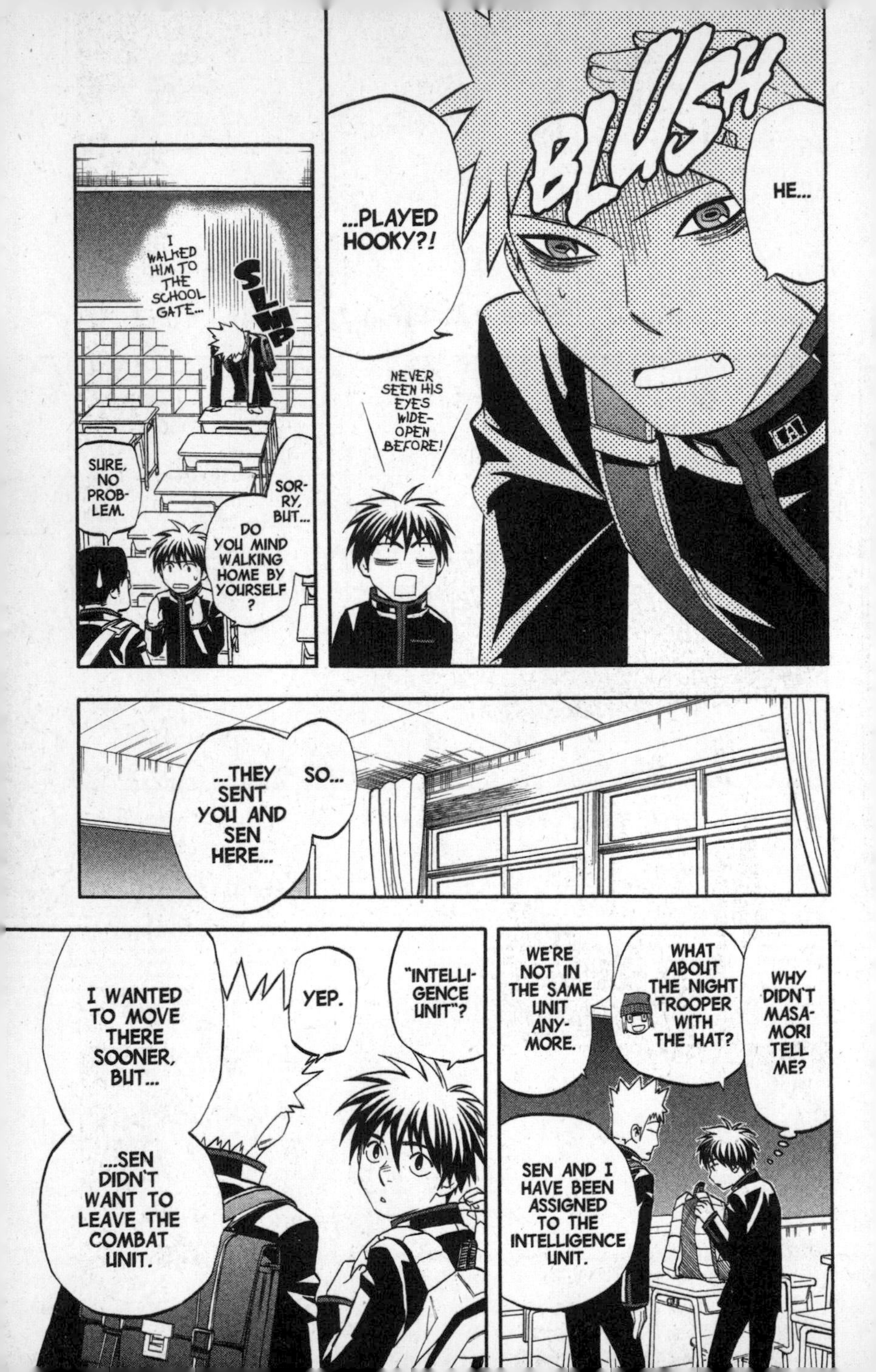
HE...
...PLAYED HOOKY?!
BLUSH
NEVER SEEN HIS EYES WIDE-OPEN BEFORE!
I WALKED HIM TO THE SCHOOL GATE...
SLUMP
SORRY, BUT... DO YOU MIND WALKING HOME BY YOURSELF?
SURE, NO PROB-LEM.
SO...
...THEY SENT YOU AND SEN HERE...
WHY DIDN'T MASAMORI TELL ME?
WHAT ABOUT THE NIGHT TROOPER WITH THE HAT?
WE'RE NOT IN THE SAME UNIT ANYMORE.
SEN AND I HAVE BEEN ASSIGNED TO THE INTELLIGENCE UNIT.
"INTELLIGENCE UNIT"?
YEP.
I WANTED TO MOVE THERE SOONER, BUT...
...SEN DIDN'T WANT TO LEAVE THE COMBAT UNIT.

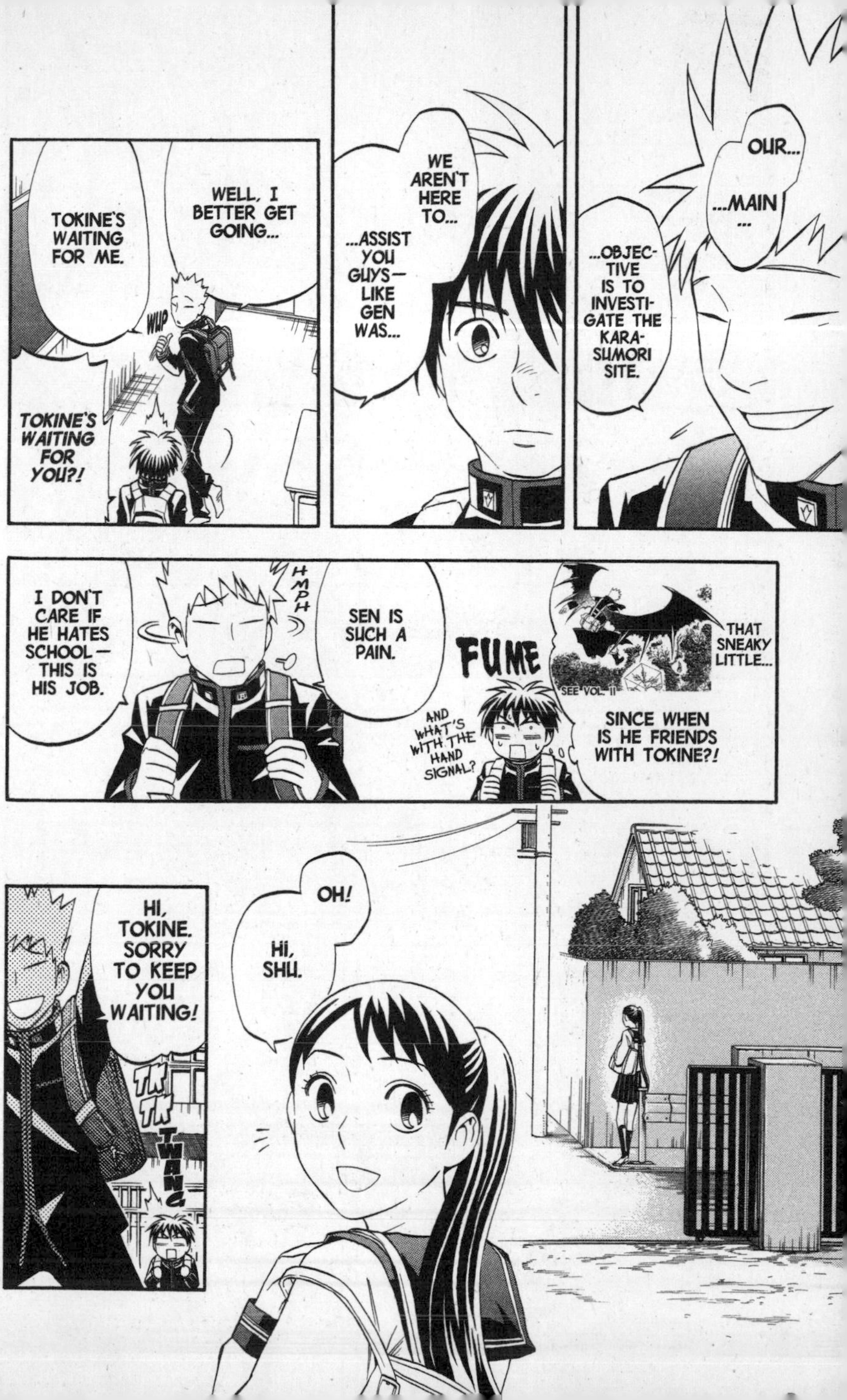
OUR...
...MAIN ...
...OBJECTIVE IS TO INVESTIGATE THE KARASUMORI SITE.
WE AREN'T HERE TO...
...ASSIST YOU GUYS—LIKE GEN WAS...
WELL, I BETTER GET GOING...
TOKINE'S WAITING FOR ME.
WUP
TOKINE'S WAITING FOR YOU?!
THAT SNEAKY LITTLE...
SEE VOL. 11
SINCE WHEN IS HE FRIENDS WITH TOKINE?!
FUME
AND WHAT'S WITH THE HAND SIGNAL?
HMPH
SEN IS SUCH A PAIN.
I DON'T CARE IF HE HATES SCHOOL—THIS IS HIS JOB.
OH!
HI, SHU.
HI, TOKINE. SORRY TO KEEP YOU WAITING!
TK TK
TWANG

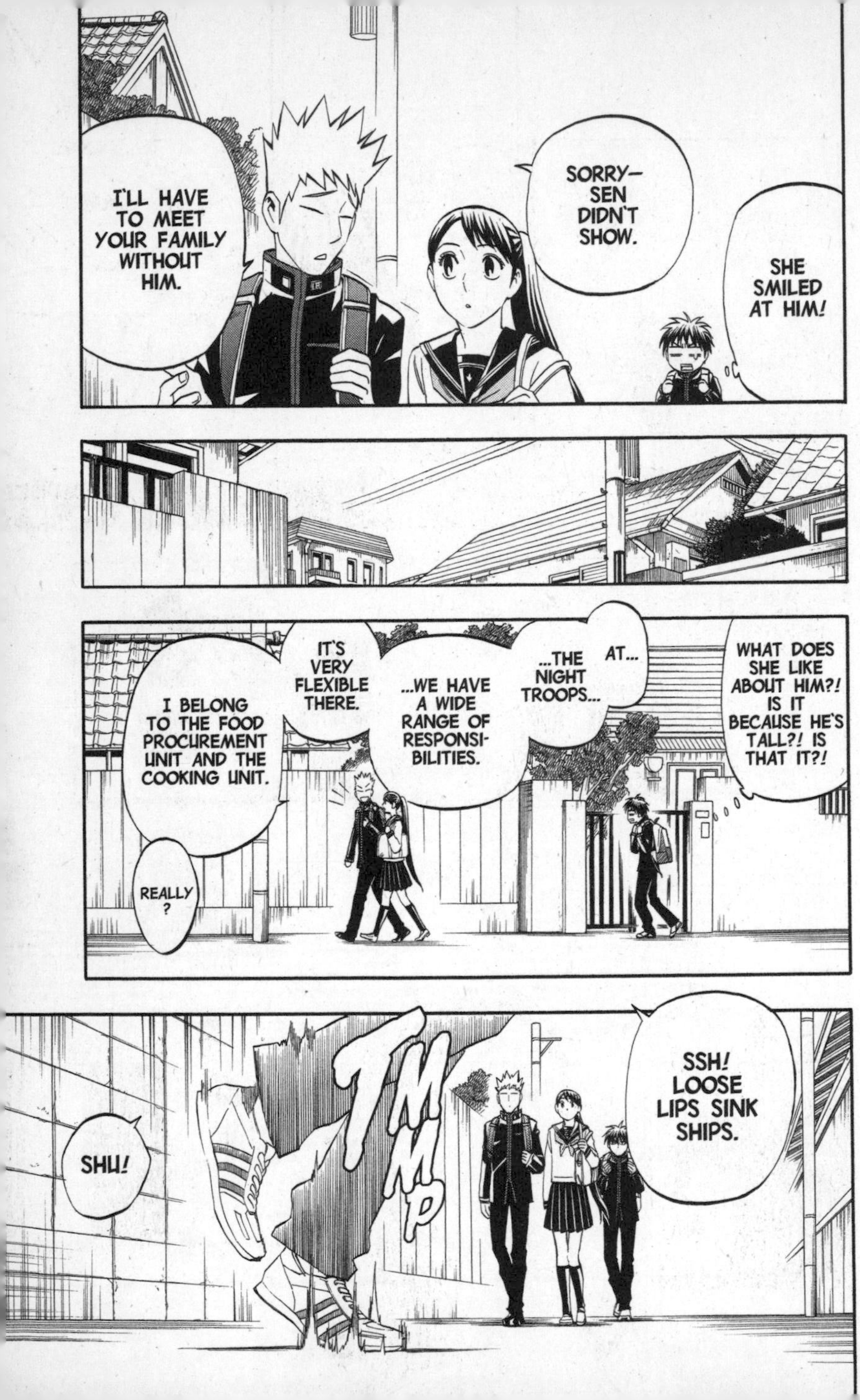
SORRY— SEN DIDN'T SHOW.
I'LL HAVE TO MEET YOUR FAMILY WITHOUT HIM.
SHE SMILED AT HIM!
WHAT DOES SHE LIKE ABOUT HIM?! IS IT BECAUSE HE'S TALL?! IS THAT IT?!
AT...
...THE NIGHT TROOPS...
...WE HAVE A WIDE RANGE OF RESPONSI-BILITIES.
IT'S VERY FLEXIBLE THERE.
I BELONG TO THE FOOD PROCUREMENT UNIT AND THE COOKING UNIT.
REALLY?
SSH! LOOSE LIPS SINK SHIPS.
TMMP
SHU!

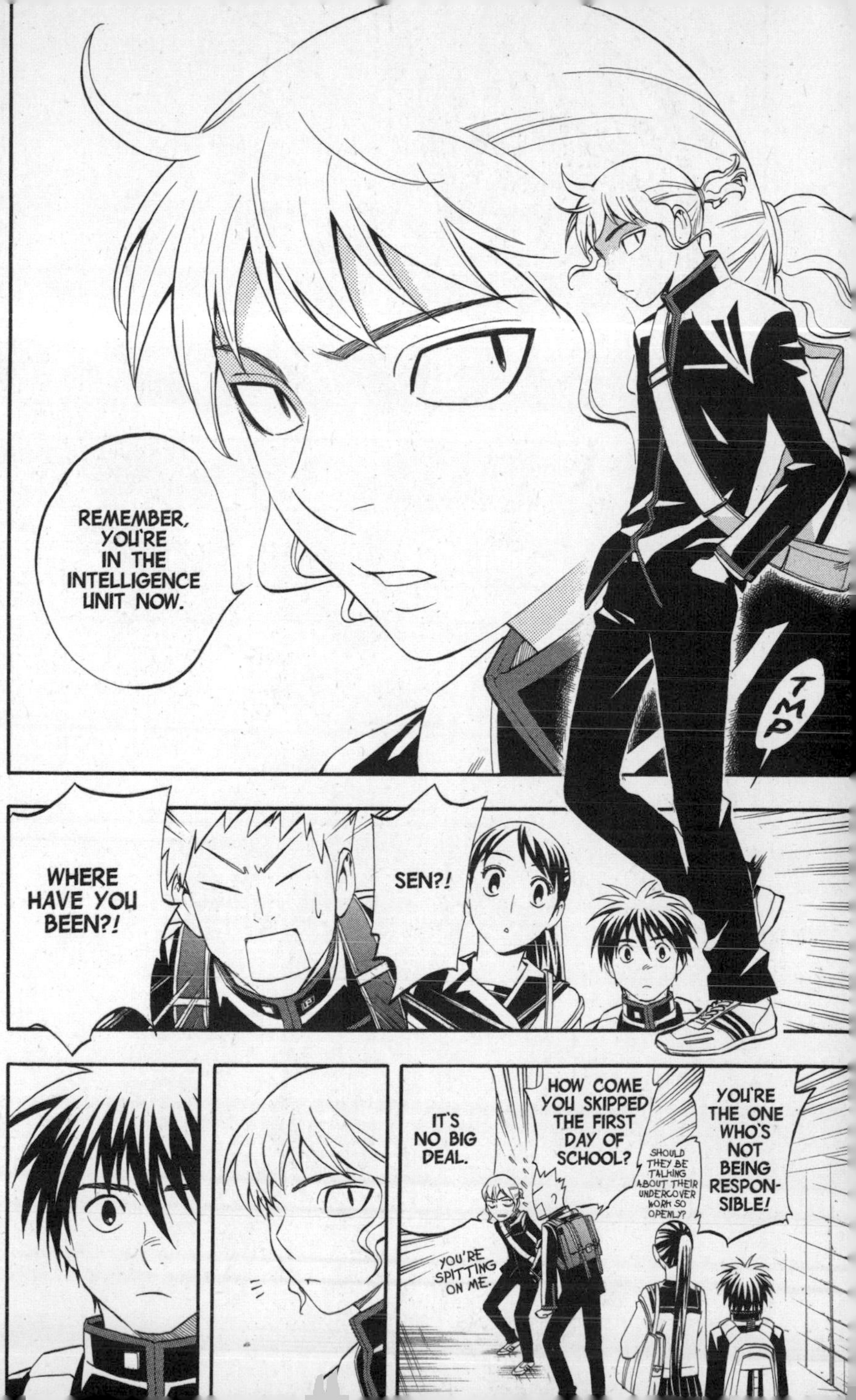
REMEMBER, YOU'RE IN THE INTELLIGENCE UNIT NOW.
TMP
SEN?!
WHERE HAVE YOU BEEN?!
YOU'RE THE ONE WHO'S NOT BEING RESPONSIBLE!
HOW COME YOU SKIPPED THE FIRST DAY OF SCHOOL?
SHOULD THEY BE TALKING ABOUT THEIR UNDERCOVER WORK SO OPENLY?
IT'S NO BIG DEAL.
YOU'RE SPITTING ON ME.

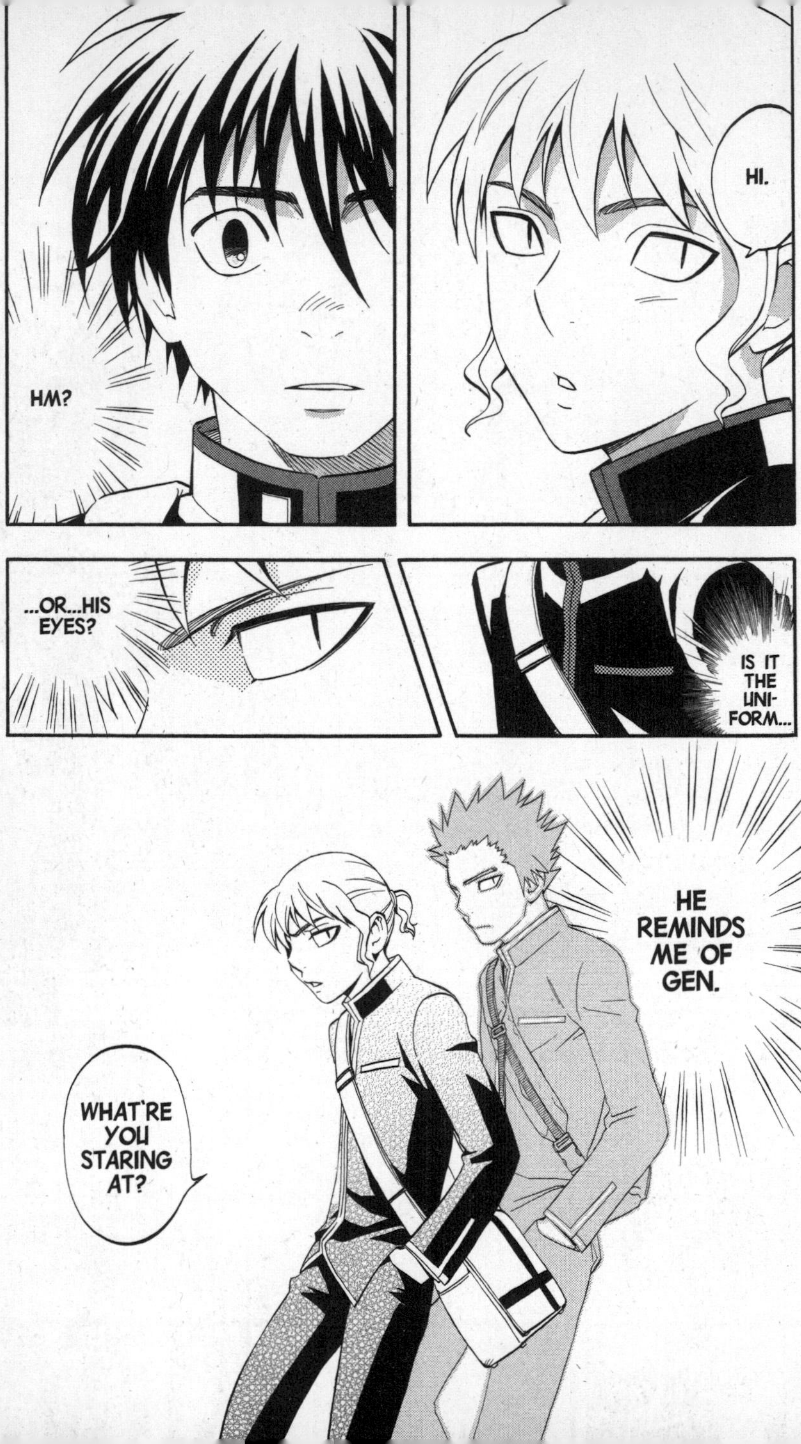
HI.
HM?
IS IT THE UNI-FORM...
...OR...HIS EYES?
HE REMINDS ME OF GEN.
WHAT'RE YOU STARING AT?

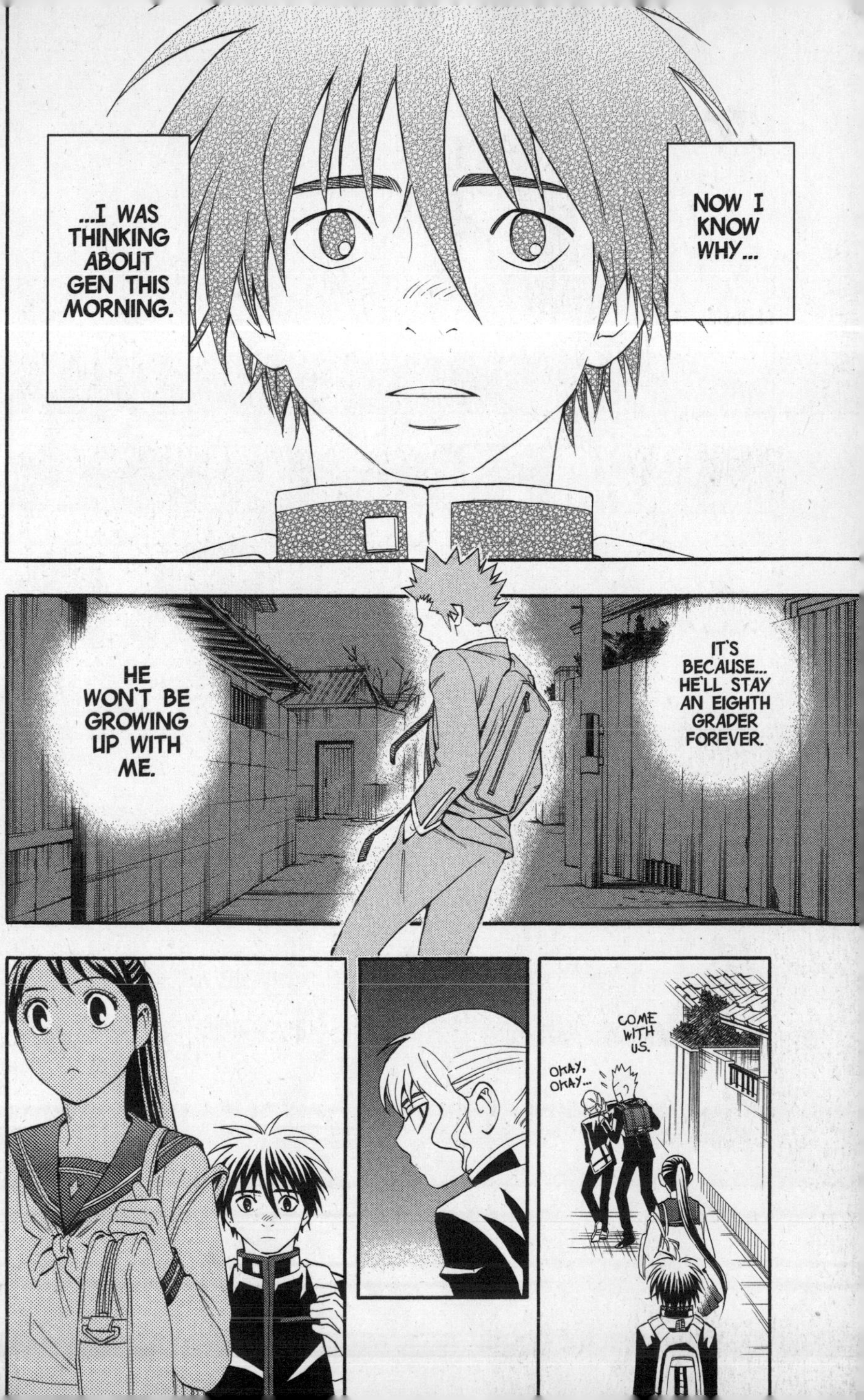
NOW I KNOW WHY...
...I WAS THINKING ABOUT GEN THIS MORNING.
IT'S BECAUSE... HE'LL STAY AN EIGHTH GRADER FOREVER.
HE WON'T BE GROWING UP WITH ME.
COME WITH US.
OKAY, OKAY...

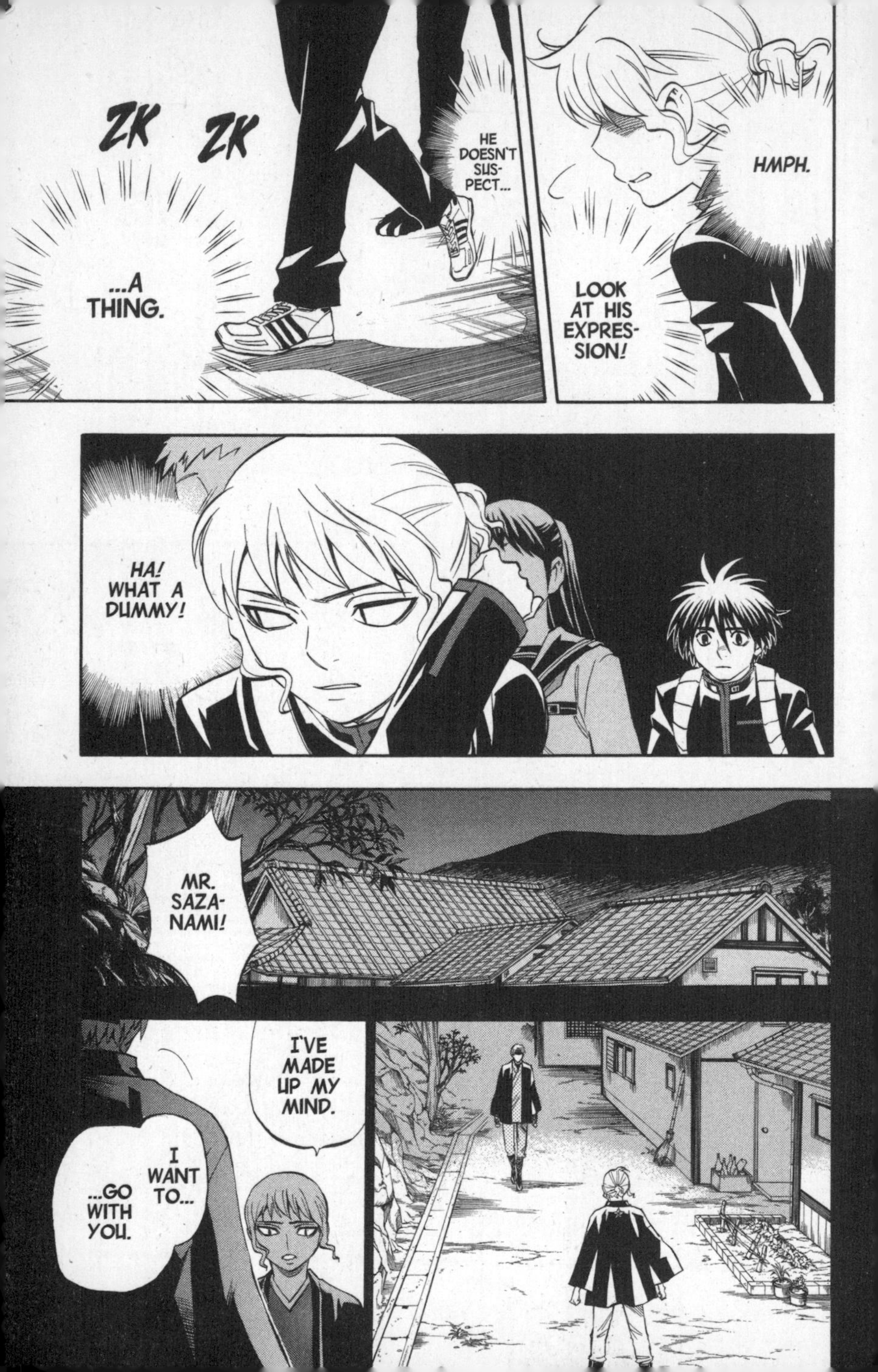
HMPH.
LOOK AT HIS EXPRESSION!
HE DOESN'T SUSPECT...
ZK ZK
...A THING.
HA! WHAT A DUMMY!
MR. SAZANAMI!
I'VE MADE UP MY MIND.
I WANT TO...
...GO WITH YOU.

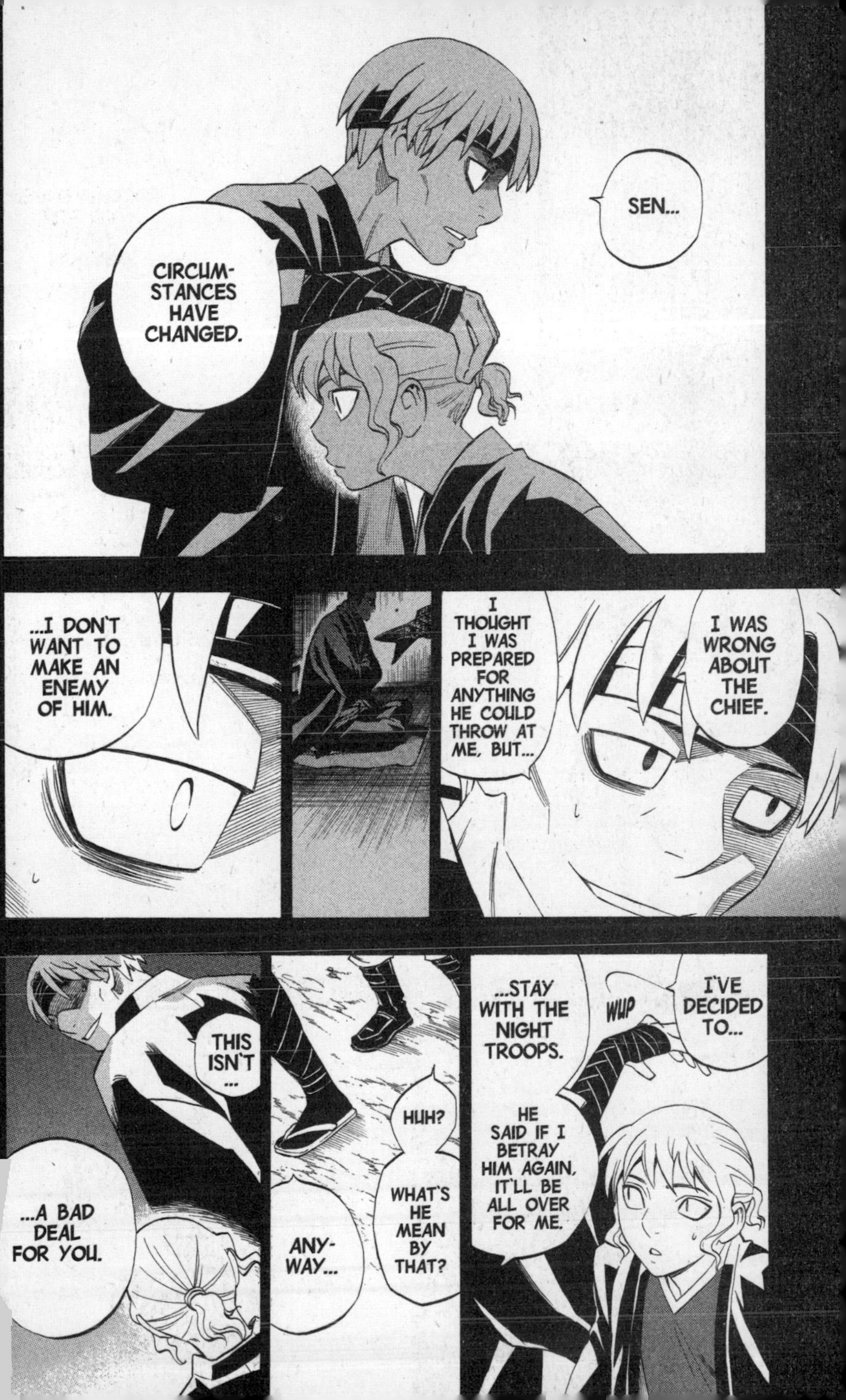
SEN...
CIRCUM-STANCES HAVE CHANGED.
I WAS WRONG ABOUT THE CHIEF.
I THOUGHT I WAS PREPARED FOR ANYTHING HE COULD THROW AT ME, BUT...
...I DON'T WANT TO MAKE AN ENEMY OF HIM.
I'VE DECIDED TO...
WUP
...STAY WITH THE NIGHT TROOPS.
HE SAID IF I BETRAY HIM AGAIN, IT'LL BE ALL OVER FOR ME.
HUH?
WHAT'S HE MEAN BY THAT?
ANY-WAY...
THIS ISN'T ...
...A BAD DEAL FOR YOU.

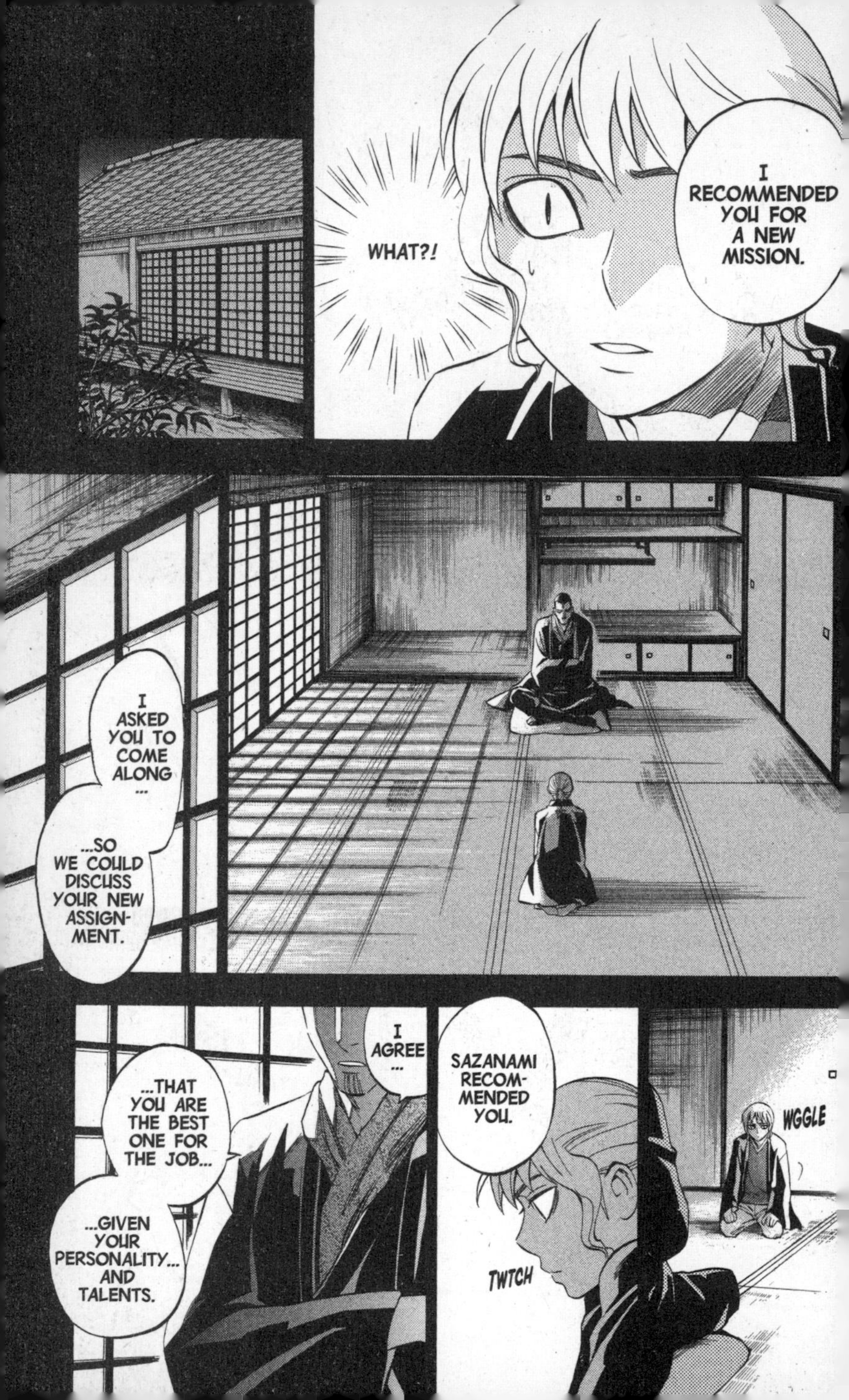
I RECOMMENDED YOU FOR A NEW MISSION.
WHAT?!
I ASKED YOU TO COME ALONG...
...SO WE COULD DISCUSS YOUR NEW ASSIGNMENT.
SAZANAMI RECOMMENDED YOU.
WGGLE
TWTCH
I AGREE...
...THAT YOU ARE THE BEST ONE FOR THE JOB...
...GIVEN YOUR PERSONALITY... AND TALENTS.

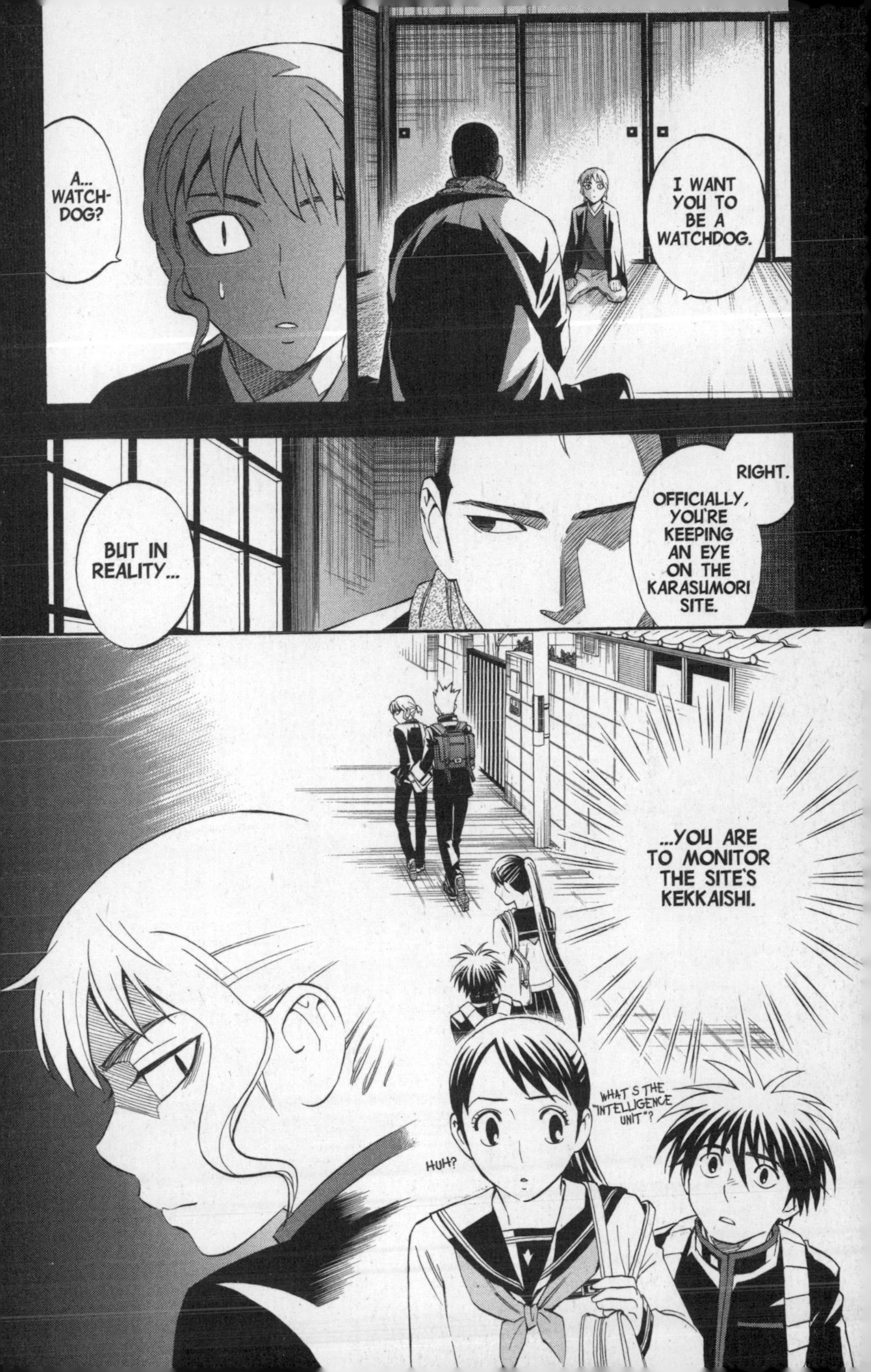
I WANT YOU TO BE A WATCHDOG.
A... WATCH-DOG?
RIGHT.
OFFICIALLY, YOU'RE KEEPING AN EYE ON THE KARASUMORI SITE.
BUT IN REALITY...
...YOU ARE TO MONITOR THE SITE'S KEKKAISHI.
WHAT'S THE "INTELLIGENCE UNIT"?
HUH?

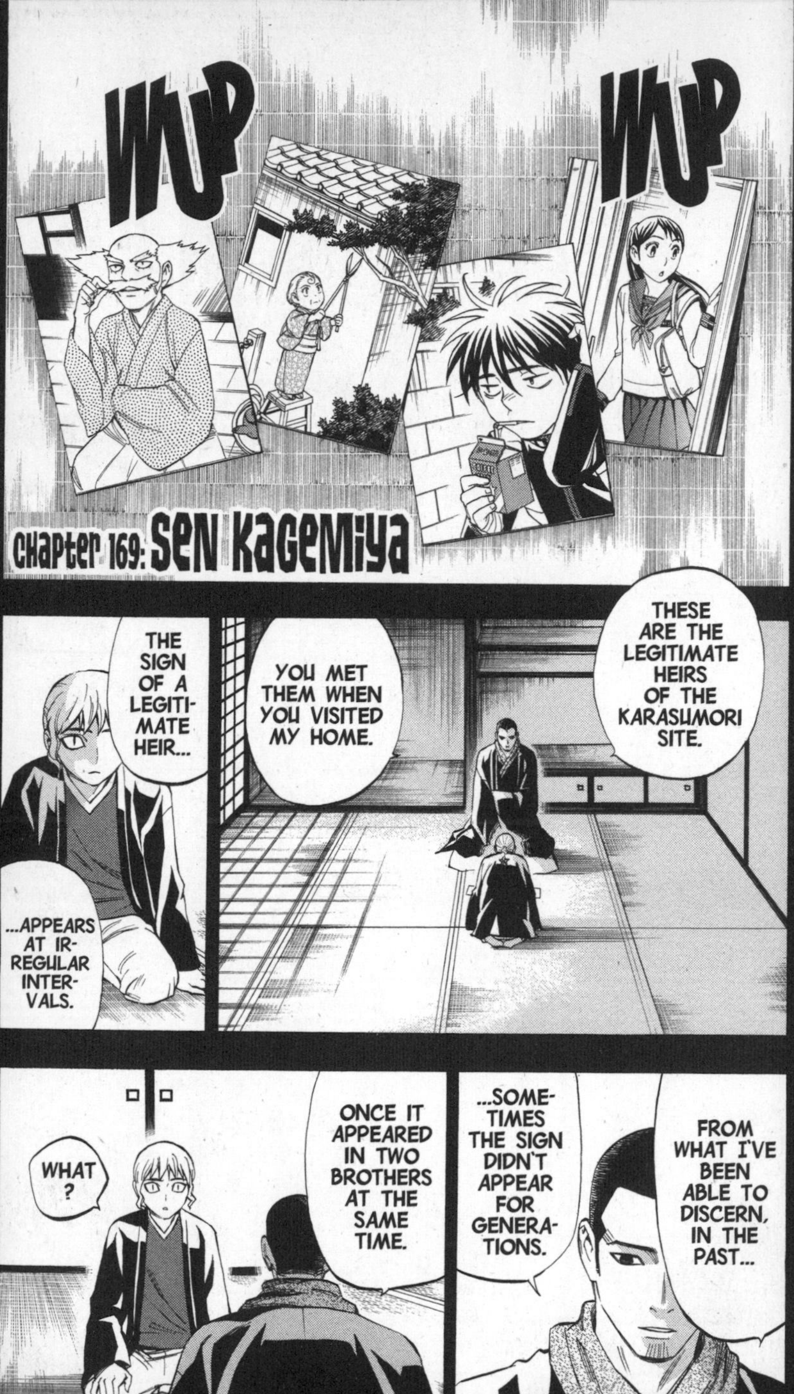
WHUP
WHUP
Chapter 169: Sen Kagemiya
THESE ARE THE LEGITIMATE HEIRS OF THE KARASUMORI SITE.
YOU MET THEM WHEN YOU VISITED MY HOME.
THE SIGN OF A LEGITI-MATE HEIR...
...APPEARS AT IR-REGULAR INTER-VALS.
FROM WHAT I'VE BEEN ABLE TO DISCERN, IN THE PAST...
...SOME-TIMES THE SIGN DIDN'T APPEAR FOR GENERA-TIONS.
ONCE IT APPEARED IN TWO BROTHERS AT THE SAME TIME.
WHAT?

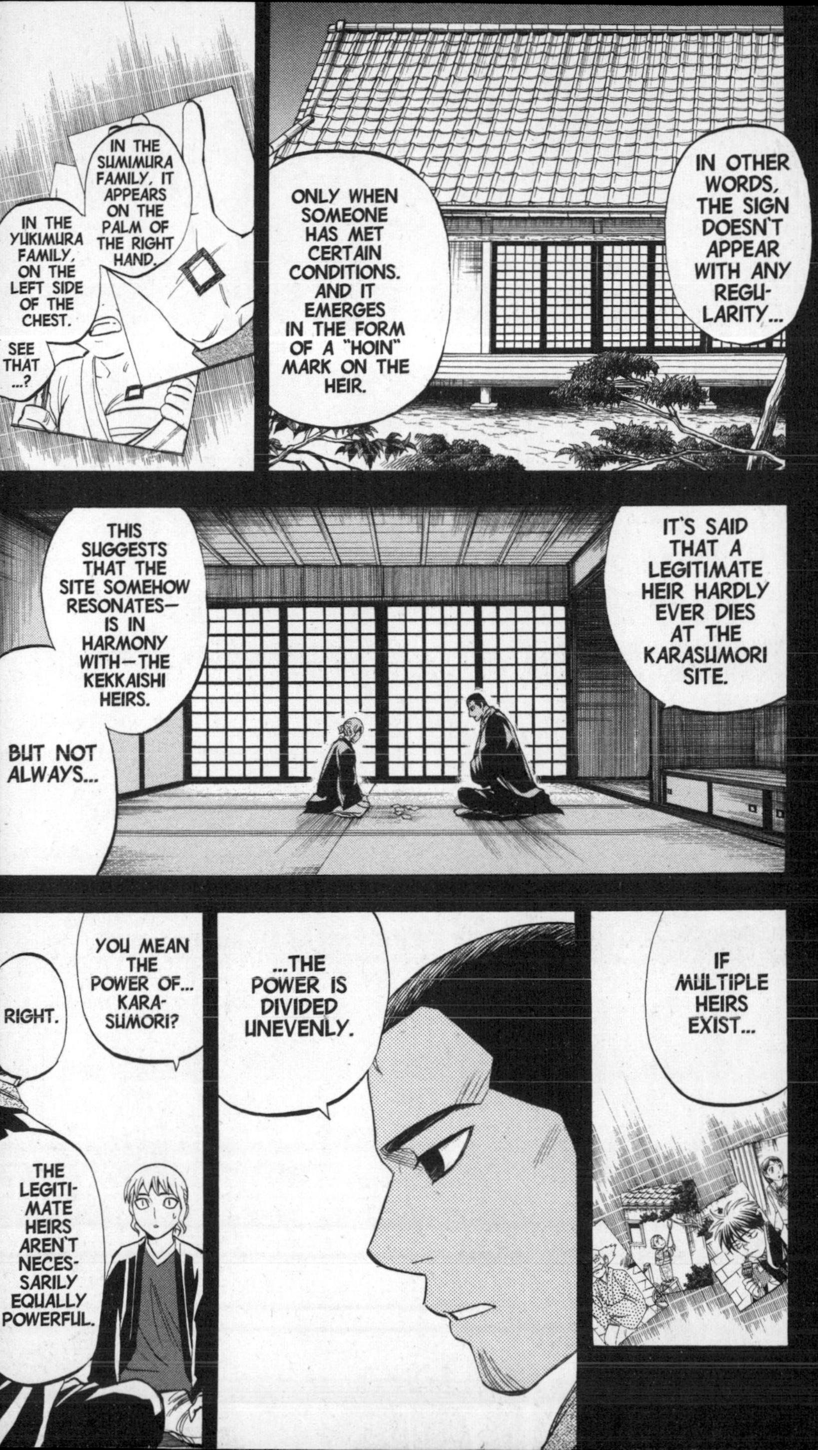
IN OTHER WORDS, THE SIGN DOESN'T APPEAR WITH ANY REGU-LARITY...
ONLY WHEN SOMEONE HAS MET CERTAIN CONDITIONS. AND IT EMERGES IN THE FORM OF A "HOIN" MARK ON THE HEIR.
IN THE SUMIMURA FAMILY, IT APPEARS ON THE PALM OF THE RIGHT HAND.
IN THE YUKIMURA FAMILY, ON THE LEFT SIDE OF THE CHEST.
SEE THAT ...?
IT'S SAID THAT A LEGITIMATE HEIR HARDLY EVER DIES AT THE KARASUMORI SITE.
THIS SUGGESTS THAT THE SITE SOMEHOW RESONATES—IS IN HARMONY WITH—THE KEKKAISHI HEIRS.
BUT NOT ALWAYS...
IF MULTIPLE HEIRS EXIST...
...THE POWER IS DIVIDED UNEVENLY.
YOU MEAN THE POWER OF... KARA-SUMORI?
RIGHT.
THE LEGITI-MATE HEIRS AREN'T NECES-SARILY EQUALLY POWERFUL.

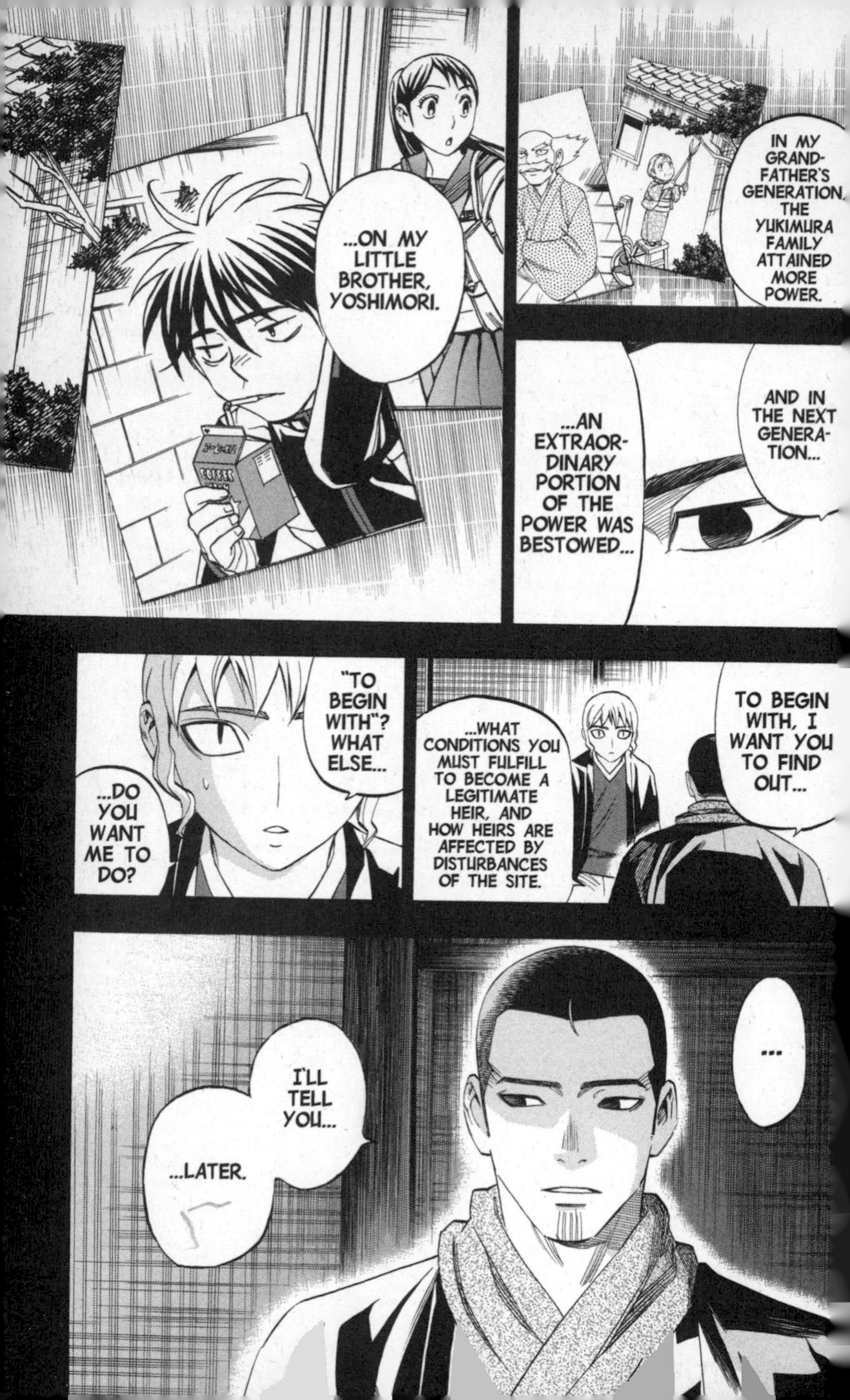
IN MY GRANDFATHER'S GENERATION, THE YUKIMURA FAMILY ATTAINED MORE POWER.
AND IN THE NEXT GENERATION...
...AN EXTRAORDINARY PORTION OF THE POWER WAS BESTOWED...
...ON MY LITTLE BROTHER, YOSHIMORI.
TO BEGIN WITH, I WANT YOU TO FIND OUT...
...WHAT CONDITIONS YOU MUST FULFILL TO BECOME A LEGITIMATE HEIR, AND HOW HEIRS ARE AFFECTED BY DISTURBANCES OF THE SITE.
"TO BEGIN WITH"? WHAT ELSE...
...DO YOU WANT ME TO DO?
...
I'LL TELL YOU...
...LATER.

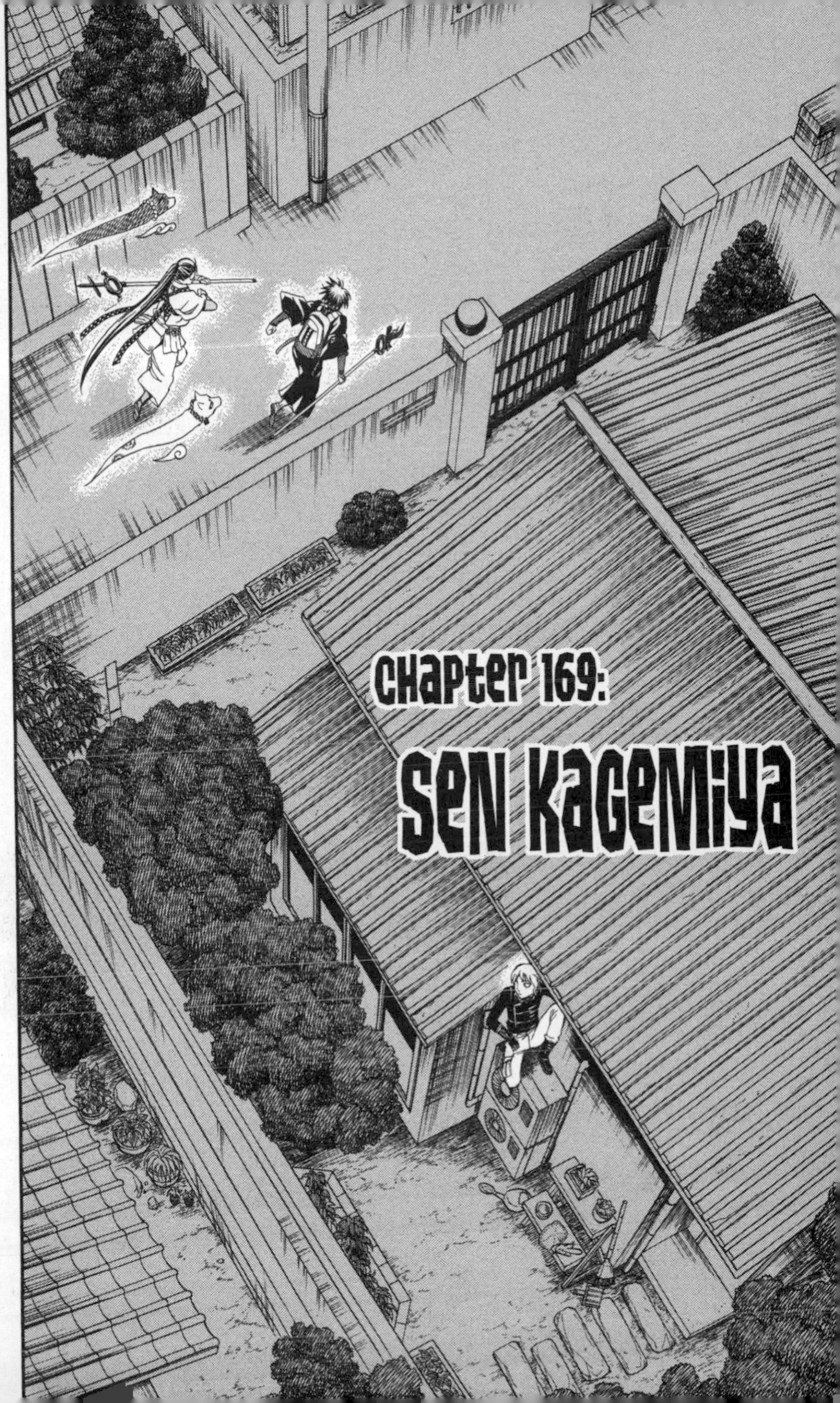
Chapter 169:
Sen Kagemiya

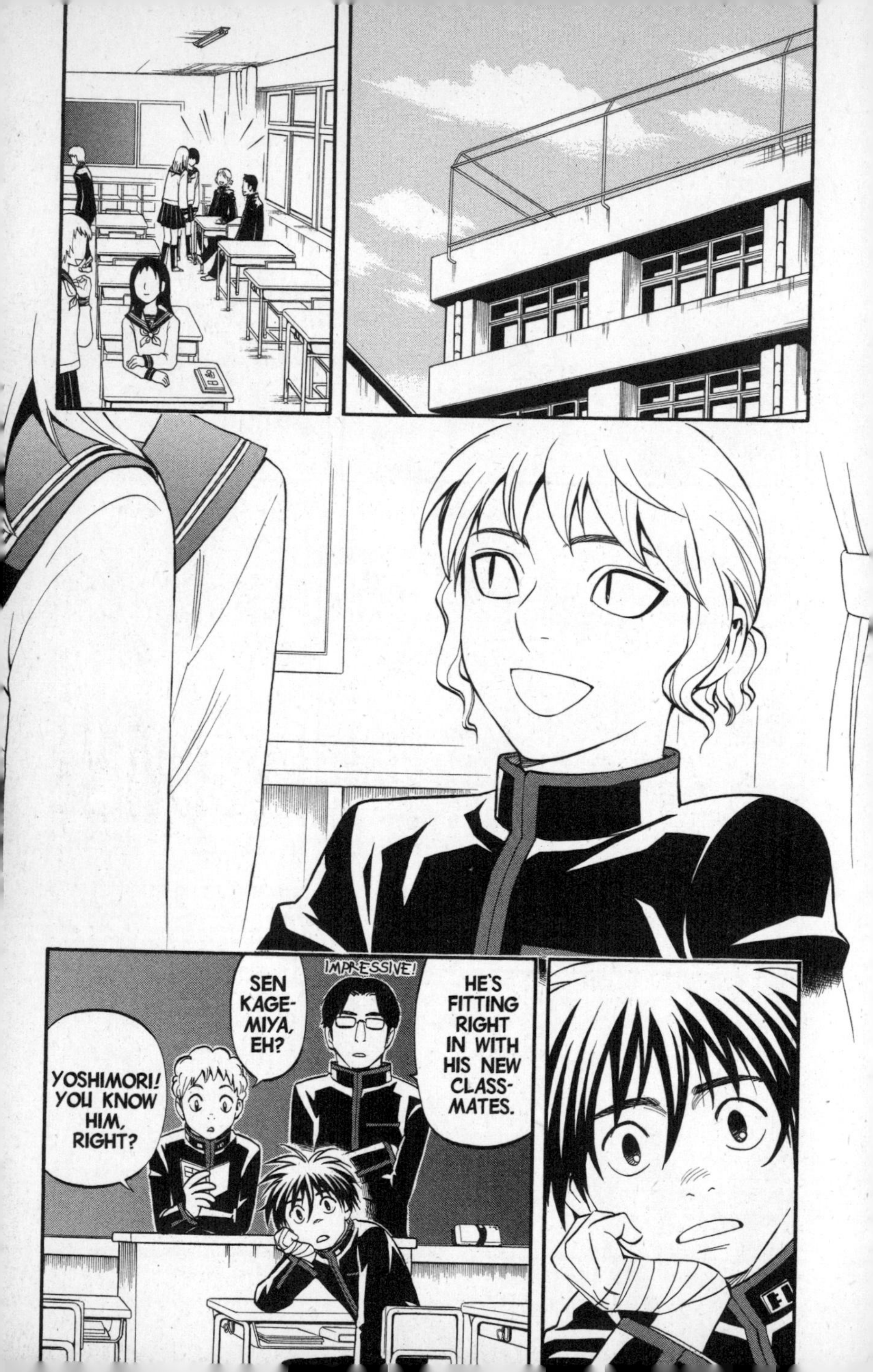
HE'S FITTING RIGHT IN WITH HIS NEW CLASSMATES.
IMPRESSIVE!
SEN KAGEMIYA, EH?
YOSHIMORI! YOU KNOW HIM, RIGHT?

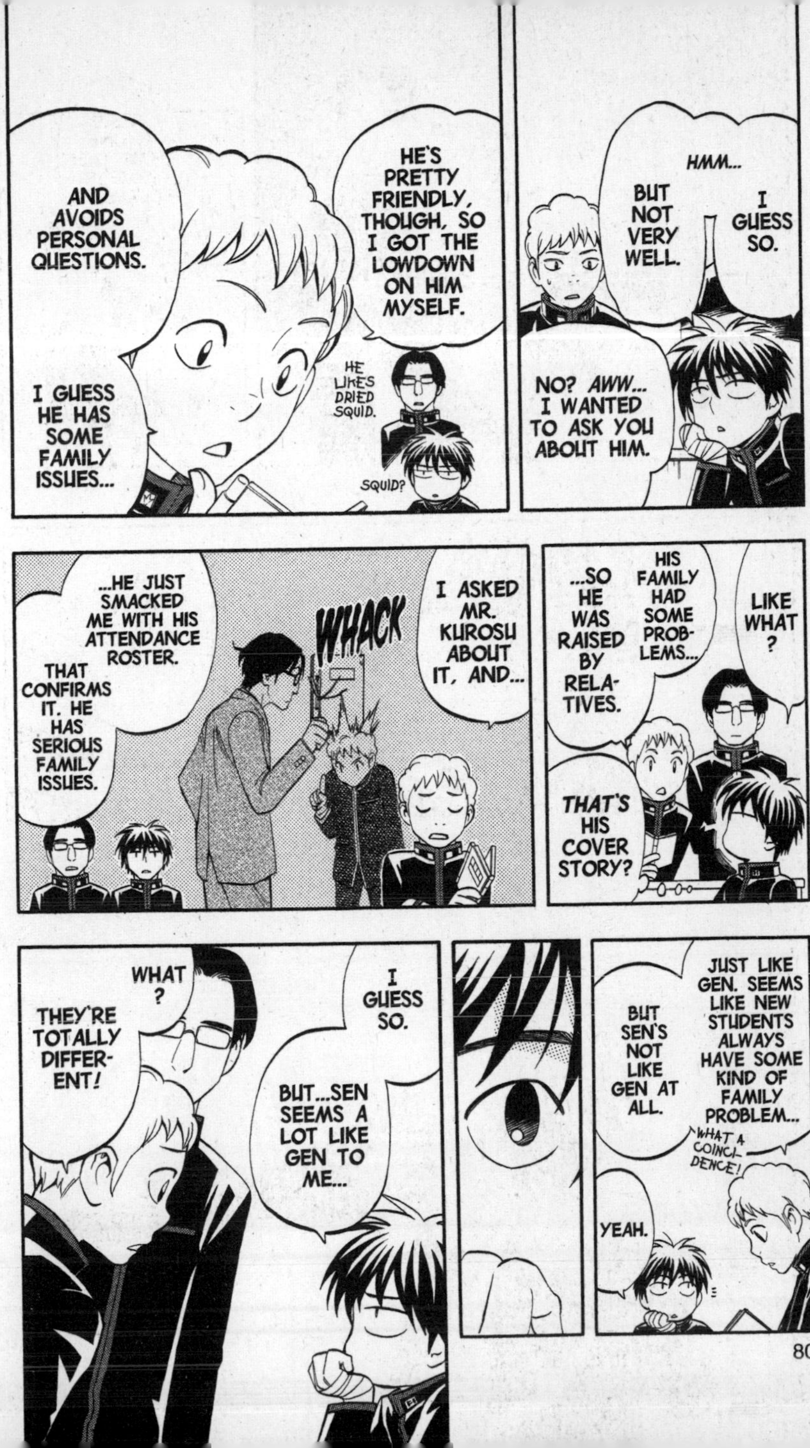
HMM...
I GUESS SO.
BUT NOT VERY WELL.
NO? AWW... I WANTED TO ASK YOU ABOUT HIM.
HE'S PRETTY FRIENDLY, THOUGH, SO I GOT THE LOWDOWN ON HIM MYSELF.
HE LIKES DRIED SQUID.
SQUID?
AND AVOIDS PERSONAL QUESTIONS.
I GUESS HE HAS SOME FAMILY ISSUES...
LIKE WHAT?
HIS FAMILY HAD SOME PROBLEMS...
...SO HE WAS RAISED BY RELATIVES.
THAT'S HIS COVER STORY?
I ASKED MR. KUROSU ABOUT IT, AND...
WHACK
...HE JUST SMACKED ME WITH HIS ATTENDANCE ROSTER.
THAT CONFIRMS IT. HE HAS SERIOUS FAMILY ISSUES.
JUST LIKE GEN. SEEMS LIKE NEW STUDENTS ALWAYS HAVE SOME KIND OF FAMILY PROBLEM...
WHAT A COINCIDENCE!
BUT SEN'S NOT LIKE GEN AT ALL.
YEAH.
I GUESS SO.
BUT...SEN SEEMS A LOT LIKE GEN TO ME...
WHAT?
THEY'RE TOTALLY DIFFERENT!

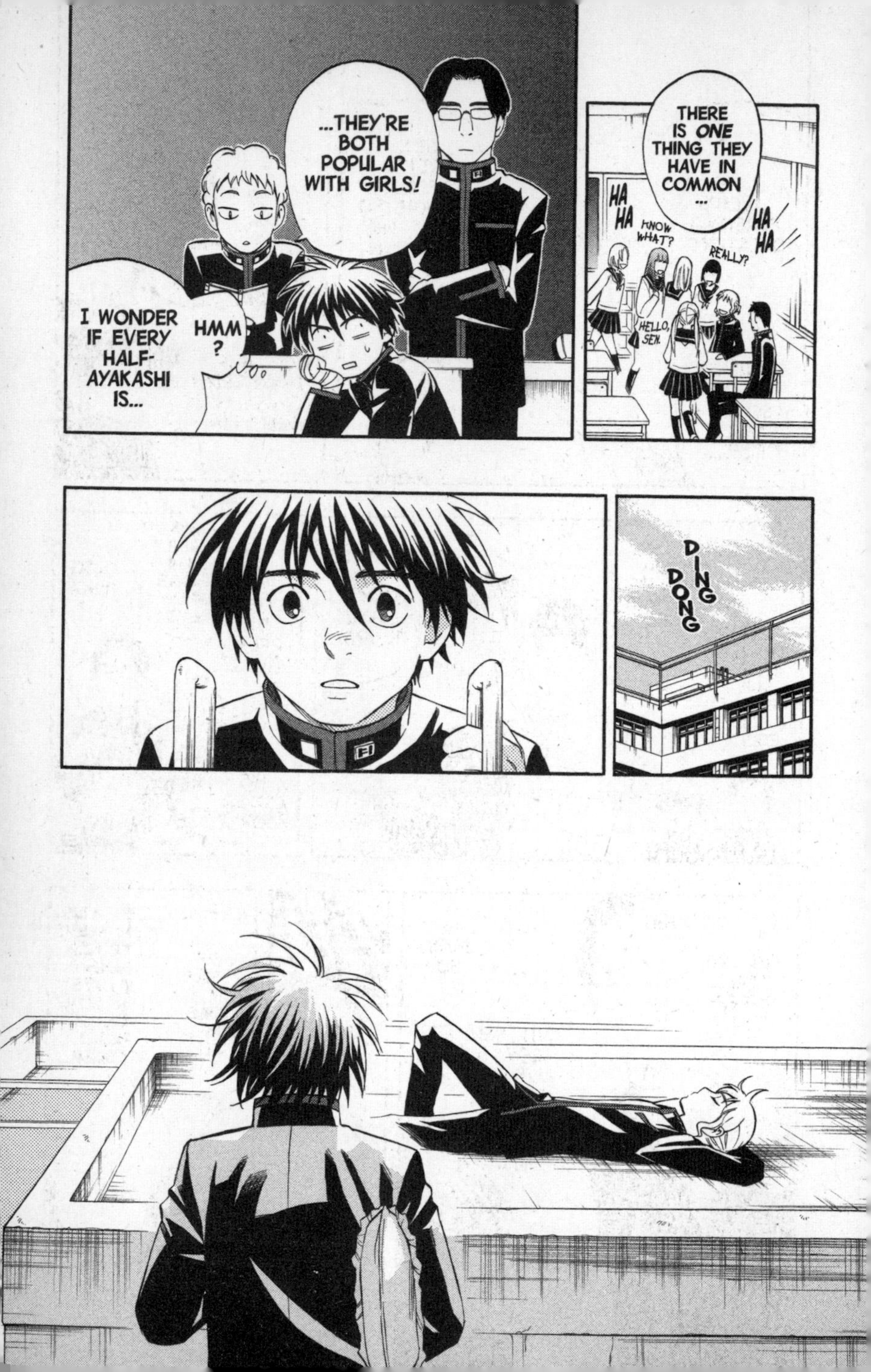
THERE IS ONE THING THEY HAVE IN COMMON ...
HA HA
REALLY?
KNOW WHAT?
HA HA
HELLO, SEN.
...THEY'RE BOTH POPULAR WITH GIRLS!
HMM ?
I WONDER IF EVERY HALF-AYAKASHI IS...
DING DONG

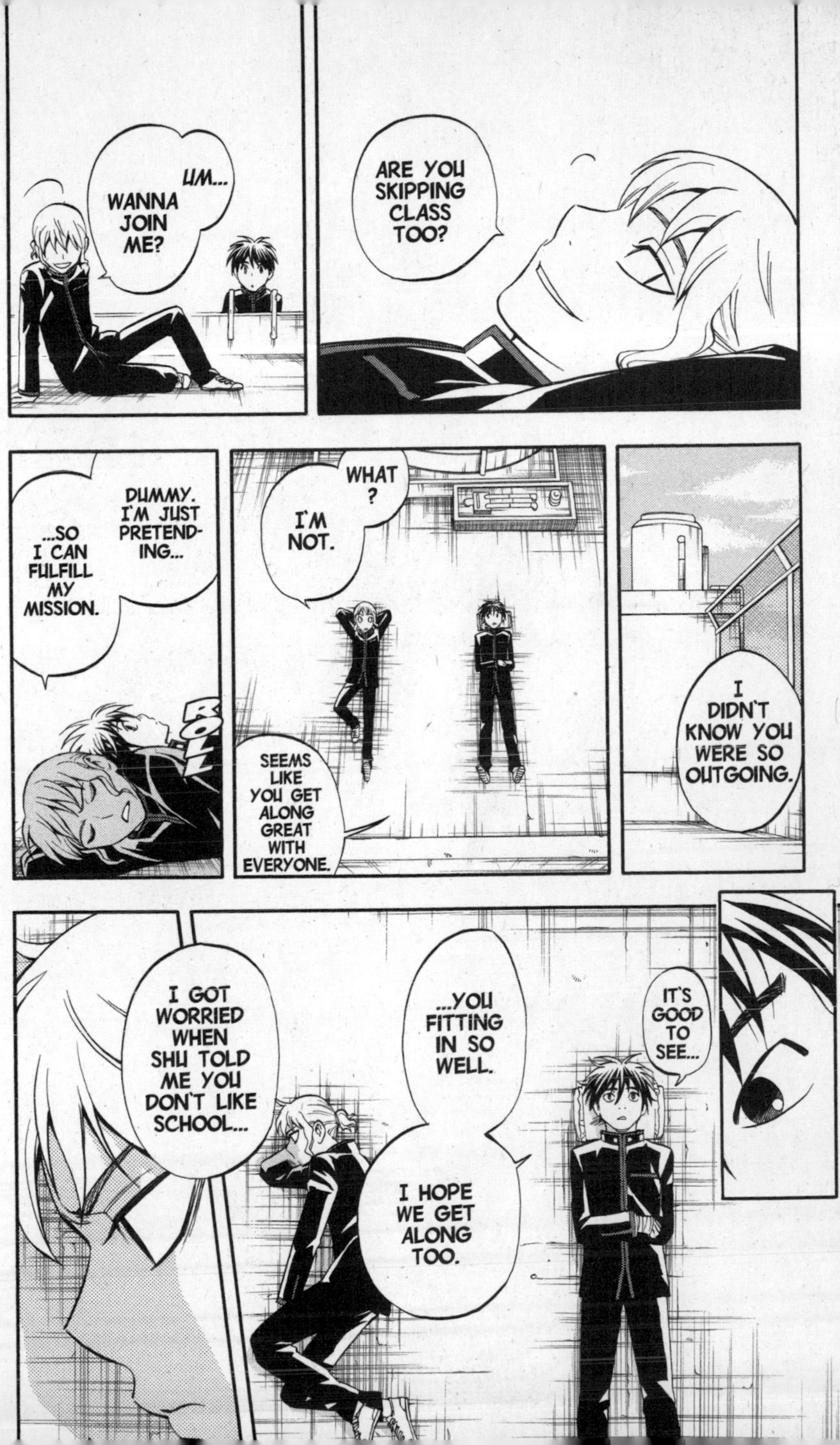
ARE YOU SKIPPING CLASS TOO?
UM... WANNA JOIN ME?
I DIDN'T KNOW YOU WERE SO OUTGOING.
SEEMS LIKE YOU GET ALONG GREAT WITH EVERYONE.
WHAT? I'M NOT.
ROLL
DUMMY. I'M JUST PRETENDING...
...SO I CAN FULFILL MY MISSION.
IT'S GOOD TO SEE...
...YOU FITTING IN SO WELL.
I HOPE WE GET ALONG TOO.
I GOT WORRIED WHEN SHU TOLD ME YOU DON'T LIKE SCHOOL...

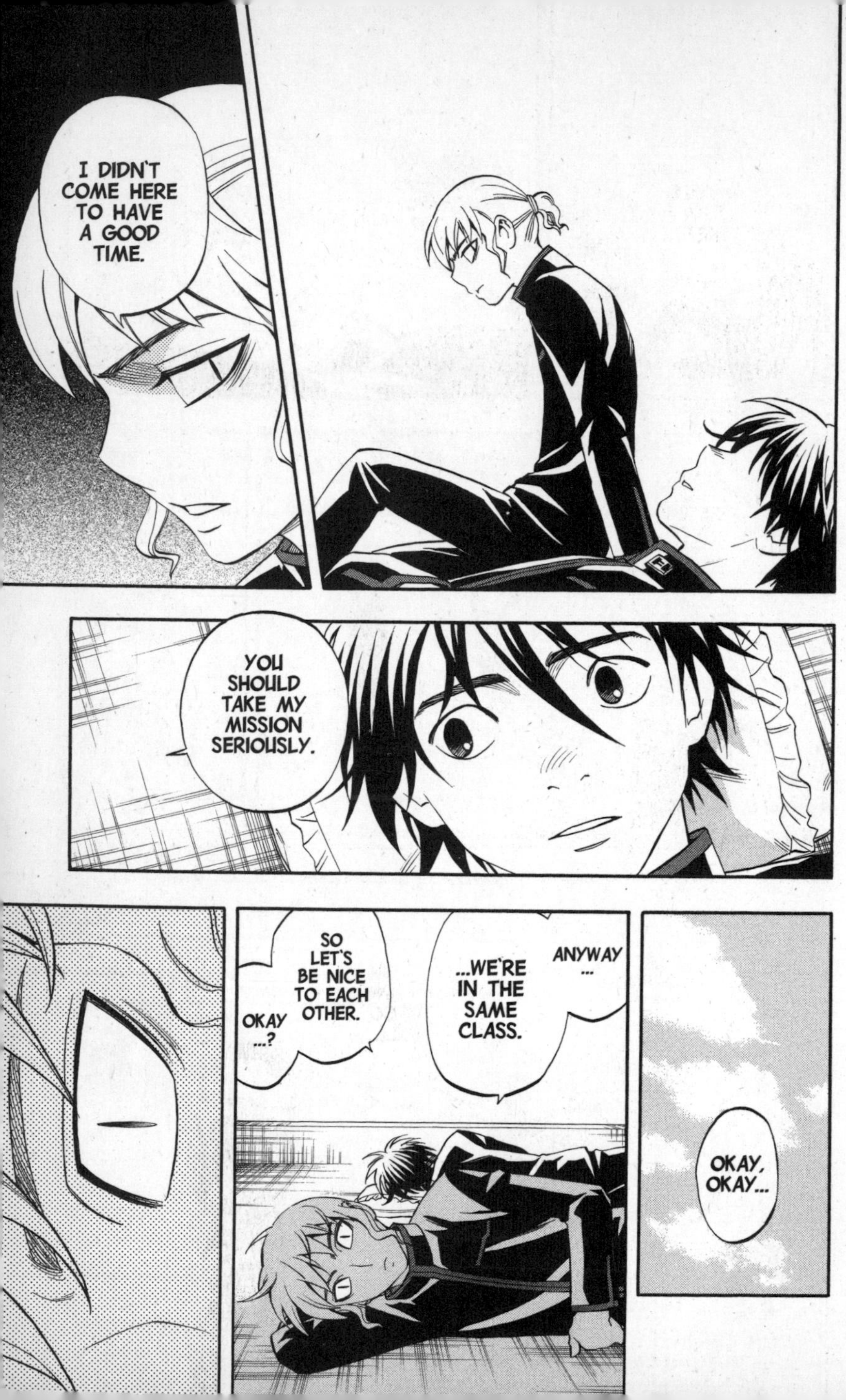
I DIDN'T COME HERE TO HAVE A GOOD TIME.
YOU SHOULD TAKE MY MISSION SERIOUSLY.
OKAY, OKAY...
ANYWAY...
...WE'RE IN THE SAME CLASS.
SO LET'S BE NICE TO EACH OTHER.
OKAY...?

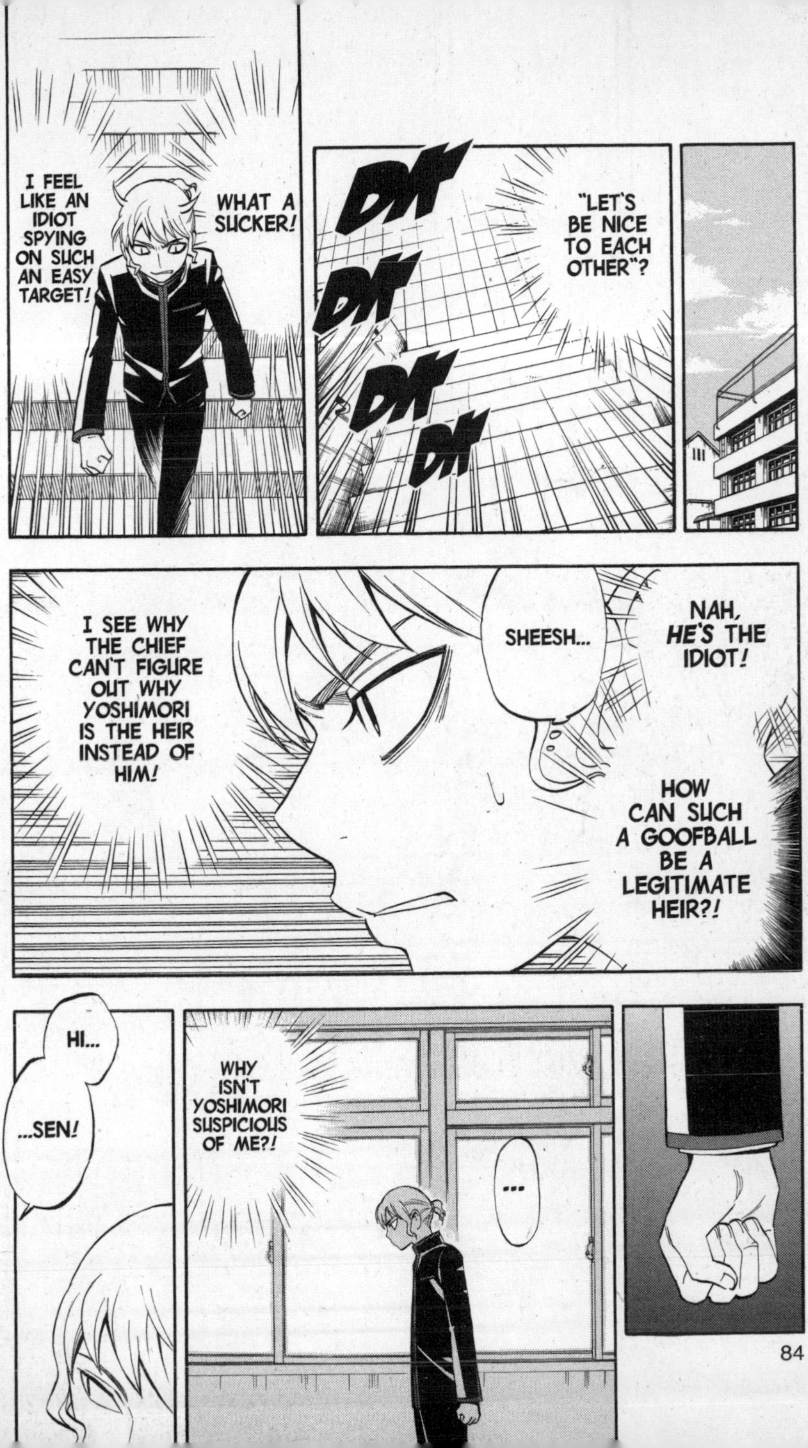
"LET'S BE NICE TO EACH OTHER"?
DF DF DF DF
WHAT A SUCKER!
I FEEL LIKE AN IDIOT SPYING ON SUCH AN EASY TARGET!
SHEESH...
NAH, HE'S THE IDIOT!
HOW CAN SUCH A GOOFBALL BE A LEGITIMATE HEIR?!
I SEE WHY THE CHIEF CAN'T FIGURE OUT WHY YOSHIMORI IS THE HEIR INSTEAD OF HIM!
...
WHY ISN'T YOSHIMORI SUSPICIOUS OF ME?!
HI...
...SEN!

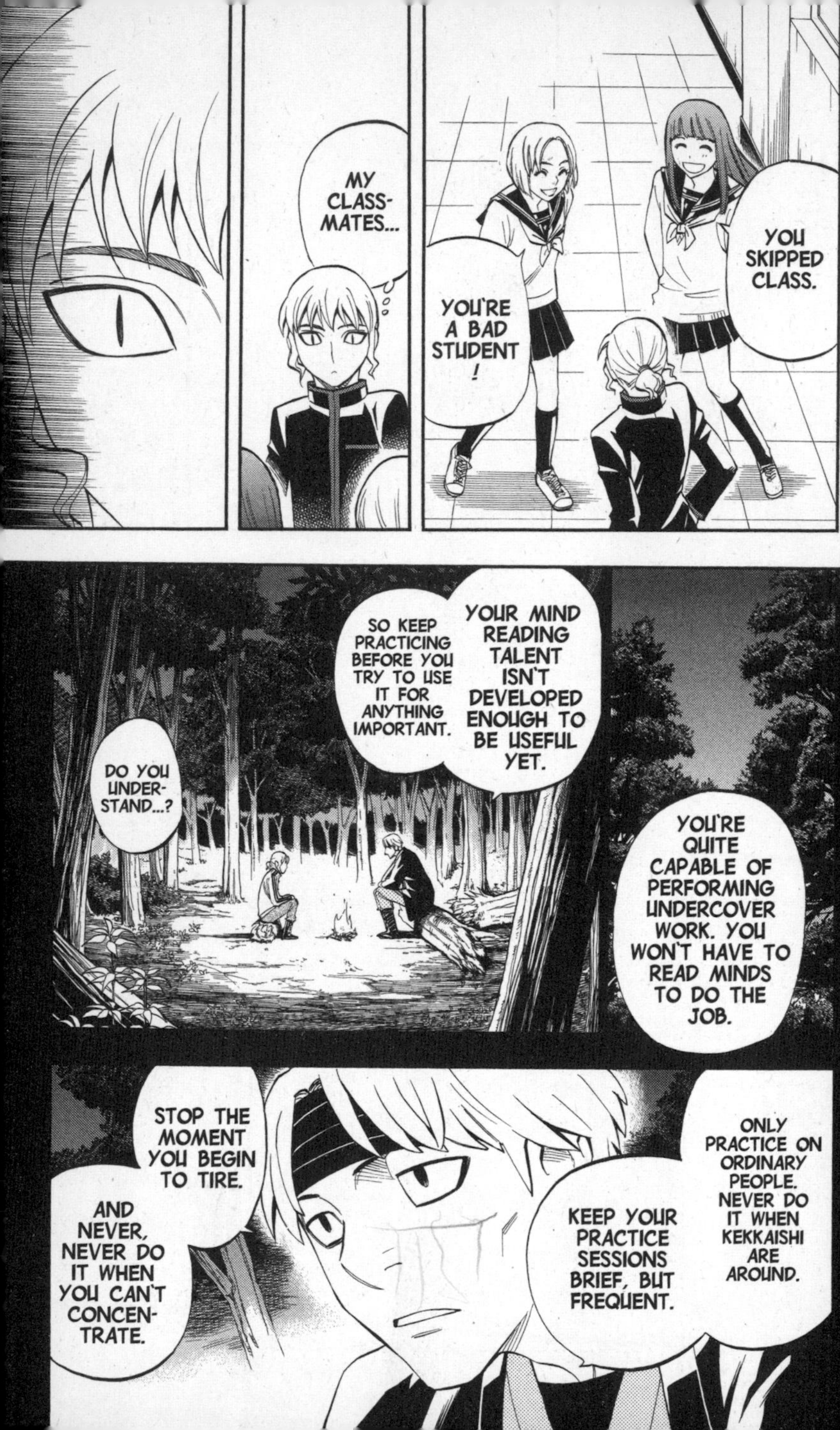
YOU SKIPPED CLASS.
YOU'RE A BAD STUDENT!
MY CLASS-MATES...
YOUR MIND READING TALENT ISN'T DEVELOPED ENOUGH TO BE USEFUL YET.
SO KEEP PRACTICING BEFORE YOU TRY TO USE IT FOR ANYTHING IMPORTANT.
YOU'RE QUITE CAPABLE OF PERFORMING UNDERCOVER WORK. YOU WON'T HAVE TO READ MINDS TO DO THE JOB.
DO YOU UNDER-STAND...?
ONLY PRACTICE ON ORDINARY PEOPLE. NEVER DO IT WHEN KEKKAISHI ARE AROUND.
KEEP YOUR PRACTICE SESSIONS BRIEF, BUT FREQUENT.
STOP THE MOMENT YOU BEGIN TO TIRE.
AND NEVER, NEVER DO IT WHEN YOU CAN'T CONCEN-TRATE.

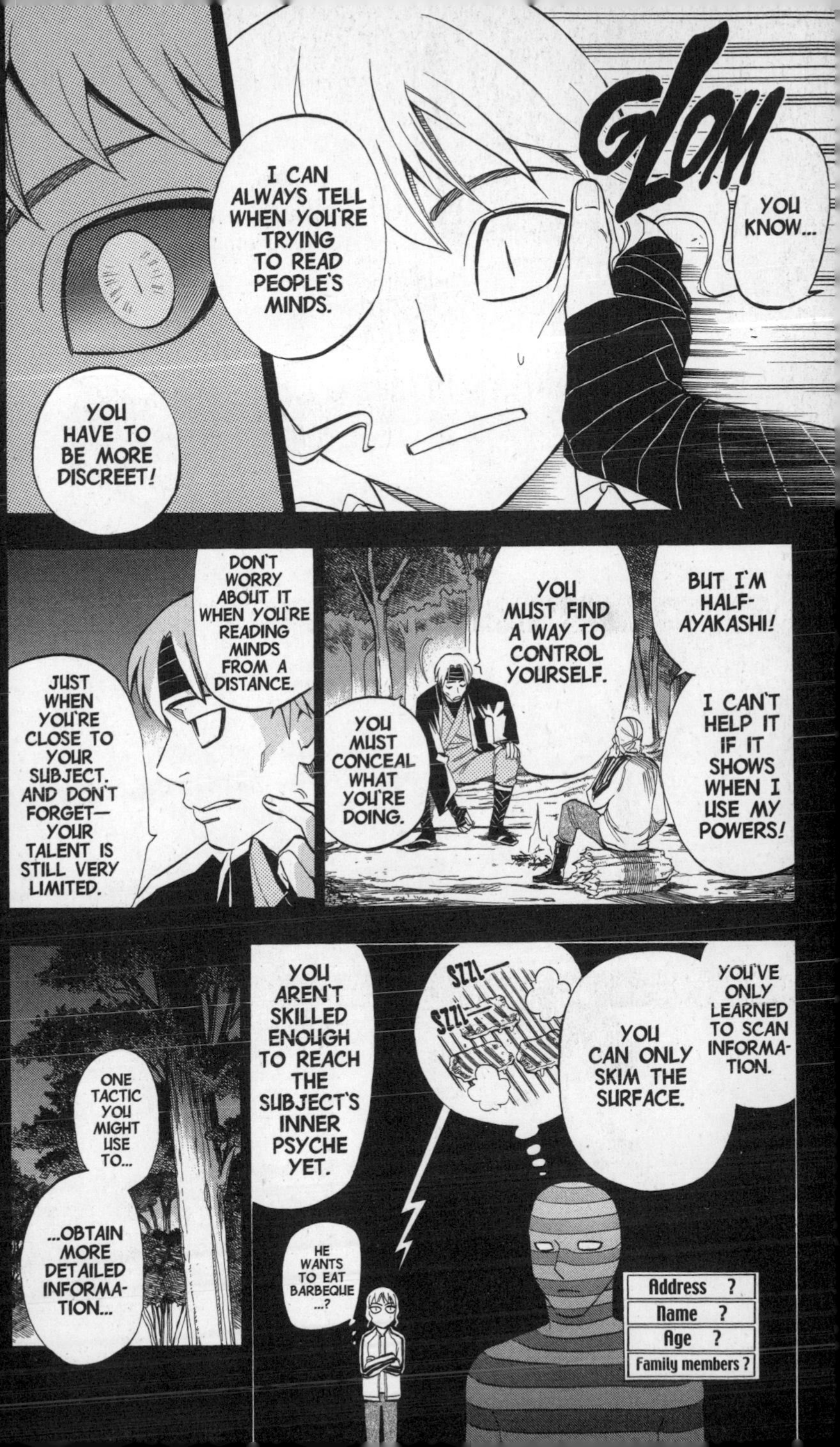
GLOM
YOU KNOW...
I CAN ALWAYS TELL WHEN YOU'RE TRYING TO READ PEOPLE'S MINDS.
YOU HAVE TO BE MORE DISCREET!
BUT I'M HALF-AYAKASHI!
I CAN'T HELP IT IF IT SHOWS WHEN I USE MY POWERS!
YOU MUST FIND A WAY TO CONTROL YOURSELF.
YOU MUST CONCEAL WHAT YOU'RE DOING.
DON'T WORRY ABOUT IT WHEN YOU'RE READING MINDS FROM A DISTANCE.
JUST WHEN YOU'RE CLOSE TO YOUR SUBJECT. AND DON'T FORGET— YOUR TALENT IS STILL VERY LIMITED.
YOU'VE ONLY LEARNED TO SCAN INFORMATION.
YOU CAN ONLY SKIM THE SURFACE.
SZZL—
SZZL—
YOU AREN'T SKILLED ENOUGH TO REACH THE SUBJECT'S INNER PSYCHE YET.
HE WANTS TO EAT BARBEQUE ...?
Address ?
Name ?
Age ?
Family members ?
ONE TACTIC YOU MIGHT USE TO...
...OBTAIN MORE DETAILED INFORMATION...

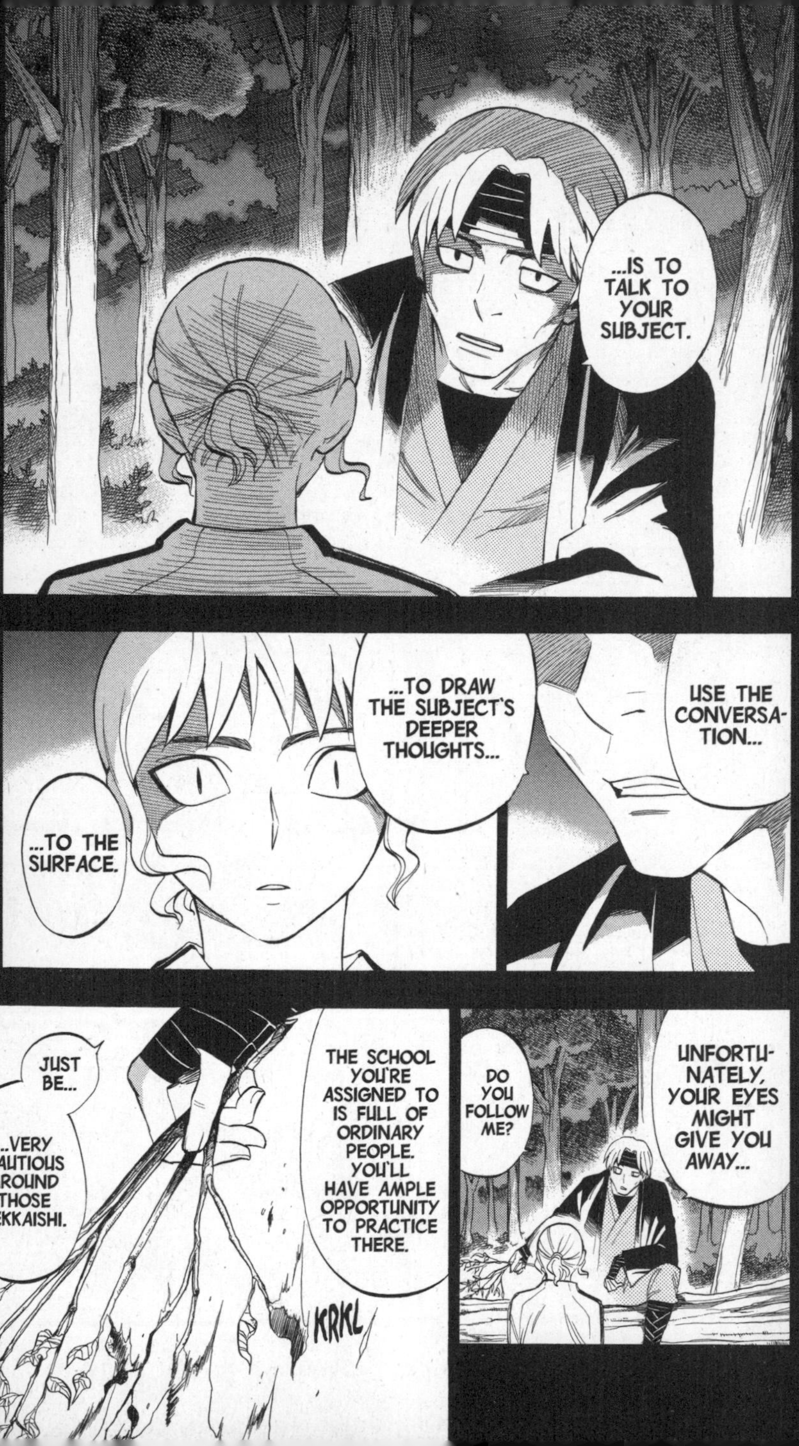
...IS TO TALK TO YOUR SUBJECT.
USE THE CONVERSA-TION...
...TO DRAW THE SUBJECT'S DEEPER THOUGHTS...
...TO THE SURFACE.
UNFORTU-NATELY, YOUR EYES MIGHT GIVE YOU AWAY...
DO YOU FOLLOW ME?
THE SCHOOL YOU'RE ASSIGNED TO IS FULL OF ORDINARY PEOPLE. YOU'LL HAVE AMPLE OPPORTUNITY TO PRACTICE THERE.
JUST BE...
...VERY CAUTIOUS AROUND THOSE KEKKAISHI.
KRKL

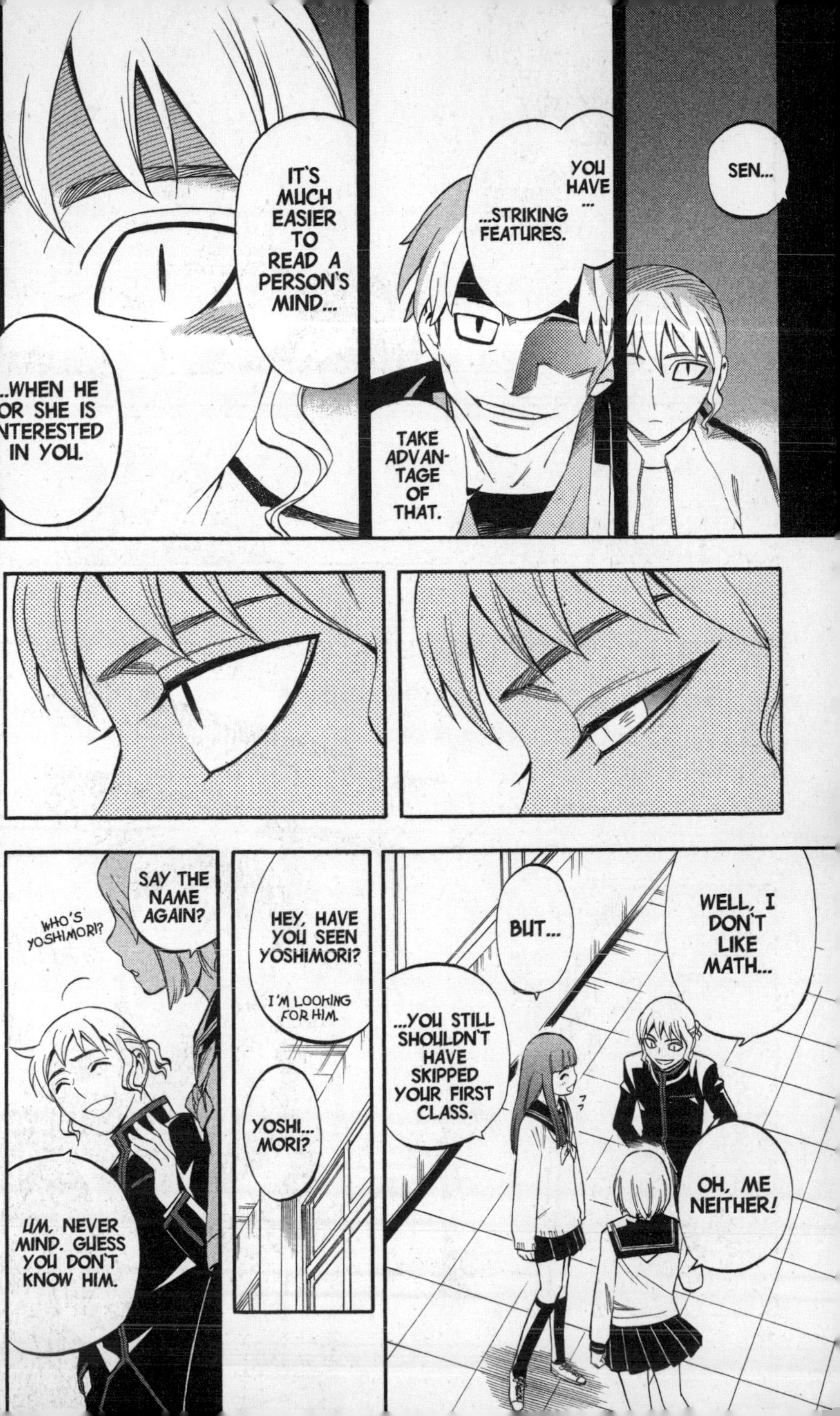
SEN...
YOU HAVE...
...STRIKING FEATURES.
TAKE ADVANTAGE OF THAT.
IT'S MUCH EASIER TO READ A PERSON'S MIND...
...WHEN HE OR SHE IS INTERESTED IN YOU.
WELL, I DON'T LIKE MATH...
OH, ME NEITHER!
BUT...
...YOU STILL SHOULDN'T HAVE SKIPPED YOUR FIRST CLASS.
HEY, HAVE YOU SEEN YOSHIMORI?
I'M LOOKING FOR HIM.
YOSHI... MORI?
SAY THE NAME AGAIN?
WHO'S YOSHIMORI?
UM, NEVER MIND. GUESS YOU DON'T KNOW HIM.

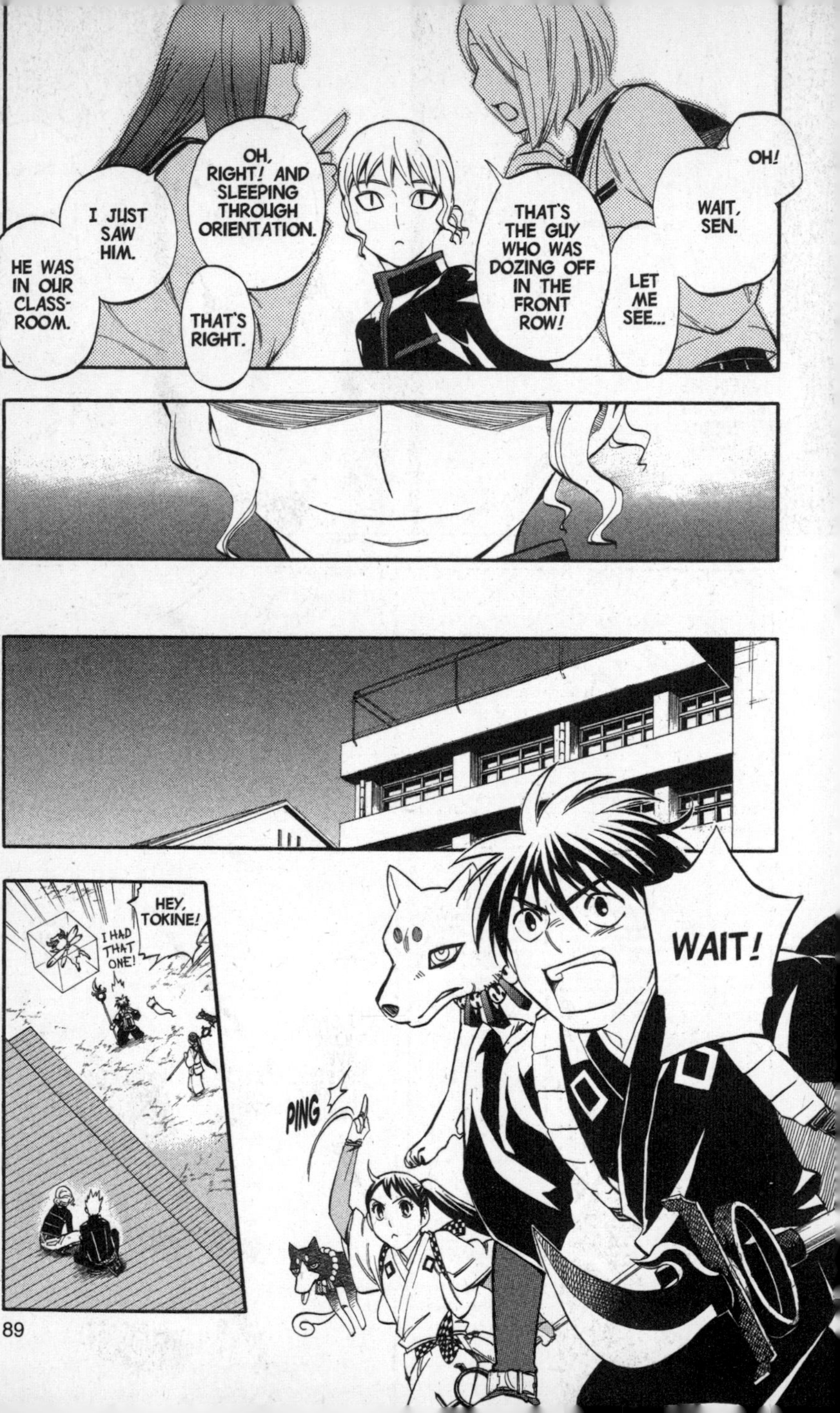
OH!
WAIT, SEN.
LET ME SEE...
THAT'S THE GUY WHO WAS DOZING OFF IN THE FRONT ROW!
OH, RIGHT! AND SLEEPING THROUGH ORIENTATION.
THAT'S RIGHT.
I JUST SAW HIM.
HE WAS IN OUR CLASS-ROOM.
WAIT!
PING
HEY, TOKINE!
I HAD THAT ONE!

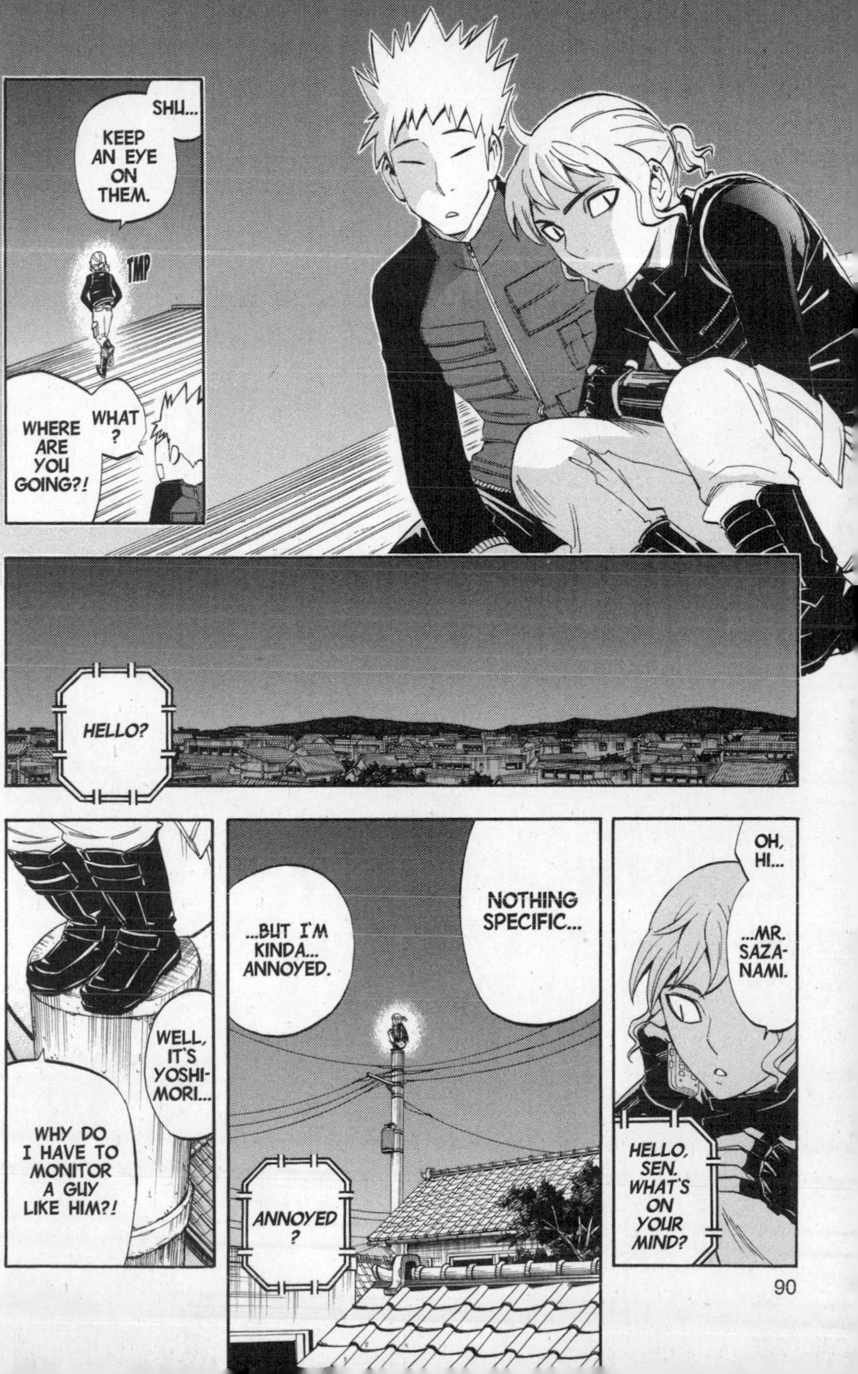
SHU... KEEP AN EYE ON THEM.
TMP
WHAT?
WHERE ARE YOU GOING?!
HELLO?
OH, HI... ...MR. SAZANAMI.
HELLO, SEN. WHAT'S ON YOUR MIND?
NOTHING SPECIFIC...
...BUT I'M KINDA... ANNOYED.
ANNOYED?
WELL, IT'S YOSHIMORI...
WHY DO I HAVE TO MONITOR A GUY LIKE HIM?!

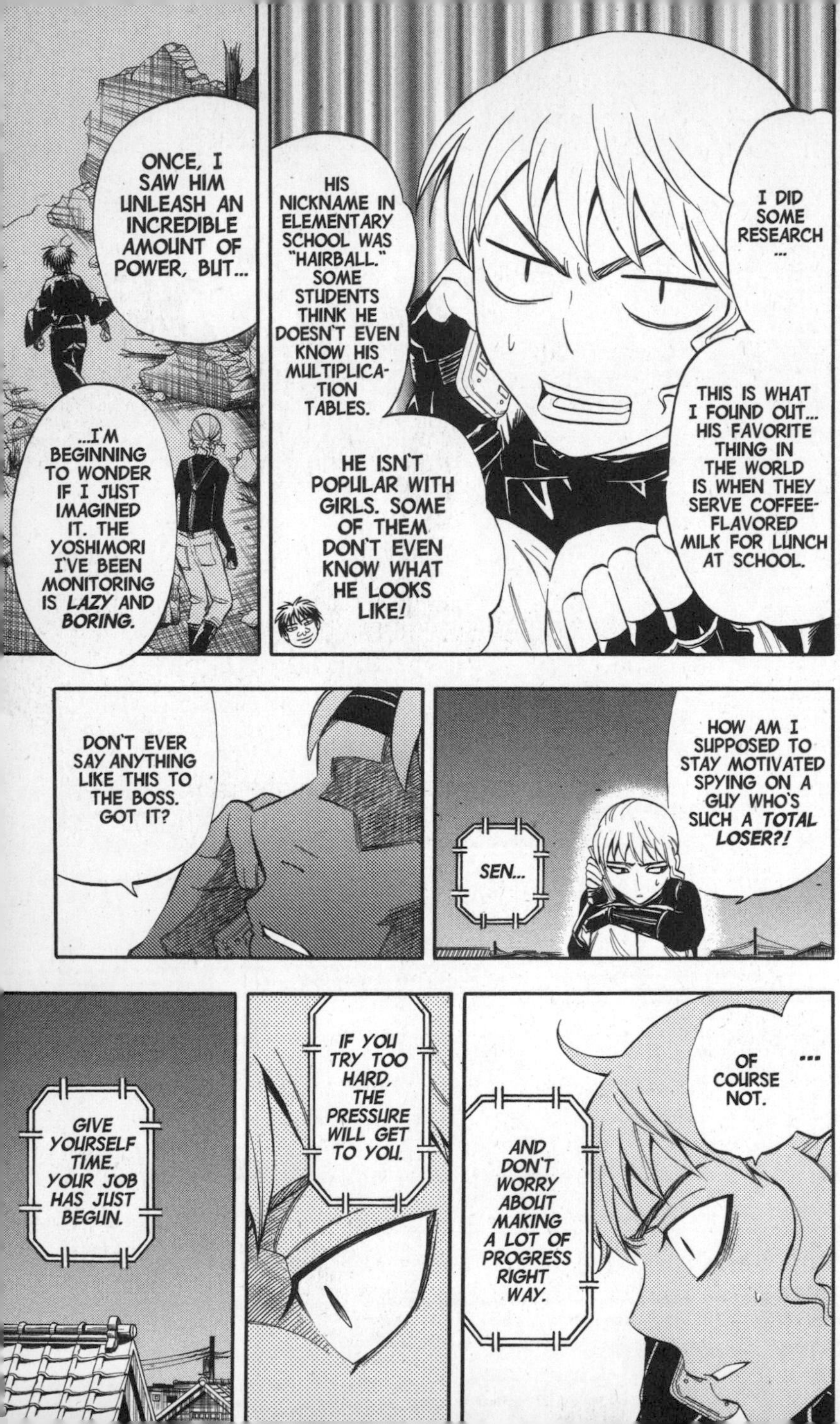
I DID SOME RESEARCH...
HIS NICKNAME IN ELEMENTARY SCHOOL WAS "HAIRBALL." SOME STUDENTS THINK HE DOESN'T EVEN KNOW HIS MULTIPLICA-TION TABLES.
THIS IS WHAT I FOUND OUT... HIS FAVORITE THING IN THE WORLD IS WHEN THEY SERVE COFFEE-FLAVORED MILK FOR LUNCH AT SCHOOL.
HE ISN'T POPULAR WITH GIRLS. SOME OF THEM DON'T EVEN KNOW WHAT HE LOOKS LIKE!
ONCE, I SAW HIM UNLEASH AN INCREDIBLE AMOUNT OF POWER, BUT...
...I'M BEGINNING TO WONDER IF I JUST IMAGINED IT. THE YOSHIMORI I'VE BEEN MONITORING IS *LAZY* AND *BORING.*
HOW AM I SUPPOSED TO STAY MOTIVATED SPYING ON A GUY WHO'S SUCH A *TOTAL LOSER?!*
SEN...
DON'T EVER SAY ANYTHING LIKE THIS TO THE BOSS. GOT IT?
OF COURSE NOT. ...
AND DON'T WORRY ABOUT MAKING A LOT OF PROGRESS RIGHT WAY.
IF YOU TRY TOO HARD, THE PRESSURE WILL GET TO YOU.
GIVE YOURSELF TIME. YOUR JOB HAS JUST BEGUN.

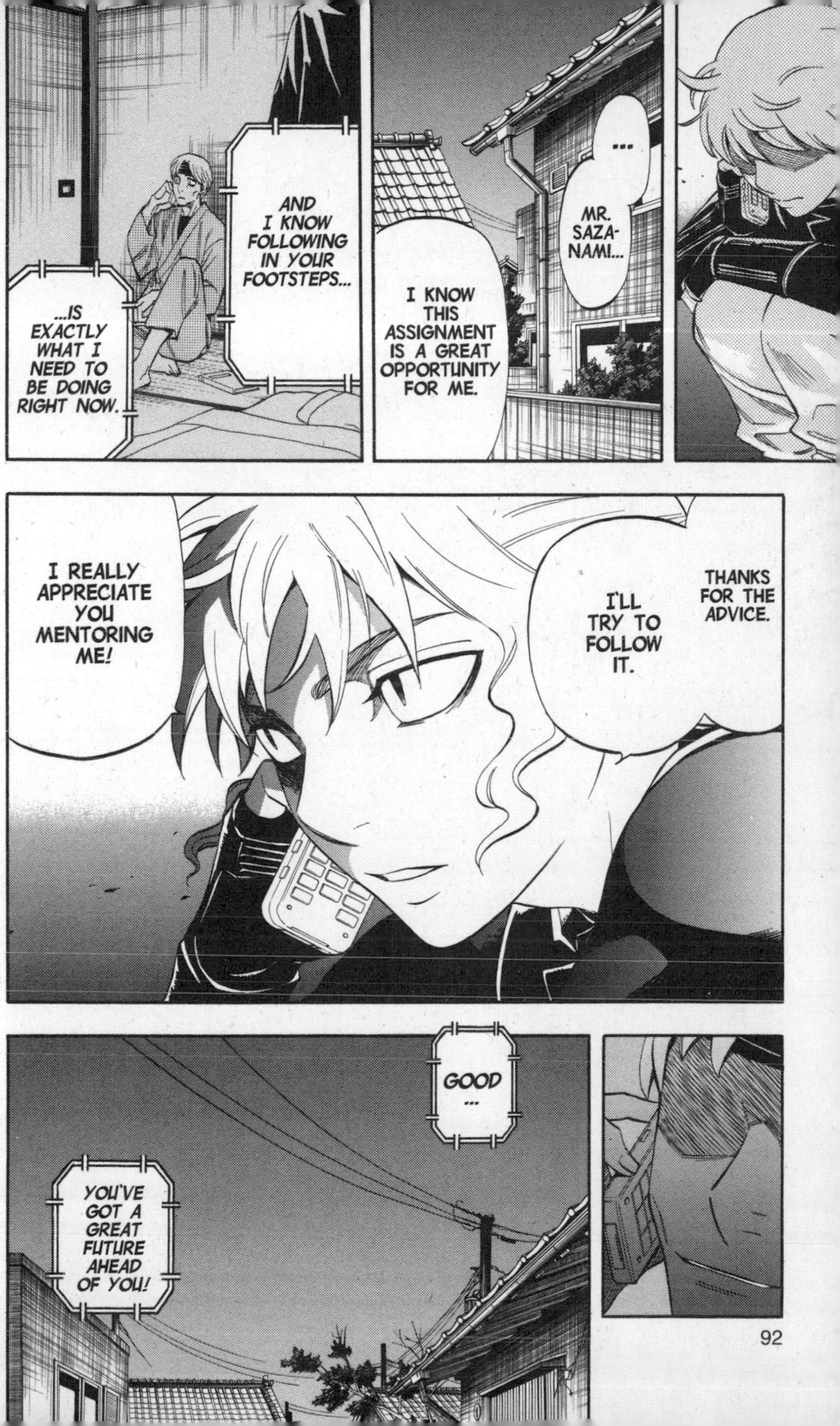
...
MR. SAZA-NAMI...
I KNOW THIS ASSIGNMENT IS A GREAT OPPORTUNITY FOR ME.
AND I KNOW FOLLOWING IN YOUR FOOTSTEPS...
...IS EXACTLY WHAT I NEED TO BE DOING RIGHT NOW.
THANKS FOR THE ADVICE.
I'LL TRY TO FOLLOW IT.
I REALLY APPRECIATE YOU MENTORING ME!
GOOD...
YOU'VE GOT A GREAT FUTURE AHEAD OF YOU!

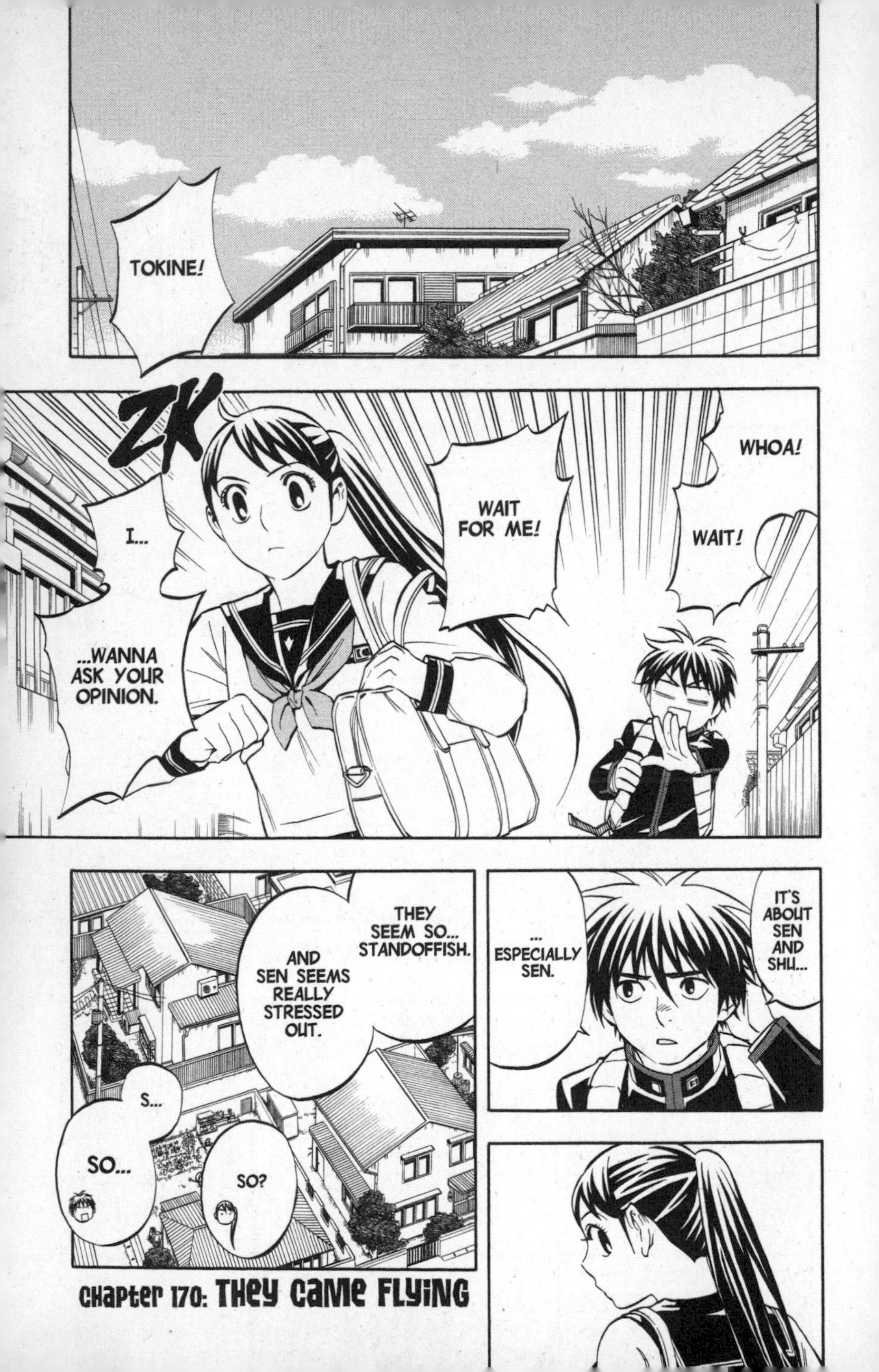
TOKINE!
WHOA!
WAIT!
WAIT FOR ME!
ZK
I...
...WANNA ASK YOUR OPINION.
IT'S ABOUT SEN AND SHU...
...ESPECIALLY SEN.
THEY SEEM SO... STANDOFFISH.
AND SEN SEEMS REALLY STRESSED OUT.
SO?
S...
SO...
Chapter 170: They Came Flying

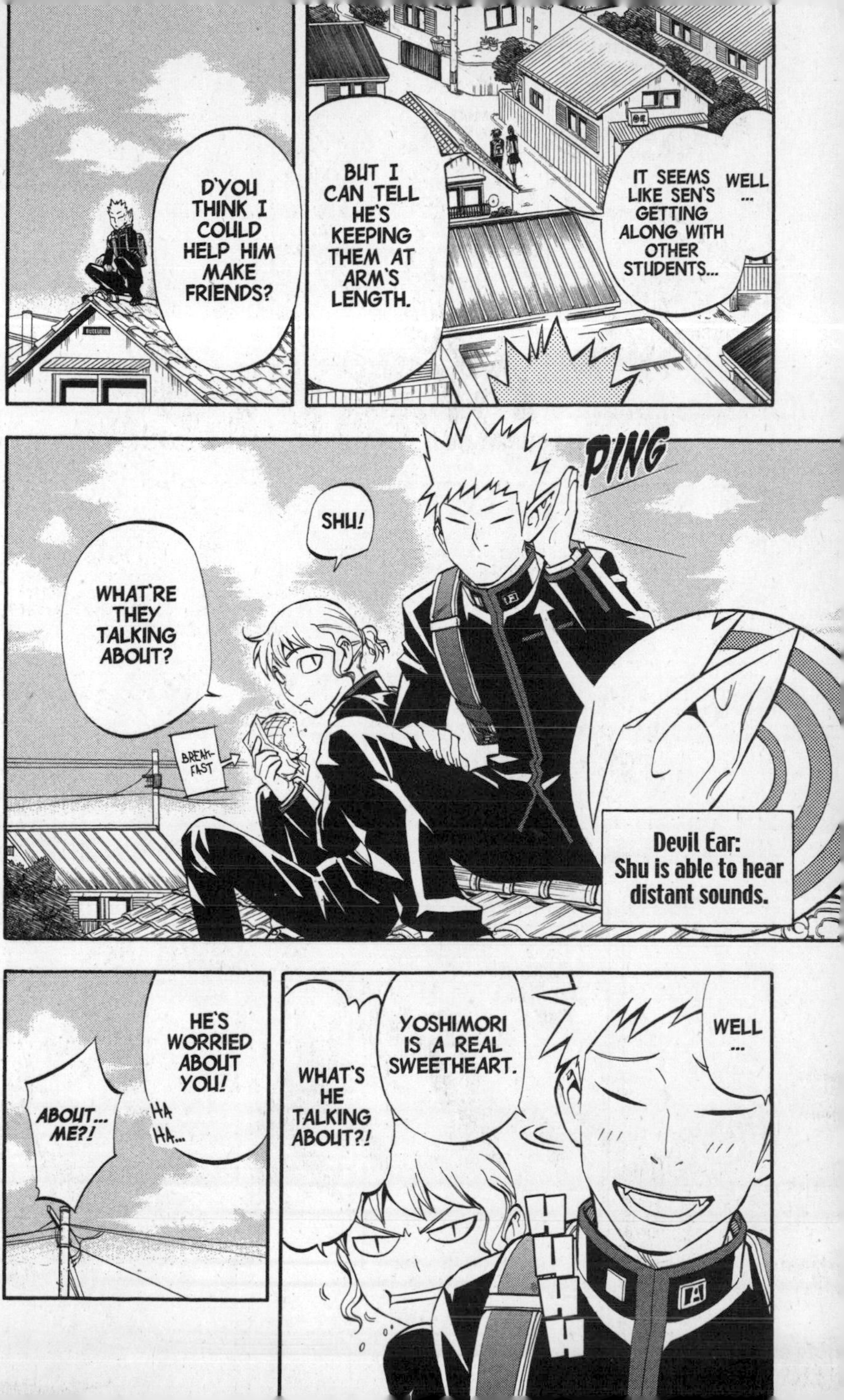
WELL ...
IT SEEMS LIKE SEN'S GETTING ALONG WITH OTHER STUDENTS...
BUT I CAN TELL HE'S KEEPING THEM AT ARM'S LENGTH.
D'YOU THINK I COULD HELP HIM MAKE FRIENDS?
PING
SHU!
WHAT'RE THEY TALKING ABOUT?
BREAK-FAST
Devil Ear: Shu is able to hear distant sounds.
WELL ...
YOSHIMORI IS A REAL SWEETHEART.
WHAT'S HE TALKING ABOUT?!
HUHH
HE'S WORRIED ABOUT YOU!
HA HA...
ABOUT... ME?!

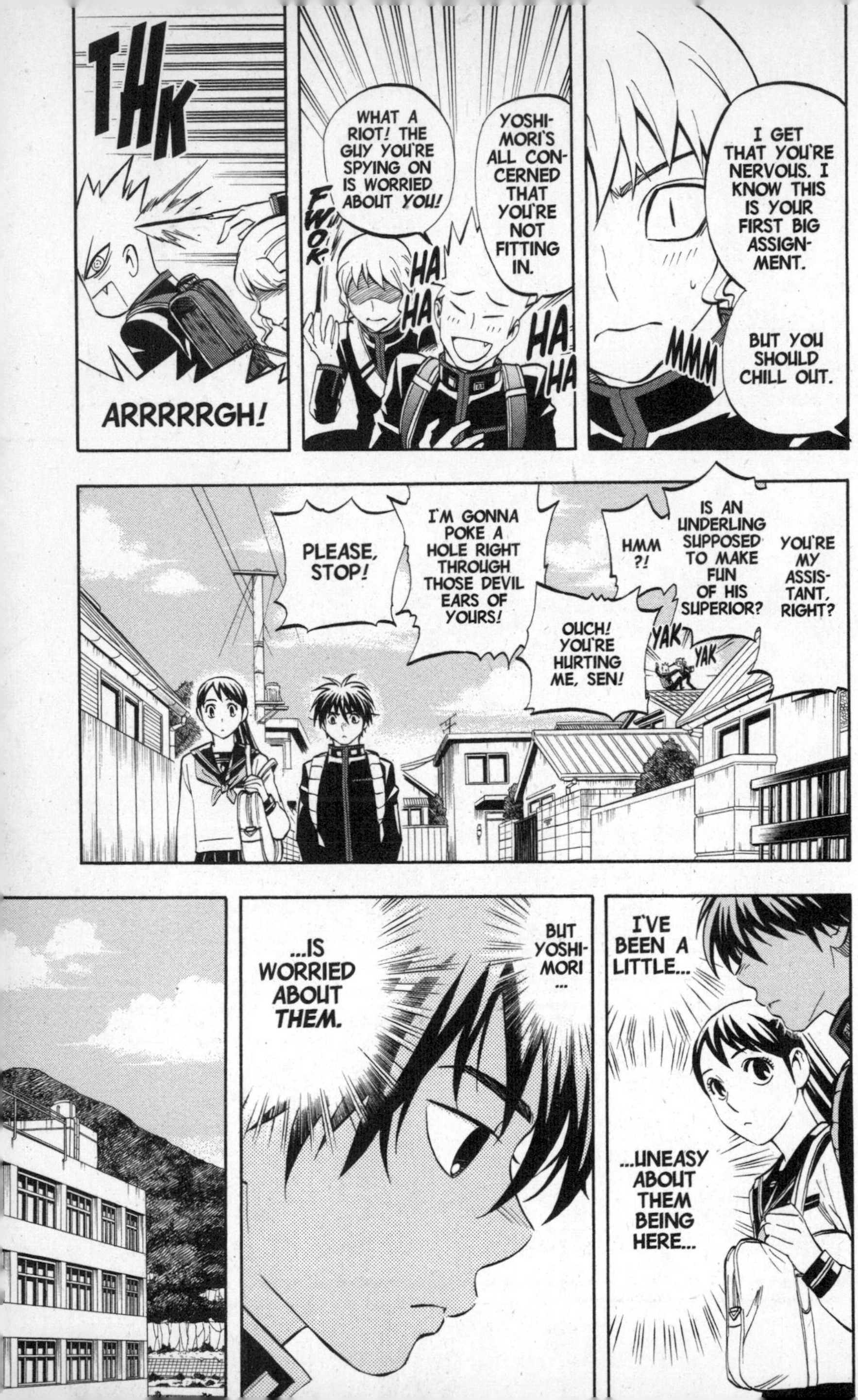
I GET THAT YOU'RE NERVOUS. I KNOW THIS IS YOUR FIRST BIG ASSIGNMENT.
MMM
BUT YOU SHOULD CHILL OUT.
YOSHI-MORI'S ALL CON-CERNED THAT YOU'RE NOT FITTING IN.
WHAT A RIOT! THE GUY YOU'RE SPYING ON IS WORRIED ABOUT *YOU*!
HA HA HA HA
FWOK
THK
ARRRRRGH!
YOU'RE MY ASSIS-TANT, RIGHT?
IS AN UNDERLING SUPPOSED TO MAKE FUN OF HIS SUPERIOR?
HMM ?!
YAK
YAK
OUCH! YOU'RE HURTING ME, SEN!
I'M GONNA POKE A HOLE RIGHT THROUGH THOSE DEVIL EARS OF YOURS!
PLEASE, STOP!
I'VE BEEN A LITTLE...
...UNEASY ABOUT THEM BEING HERE...
BUT YOSHI-MORI ...
...IS WORRIED ABOUT *THEM*.

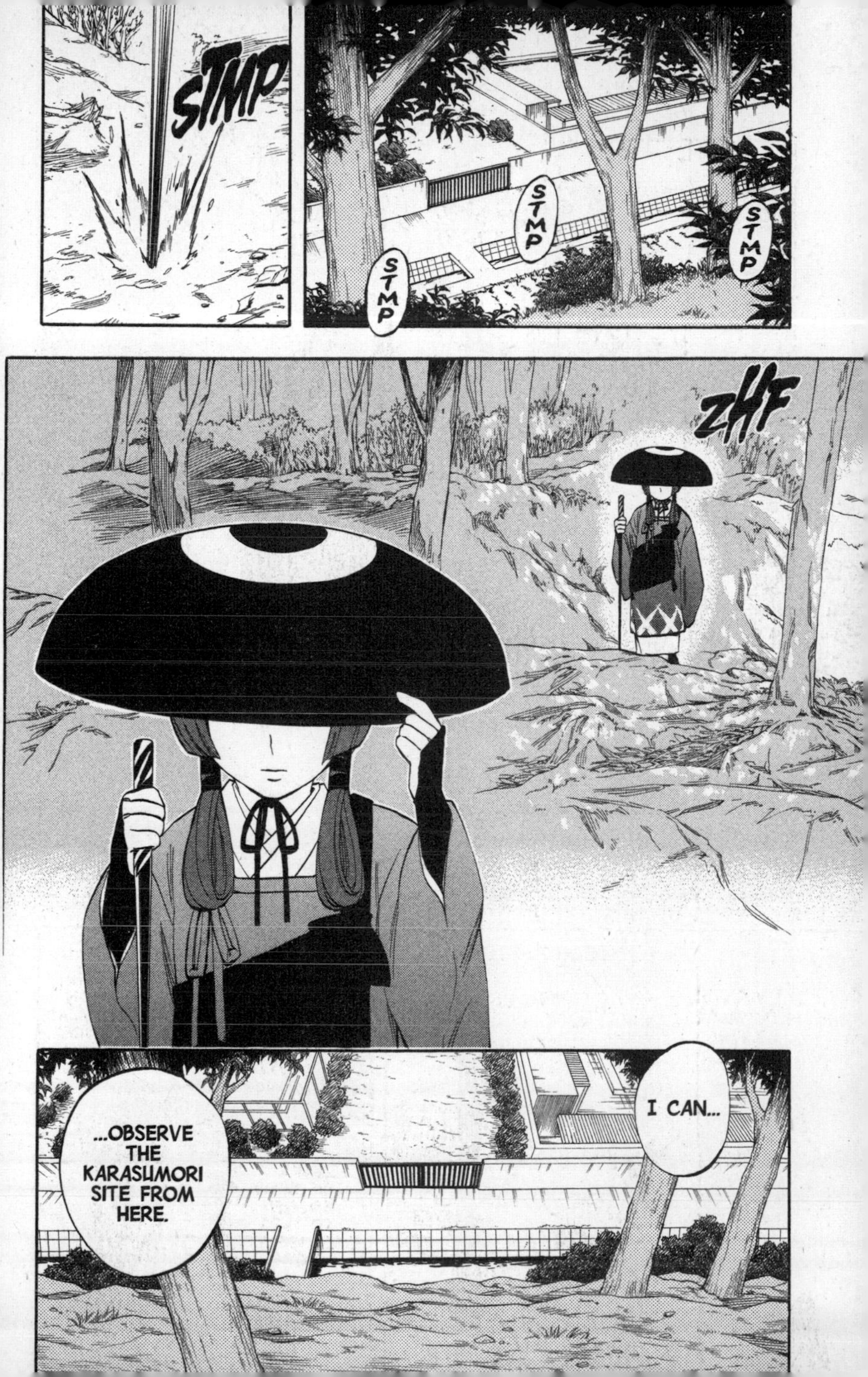
STMP
STMP
STMP
STMP
ZHF
I CAN...
...OBSERVE THE KARASUMORI SITE FROM HERE.

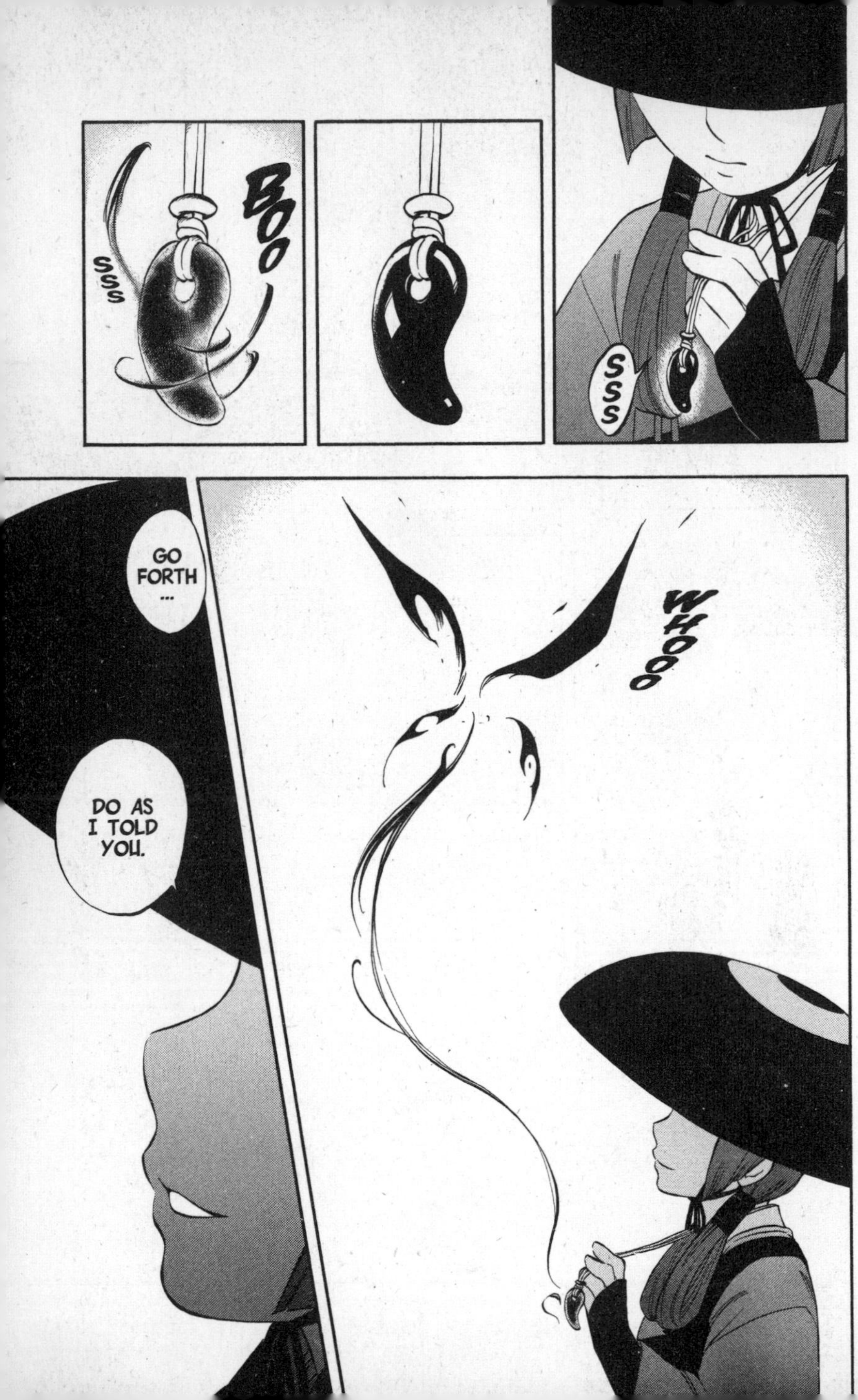
SSS
BOOO
SSS
WHOOOO
GO FORTH ...
DO AS I TOLD YOU.

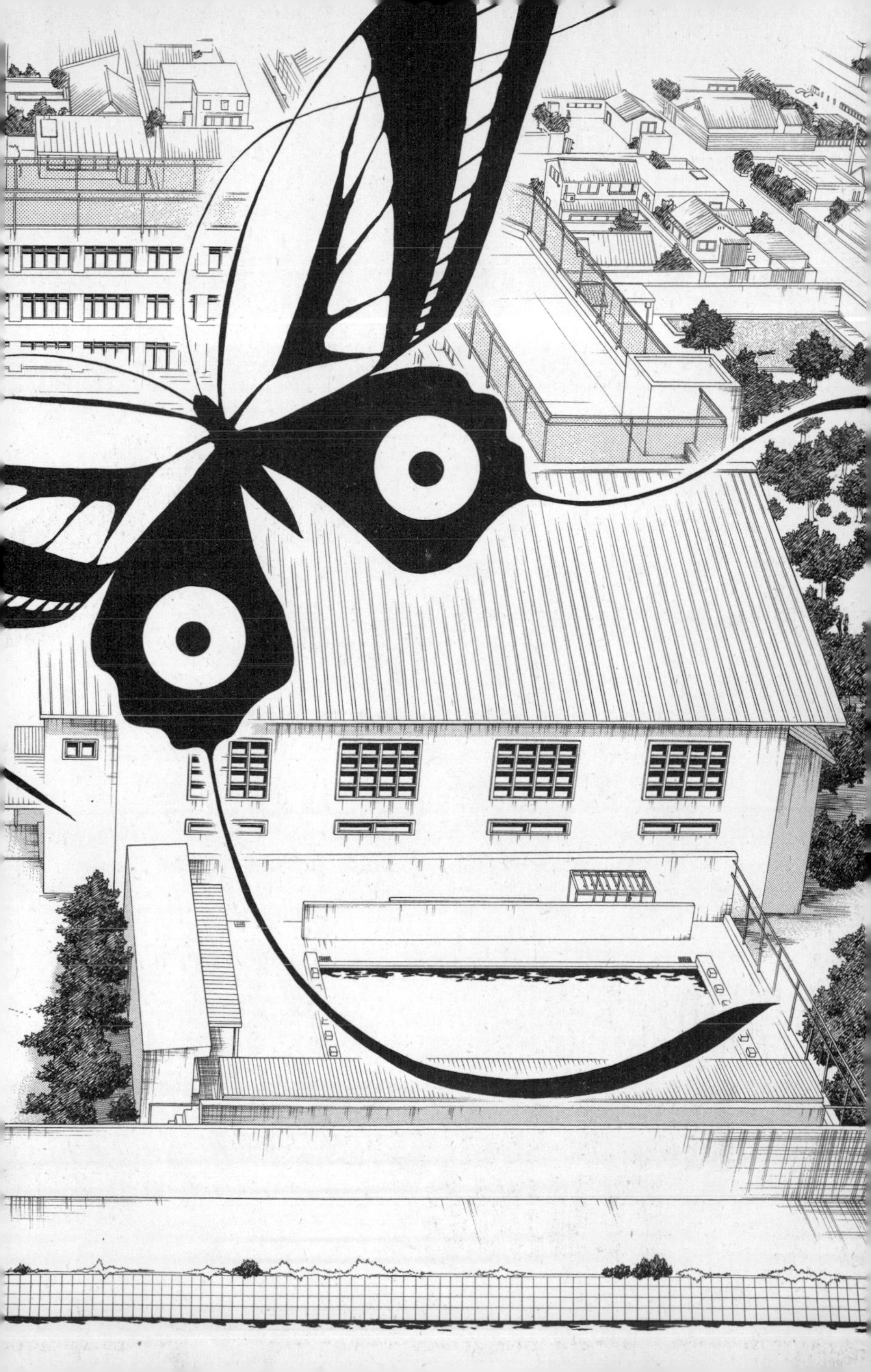

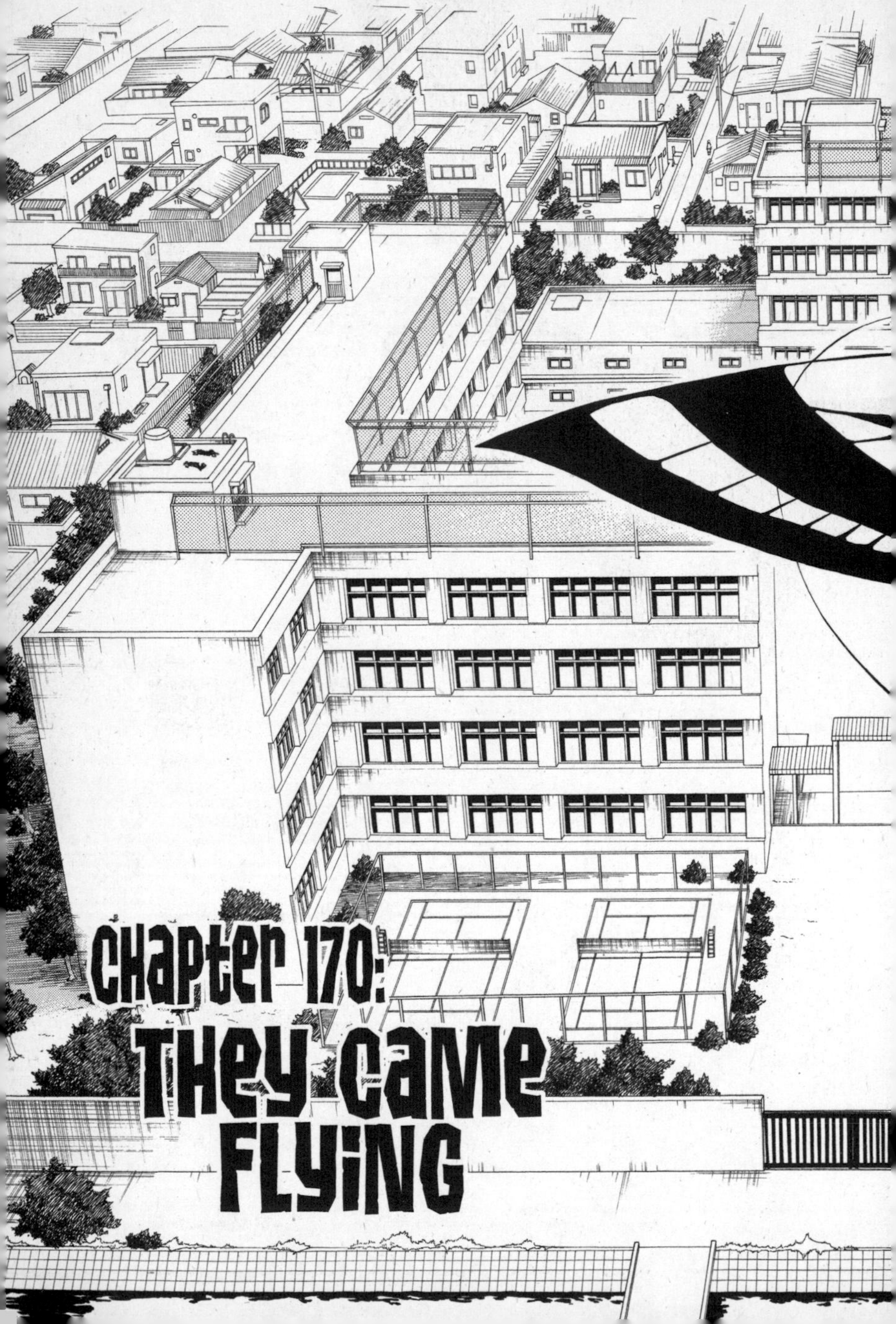
Chapter 170:
They Came Flying

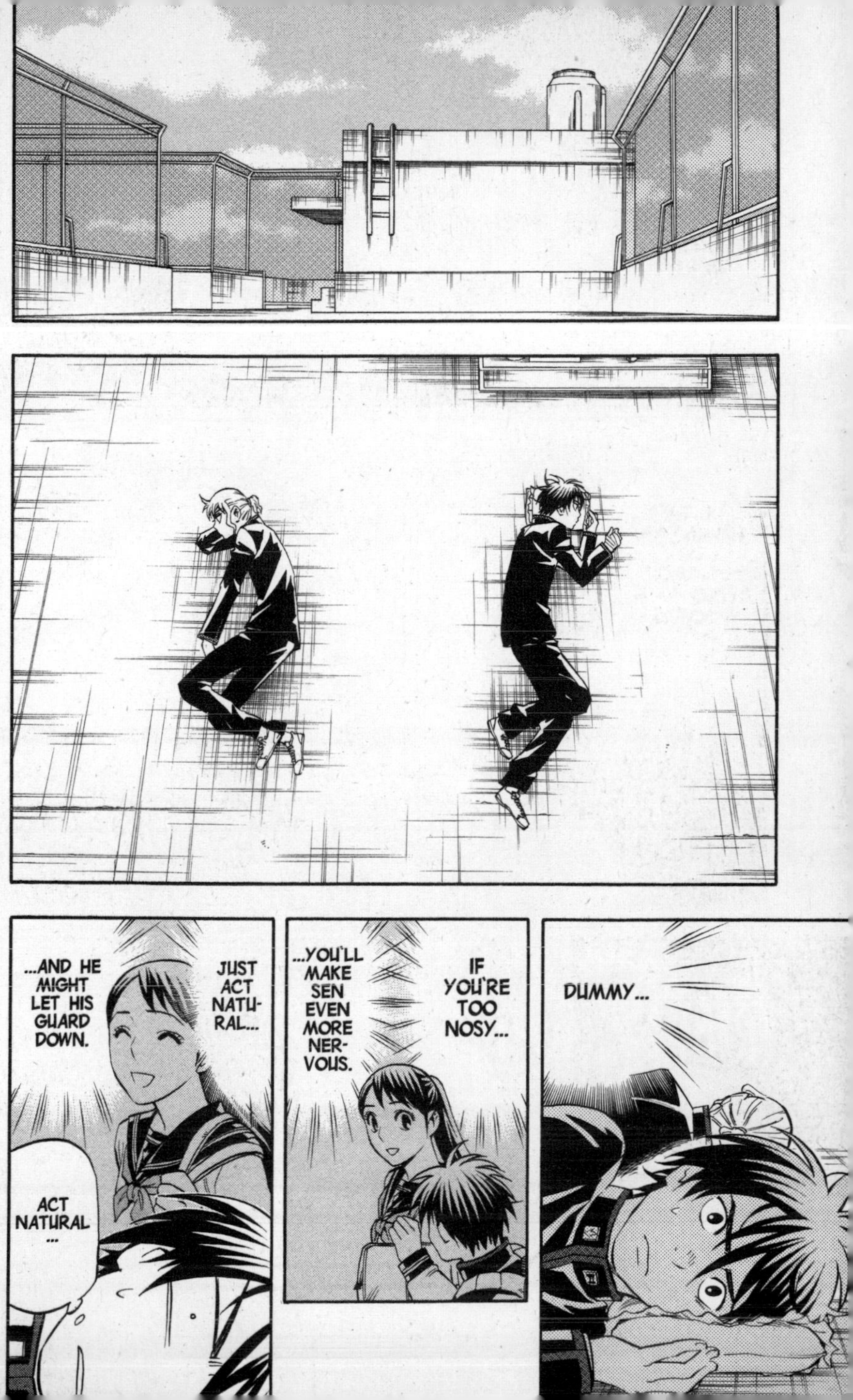
DUMMY...
IF YOU'RE TOO NOSY...
...YOU'LL MAKE SEN EVEN MORE NER-VOUS.
JUST ACT NATU-RAL...
...AND HE MIGHT LET HIS GUARD DOWN.
ACT NATURAL ...

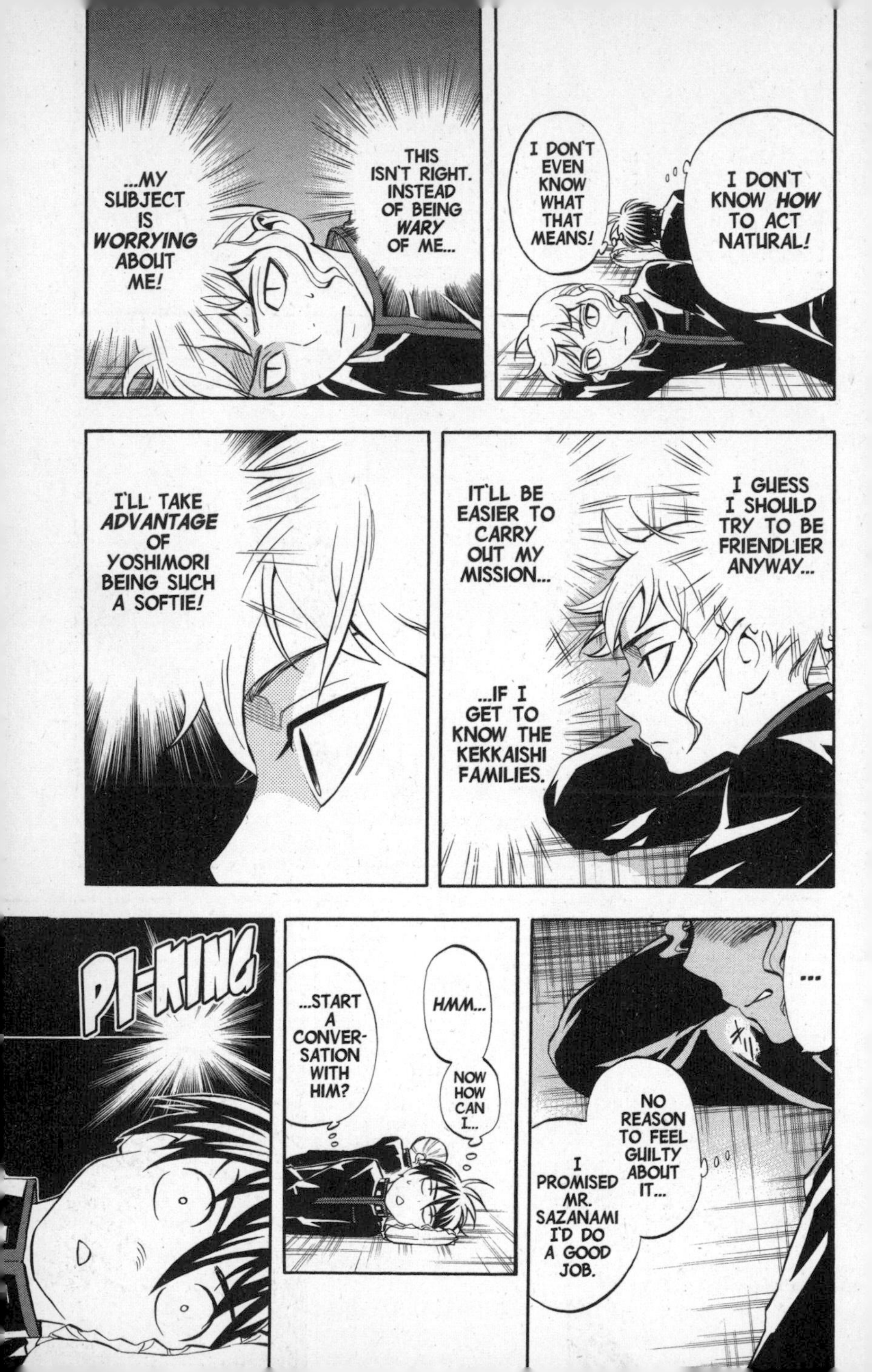
I DON'T KNOW HOW TO ACT NATURAL!
I DON'T EVEN KNOW WHAT THAT MEANS!
THIS ISN'T RIGHT. INSTEAD OF BEING WARY OF ME...
...MY SUBJECT IS WORRYING ABOUT ME!
I GUESS I SHOULD TRY TO BE FRIENDLIER ANYWAY...
IT'LL BE EASIER TO CARRY OUT MY MISSION...
...IF I GET TO KNOW THE KEKKAISHI FAMILIES.
I'LL TAKE ADVANTAGE OF YOSHIMORI BEING SUCH A SOFTIE!
...
NO REASON TO FEEL GUILTY ABOUT IT...
I PROMISED MR. SAZANAMI I'D DO A GOOD JOB.
HMM...
NOW HOW CAN I...
...START A CONVERSATION WITH HIM?
PI-KING

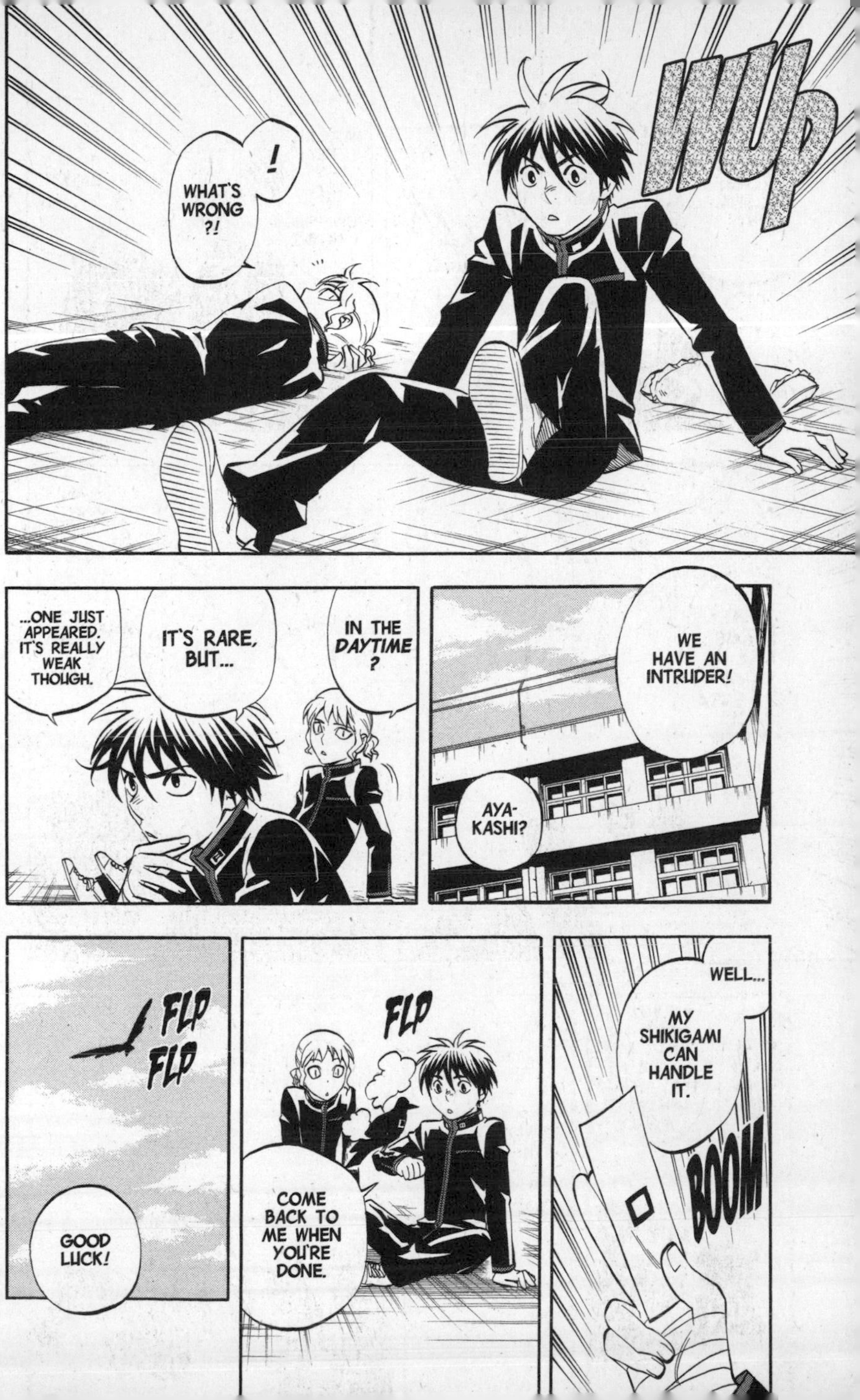
WUP
!
WHAT'S WRONG ?!
WE HAVE AN INTRUDER!
AYA-KASHI?
IN THE DAYTIME ?
IT'S RARE, BUT...
...ONE JUST APPEARED. IT'S REALLY WEAK THOUGH.
WELL...
MY SHIKIGAMI CAN HANDLE IT.
BOOM
FLP
COME BACK TO ME WHEN YOU'RE DONE.
FLP FLP
GOOD LUCK!

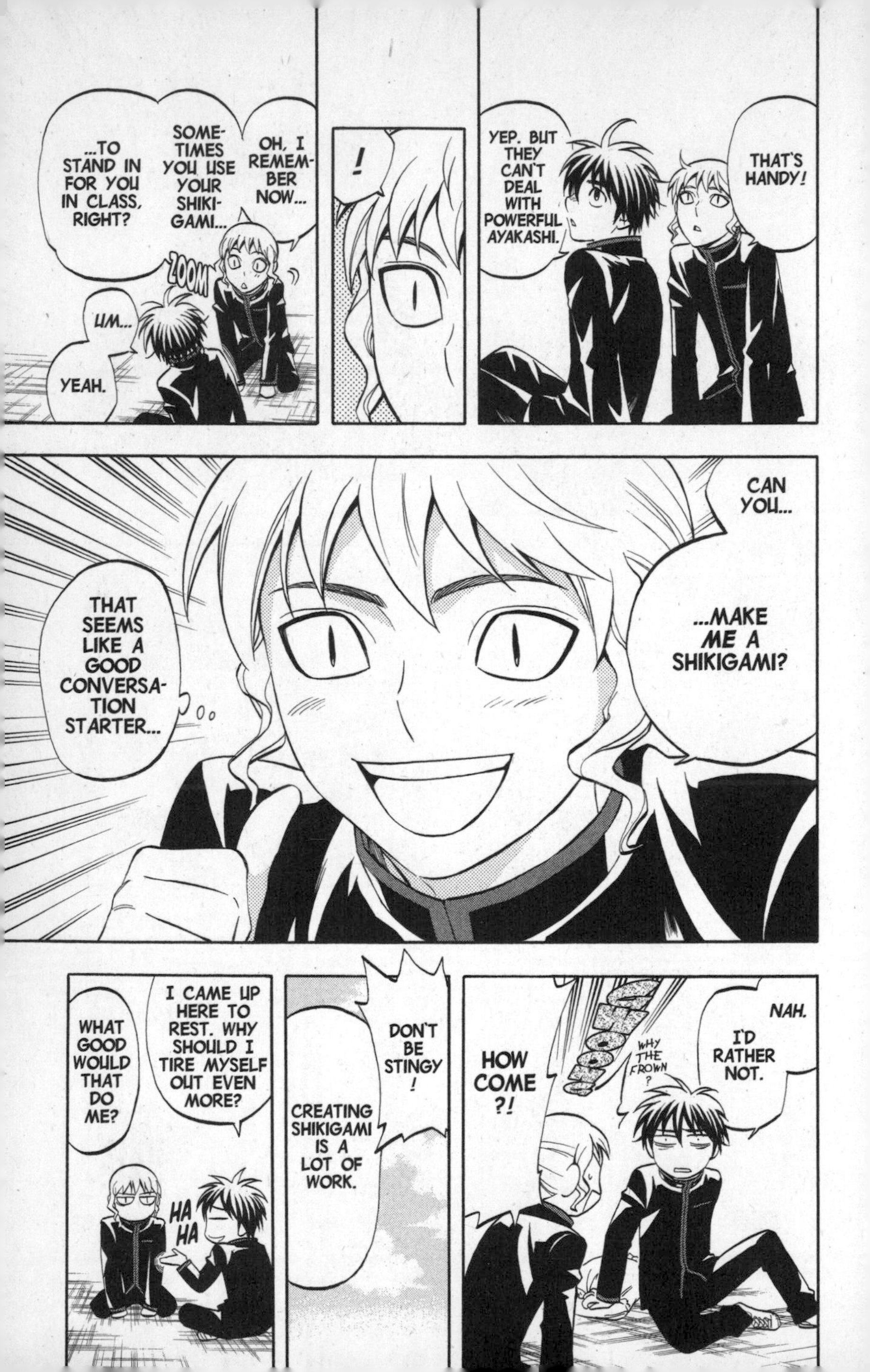
THAT'S HANDY!
YEP. BUT THEY CAN'T DEAL WITH POWERFUL AYAKASHI.
!
OH, I REMEMBER NOW...
SOMETIMES YOU USE YOUR SHIKIGAMI...
...TO STAND IN FOR YOU IN CLASS, RIGHT?
ZOOM
UM...
YEAH.
CAN YOU...
...MAKE ME A SHIKIGAMI?
THAT SEEMS LIKE A GOOD CONVERSATION STARTER...
NAH.
I'D RATHER NOT.
WHY THE FROWN?
HOW COME?!
DON'T BE STINGY!
CREATING SHIKIGAMI IS A LOT OF WORK.
I CAME UP HERE TO REST. WHY SHOULD I TIRE MYSELF OUT EVEN MORE?
WHAT GOOD WOULD THAT DO ME?
HA HA

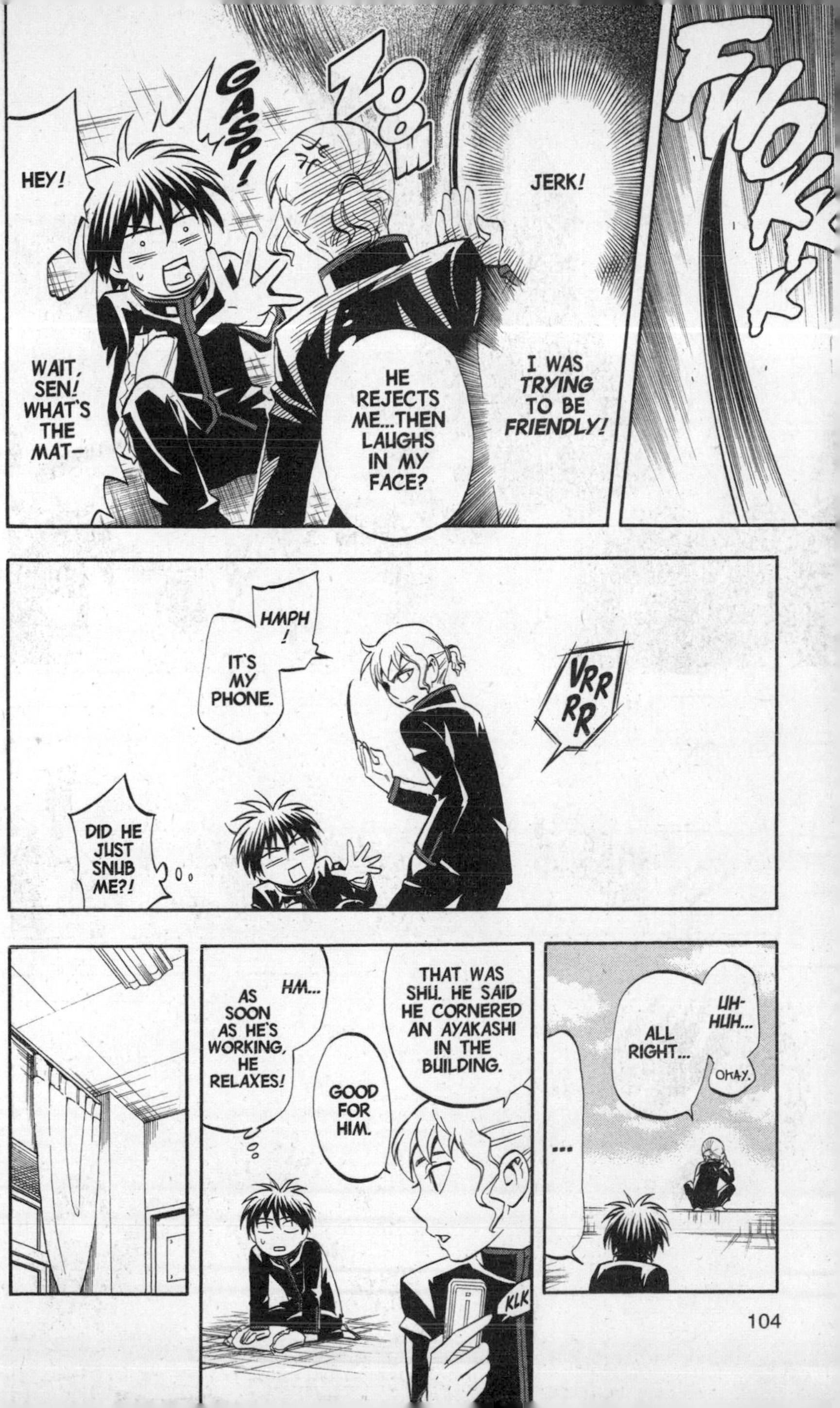
FWOKKK
JERK!
ZOOM
GASP!
HEY!
I WAS TRYING TO BE FRIENDLY!
HE REJECTS ME...THEN LAUGHS IN MY FACE?
WAIT, SEN! WHAT'S THE MAT—
VRRRR
HMPH!
IT'S MY PHONE.
DID HE JUST SNUB ME?!
UH-HUH...
ALL RIGHT...
OKAY.
...
THAT WAS SHU. HE SAID HE CORNERED AN AYAKASHI IN THE BUILDING.
HM...
AS SOON AS HE'S WORKING, HE RELAXES!
GOOD FOR HIM.
KLK

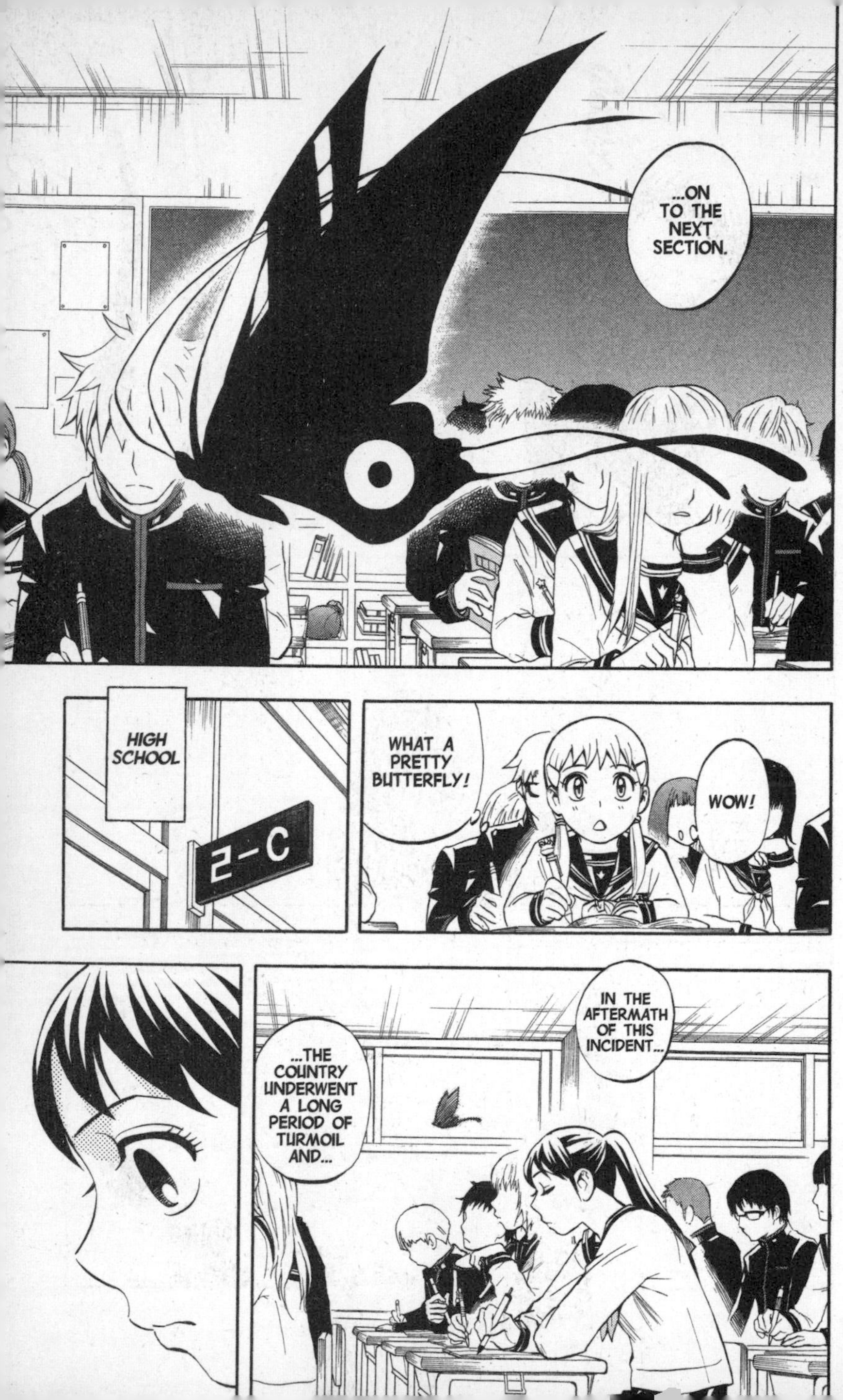
...ON TO THE NEXT SECTION.
WOW!
WHAT A PRETTY BUTTERFLY!
HIGH SCHOOL
2-C
IN THE AFTERMATH OF THIS INCIDENT...
...THE COUNTRY UNDERWENT A LONG PERIOD OF TURMOIL AND...

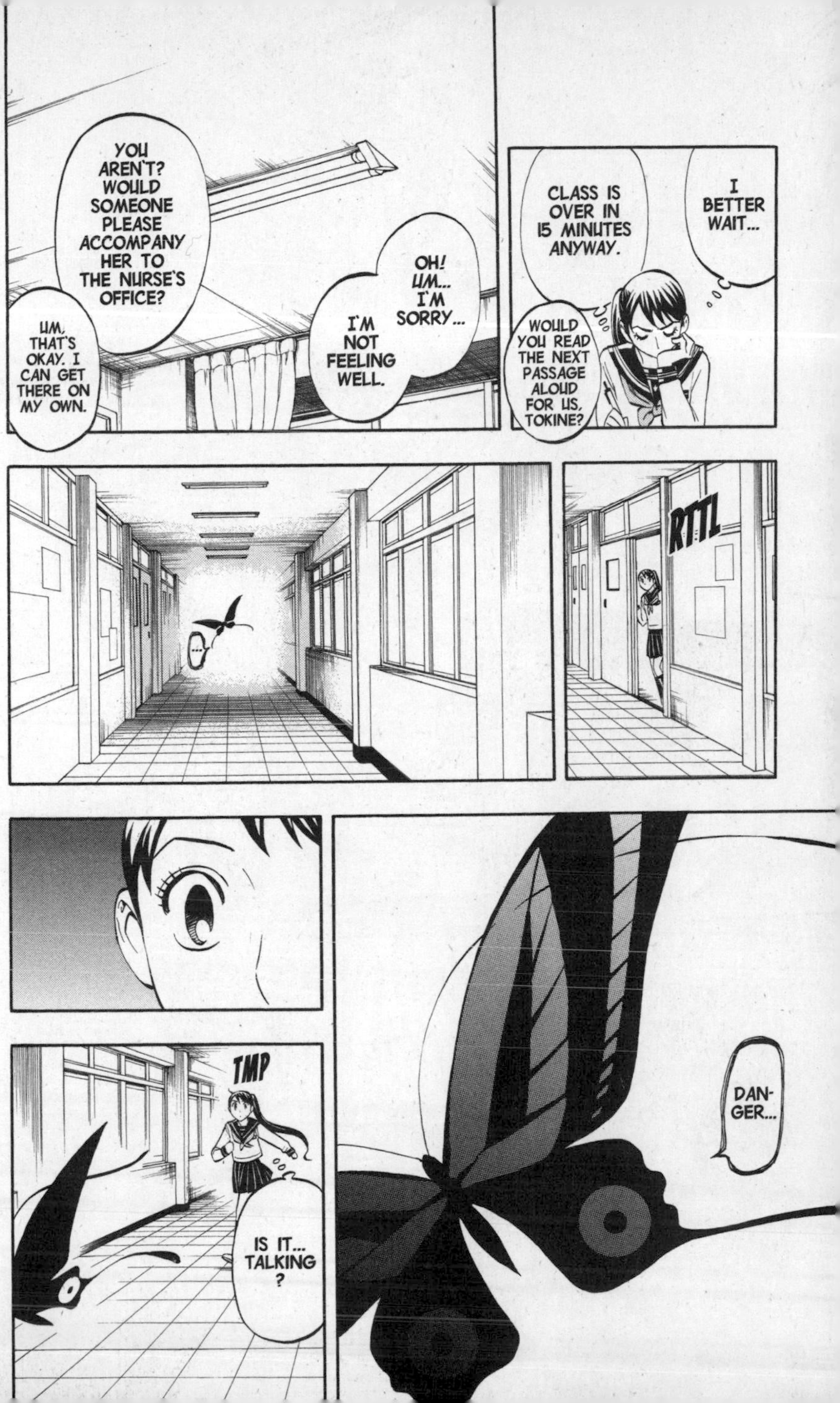
I BETTER WAIT...
CLASS IS OVER IN 15 MINUTES ANYWAY.
WOULD YOU READ THE NEXT PASSAGE ALOUD FOR US, TOKINE?
OH! UM... I'M SORRY...
I'M NOT FEELING WELL.
YOU AREN'T? WOULD SOMEONE PLEASE ACCOMPANY HER TO THE NURSE'S OFFICE?
UM, THAT'S OKAY. I CAN GET THERE ON MY OWN.
RTTL
...
DAN-GER...
TMP
IS IT... TALKING ?

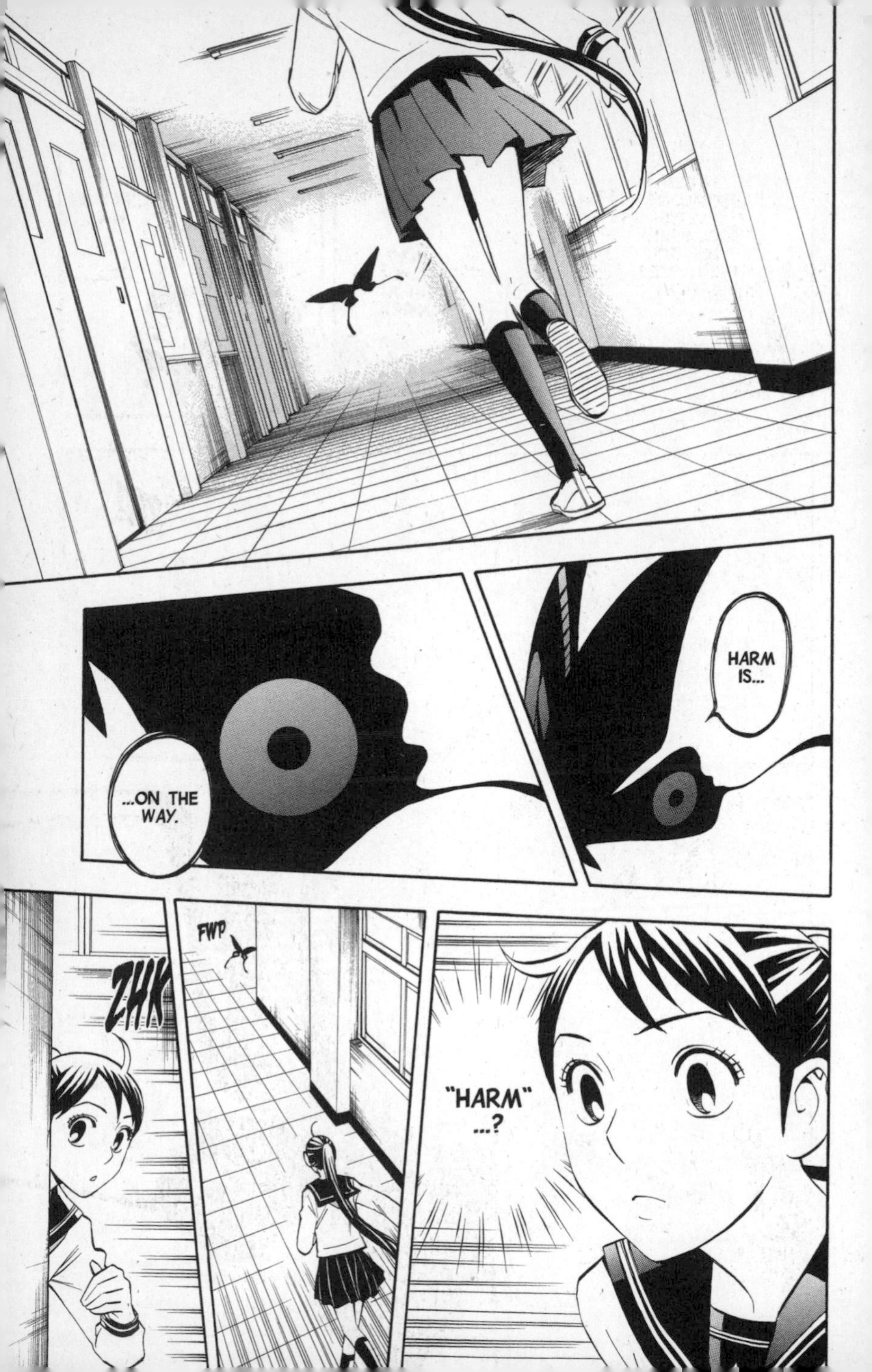
HARM IS...
...ON THE WAY.
"HARM" ...?
FWP
ZHK

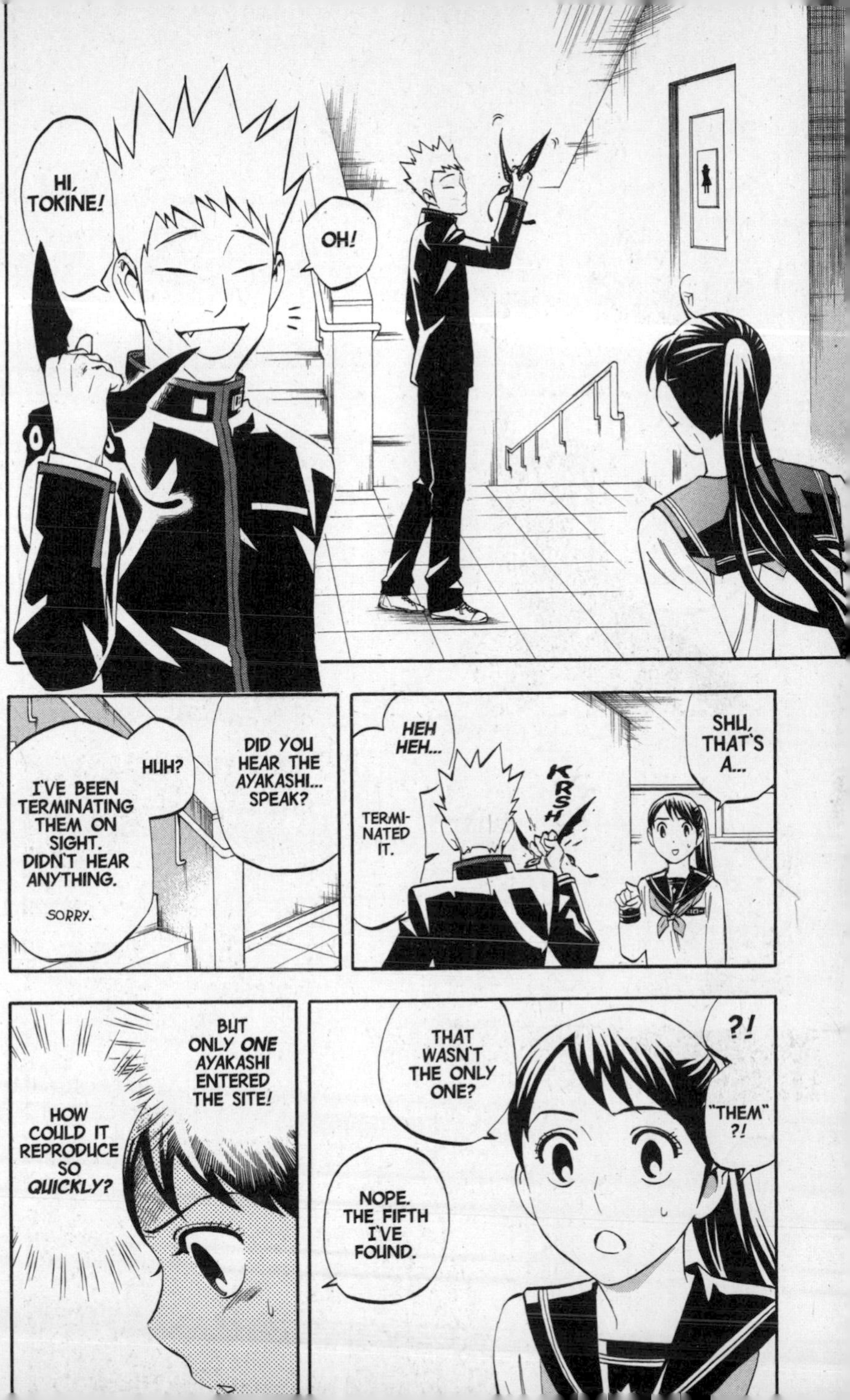
OH!
HI, TOKINE!
SHU, THAT'S A...
HEH HEH...
KRSH
TERMINATED IT.
DID YOU HEAR THE AYAKASHI... SPEAK?
HUH?
I'VE BEEN TERMINATING THEM ON SIGHT. DIDN'T HEAR ANYTHING.
SORRY.
?!
"THEM" ?!
THAT WASN'T THE ONLY ONE?
NOPE. THE FIFTH I'VE FOUND.
BUT ONLY *ONE* AYAKASHI ENTERED THE SITE!
HOW COULD IT REPRODUCE SO *QUICKLY?*

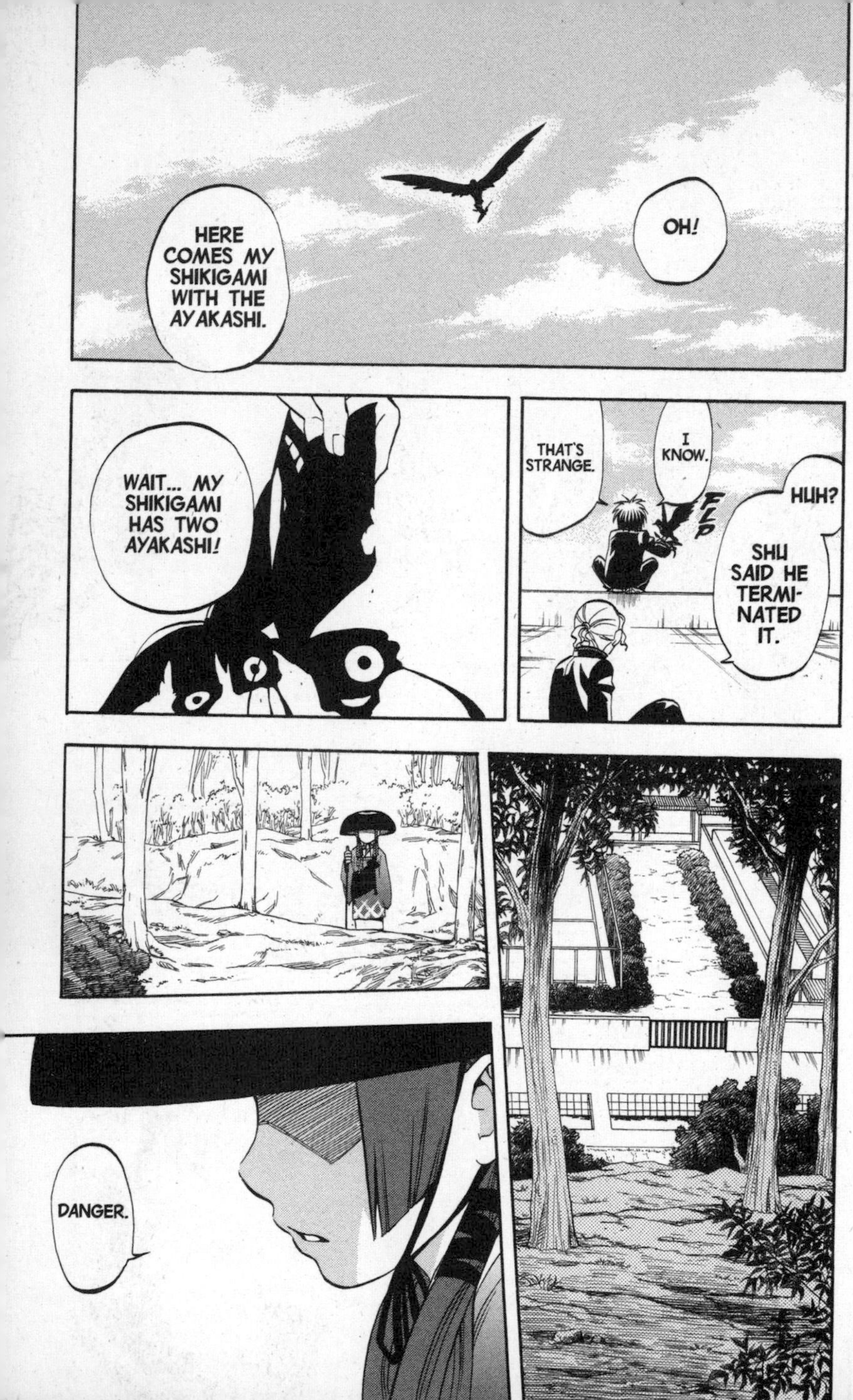
OH!
HERE COMES MY SHIKIGAMI WITH THE AYAKASHI.
HUH?
SHU SAID HE TERMINATED IT.
I KNOW.
FLP
THAT'S STRANGE.
WAIT... MY SHIKIGAMI HAS TWO AYAKASHI!
DANGER.

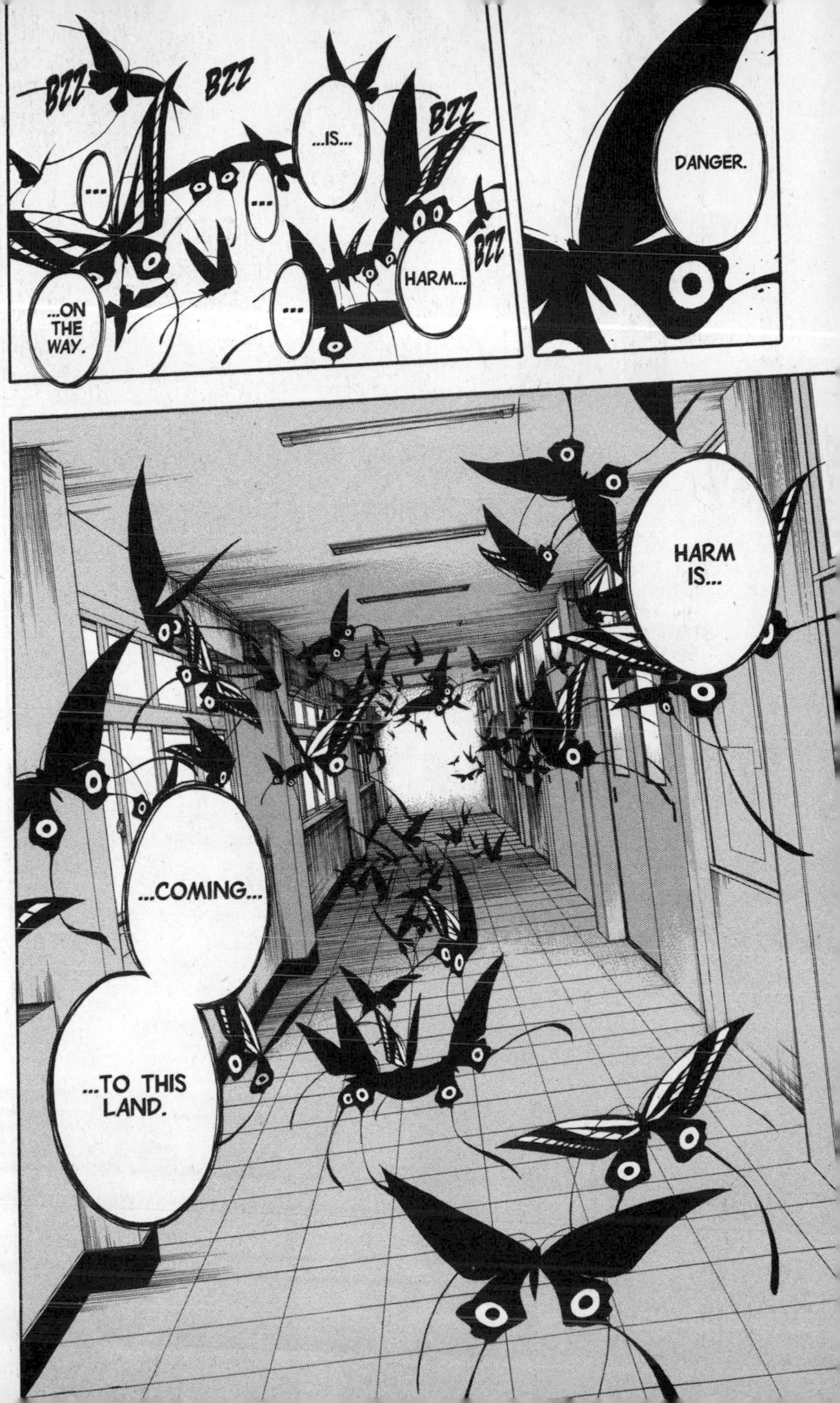
DANGER.
BZZ
...IS...
HARM...
BZZ
...
...
BZZ
BZZ
...
...ON THE WAY.
HARM IS...
...COMING...
...TO THIS LAND.

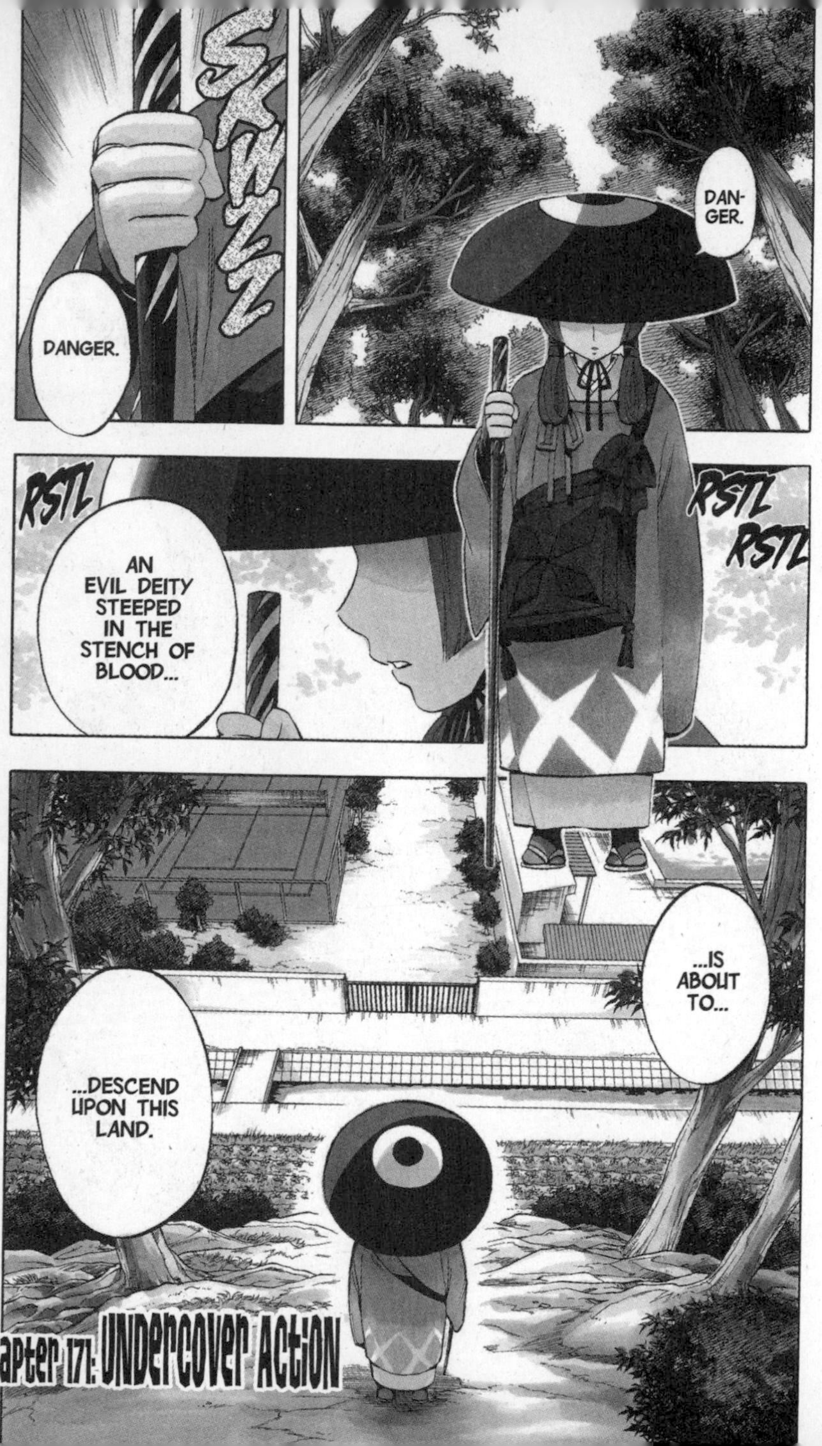
DAN-GER.
SKWZZ
DANGER.
RSTL RSTL
AN EVIL DEITY STEEPED IN THE STENCH OF BLOOD...
RSTL
...IS ABOUT TO...
...DESCEND UPON THIS LAND.
Chapter 171: Undercover Action

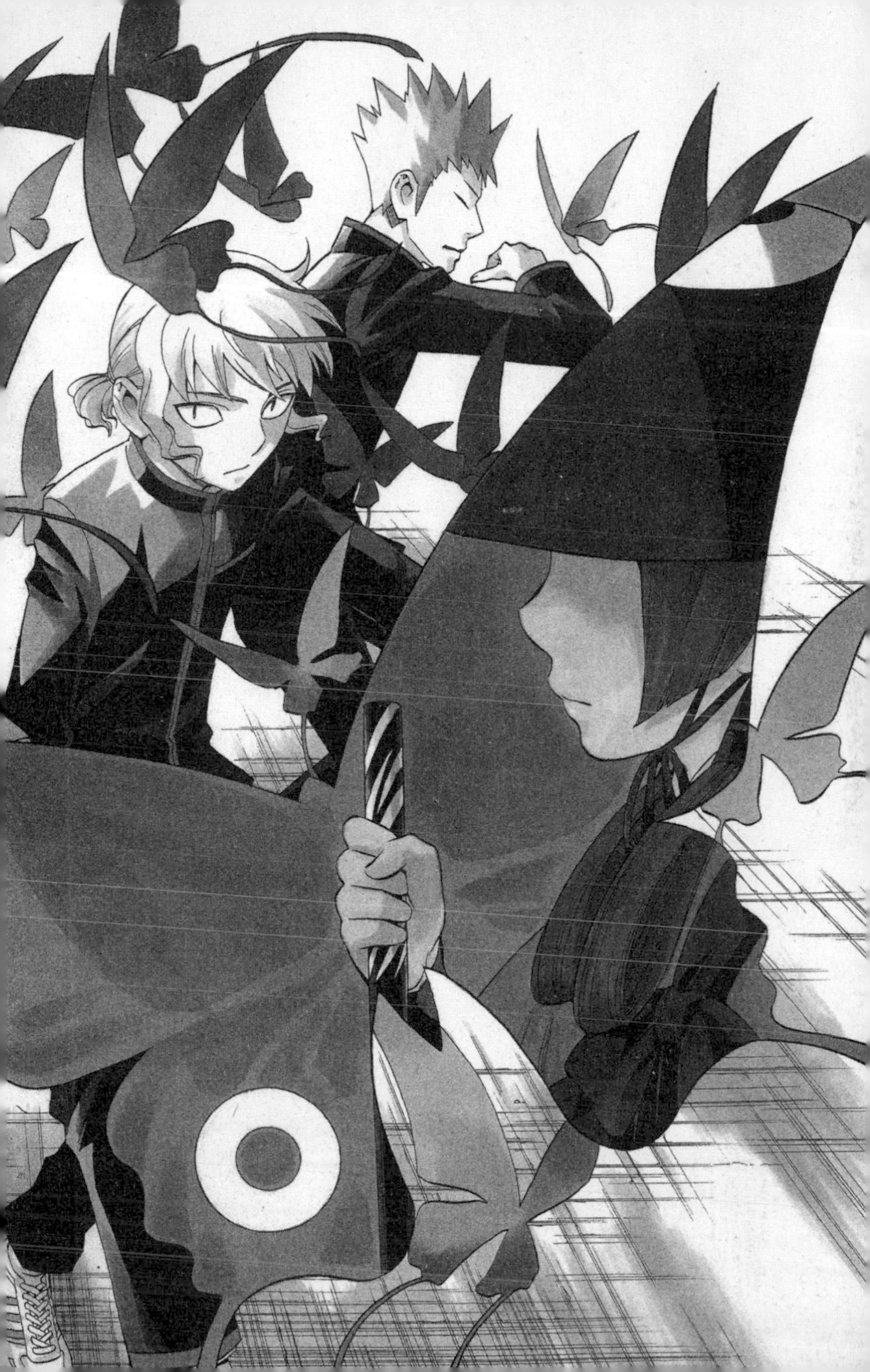

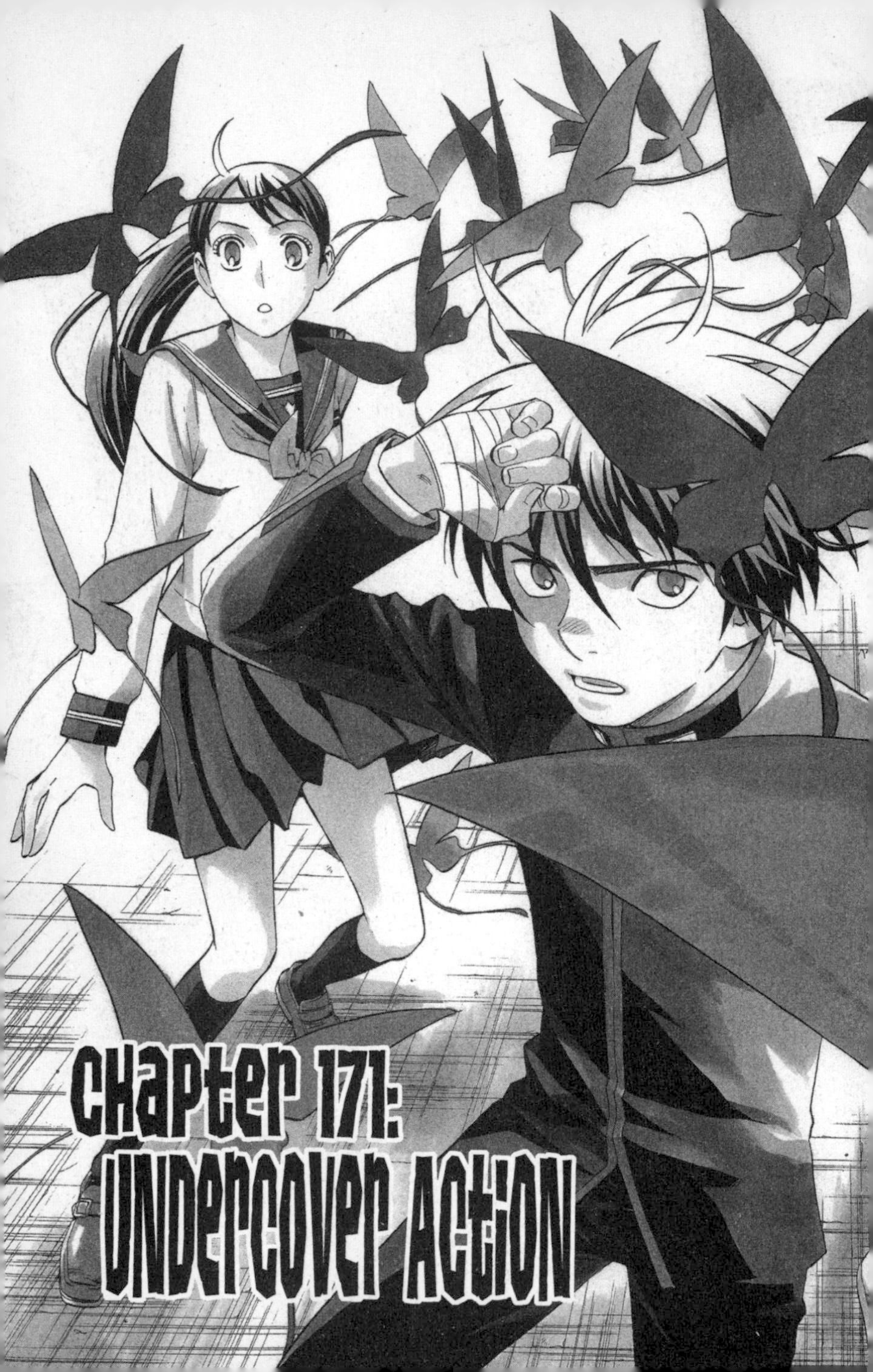
Chapter 171:
Undercover Action

結界師

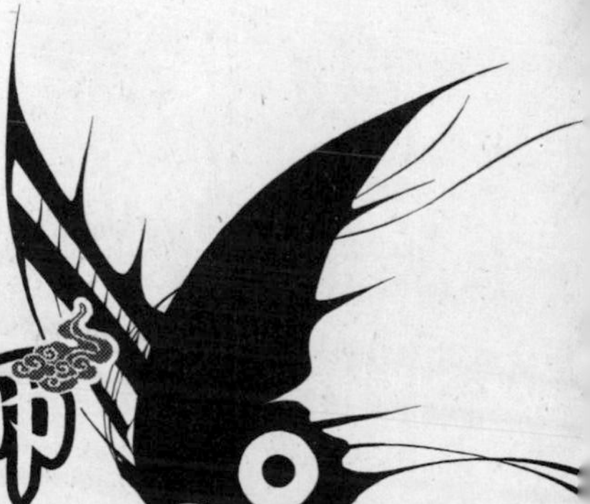

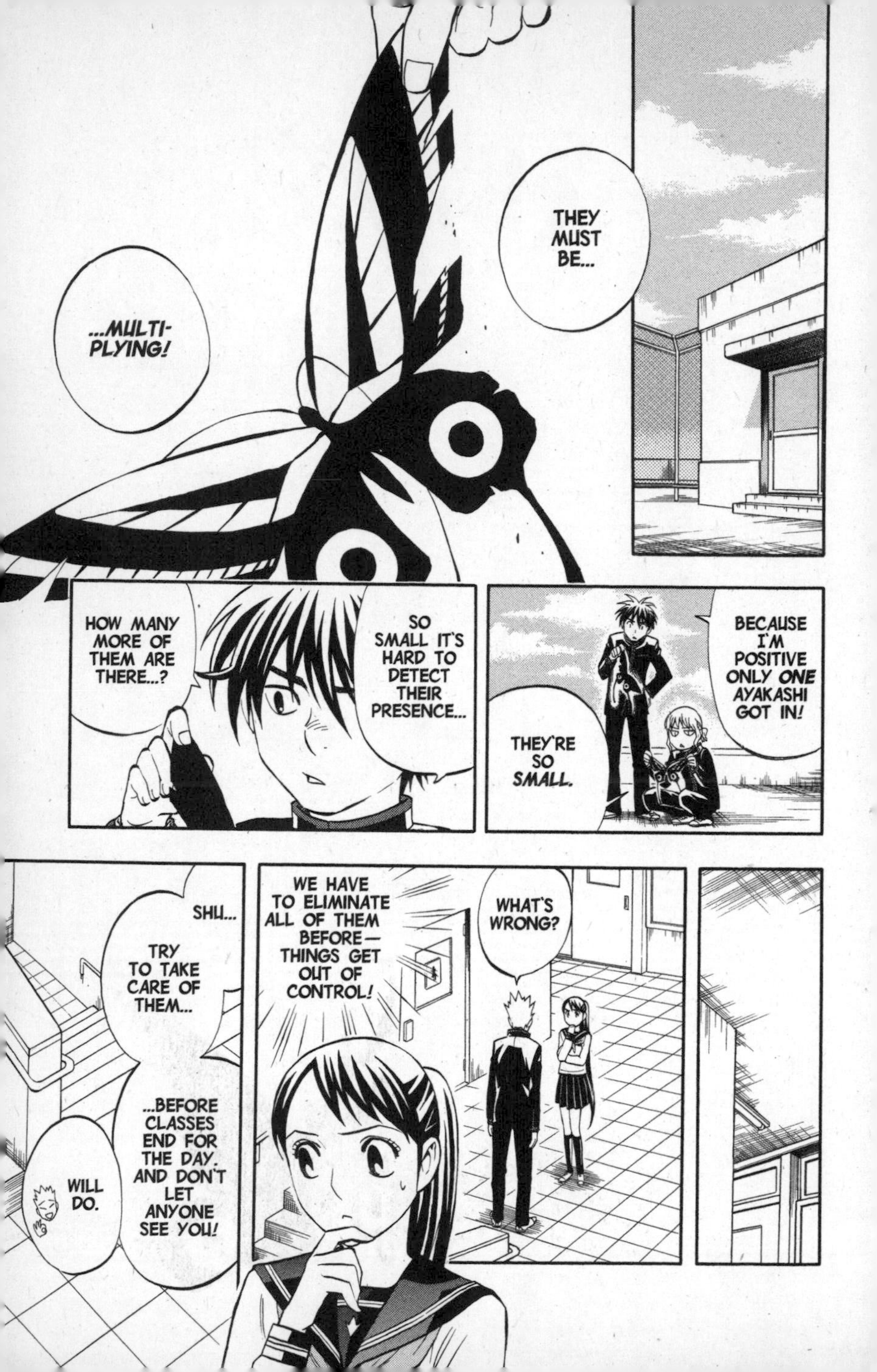
THEY MUST BE...
...MULTI-PLYING!
BECAUSE I'M POSITIVE ONLY ONE AYAKASHI GOT IN!
THEY'RE SO SMALL.
SO SMALL IT'S HARD TO DETECT THEIR PRESENCE...
HOW MANY MORE OF THEM ARE THERE...?
WHAT'S WRONG?
WE HAVE TO ELIMINATE ALL OF THEM BEFORE—THINGS GET OUT OF CONTROL!
SHU...
TRY TO TAKE CARE OF THEM...
...BEFORE CLASSES END FOR THE DAY. AND DON'T LET ANYONE SEE YOU!
WILL DO.

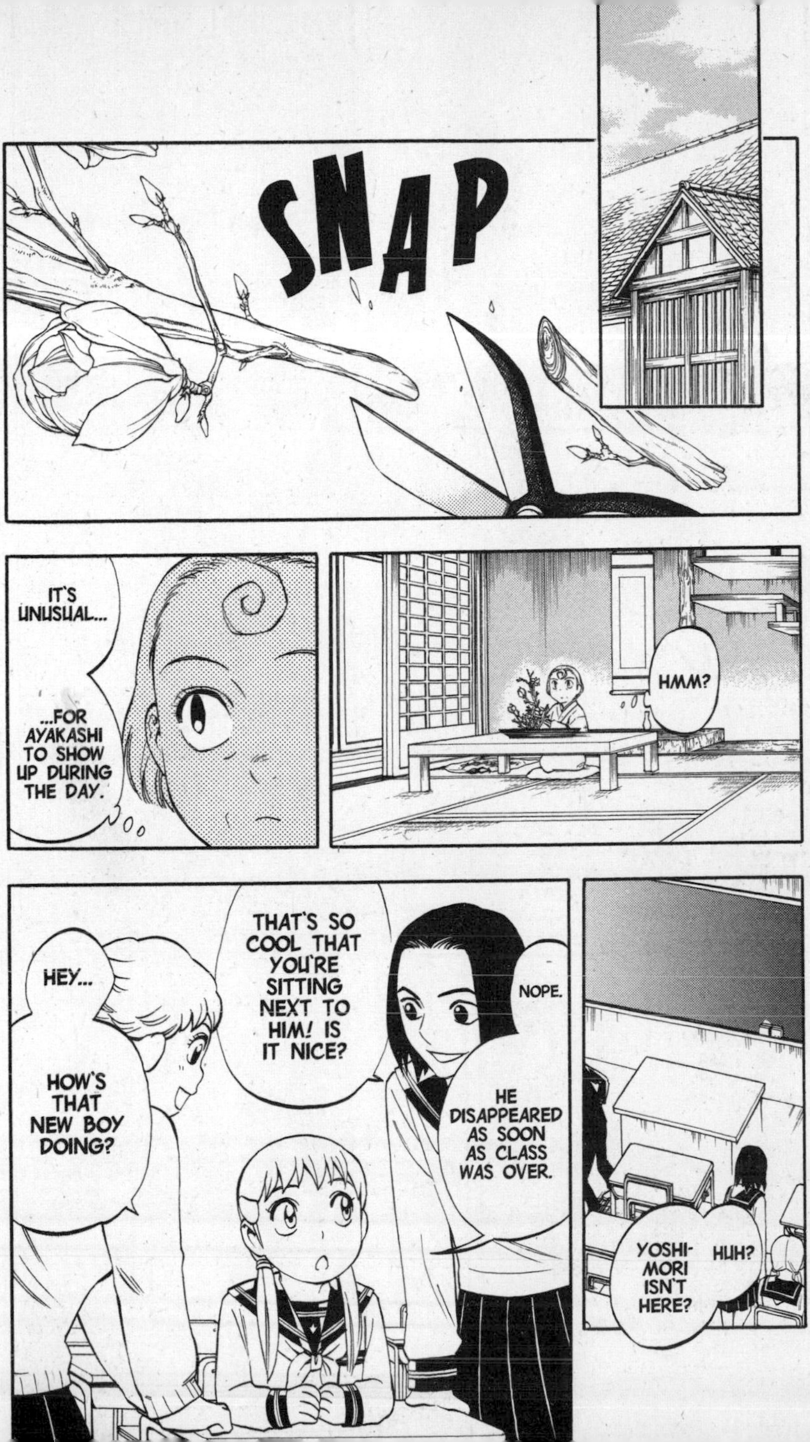
SNAP
HMM?
IT'S UNUSUAL...
...FOR AYAKASHI TO SHOW UP DURING THE DAY.
HUH?
YOSHI-MORI ISN'T HERE?
HEY...
HOW'S THAT NEW BOY DOING?
THAT'S SO COOL THAT YOU'RE SITTING NEXT TO HIM! IS IT NICE?
NOPE.
HE DISAPPEARED AS SOON AS CLASS WAS OVER.

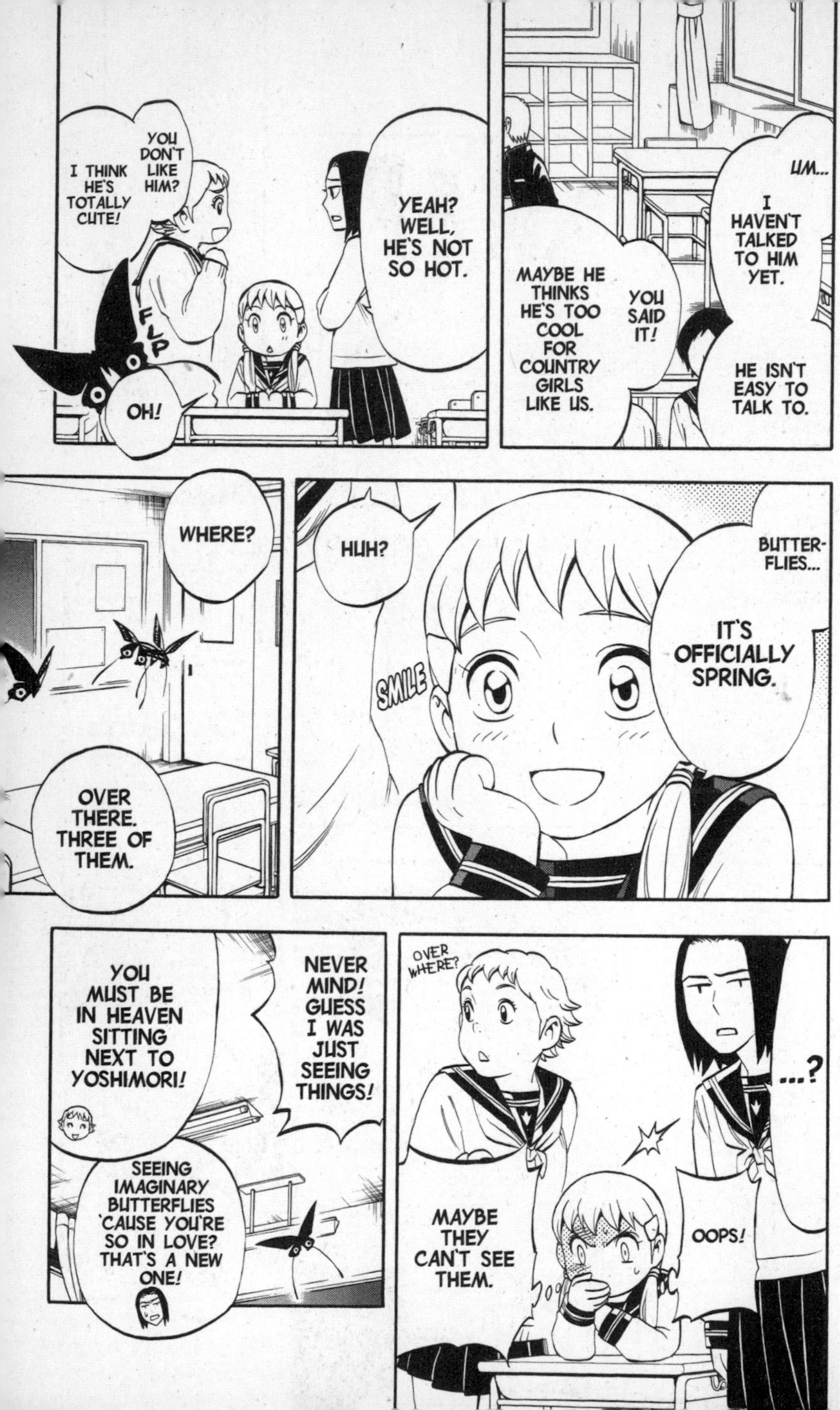
UM... I HAVEN'T TALKED TO HIM YET.
HE ISN'T EASY TO TALK TO.
MAYBE HE THINKS HE'S TOO COOL FOR COUNTRY GIRLS LIKE US.
YOU SAID IT!
YEAH? WELL, HE'S NOT SO HOT.
YOU DON'T LIKE HIM?
I THINK HE'S TOTALLY CUTE!
FLP
OH!
BUTTER-FLIES...
IT'S OFFICIALLY SPRING.
SMILE
HUH?
WHERE?
OVER THERE. THREE OF THEM.
...?
OVER WHERE?
OOPS!
MAYBE THEY CAN'T SEE THEM.
NEVER MIND! GUESS I WAS JUST SEEING THINGS!
YOU MUST BE IN HEAVEN SITTING NEXT TO YOSHIMORI!
SEEING IMAGINARY BUTTERFLIES 'CAUSE YOU'RE SO IN LOVE? THAT'S A NEW ONE!

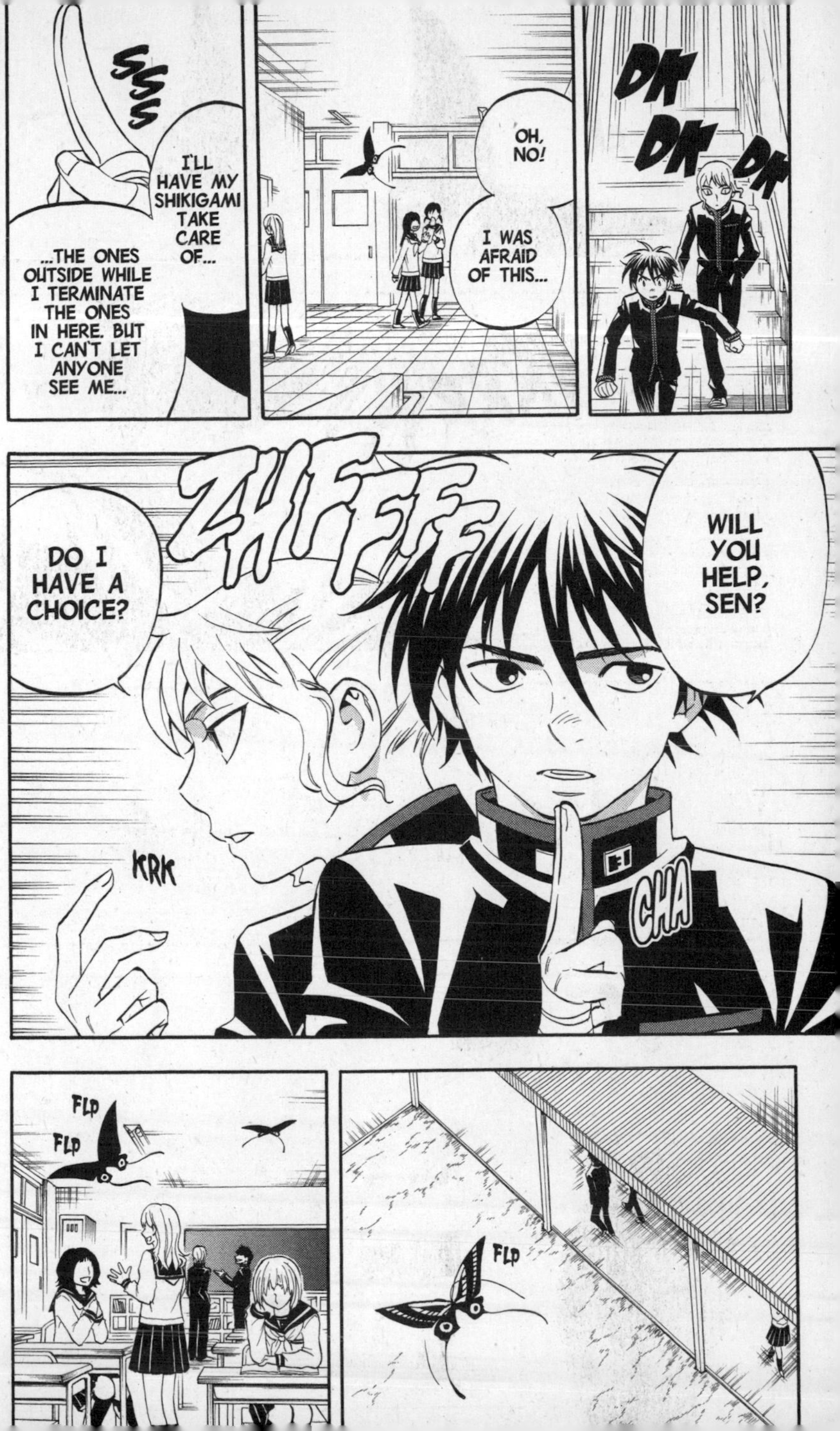
DK
DK
DK
OH, NO!
I WAS AFRAID OF THIS...
SSS
I'LL HAVE MY SHIKIGAMI TAKE CARE OF...
...THE ONES OUTSIDE WHILE I TERMINATE THE ONES IN HERE. BUT I CAN'T LET ANYONE SEE ME...
WILL YOU HELP, SEN?
ZHFFF
CHA
DO I HAVE A CHOICE?
KRK
FLP
FLP
FLP

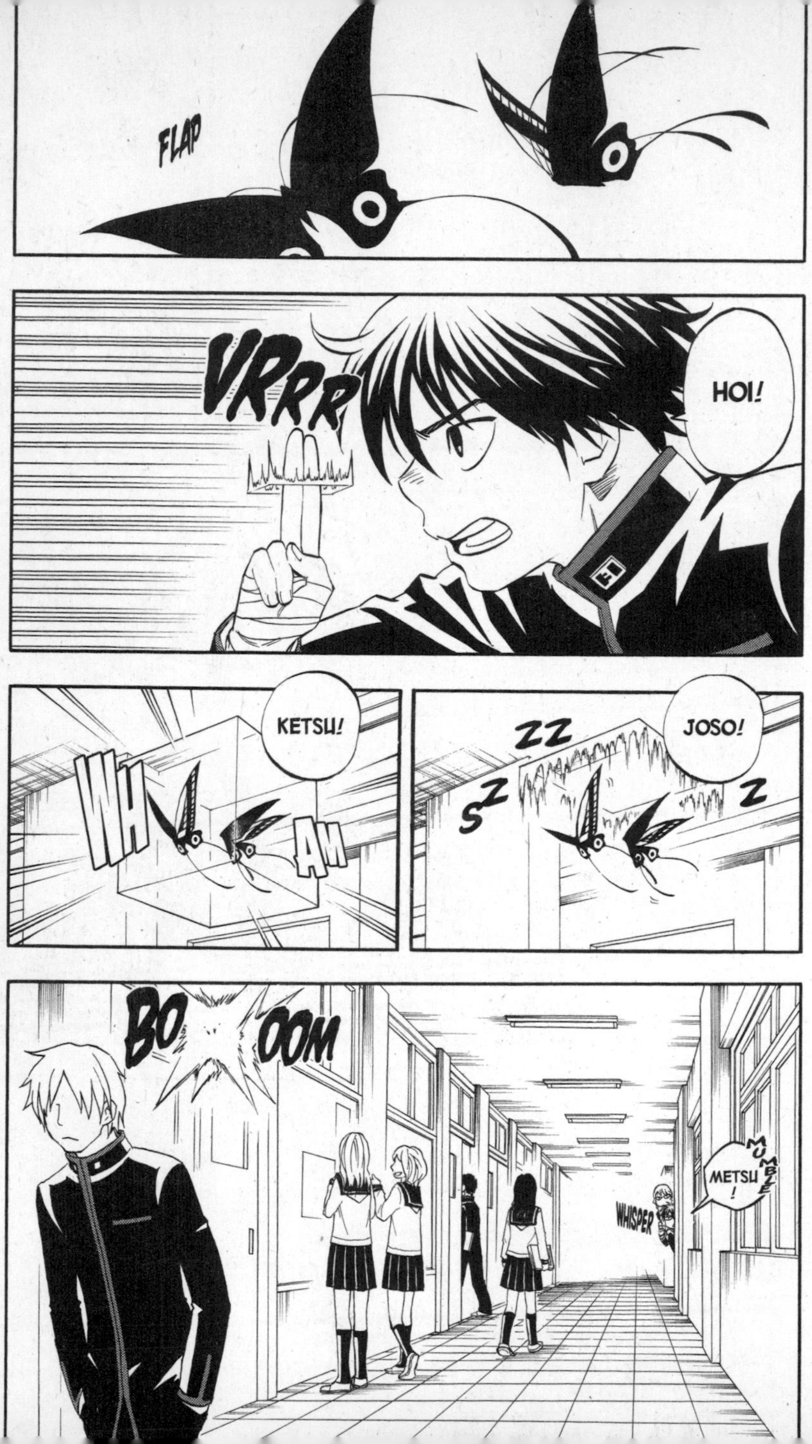
FLAP
HOI!
VRRR
JOSO!
ZZ
SZ
Z
KETSU!
WH
AM
METSU!
MUMBLE!
WHISPER
BO
OOM

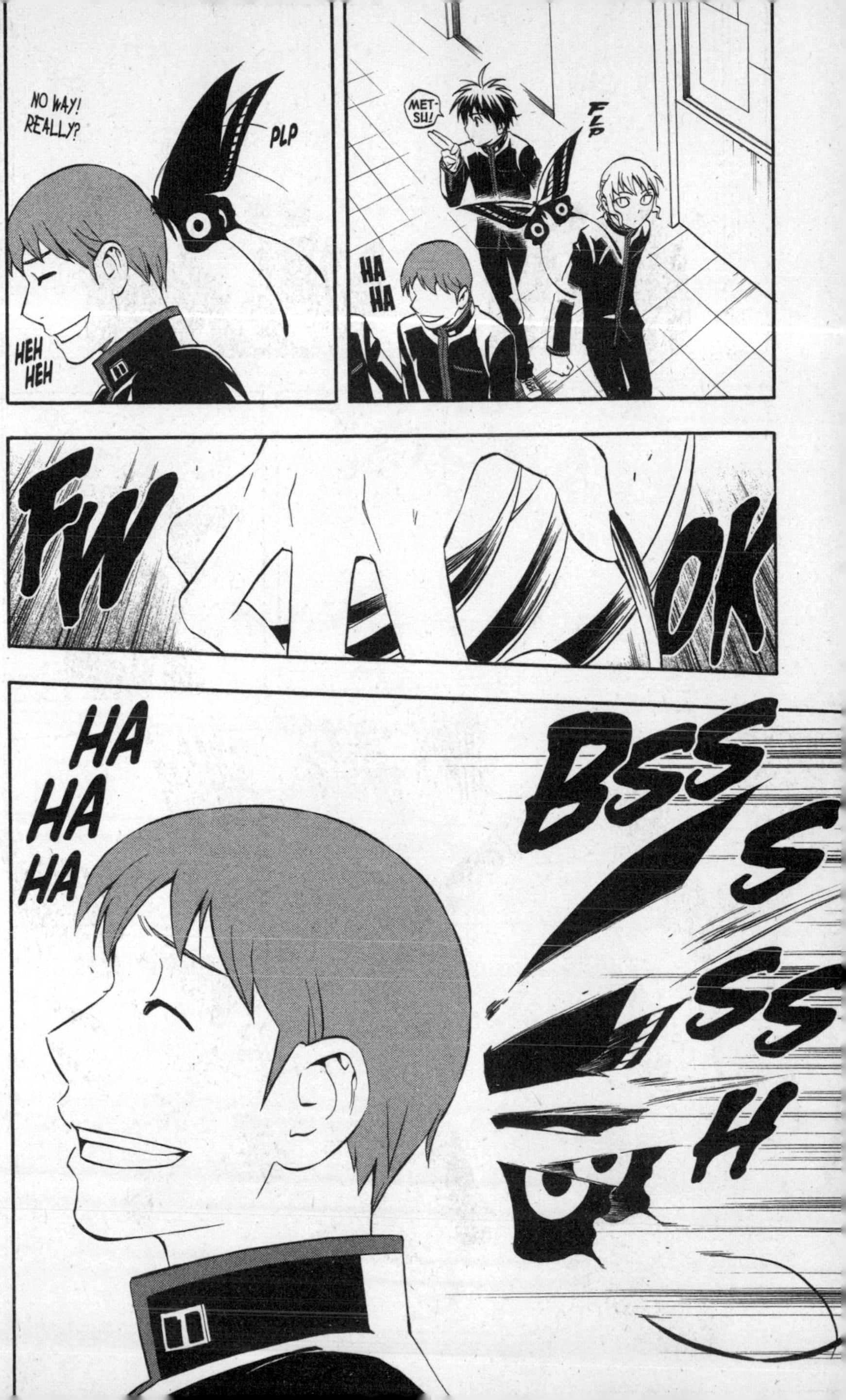

MET-SU!
FLP
HA HA
NO WAY! REALLY?
PLP
HEH HEH
FWOK
HA HA HA
BSSSSSH

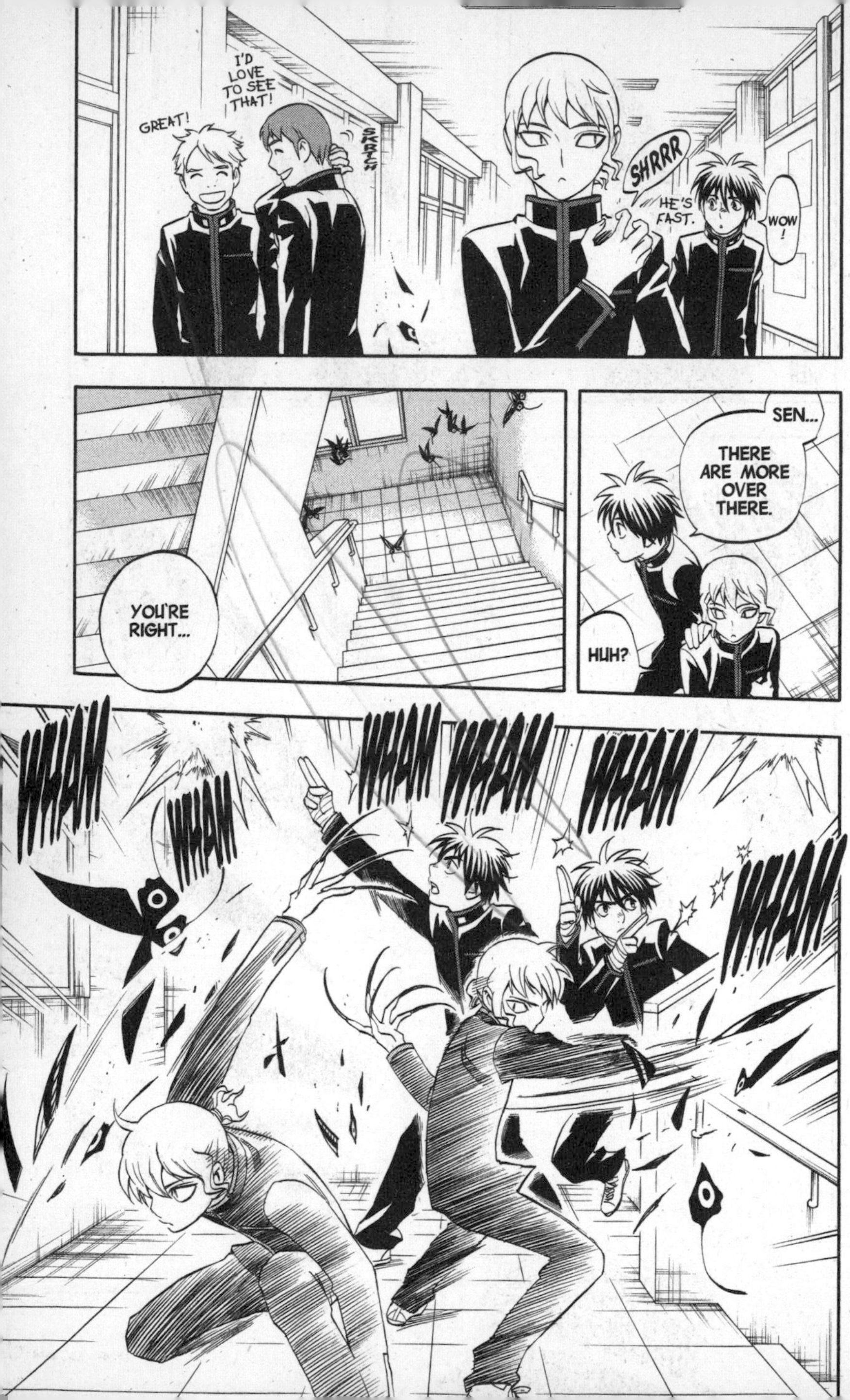
WOW!
SHRRR
HE'S FAST.
SKRTCH
I'D LOVE TO SEE THAT!
GREAT!
SEN...
THERE ARE MORE OVER THERE.
HUH?
YOU'RE RIGHT...
WHAM
WHAM
WHAM
WHAM
WHAM
WHAM
WHAM

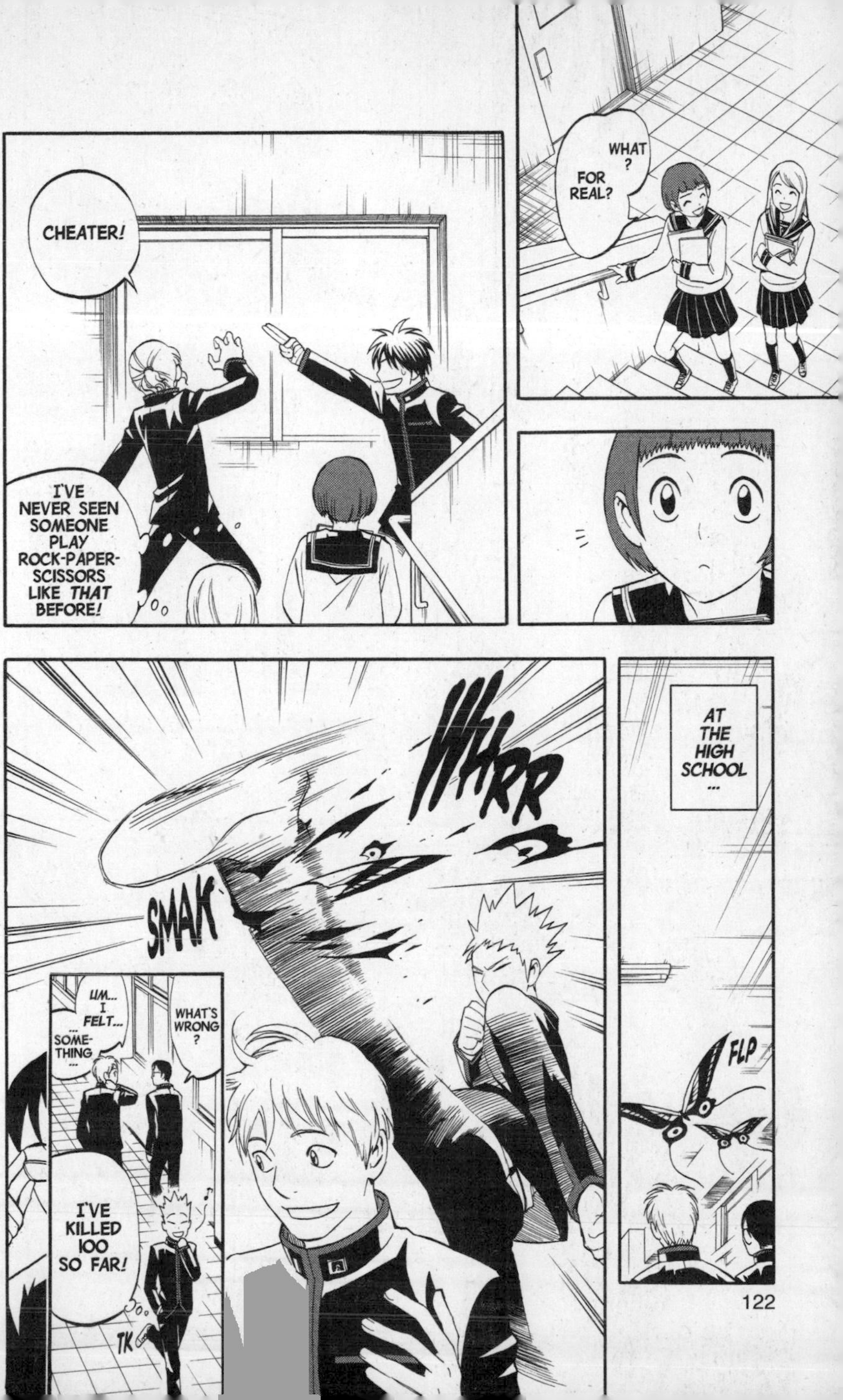
WHAT? FOR REAL?
CHEATER!
I'VE NEVER SEEN SOMEONE PLAY ROCK-PAPER-SCISSORS LIKE *THAT* BEFORE!
AT THE HIGH SCHOOL...
FLP
WHRR
SMAK
WHAT'S WRONG?
UM... I FELT... ...SOMETHING...
I'VE KILLED 100 SO FAR!
TK

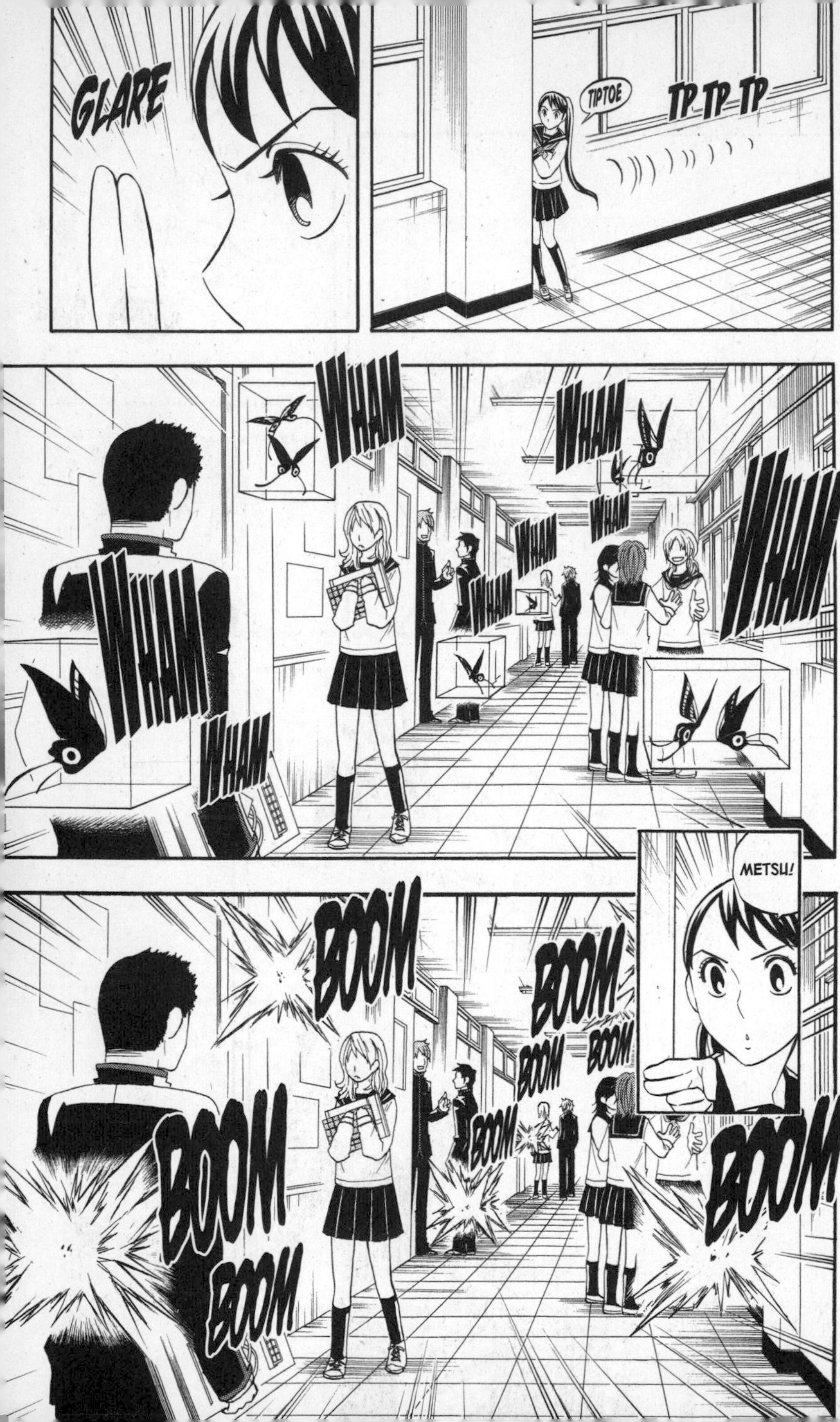
TIPTOE
TP TP TP
GLARE
WHAM
WHAM
WHAM
WHAM
WHAM
WHAM
WHAM
WHAM
METSU!
BOOM
BOOM
BOOM
BOOM
BOOM
BOOM
BOOM
BOOM

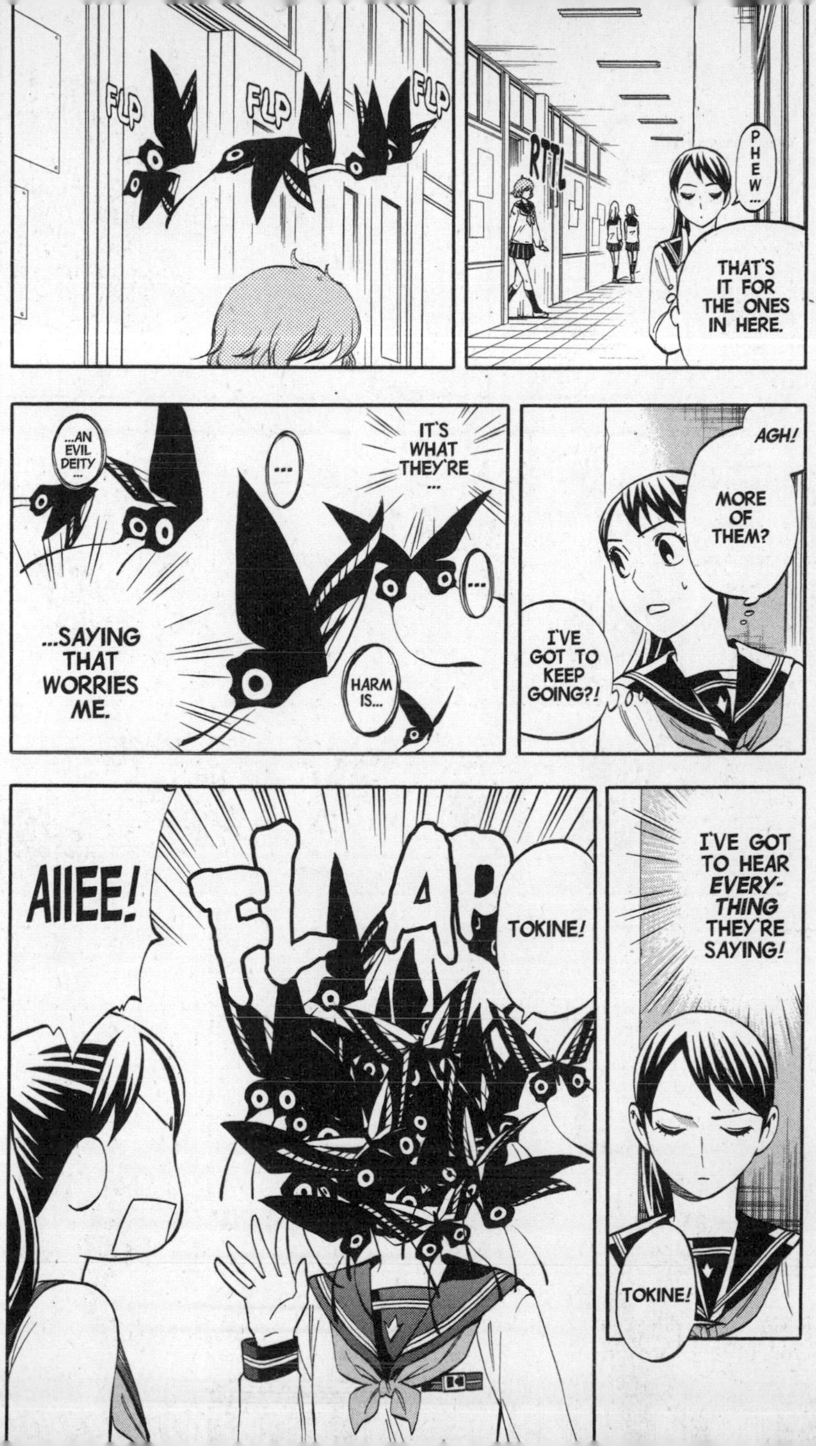
PHEW...
THAT'S IT FOR THE ONES IN HERE.
RTTL
FLP
FLP
FLP
AGH!
MORE OF THEM?
I'VE GOT TO KEEP GOING?!
IT'S WHAT THEY'RE...
...
...AN EVIL DEITY...
...
HARM IS...
...SAYING THAT WORRIES ME.
I'VE GOT TO HEAR EVERYTHING THEY'RE SAYING!
TOKINE!
TOKINE!
FLAP
AIIEE!

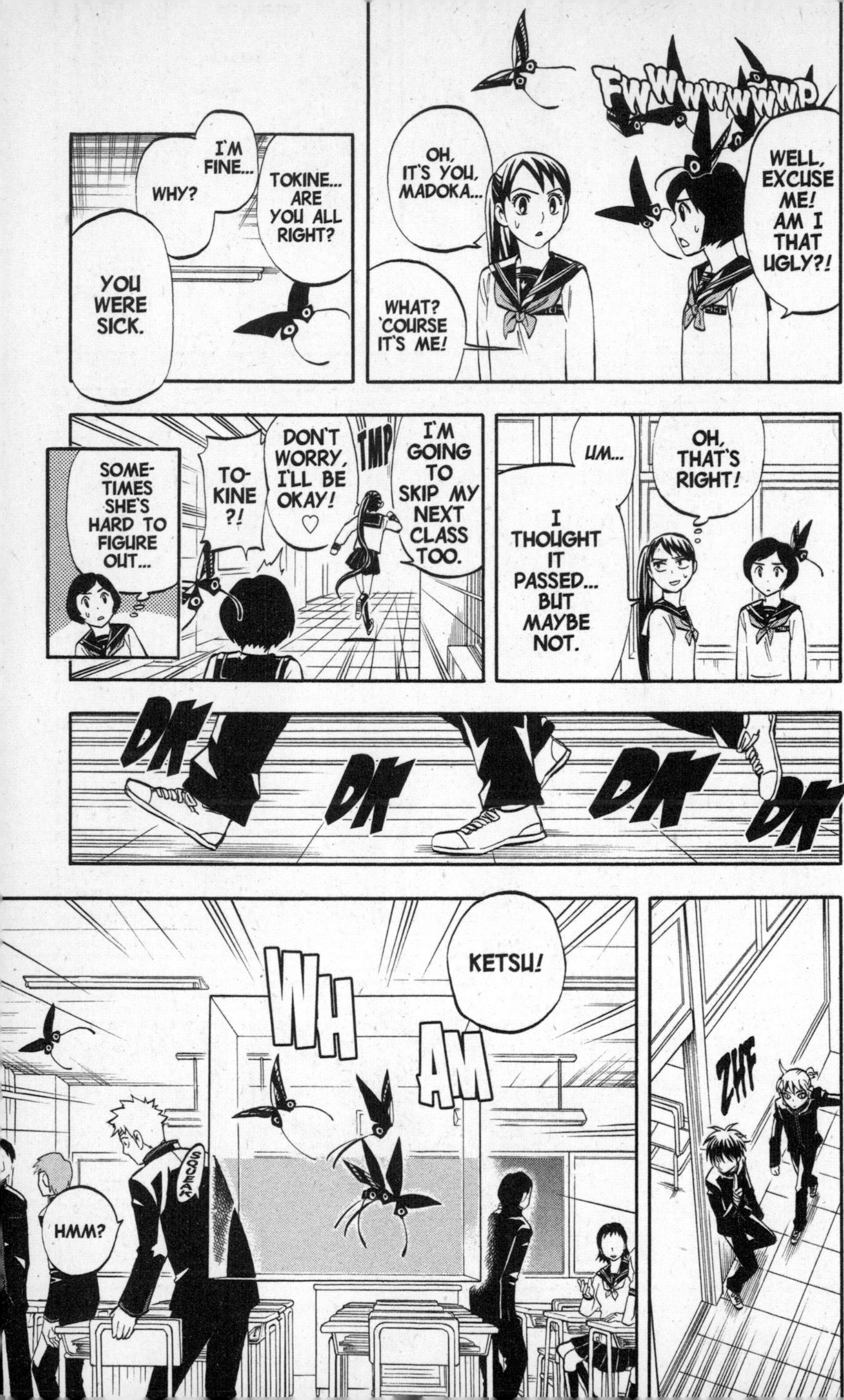
FWWWWWWWP
WELL, EXCUSE ME! AM I THAT UGLY?!
OH, IT'S YOU, MADOKA...
WHAT? 'COURSE IT'S ME!
TOKINE... ARE YOU ALL RIGHT?
I'M FINE... WHY?
YOU WERE SICK.
OH, THAT'S RIGHT!
UM...
I THOUGHT IT PASSED... BUT MAYBE NOT.
I'M GOING TO SKIP MY NEXT CLASS TOO.
TMP
DON'T WORRY, I'LL BE OKAY! ♡
TO-KINE?!
SOME-TIMES SHE'S HARD TO FIGURE OUT...
DK
DK
DK
DK
ZHF
KETSU!
WH
AM
SQUEAK
HMM?

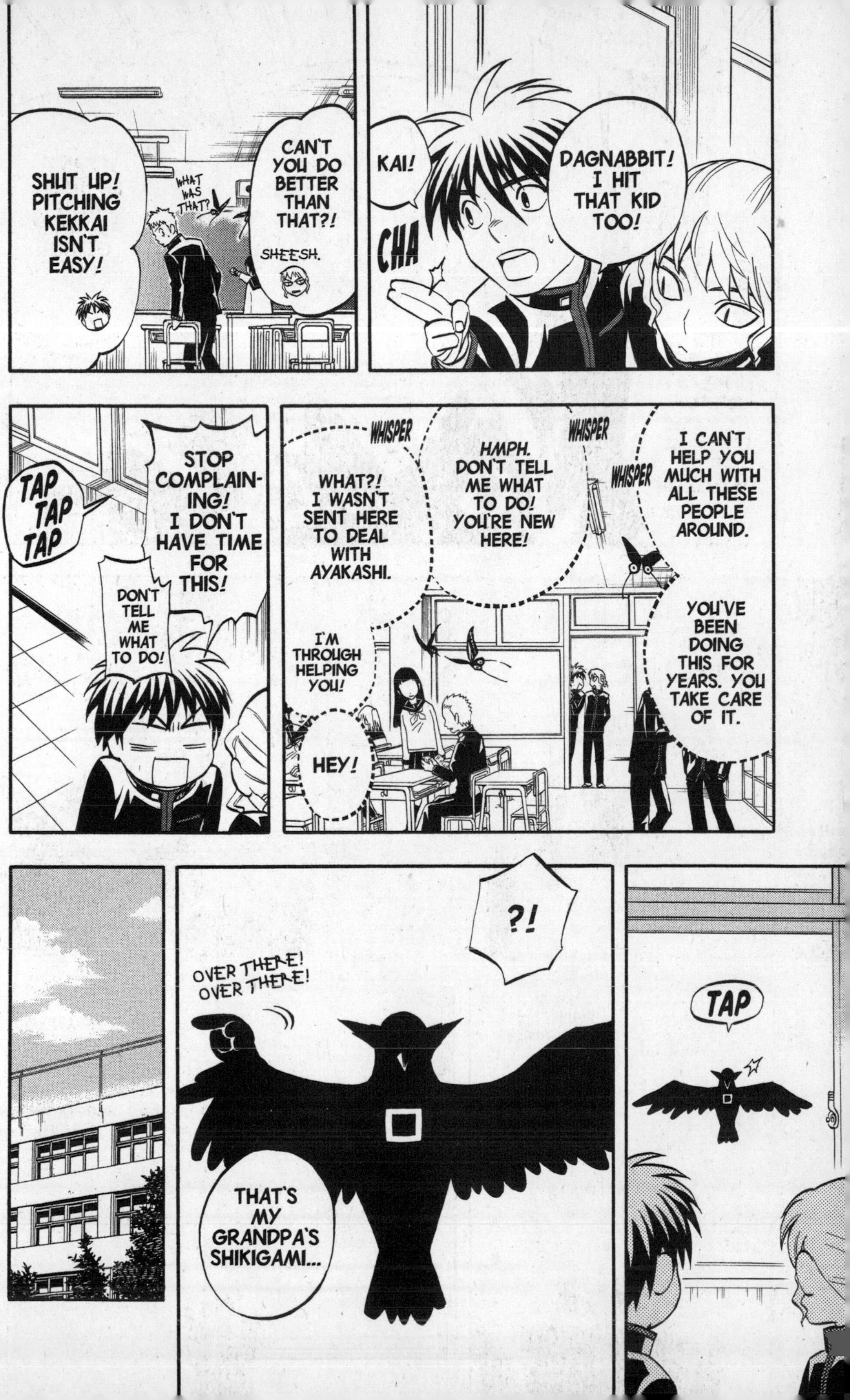
DAGNABBIT! I HIT THAT KID TOO!
KAI!
CHA
CAN'T YOU DO BETTER THAN THAT?!
SHEESH.
WHAT WAS THAT?
SHUT UP! PITCHING KEKKAI ISN'T EASY!
WHISPER
I CAN'T HELP YOU MUCH WITH ALL THESE PEOPLE AROUND.
WHISPER
HMPH. DON'T TELL ME WHAT TO DO! YOU'RE NEW HERE!
WHISPER
WHAT?! I WASN'T SENT HERE TO DEAL WITH AYAKASHI.
YOU'VE BEEN DOING THIS FOR YEARS. YOU TAKE CARE OF IT.
I'M THROUGH HELPING YOU!
HEY!
STOP COMPLAINING! I DON'T HAVE TIME FOR THIS!
DON'T TELL ME WHAT TO DO!
TAP TAP TAP
TAP
?!
OVER THERE! OVER THERE!
THAT'S MY GRANDPA'S SHIKIGAMI...

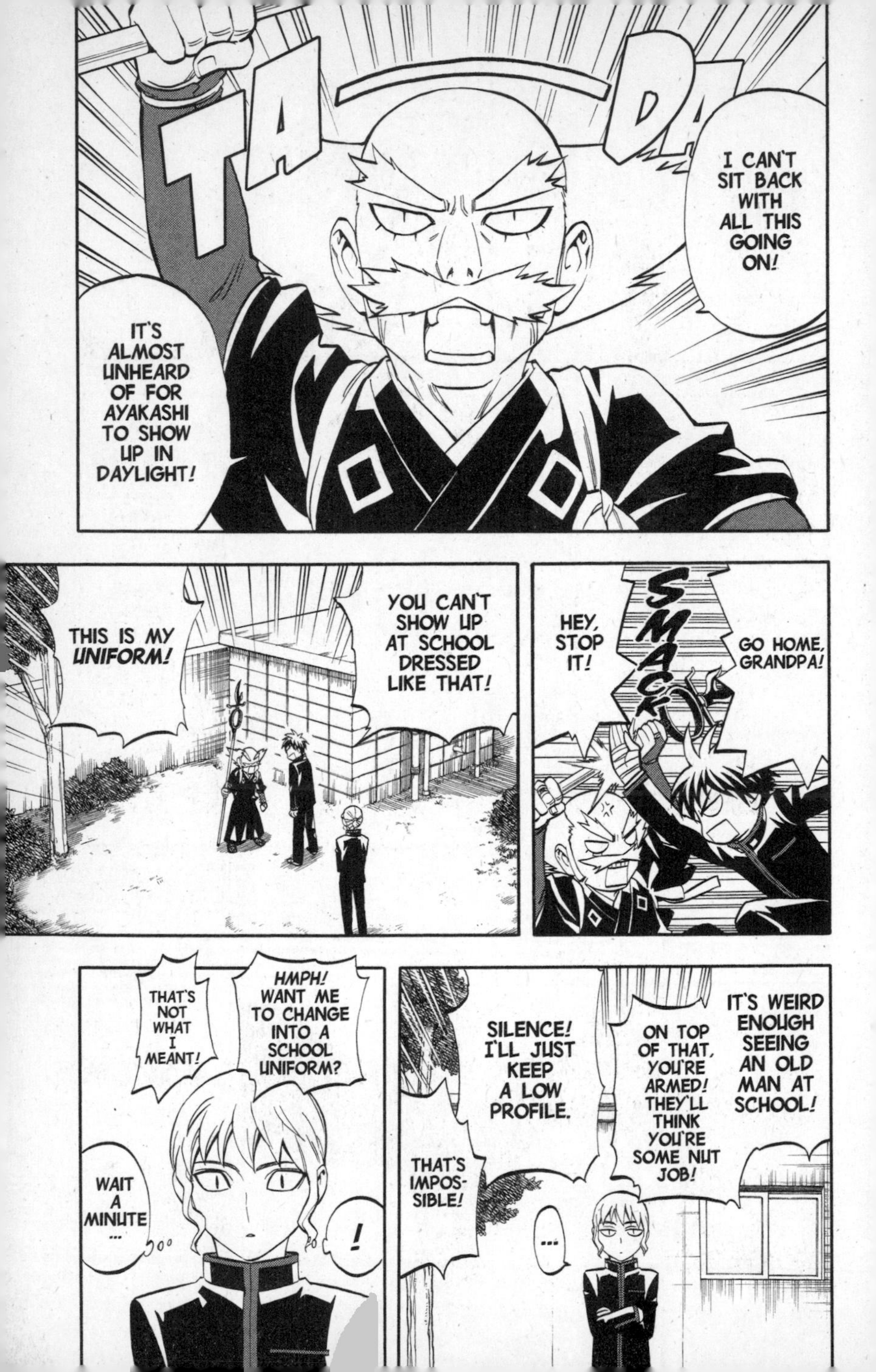
TA—DA
I CAN'T SIT BACK WITH ALL THIS GOING ON!
IT'S ALMOST UNHEARD OF FOR AYAKASHI TO SHOW UP IN DAYLIGHT!
GO HOME, GRANDPA!
SMACK
HEY, STOP IT!
YOU CAN'T SHOW UP AT SCHOOL DRESSED LIKE THAT!
THIS IS MY *UNIFORM!*
IT'S WEIRD ENOUGH SEEING AN OLD MAN AT SCHOOL!
ON TOP OF THAT, YOU'RE ARMED! THEY'LL THINK YOU'RE SOME NUT JOB!
SILENCE! I'LL JUST KEEP A LOW PROFILE.
THAT'S IMPOSSIBLE!
...
HMPH! WANT ME TO CHANGE INTO A SCHOOL UNIFORM?
THAT'S NOT WHAT I MEANT!
!
WAIT A MINUTE...

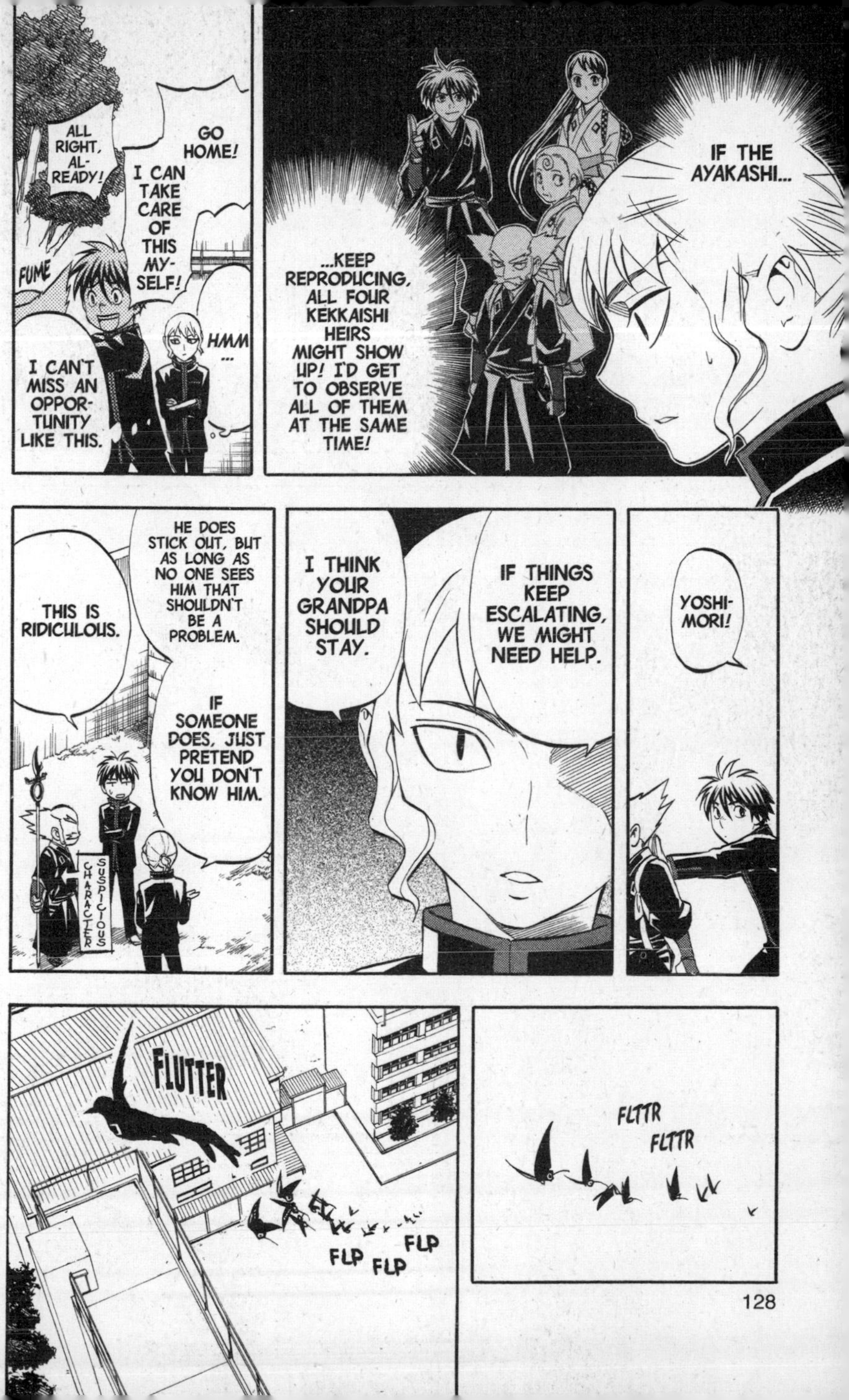
IF THE AYAKASHI...
...KEEP REPRODUCING, ALL FOUR KEKKAISHI HEIRS MIGHT SHOW UP! I'D GET TO OBSERVE ALL OF THEM AT THE SAME TIME!
GO HOME! I CAN TAKE CARE OF THIS MYSELF!
ALL RIGHT, ALREADY!
FUME
HMM...
I CAN'T MISS AN OPPORTUNITY LIKE THIS.
YOSHIMORI!
IF THINGS KEEP ESCALATING, WE MIGHT NEED HELP.
I THINK YOUR GRANDPA SHOULD STAY.
HE DOES STICK OUT, BUT AS LONG AS NO ONE SEES HIM THAT SHOULDN'T BE A PROBLEM.
THIS IS RIDICULOUS.
IF SOMEONE DOES, JUST PRETEND YOU DON'T KNOW HIM.
SUSPICIOUS CHARACTER
FLTTR
FLTTR
FLUTTER
FLP
FLP
FLP

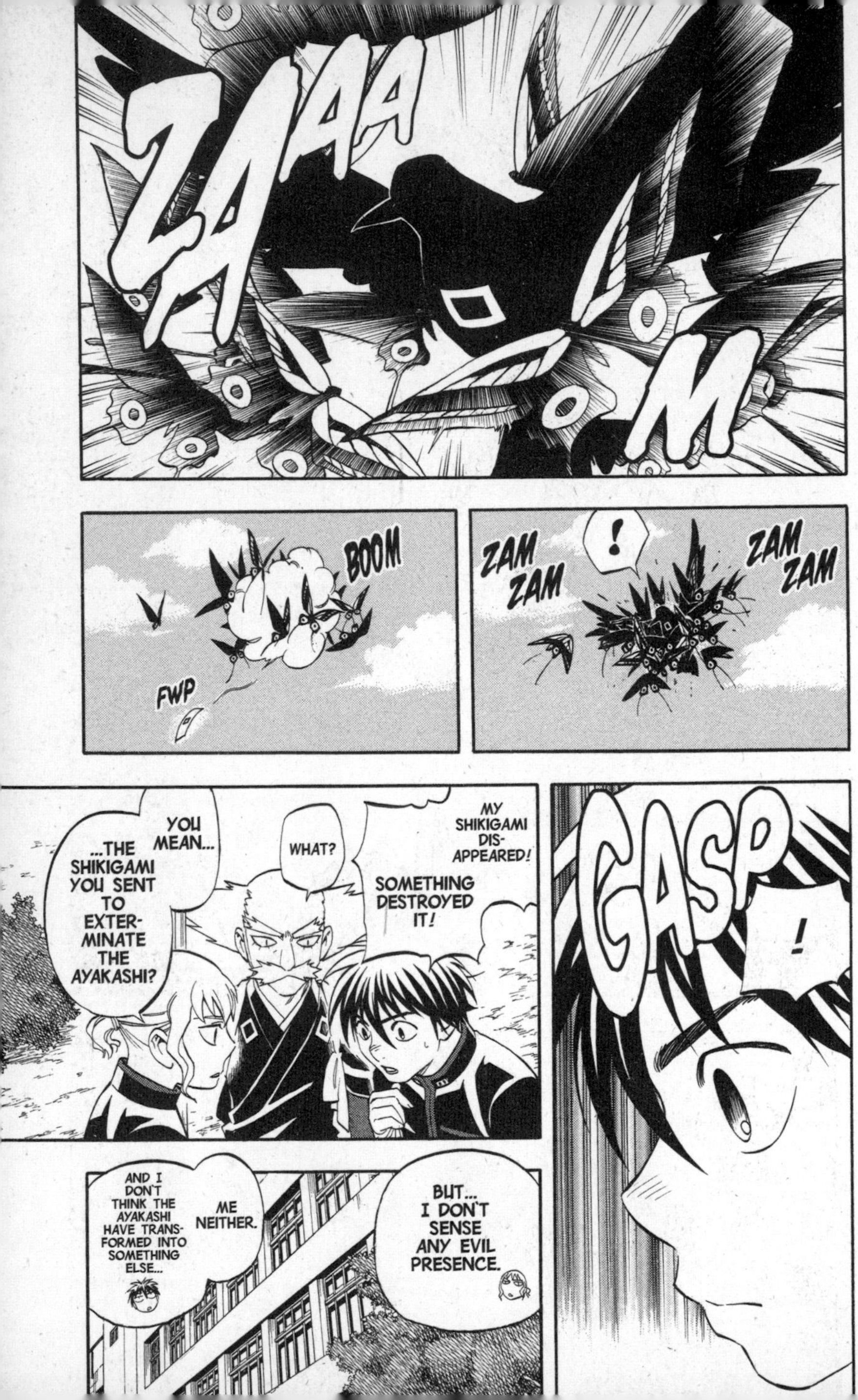
ZAAAM
ZAM ZAM
!
ZAM ZAM
BOOM
FWP
GASP
!
MY SHIKIGAMI DIS-APPEARED!
SOMETHING DESTROYED IT!
WHAT?
YOU MEAN...
...THE SHIKIGAMI YOU SENT TO EXTER-MINATE THE AYAKASHI?
BUT... I DON'T SENSE ANY EVIL PRESENCE.
ME NEITHER.
AND I DON'T THINK THE AYAKASHI HAVE TRANS-FORMED INTO SOMETHING ELSE...

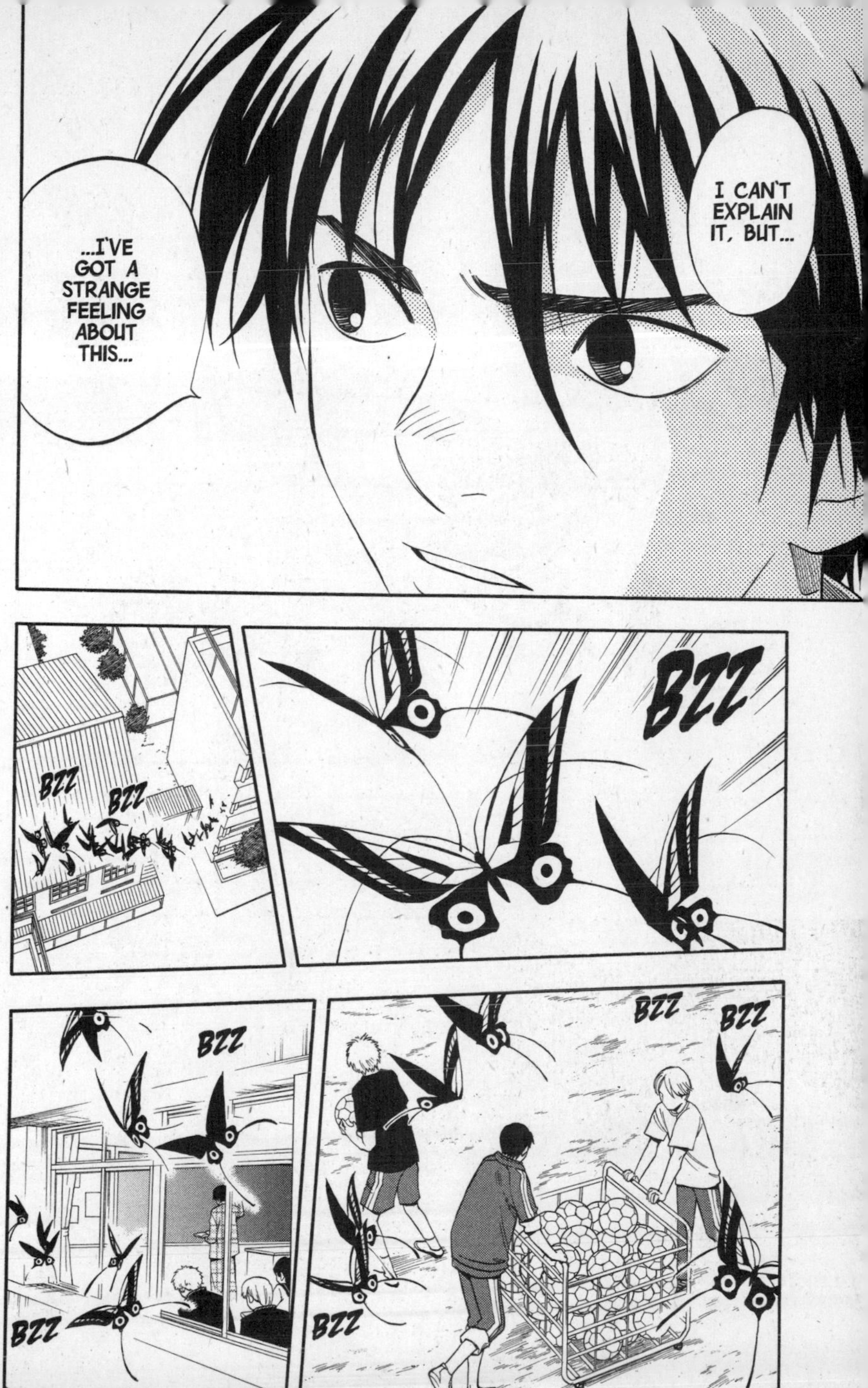
I CAN'T EXPLAIN IT, BUT...
...I'VE GOT A STRANGE FEELING ABOUT THIS...
BZZ
BZZ
BZZ
BZZ
BZZ
BZZ
BZZ
BZZ

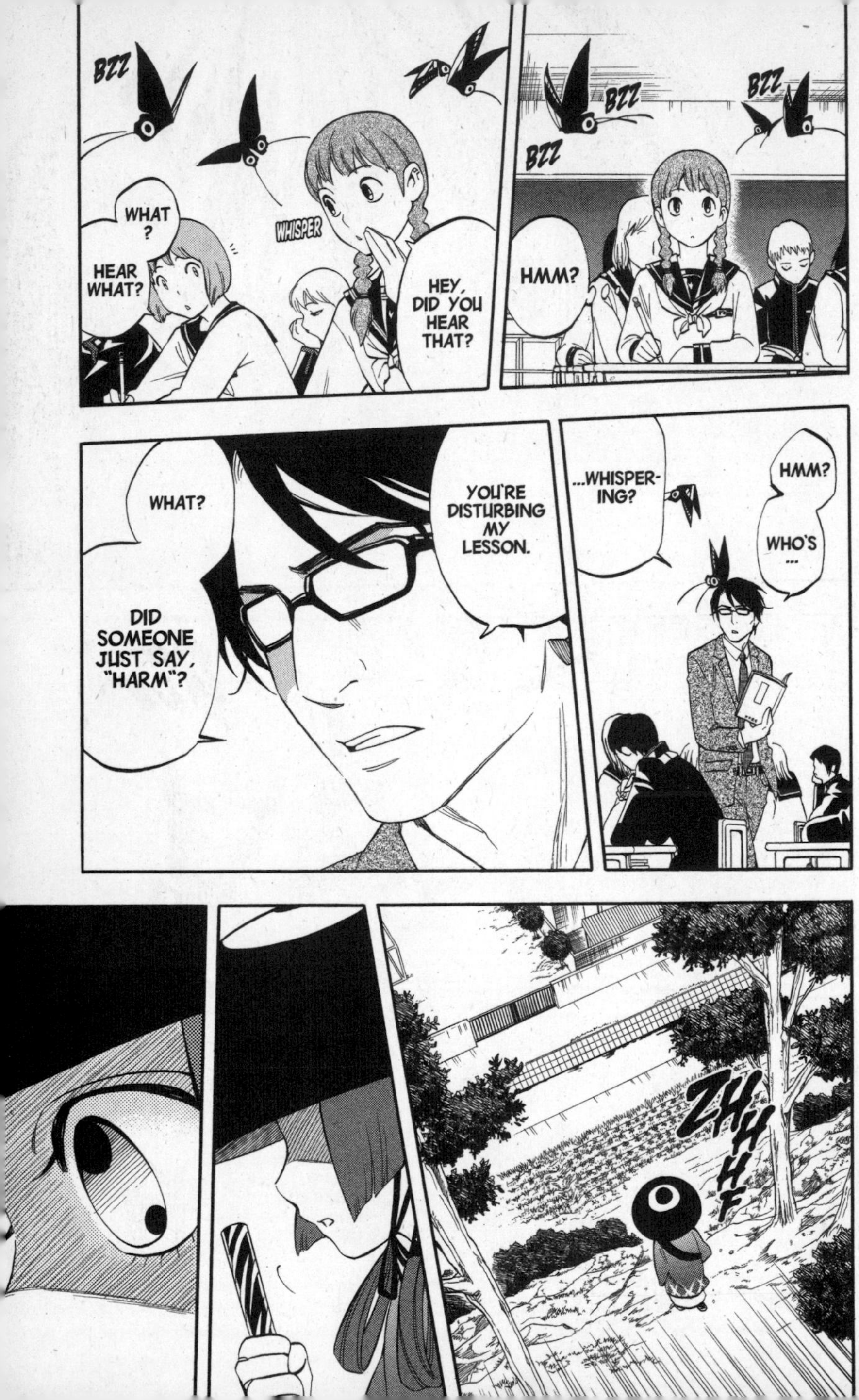
BZZ
BZZ
BZZ
HMM?
BZZ
WHISPER
HEY, DID YOU HEAR THAT?
WHAT? HEAR WHAT?
HMM? WHO'S ...
...WHISPER-ING?
YOU'RE DISTURBING MY LESSON.
WHAT? DID SOMEONE JUST SAY, "HARM"?
ZHHHHF

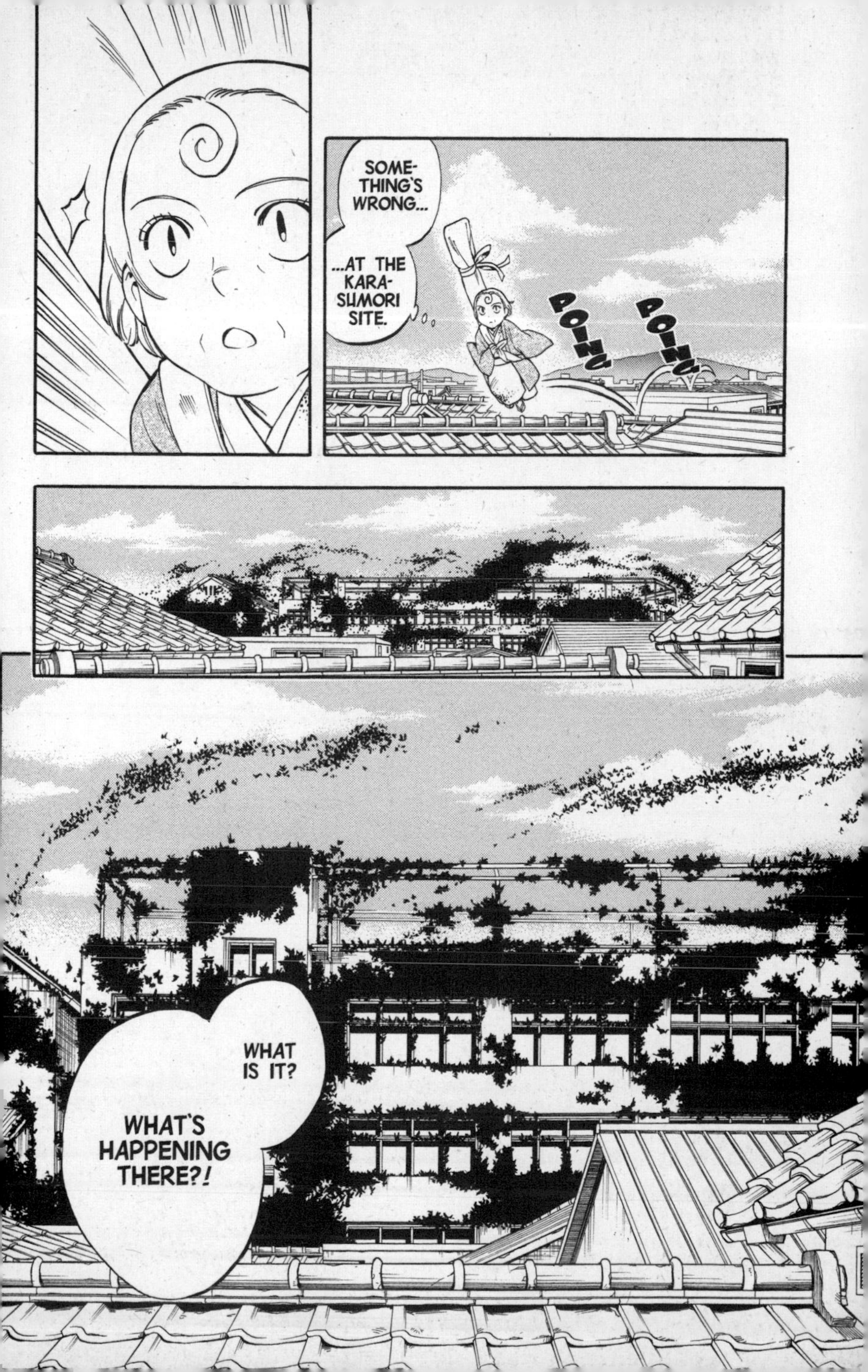
SOMETHING'S WRONG...
...AT THE KARASUMORI SITE.
POING
POING
WHAT IS IT?
WHAT'S HAPPENING THERE?!

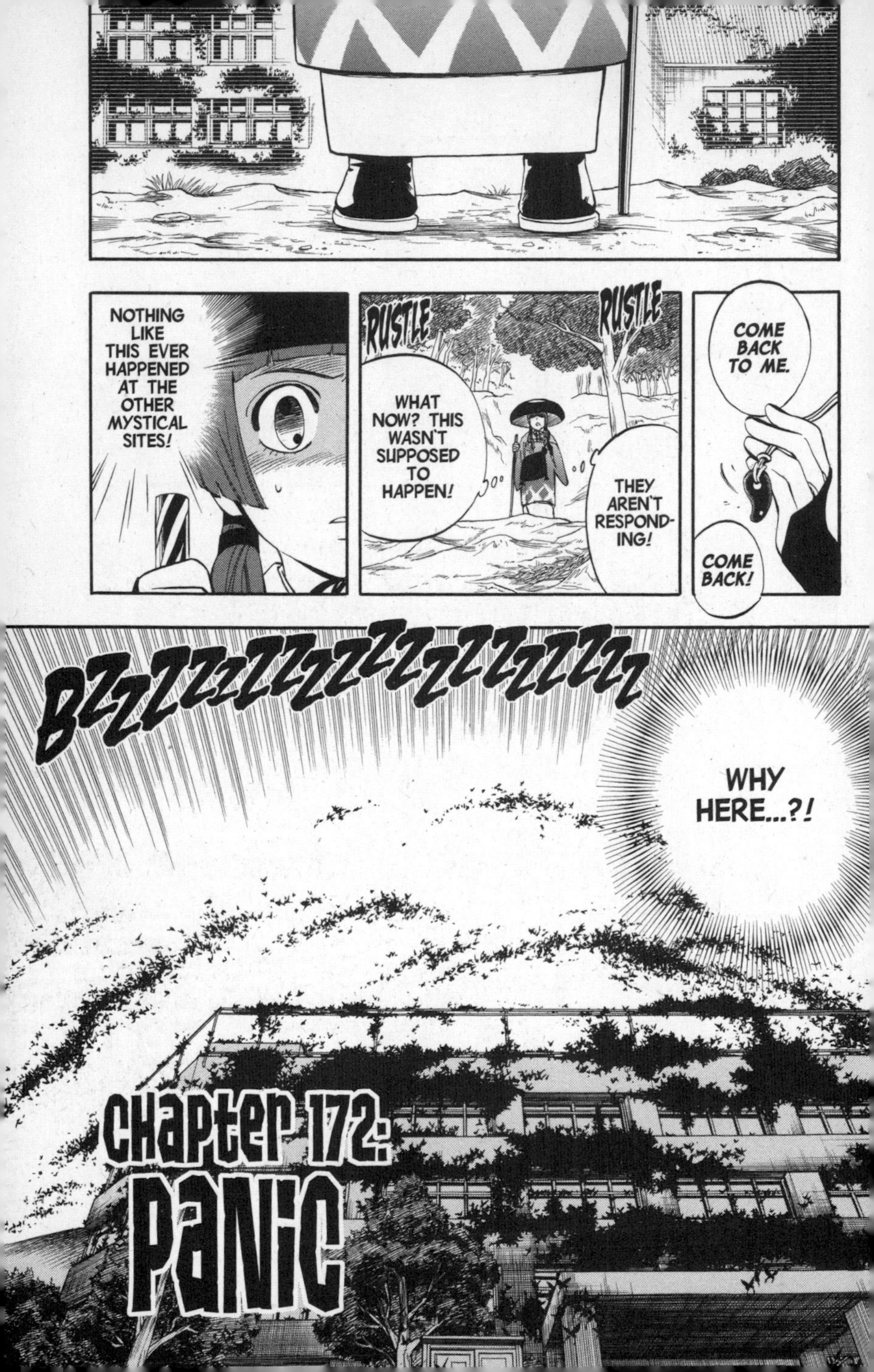
COME BACK TO ME.
COME BACK!
RUSTLE
RUSTLE
THEY AREN'T RESPOND-ING!
WHAT NOW? THIS WASN'T SUPPOSED TO HAPPEN!
NOTHING LIKE THIS EVER HAPPENED AT THE OTHER MYSTICAL SITES!
BZZZZZZZZZZZZZZZZZ
WHY HERE...?!
CHAPTER 172: PANIC

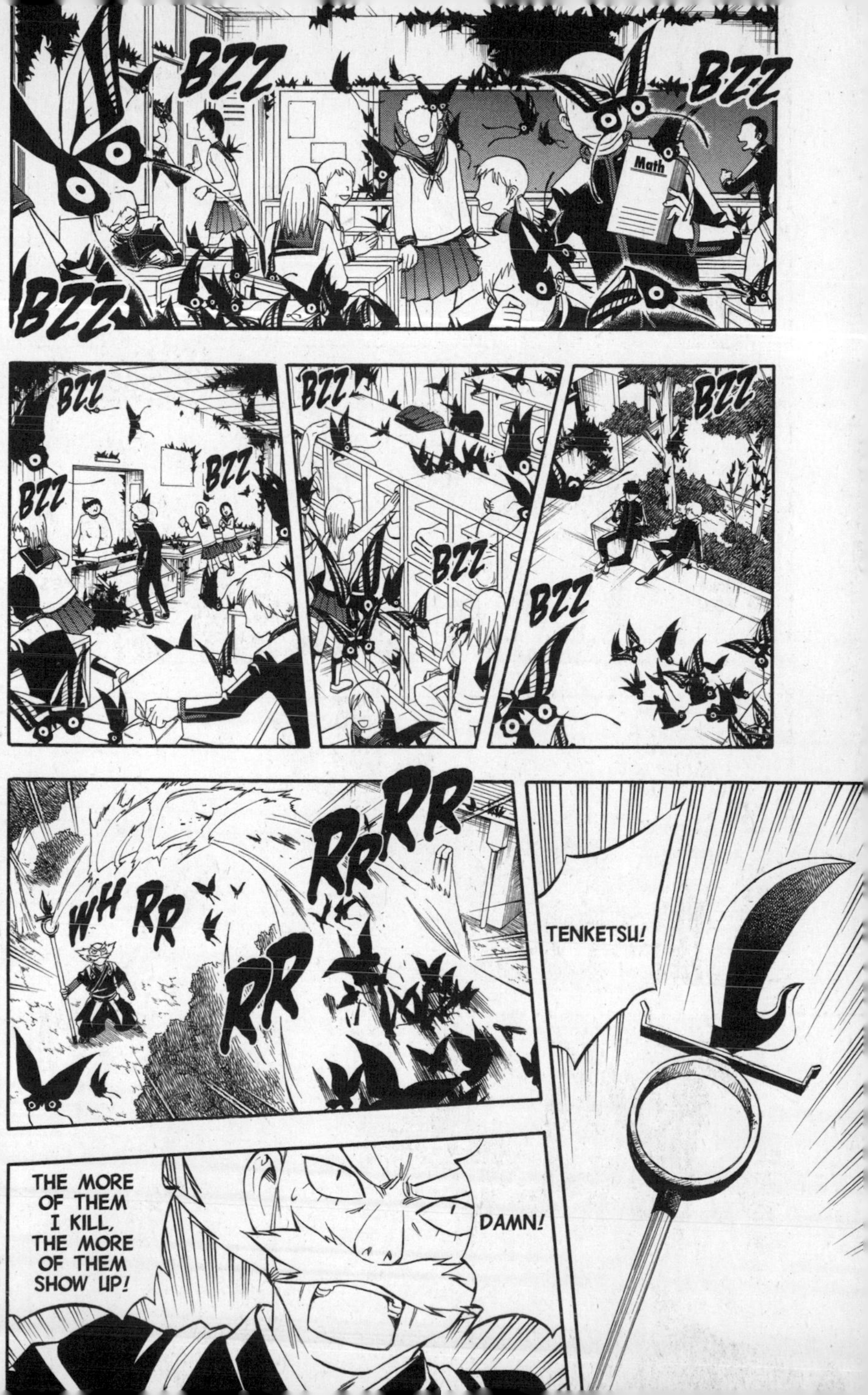
BZZ
BZZ
Math
BZZ
BZZ
BZZ
BZZ
BZZ
BZZ
BZZ
BZZ
TENKETSU!
RRRR
WHRR
RR
DAMN!
THE MORE OF THEM I KILL, THE MORE OF THEM SHOW UP!

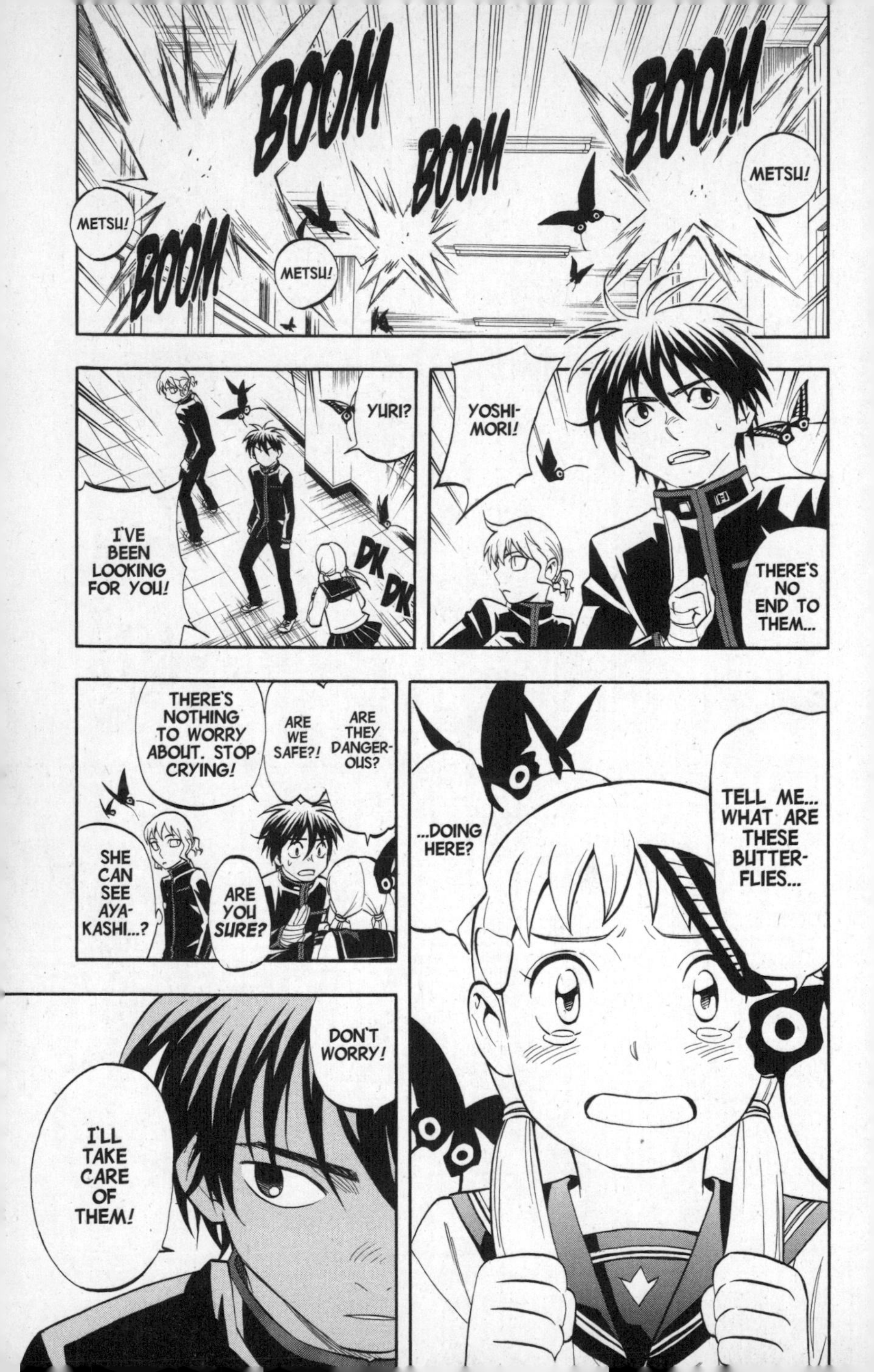
BOOM
METSU!
BOOM
METSU!
BOOM
METSU!
BOOM
YOSHI-MORI!
THERE'S NO END TO THEM...
YURI?
I'VE BEEN LOOKING FOR YOU!
DK DK
TELL ME... WHAT ARE THESE BUTTER-FLIES...
...DOING HERE?
ARE THEY DANGER-OUS?
ARE WE SAFE?!
THERE'S NOTHING TO WORRY ABOUT. STOP CRYING!
ARE YOU SURE?
SHE CAN SEE AYA-KASHI...?
DON'T WORRY!
I'LL TAKE CARE OF THEM!

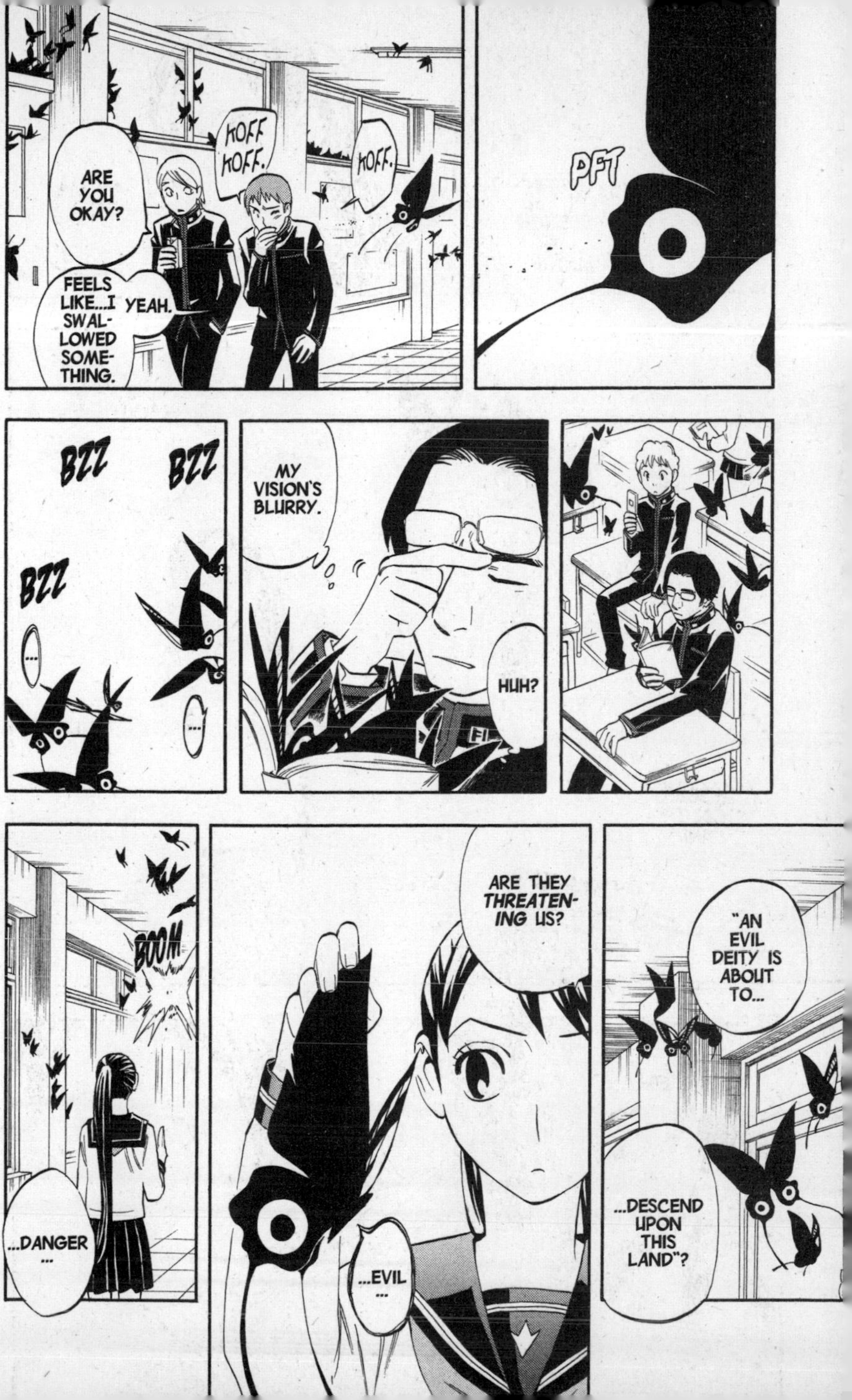
PFT
KOFF.
KOFF KOFF.
ARE YOU OKAY?
YEAH.
FEELS LIKE...I SWALLOWED SOMETHING.
MY VISION'S BLURRY.
HUH?
BZZ
BZZ
BZZ
...
...
"AN EVIL DEITY IS ABOUT TO...
...DESCEND UPON THIS LAND"?
ARE THEY THREATENING US?
...EVIL ...
BOOM
...DANGER ...

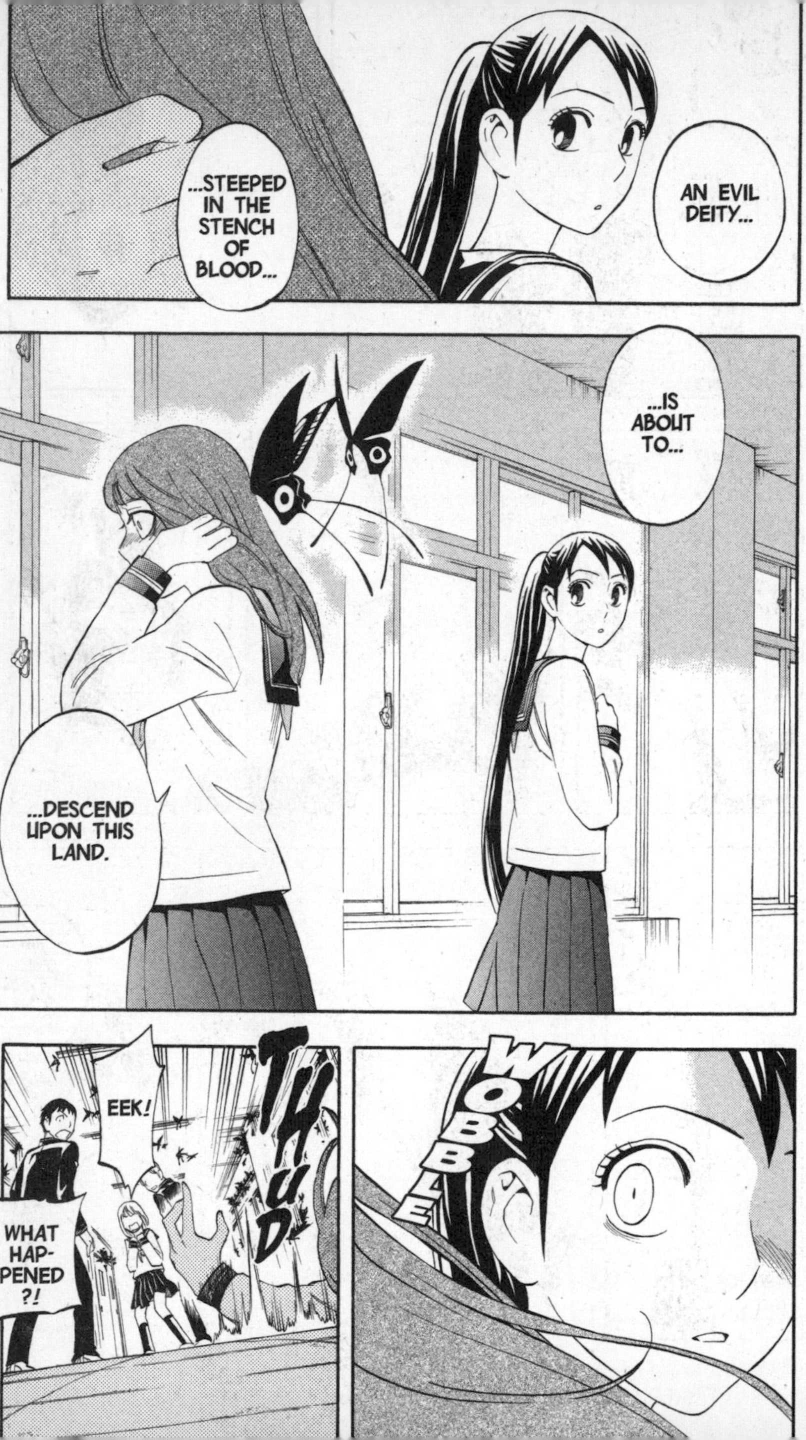
AN EVIL DEITY...
...STEEPED IN THE STENCH OF BLOOD...
...IS ABOUT TO...
...DESCEND UPON THIS LAND.
WOBBLE
THUD
EEK!
WHAT HAP-PENED?!

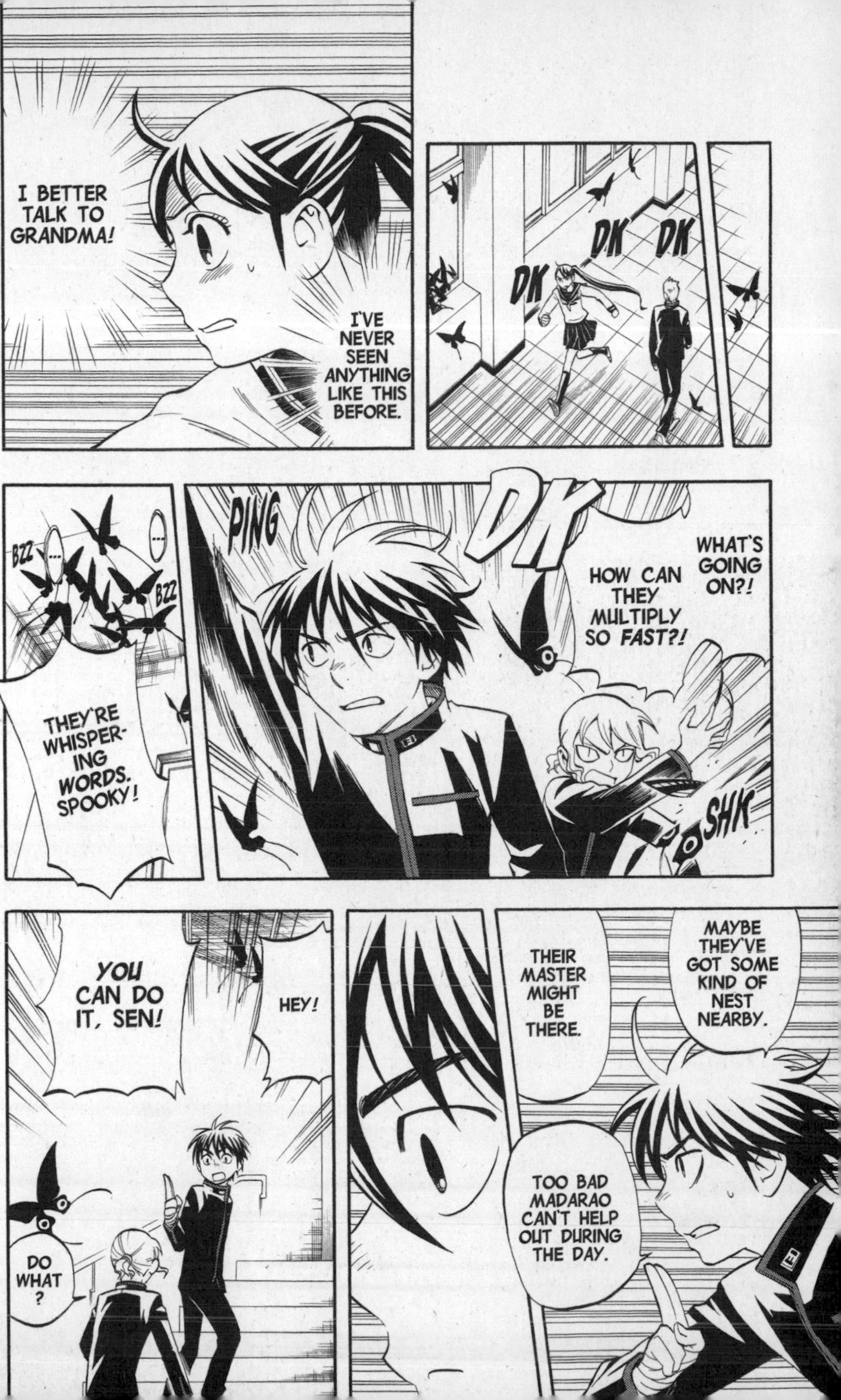
DK
DK
DK
I'VE NEVER SEEN ANYTHING LIKE THIS BEFORE.
I BETTER TALK TO GRANDMA!
DK
WHAT'S GOING ON?!
HOW CAN THEY MULTIPLY SO FAST?!
PING
SHK
...
...
BZZ
BZZ
THEY'RE WHISPER-ING WORDS. SPOOKY!
MAYBE THEY'VE GOT SOME KIND OF NEST NEARBY.
THEIR MASTER MIGHT BE THERE.
TOO BAD MADARAO CAN'T HELP OUT DURING THE DAY.
HEY!
YOU CAN DO IT, SEN!
DO WHAT?

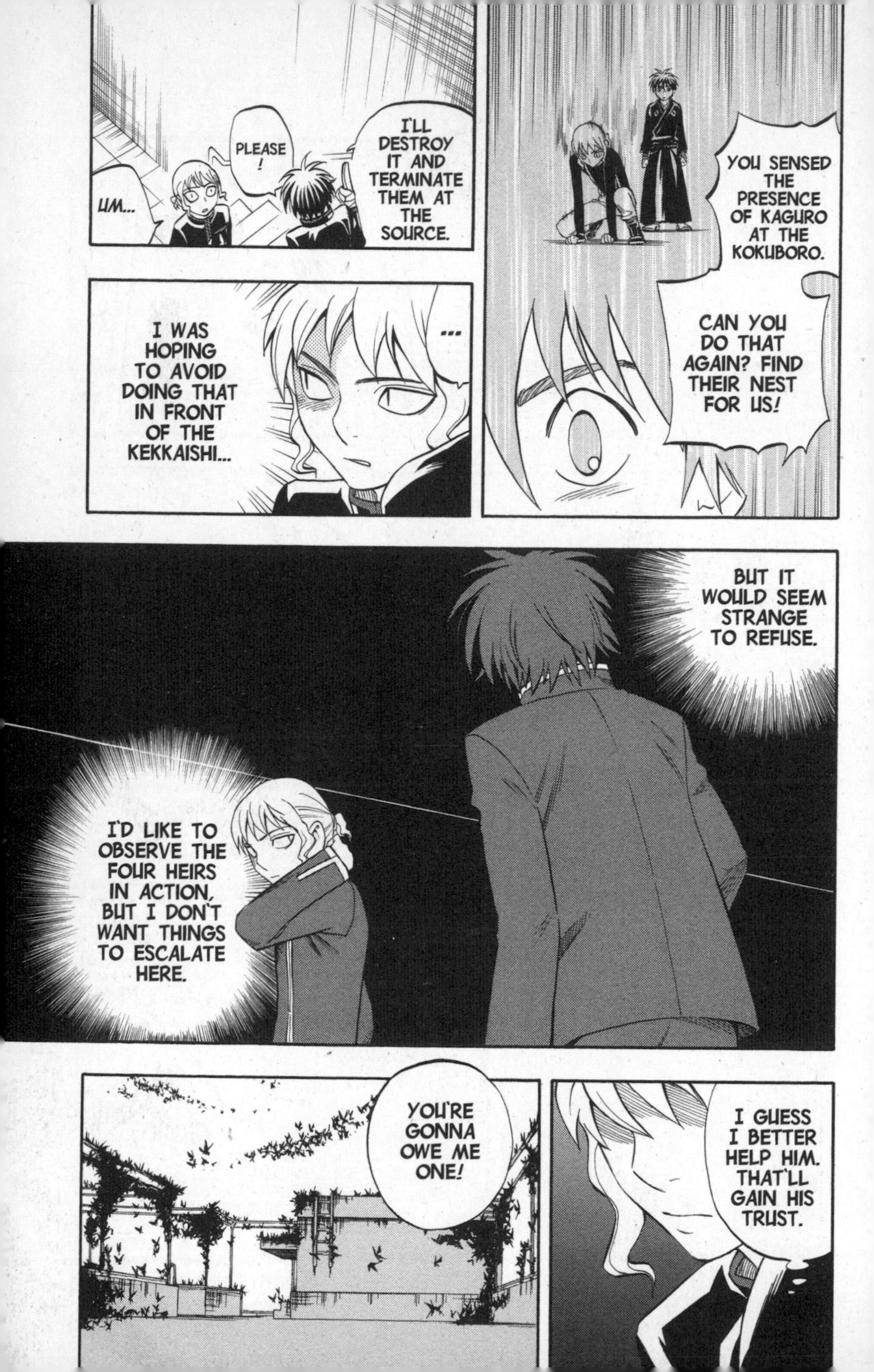
YOU SENSED THE PRESENCE OF KAGURO AT THE KOKUBORO.
CAN YOU DO THAT AGAIN? FIND THEIR NEST FOR US!
I'LL DESTROY IT AND TERMINATE THEM AT THE SOURCE.
PLEASE!
UM...
...
I WAS HOPING TO AVOID DOING THAT IN FRONT OF THE KEKKAISHI...
BUT IT WOULD SEEM STRANGE TO REFUSE.
I'D LIKE TO OBSERVE THE FOUR HEIRS IN ACTION, BUT I DON'T WANT THINGS TO ESCALATE HERE.
I GUESS I BETTER HELP HIM. THAT'LL GAIN HIS TRUST.
YOU'RE GONNA OWE ME ONE!

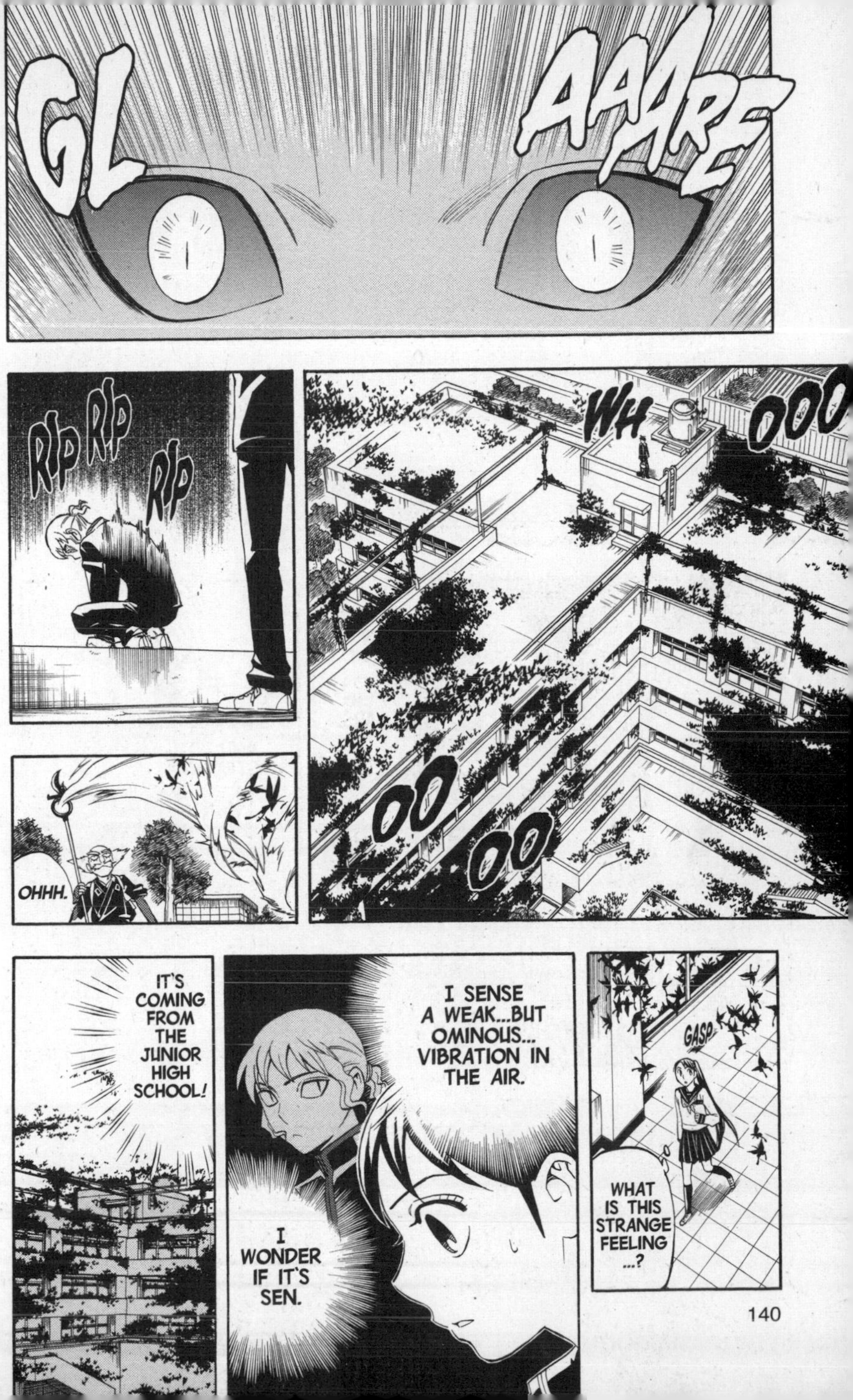
GL AAARE
WH OOO OO OO
RIP RIP RIP
OHHH.
GASP
WHAT IS THIS STRANGE FEELING ...?
I SENSE A WEAK...BUT OMINOUS... VIBRATION IN THE AIR.
I WONDER IF IT'S SEN.
IT'S COMING FROM THE JUNIOR HIGH SCHOOL!

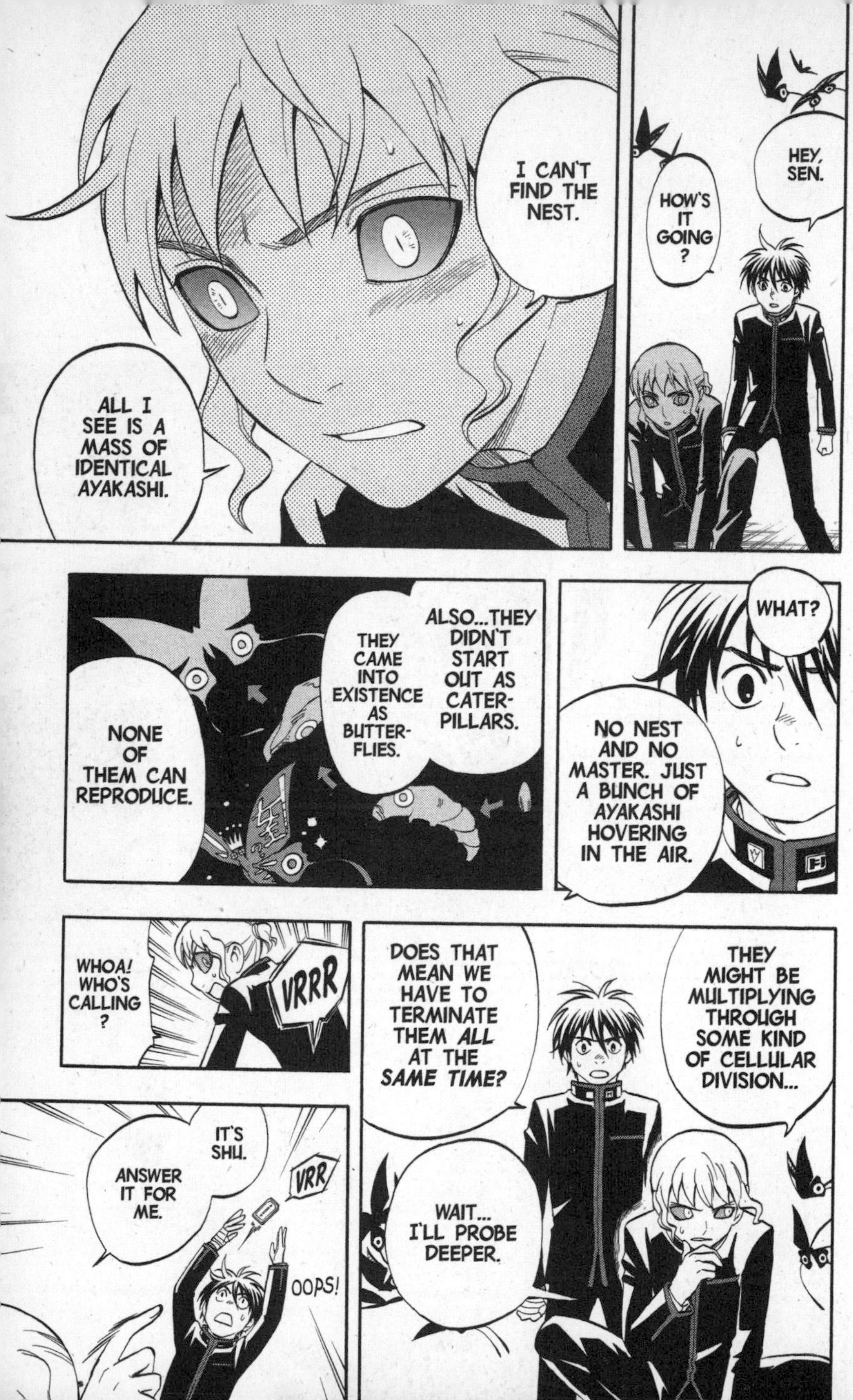
HEY, SEN.
HOW'S IT GOING?
I CAN'T FIND THE NEST.
ALL I SEE IS A MASS OF IDENTICAL AYAKASHI.
WHAT?
NO NEST AND NO MASTER. JUST A BUNCH OF AYAKASHI HOVERING IN THE AIR.
ALSO...THEY DIDN'T START OUT AS CATER-PILLARS.
THEY CAME INTO EXISTENCE AS BUTTER-FLIES.
NONE OF THEM CAN REPRODUCE.
THEY MIGHT BE MULTIPLYING THROUGH SOME KIND OF CELLULAR DIVISION...
DOES THAT MEAN WE HAVE TO TERMINATE THEM *ALL* AT THE *SAME TIME?*
WAIT... I'LL PROBE DEEPER.
WHOA! WHO'S CALLING?
VRRR
IT'S SHU.
ANSWER IT FOR ME.
VRR
OOPS!

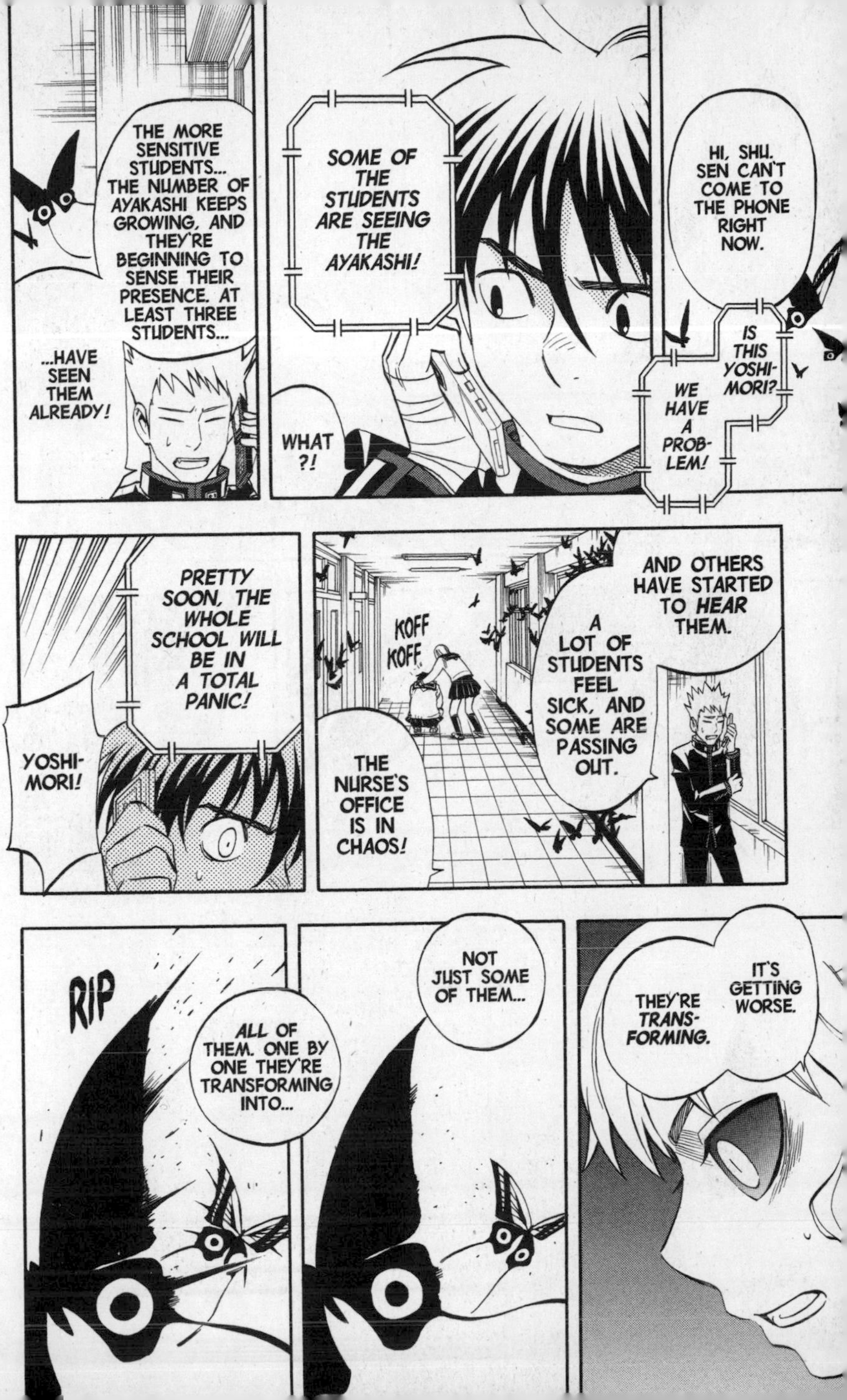
HI, SHU. SEN CAN'T COME TO THE PHONE RIGHT NOW.
IS THIS YOSHIMORI?
WE HAVE A PROBLEM!
SOME OF THE STUDENTS ARE SEEING THE AYAKASHI!
WHAT?!
THE MORE SENSITIVE STUDENTS... THE NUMBER OF AYAKASHI KEEPS GROWING, AND THEY'RE BEGINNING TO SENSE THEIR PRESENCE. AT LEAST THREE STUDENTS...
...HAVE SEEN THEM ALREADY!
AND OTHERS HAVE STARTED TO HEAR THEM.
A LOT OF STUDENTS FEEL SICK, AND SOME ARE PASSING OUT.
KOFF KOFF
THE NURSE'S OFFICE IS IN CHAOS!
PRETTY SOON, THE WHOLE SCHOOL WILL BE IN A TOTAL PANIC!
YOSHIMORI!
IT'S GETTING WORSE.
THEY'RE TRANSFORMING.
NOT JUST SOME OF THEM...
ALL OF THEM. ONE BY ONE THEY'RE TRANSFORMING INTO...
RIP

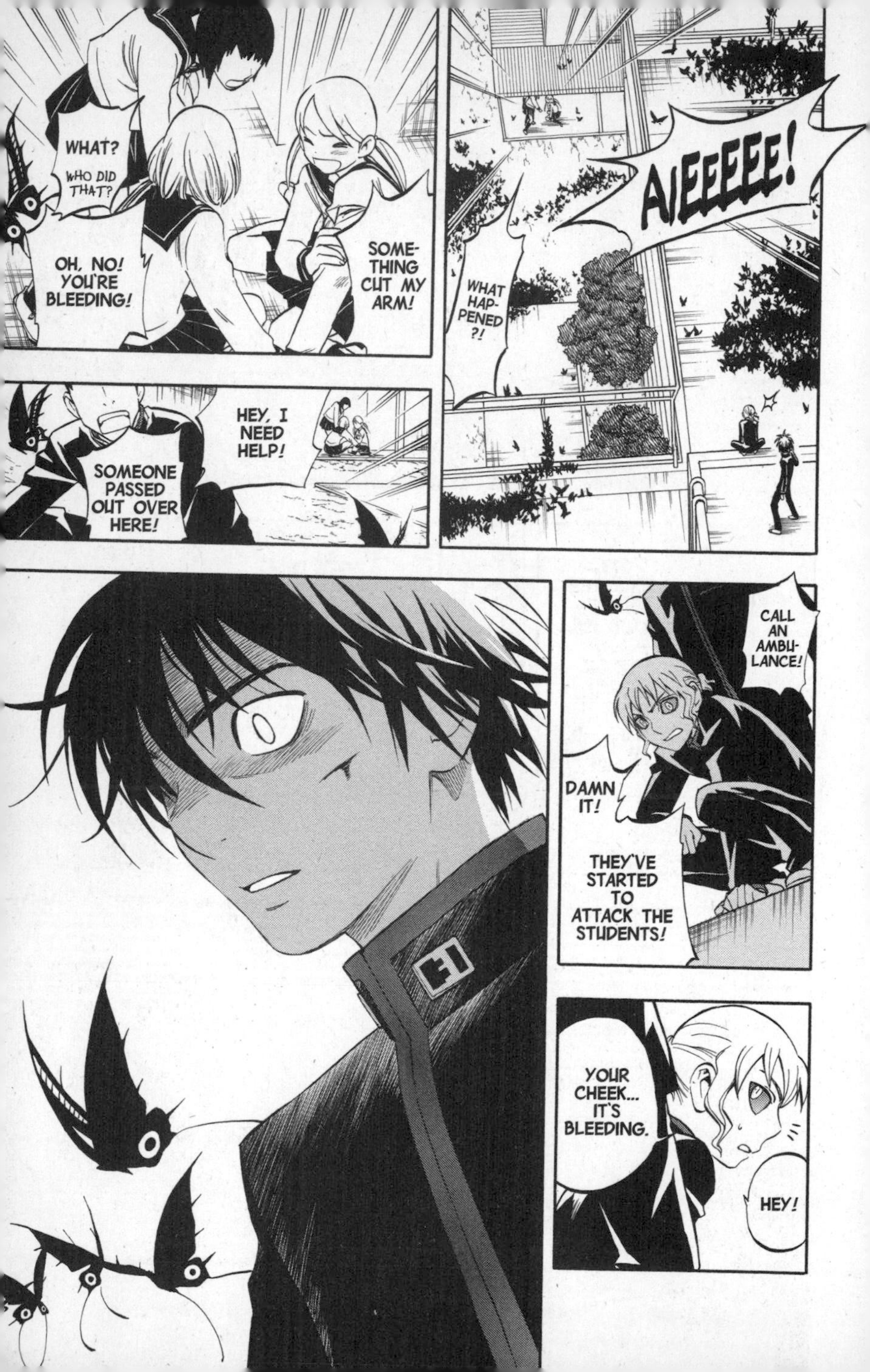
AIEEEEE!
WHAT HAPPENED?!
SOMETHING CUT MY ARM!
WHAT? WHO DID THAT?
OH, NO! YOU'RE BLEEDING!
HEY, I NEED HELP!
SOMEONE PASSED OUT OVER HERE!
CALL AN AMBULANCE!
DAMN IT!
THEY'VE STARTED TO ATTACK THE STUDENTS!
YOUR CHEEK... IT'S BLEEDING.
HEY!

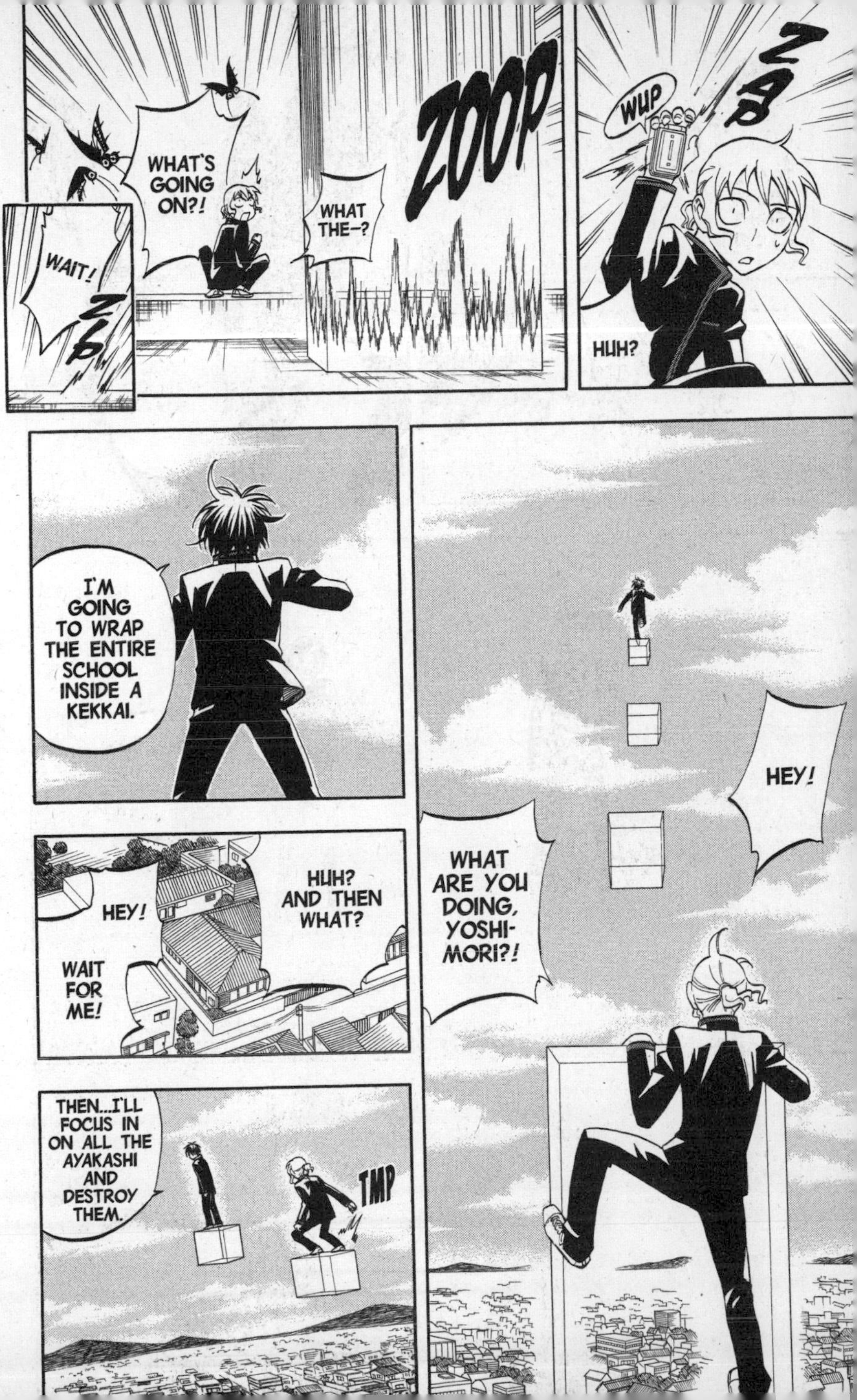
ZAP
WUP
HUH?
ZOOP
WHAT THE-?
WHAT'S GOING ON?!
WAIT!
ZAP
HEY!
WHAT ARE YOU DOING, YOSHIMORI?!
I'M GOING TO WRAP THE ENTIRE SCHOOL INSIDE A KEKKAI.
HUH? AND THEN WHAT?
HEY!
WAIT FOR ME!
THEN...I'LL FOCUS IN ON ALL THE AYAKASHI AND DESTROY THEM.
TMP

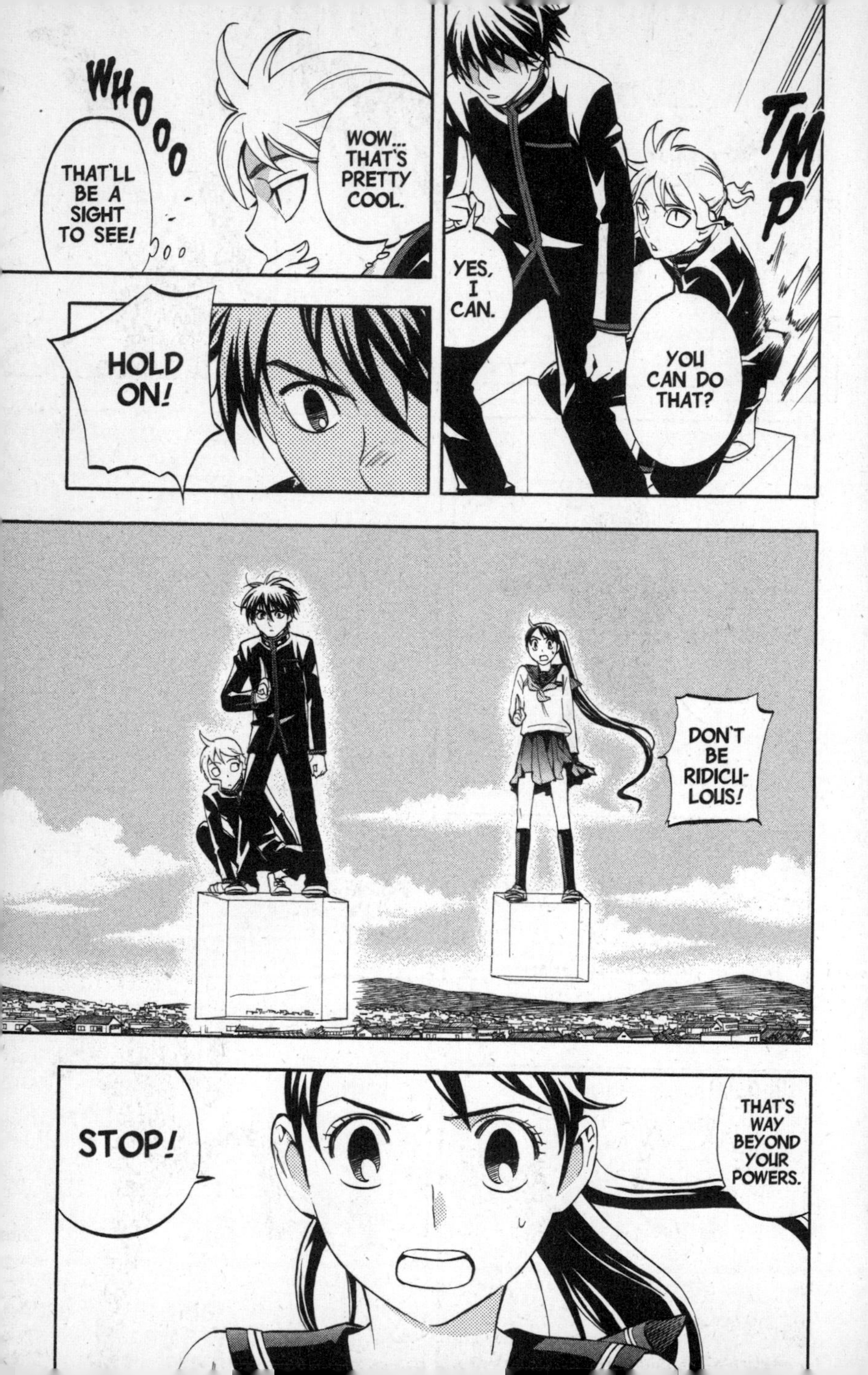
TMP
YOU CAN DO THAT?
YES, I CAN.
WOW... THAT'S PRETTY COOL.
WHOOOO
THAT'LL BE A SIGHT TO SEE!
HOLD ON!
DON'T BE RIDICU-LOUS!
THAT'S WAY BEYOND YOUR POWERS.
STOP!

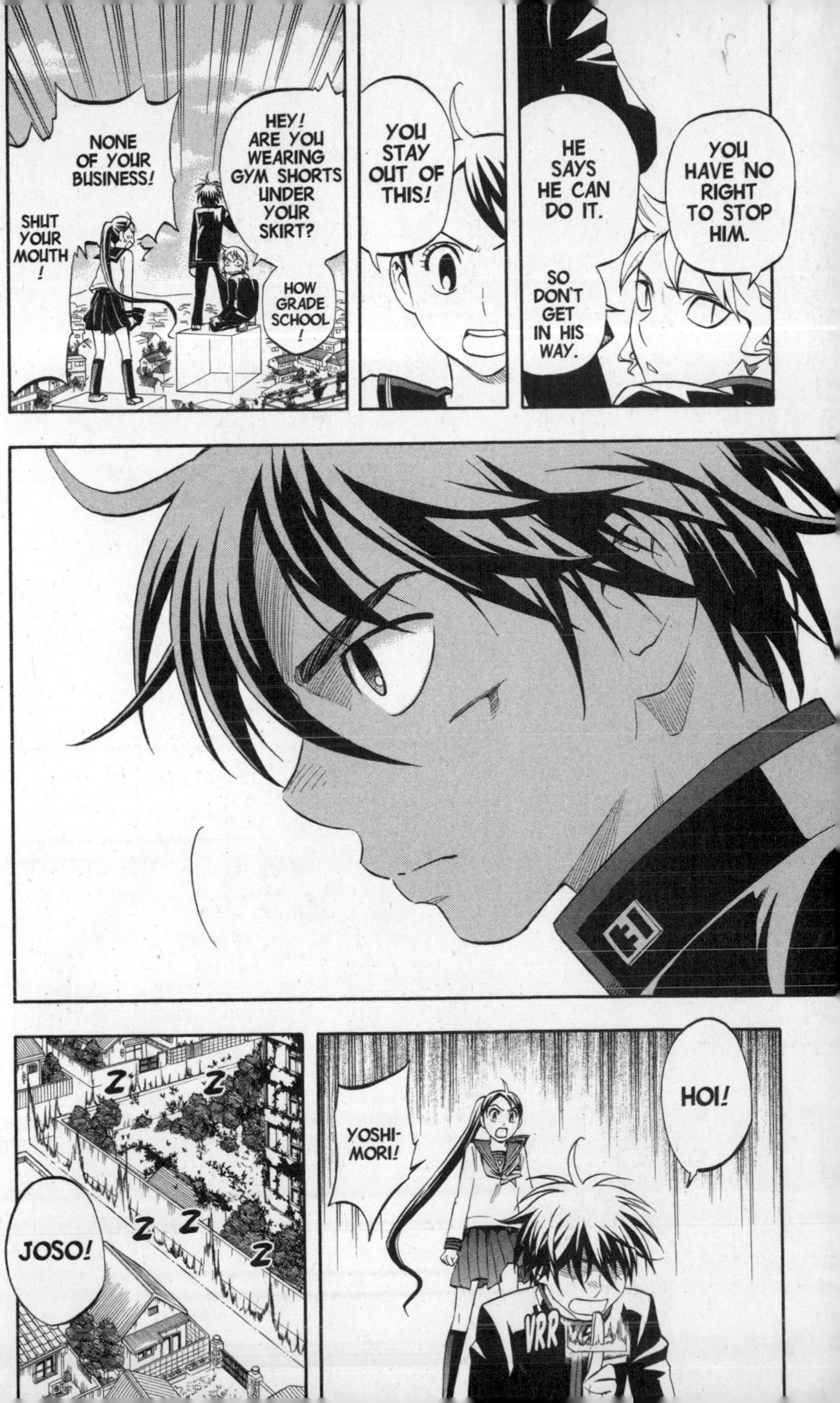
YOU HAVE NO RIGHT TO STOP HIM.
HE SAYS HE CAN DO IT.
SO DON'T GET IN HIS WAY.
YOU STAY OUT OF THIS!
HEY! ARE YOU WEARING GYM SHORTS UNDER YOUR SKIRT?
HOW GRADE SCHOOL!
NONE OF YOUR BUSINESS!
SHUT YOUR MOUTH!
HOI!
YOSHI-MORI!
VRR
Z Z
JOSO!
Z Z Z

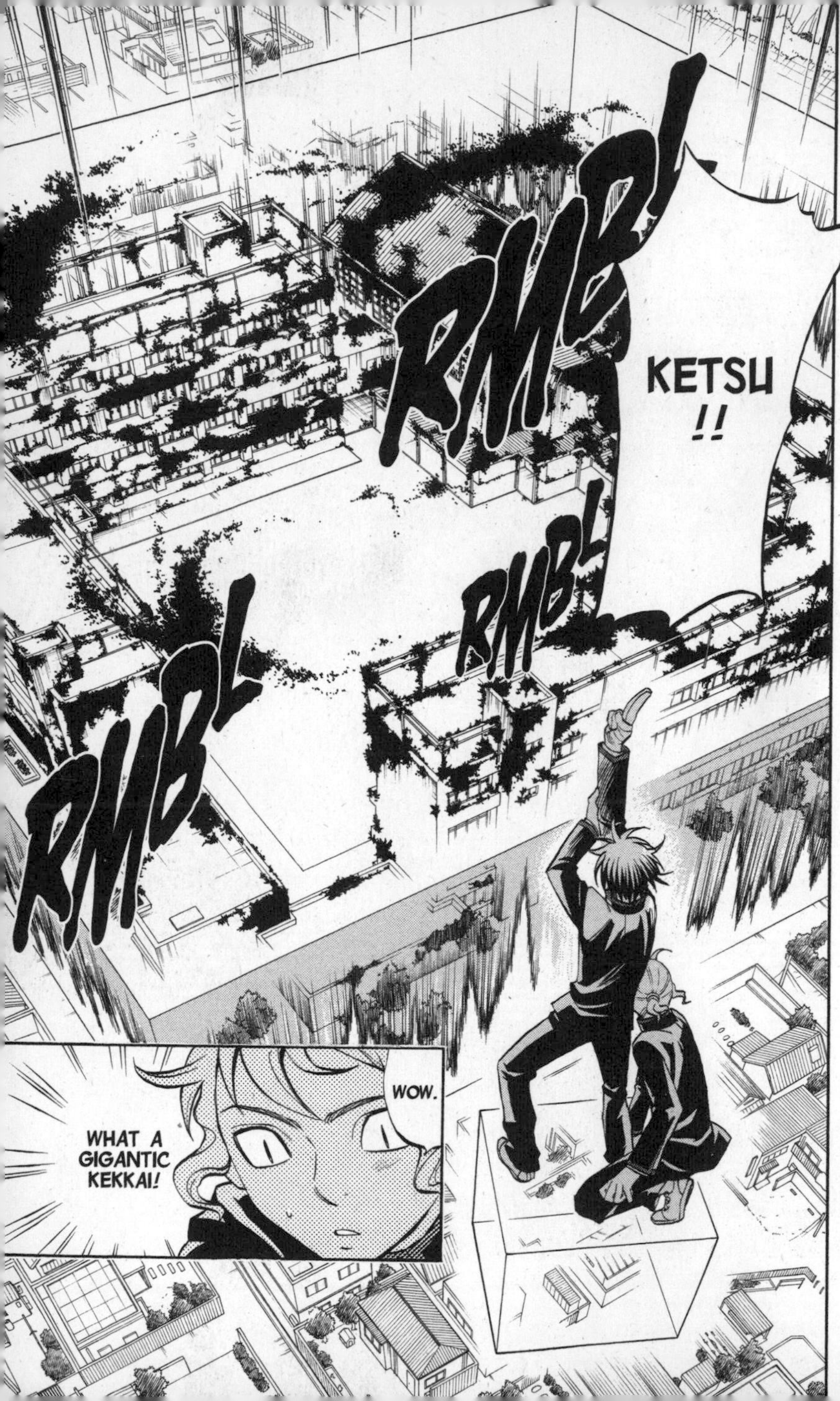

RMBL
KETSU !!
RMBL
RMBL
WOW.
WHAT A GIGANTIC KEKKAI!

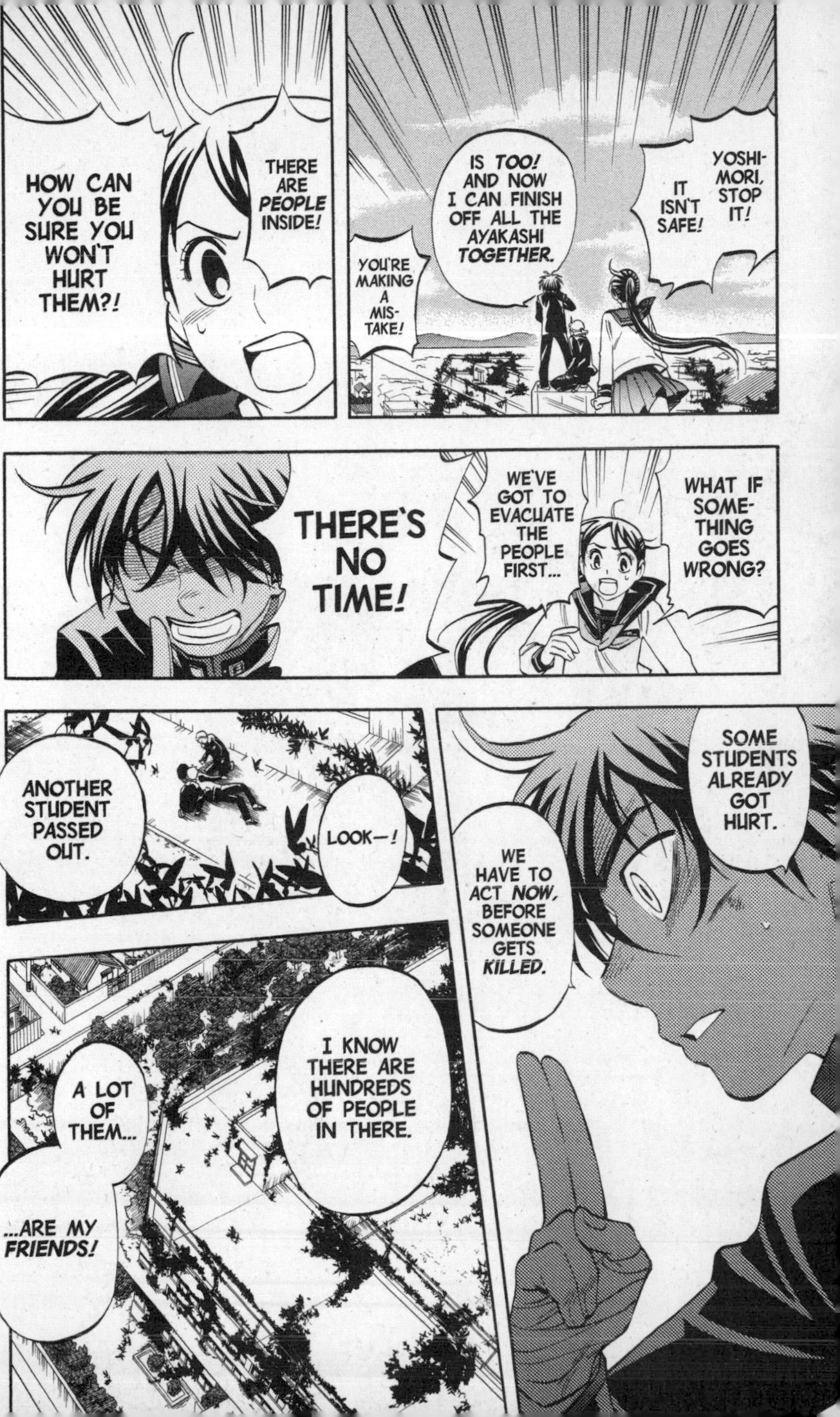
YOSHI-MORI, STOP IT!
IT ISN'T SAFE!
IS *TOO!* AND NOW I CAN FINISH OFF ALL THE AYAKASHI *TOGETHER.*
YOU'RE MAKING A MIS-TAKE!
THERE ARE *PEOPLE* INSIDE!
HOW CAN YOU BE SURE YOU WON'T HURT THEM?!
WHAT IF SOME-THING GOES WRONG?
WE'VE GOT TO EVACUATE THE PEOPLE FIRST...
THERE'S NO TIME!
SOME STUDENTS ALREADY GOT HURT.
WE HAVE TO ACT *NOW,* BEFORE SOMEONE GETS *KILLED.*
LOOK—!
ANOTHER STUDENT PASSED OUT.
I KNOW THERE ARE HUNDREDS OF PEOPLE IN THERE.
A LOT OF THEM...
...ARE MY *FRIENDS!*

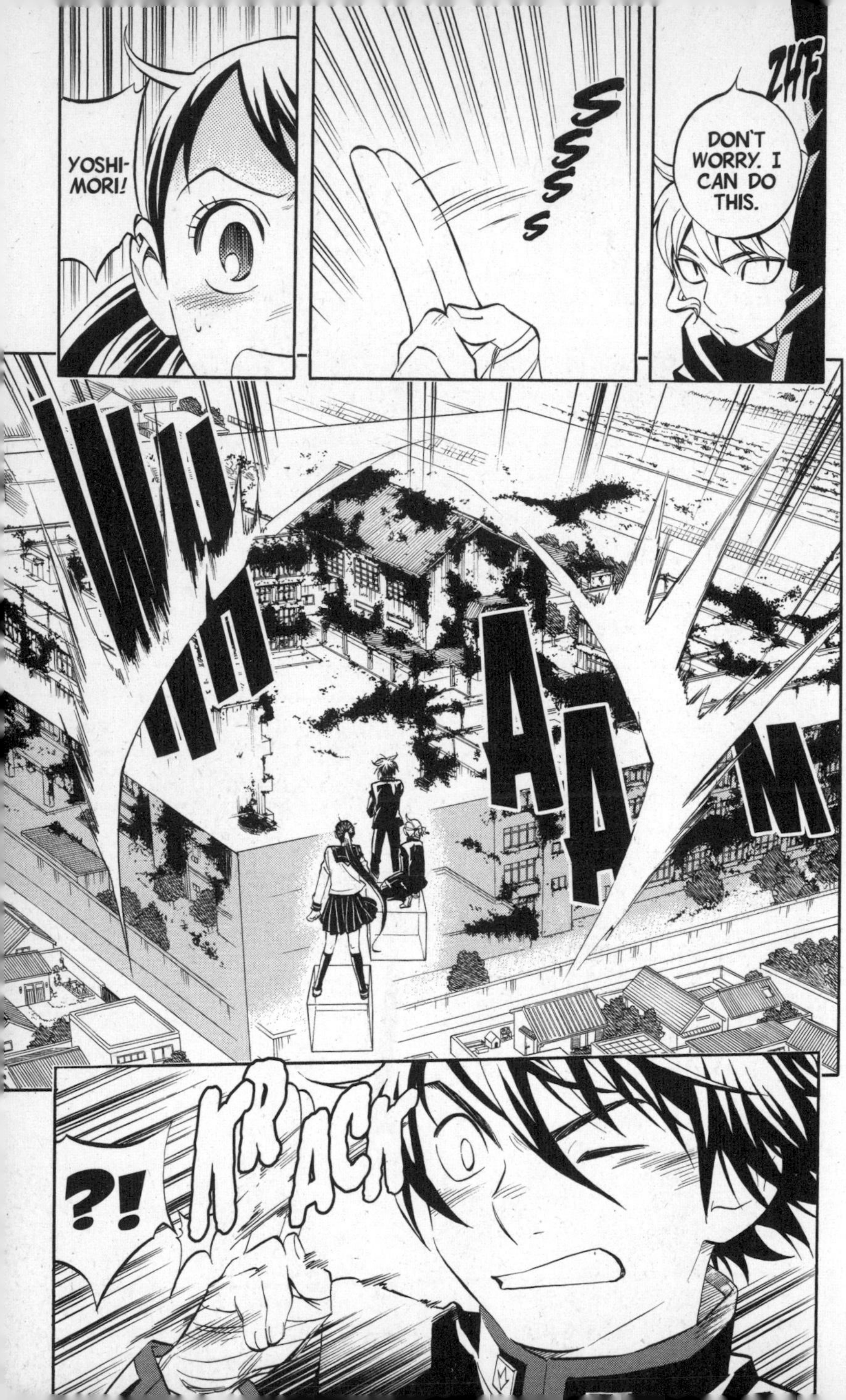
ZHF
DON'T WORRY. I CAN DO THIS.
SSSSS
YOSHIMORI!
WHAAM
KRACK
?!

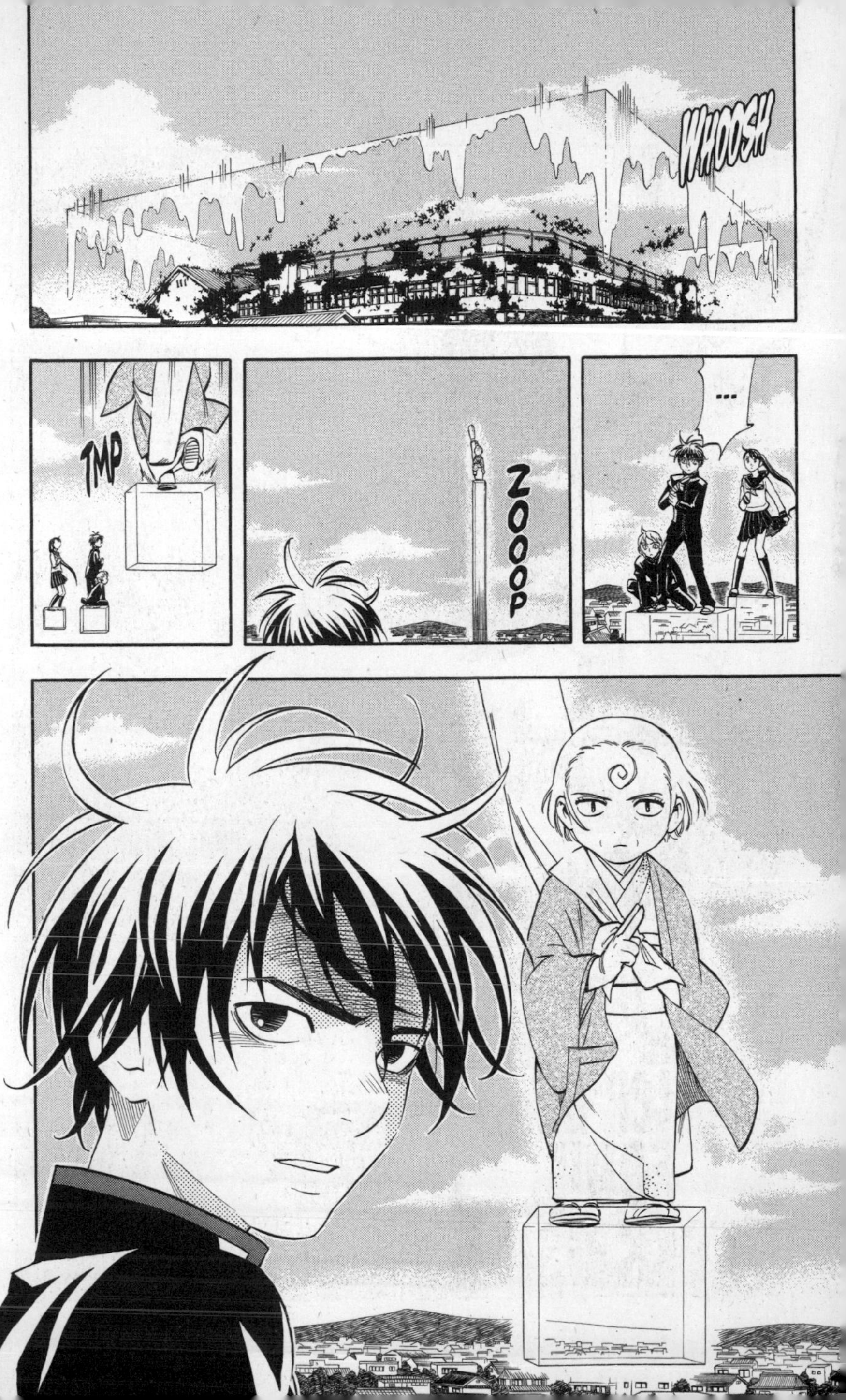
WHOOSH
...
ZOOOOP
TMP

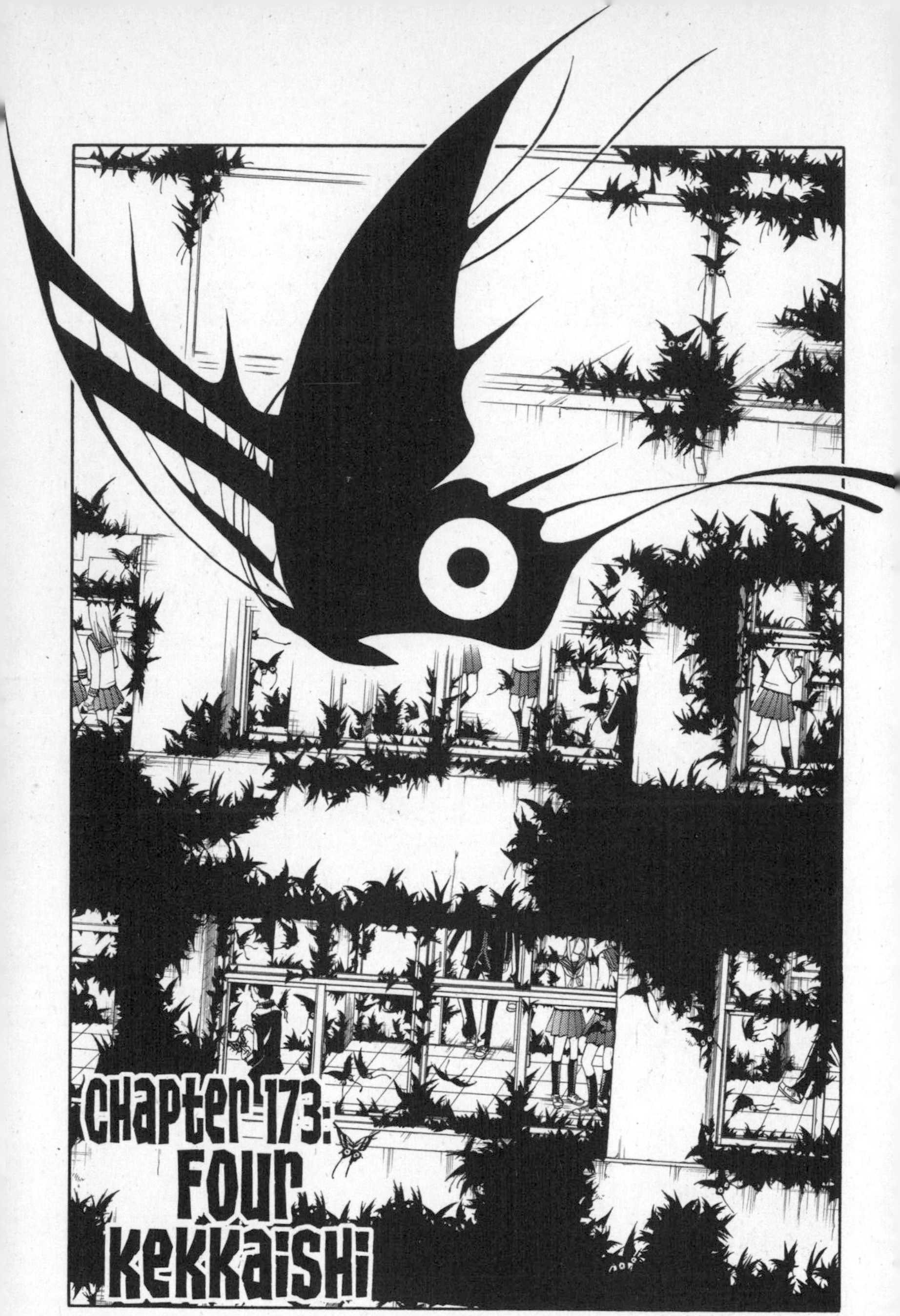
Chapter 173:
Four Kekkaishi

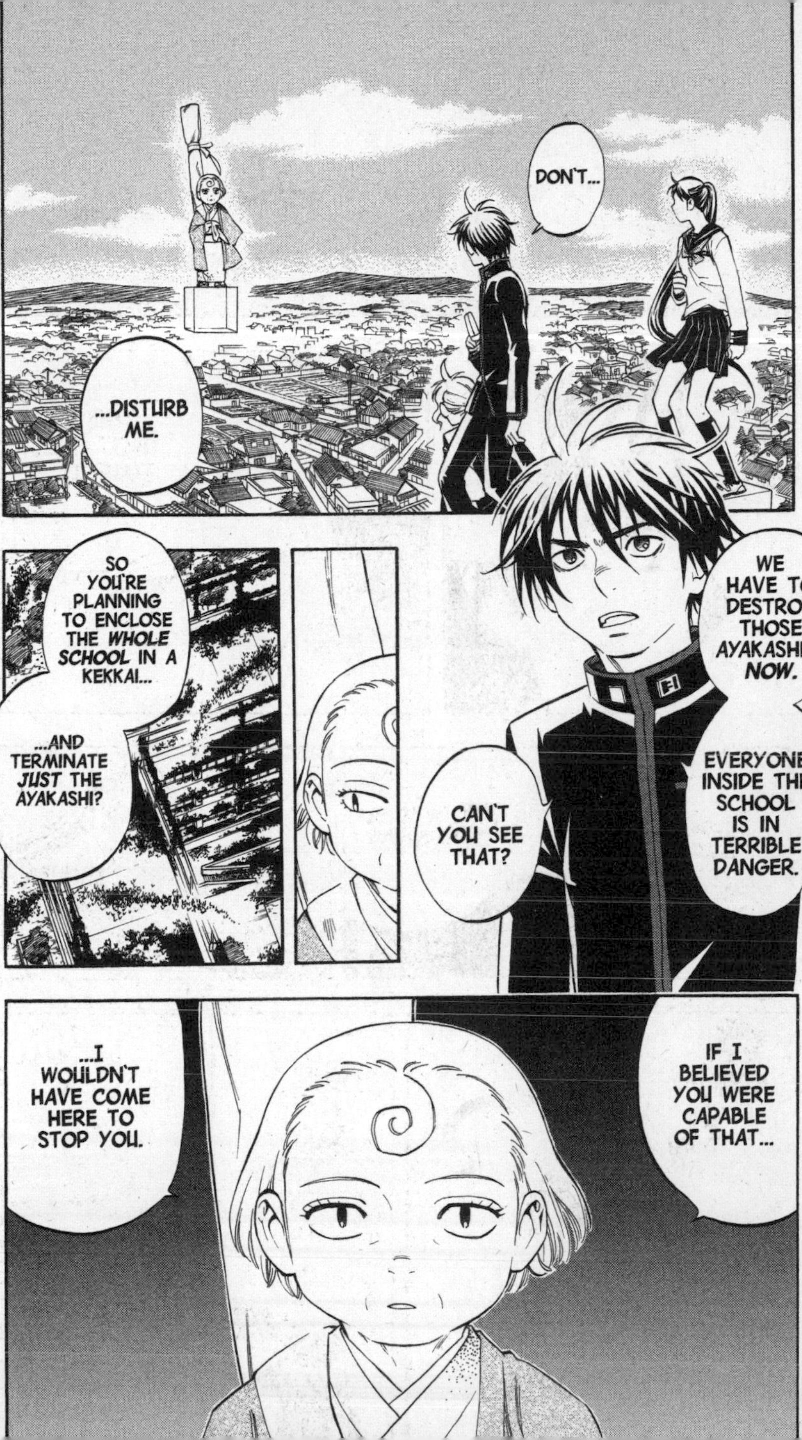
DON'T...
...DISTURB ME.
WE HAVE TO DESTROY THOSE AYAKASHI—NOW.
EVERYONE INSIDE THE SCHOOL IS IN TERRIBLE DANGER.
CAN'T YOU SEE THAT?
SO YOU'RE PLANNING TO ENCLOSE THE WHOLE SCHOOL IN A KEKKAI...
...AND TERMINATE JUST THE AYAKASHI?
IF I BELIEVED YOU WERE CAPABLE OF THAT...
...I WOULDN'T HAVE COME HERE TO STOP YOU.

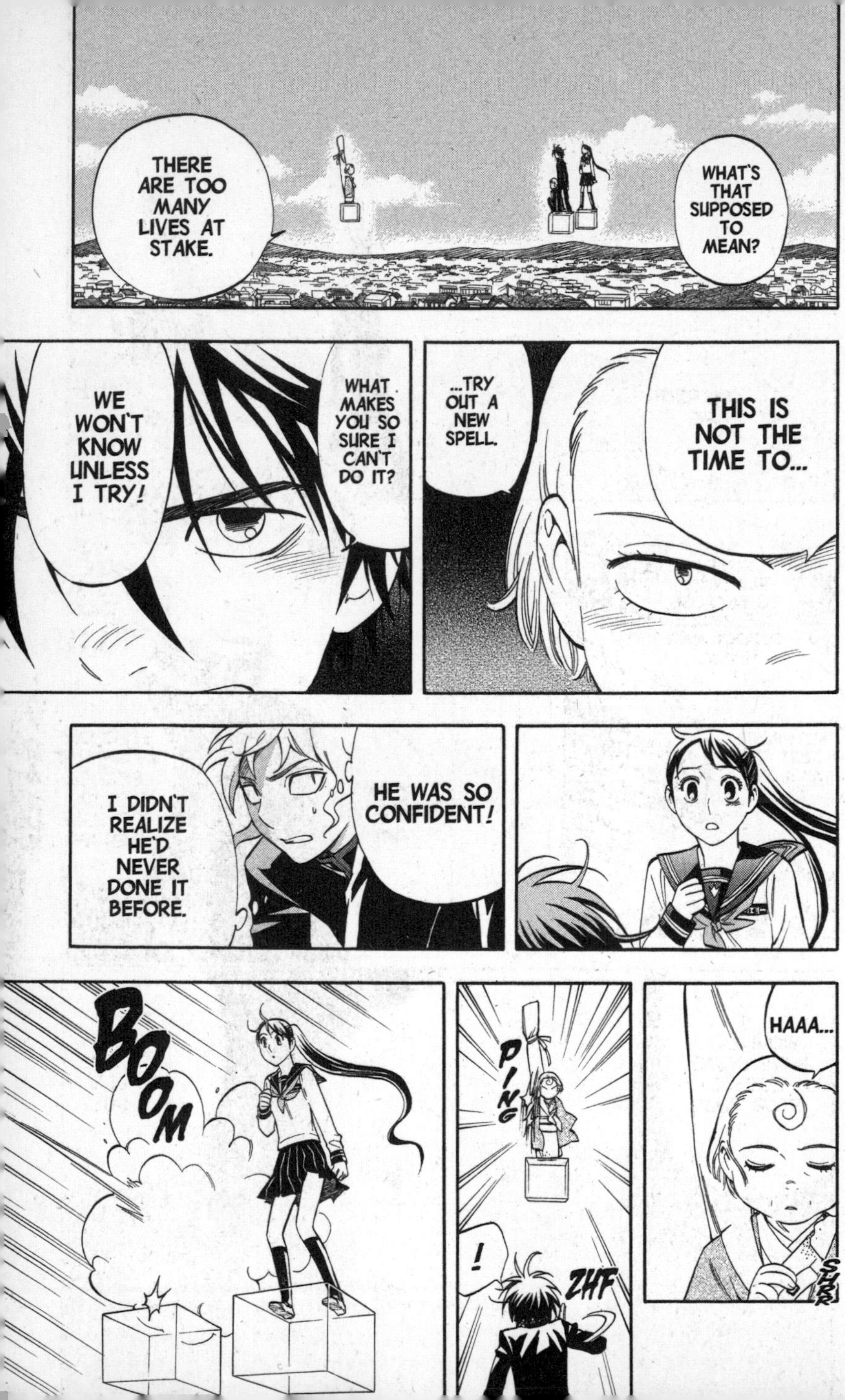
WHAT'S THAT SUPPOSED TO MEAN?
THERE ARE TOO MANY LIVES AT STAKE.
THIS IS NOT THE TIME TO...
...TRY OUT A NEW SPELL.
WHAT MAKES YOU SO SURE I CAN'T DO IT?
WE WON'T KNOW UNLESS I TRY!
HE WAS SO CONFIDENT!
I DIDN'T REALIZE HE'D NEVER DONE IT BEFORE.
HAAA...
SHRR
PING
!
ZHF
BOOM

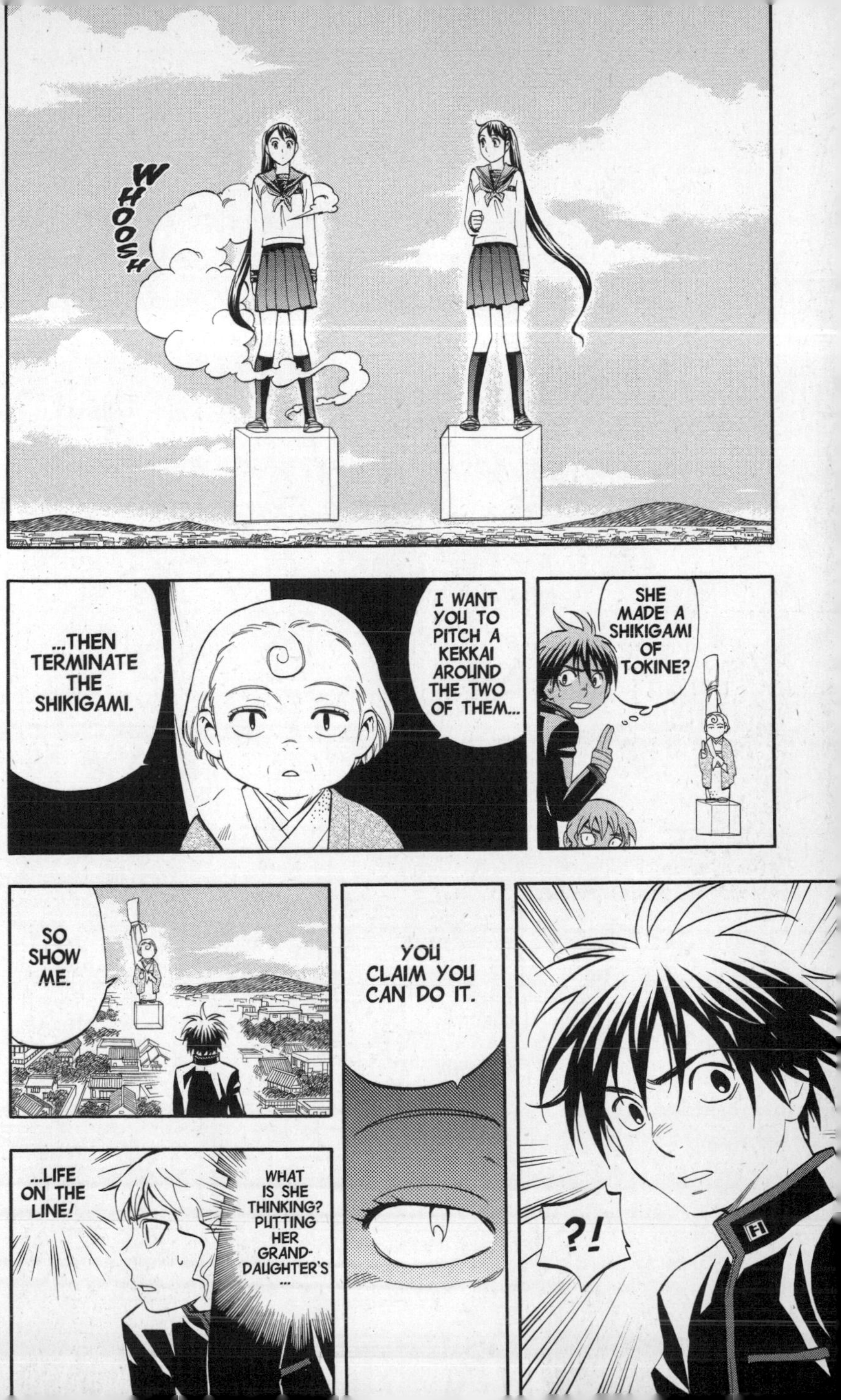
WHOOSH
SHE MADE A SHIKIGAMI OF TOKINE?
I WANT YOU TO PITCH A KEKKAI AROUND THE TWO OF THEM...
...THEN TERMINATE THE SHIKIGAMI.
?!
YOU CLAIM YOU CAN DO IT.
SO SHOW ME.
WHAT IS SHE THINKING? PUTTING HER GRAND-DAUGHTER'S ...
...LIFE ON THE LINE!

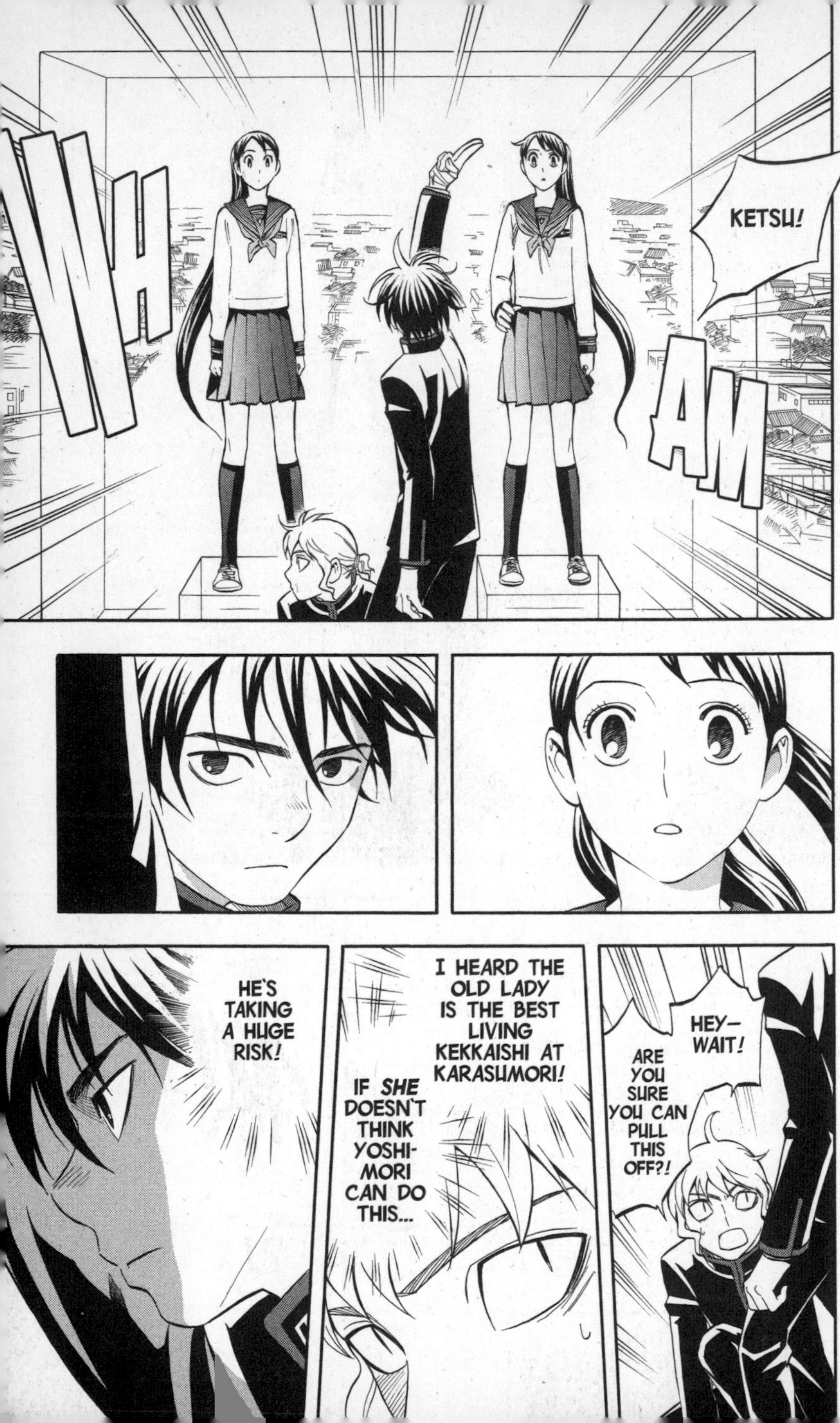
KETSU!
WHAM
HEY— WAIT!
ARE YOU SURE YOU CAN PULL THIS OFF?!
I HEARD THE OLD LADY IS THE BEST LIVING KEKKAISHI AT KARASUMORI!
IF *SHE* DOESN'T THINK YOSHIMORI CAN DO THIS...
HE'S TAKING A HUGE RISK!

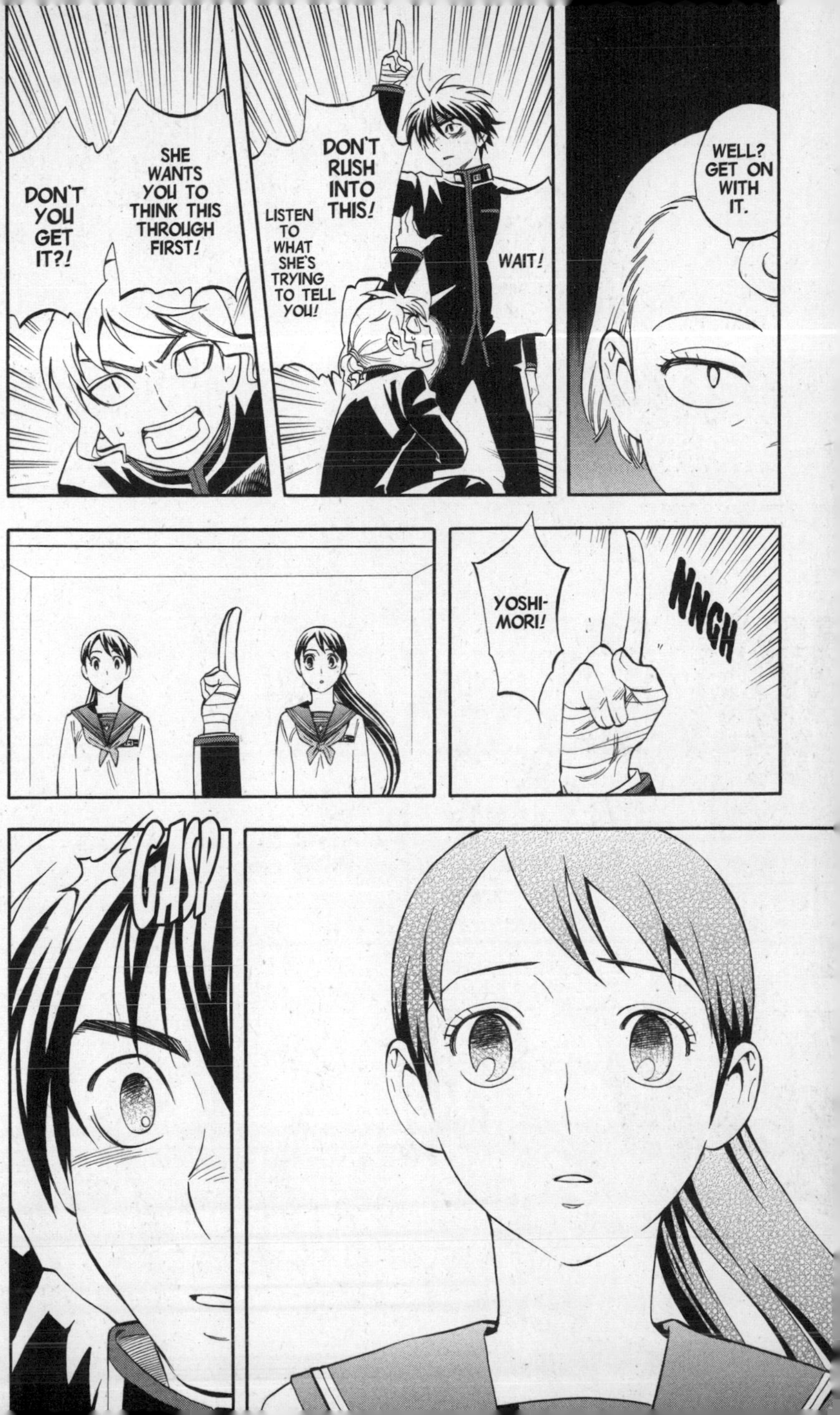
WELL? GET ON WITH IT.
WAIT!
DON'T RUSH INTO THIS!
LISTEN TO WHAT SHE'S TRYING TO TELL YOU!
SHE WANTS YOU TO THINK THIS THROUGH FIRST!
DON'T YOU GET IT?!
YOSHI-MORI!
NNGH
GASP!

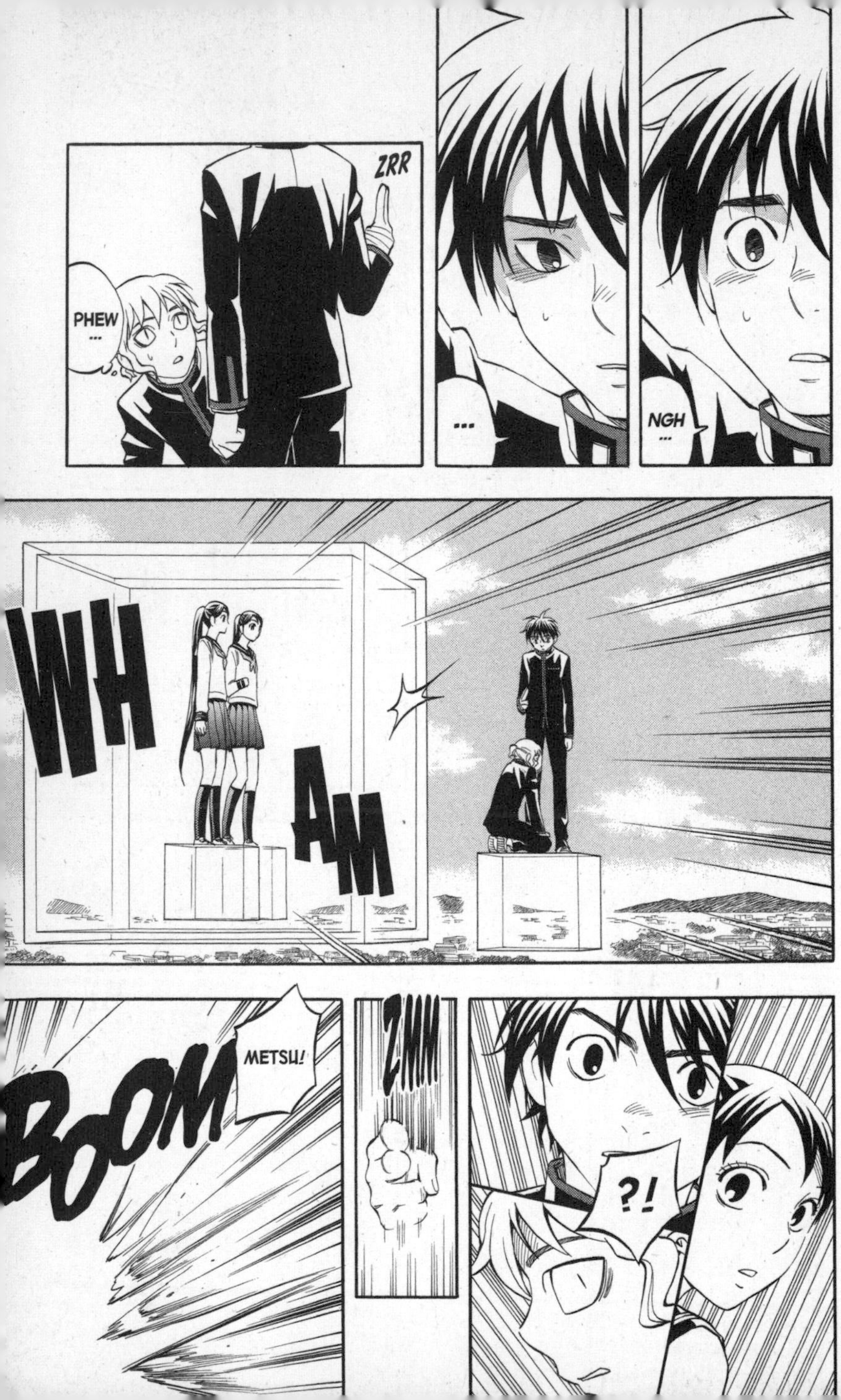
NGH ...
...
ZRR
PHEW ...
WHAM
?!
ZMM
METSU!
BOOM

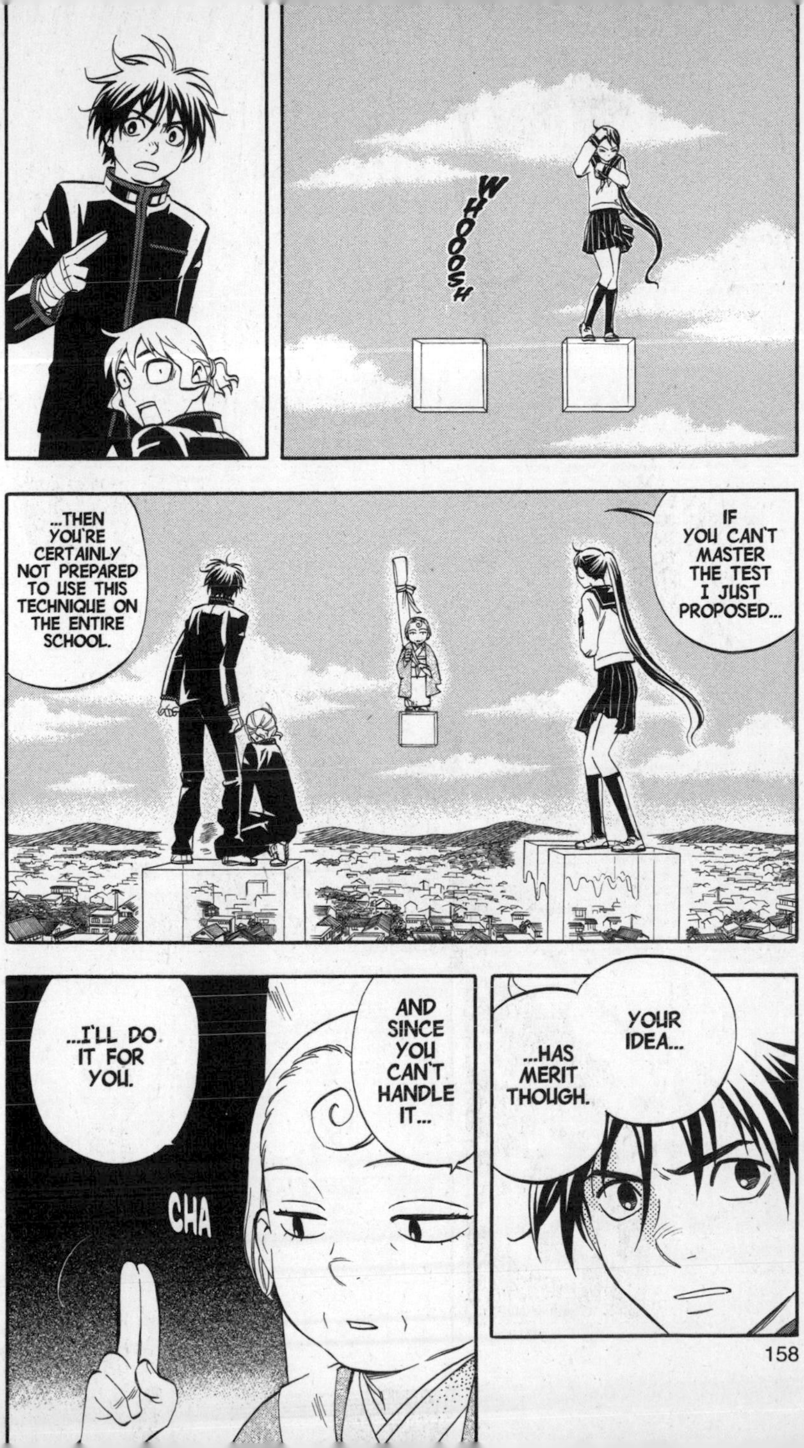
WHOOOOSH
IF YOU CAN'T MASTER THE TEST I JUST PROPOSED...
...THEN YOU'RE CERTAINLY NOT PREPARED TO USE THIS TECHNIQUE ON THE ENTIRE SCHOOL.
YOUR IDEA...
...HAS MERIT THOUGH.
AND SINCE YOU CAN'T HANDLE IT...
...I'LL DO IT FOR YOU.
CHA

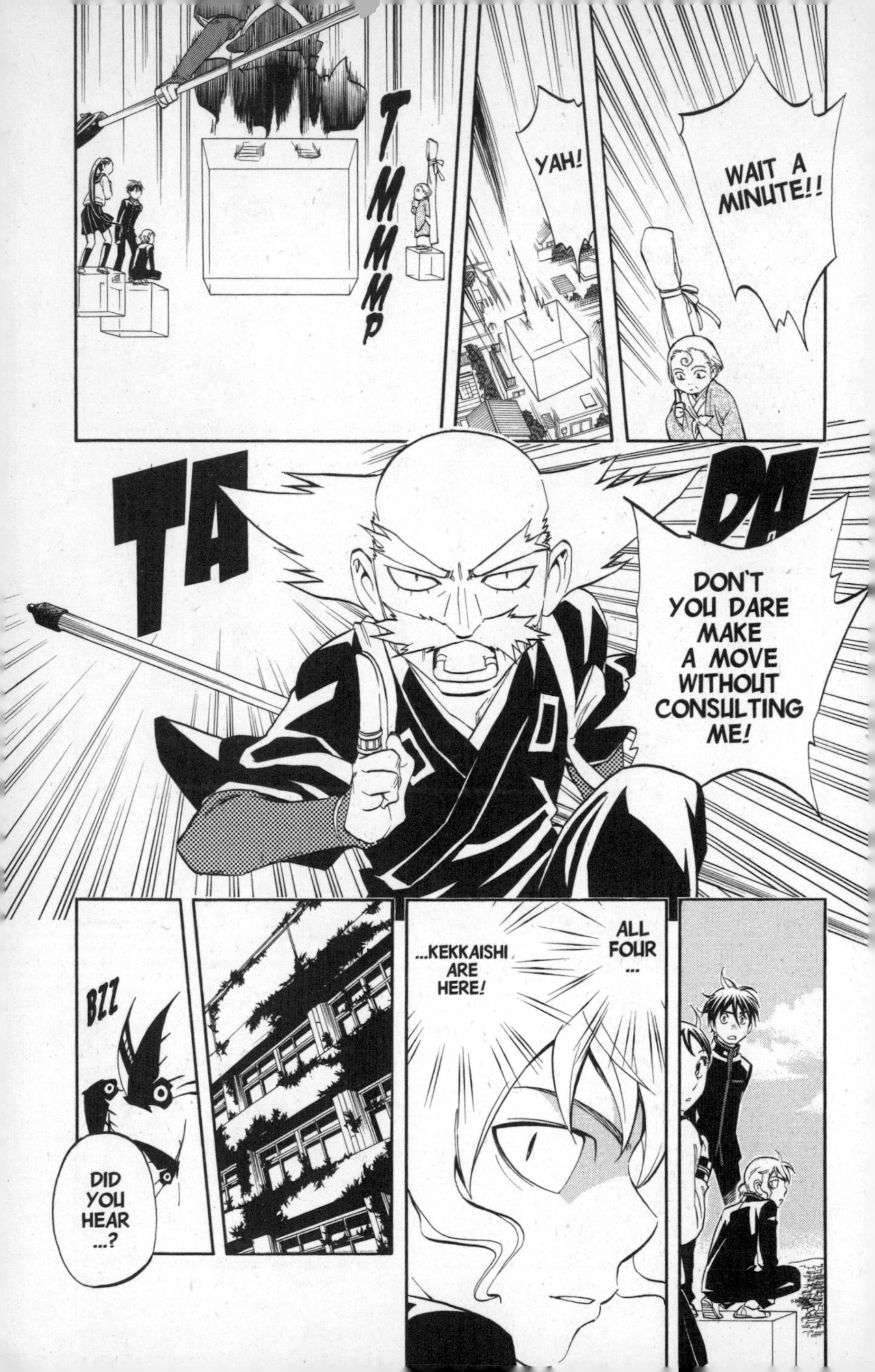
WAIT A MINUTE!!
YAH!
TMMMMP
TA DA
DON'T YOU DARE MAKE A MOVE WITHOUT CONSULTING ME!
ALL FOUR ...
...KEKKAISHI ARE HERE!
BZZ
DID YOU HEAR ...?

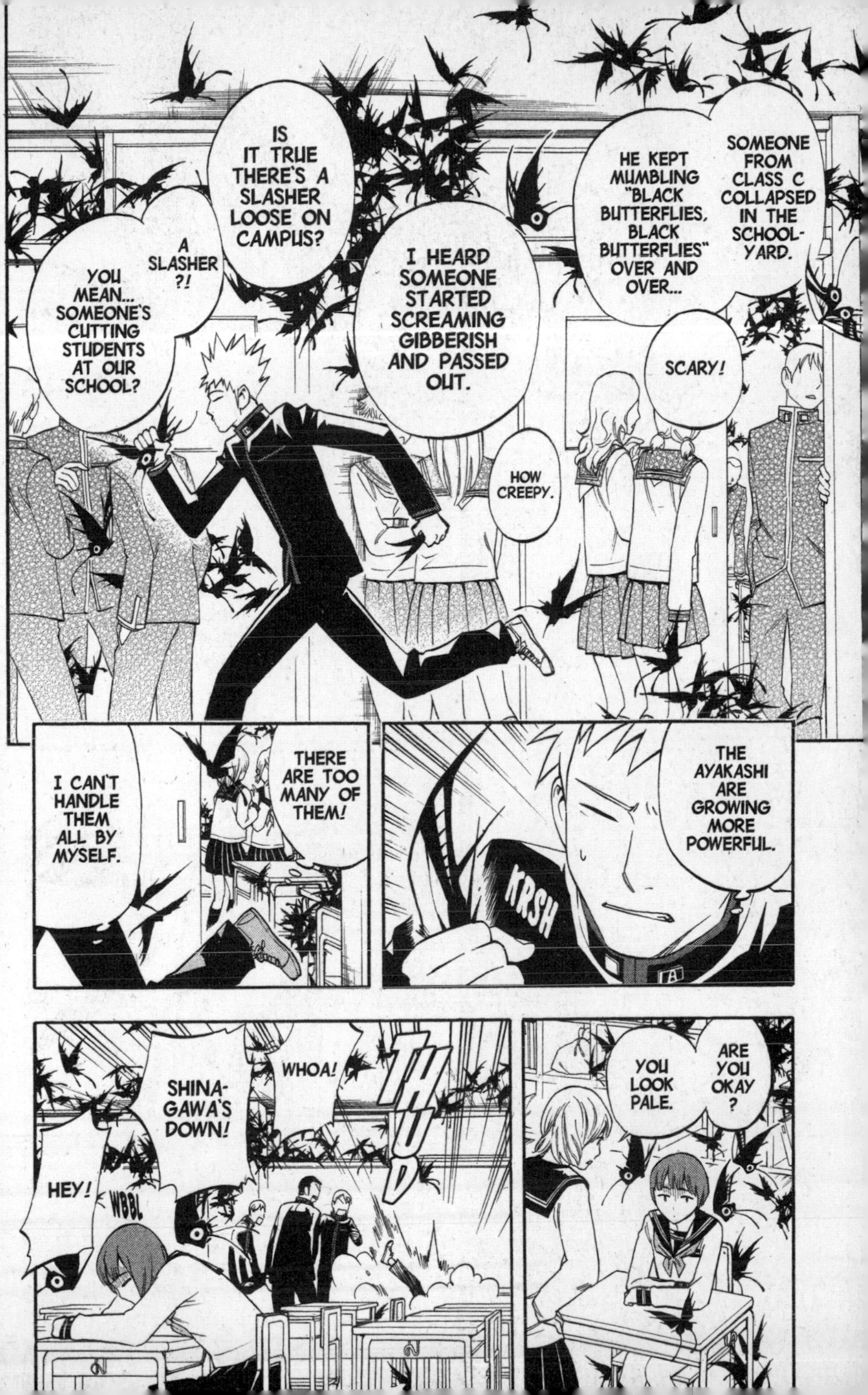
SOMEONE FROM CLASS C COLLAPSED IN THE SCHOOL-YARD.
HE KEPT MUMBLING "BLACK BUTTERFLIES, BLACK BUTTERFLIES" OVER AND OVER...
SCARY!
HOW CREEPY.
I HEARD SOMEONE STARTED SCREAMING GIBBERISH AND PASSED OUT.
IS IT TRUE THERE'S A SLASHER LOOSE ON CAMPUS?
A SLASHER?!
YOU MEAN... SOMEONE'S CUTTING STUDENTS AT OUR SCHOOL?
THE AYAKASHI ARE GROWING MORE POWERFUL.
KRSH
THERE ARE TOO MANY OF THEM!
I CAN'T HANDLE THEM ALL BY MYSELF.
ARE YOU OKAY?
YOU LOOK PALE.
THUD
WHOA!
SHINA-GAWA'S DOWN!
HEY!
WBBL

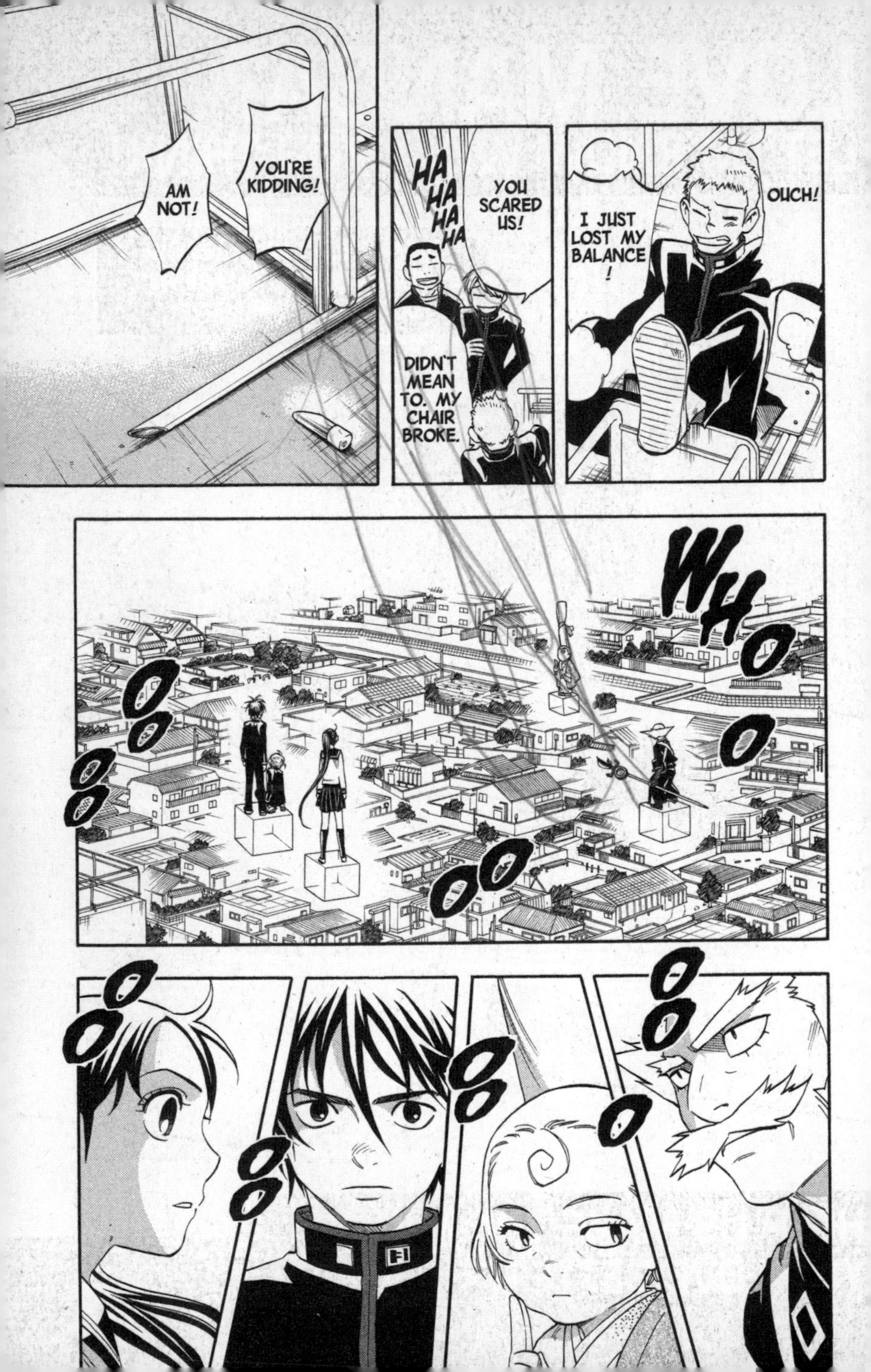
OUCH!
I JUST LOST MY BALANCE!
HA HA HA HA
YOU SCARED US!
DIDN'T MEAN TO. MY CHAIR BROKE.
YOU'RE KIDDING!
AM NOT!
WHO

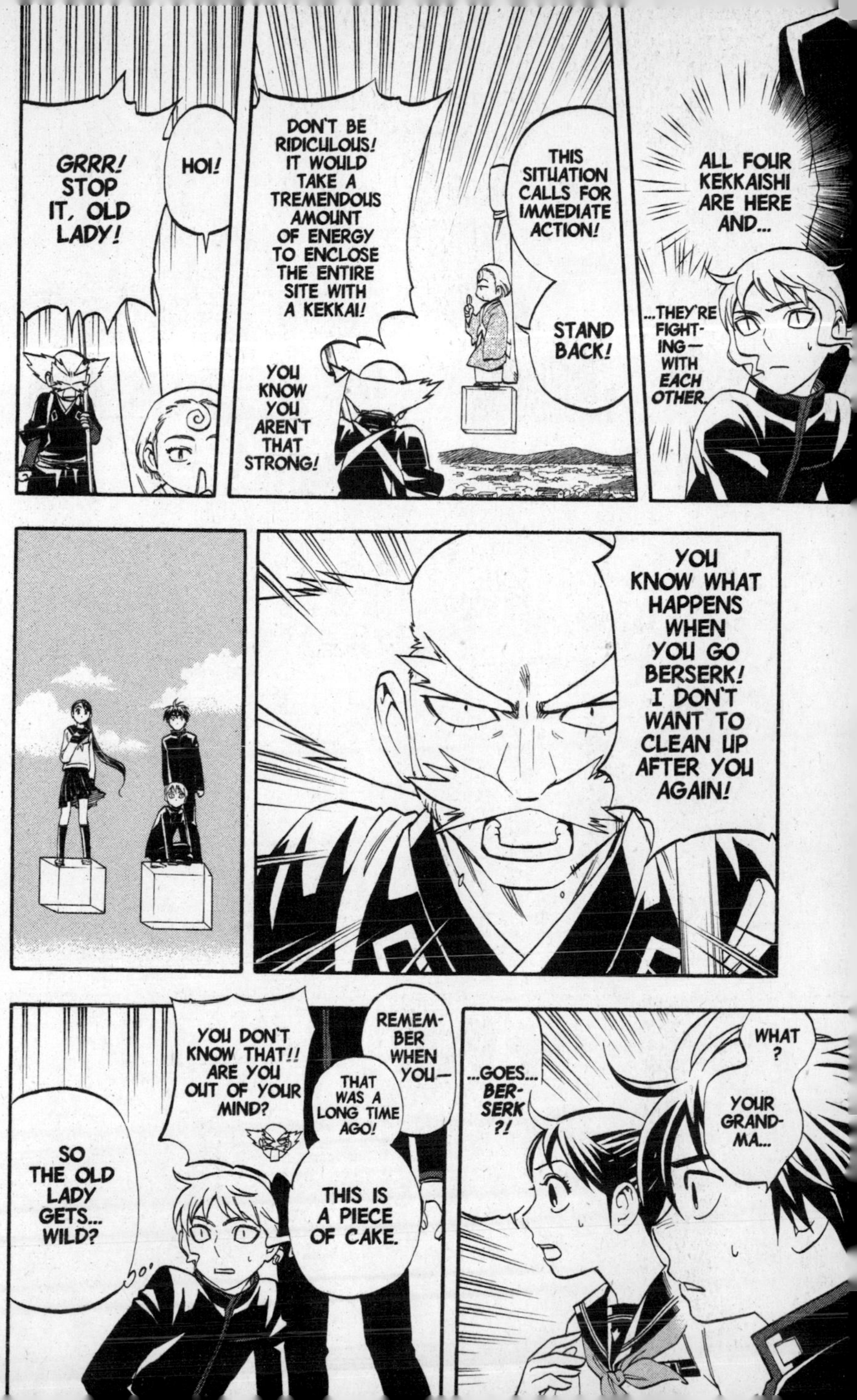
ALL FOUR KEKKAISHI ARE HERE AND...
...THEY'RE FIGHT-ING—WITH EACH OTHER.
THIS SITUATION CALLS FOR IMMEDIATE ACTION!
STAND BACK!
DON'T BE RIDICULOUS! IT WOULD TAKE A TREMENDOUS AMOUNT OF ENERGY TO ENCLOSE THE ENTIRE SITE WITH A KEKKAI!
YOU KNOW YOU AREN'T THAT STRONG!
HOI!
GRRR! STOP IT, OLD LADY!
YOU KNOW WHAT HAPPENS WHEN YOU GO BERSERK! I DON'T WANT TO CLEAN UP AFTER YOU AGAIN!
WHAT?
YOUR GRAND-MA...
...GOES... BER-SERK?!
REMEM-BER WHEN YOU—
THAT WAS A LONG TIME AGO!
YOU DON'T KNOW THAT!! ARE YOU OUT OF YOUR MIND?
THIS IS A PIECE OF CAKE.
SO THE OLD LADY GETS... WILD?

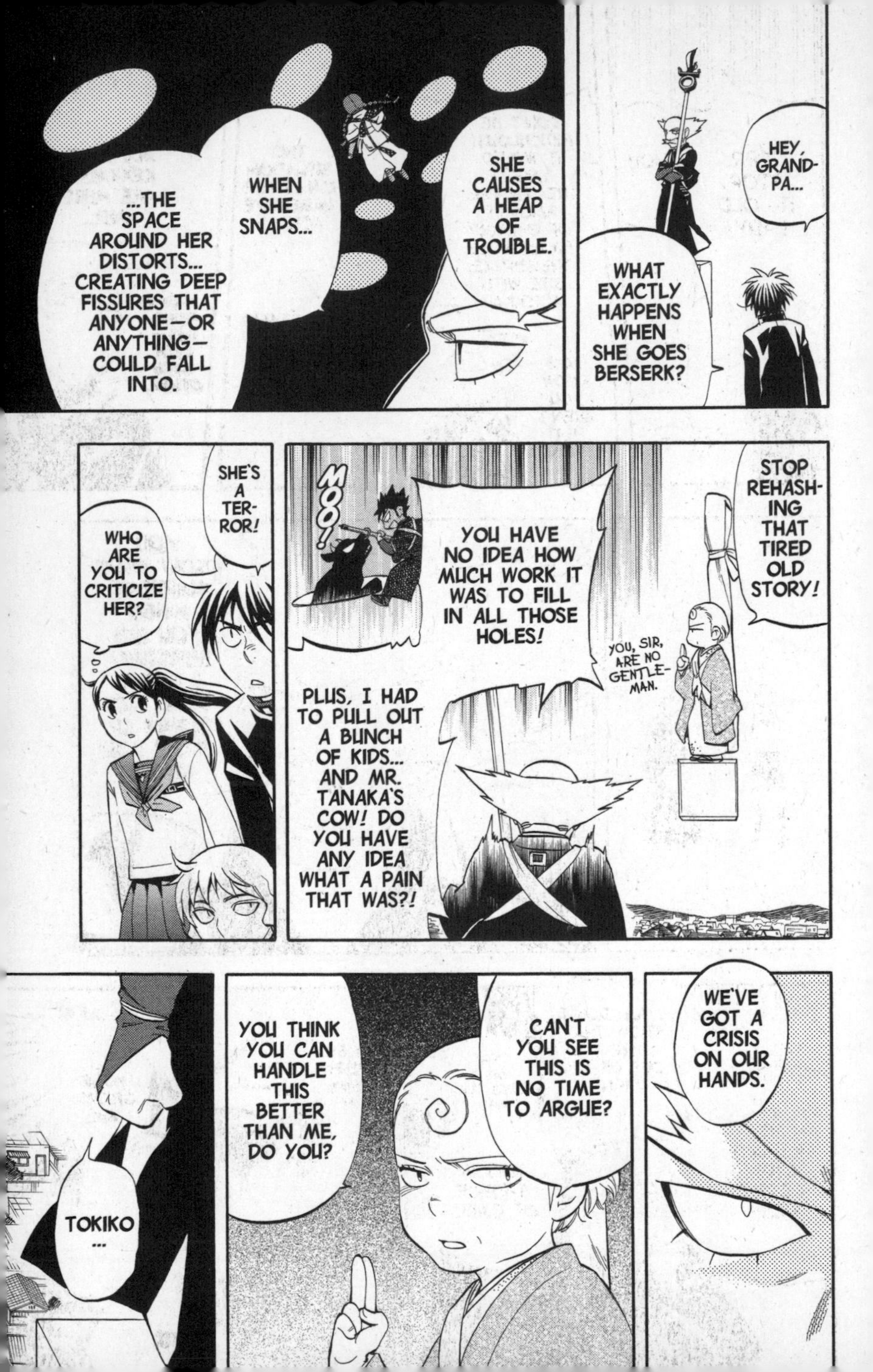
HEY, GRANDPA...
WHAT EXACTLY HAPPENS WHEN SHE GOES BERSERK?
SHE CAUSES A HEAP OF TROUBLE.
WHEN SHE SNAPS...
...THE SPACE AROUND HER DISTORTS... CREATING DEEP FISSURES THAT ANYONE—OR ANYTHING—COULD FALL INTO.
STOP REHASHING THAT TIRED OLD STORY!
YOU, SIR, ARE NO GENTLEMAN.
YOU HAVE NO IDEA HOW MUCH WORK IT WAS TO FILL IN ALL THOSE HOLES!
MOO!
PLUS, I HAD TO PULL OUT A BUNCH OF KIDS... AND MR. TANAKA'S COW! DO YOU HAVE ANY IDEA WHAT A PAIN THAT WAS?!
SHE'S A TERROR!
WHO ARE YOU TO CRITICIZE HER?
WE'VE GOT A CRISIS ON OUR HANDS.
CAN'T YOU SEE THIS IS NO TIME TO ARGUE?
YOU THINK YOU CAN HANDLE THIS BETTER THAN ME, DO YOU?
TOKIKO...

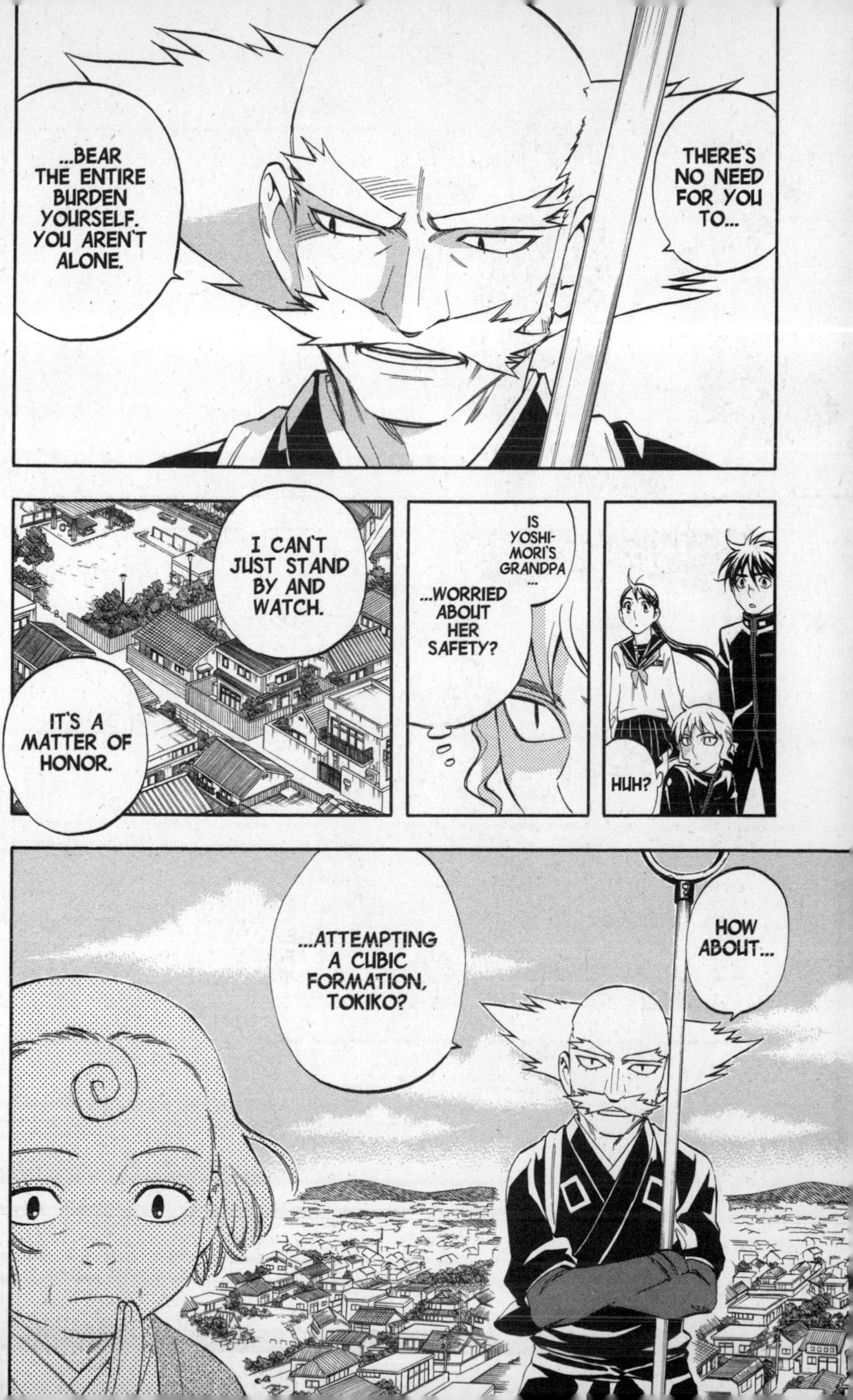
THERE'S NO NEED FOR YOU TO...
...BEAR THE ENTIRE BURDEN YOURSELF. YOU AREN'T ALONE.
HUH?
IS YOSHI-MORI'S GRANDPA ...
...WORRIED ABOUT HER SAFETY?
I CAN'T JUST STAND BY AND WATCH.
IT'S A MATTER OF HONOR.
HOW ABOUT...
...ATTEMPTING A CUBIC FORMATION, TOKIKO?

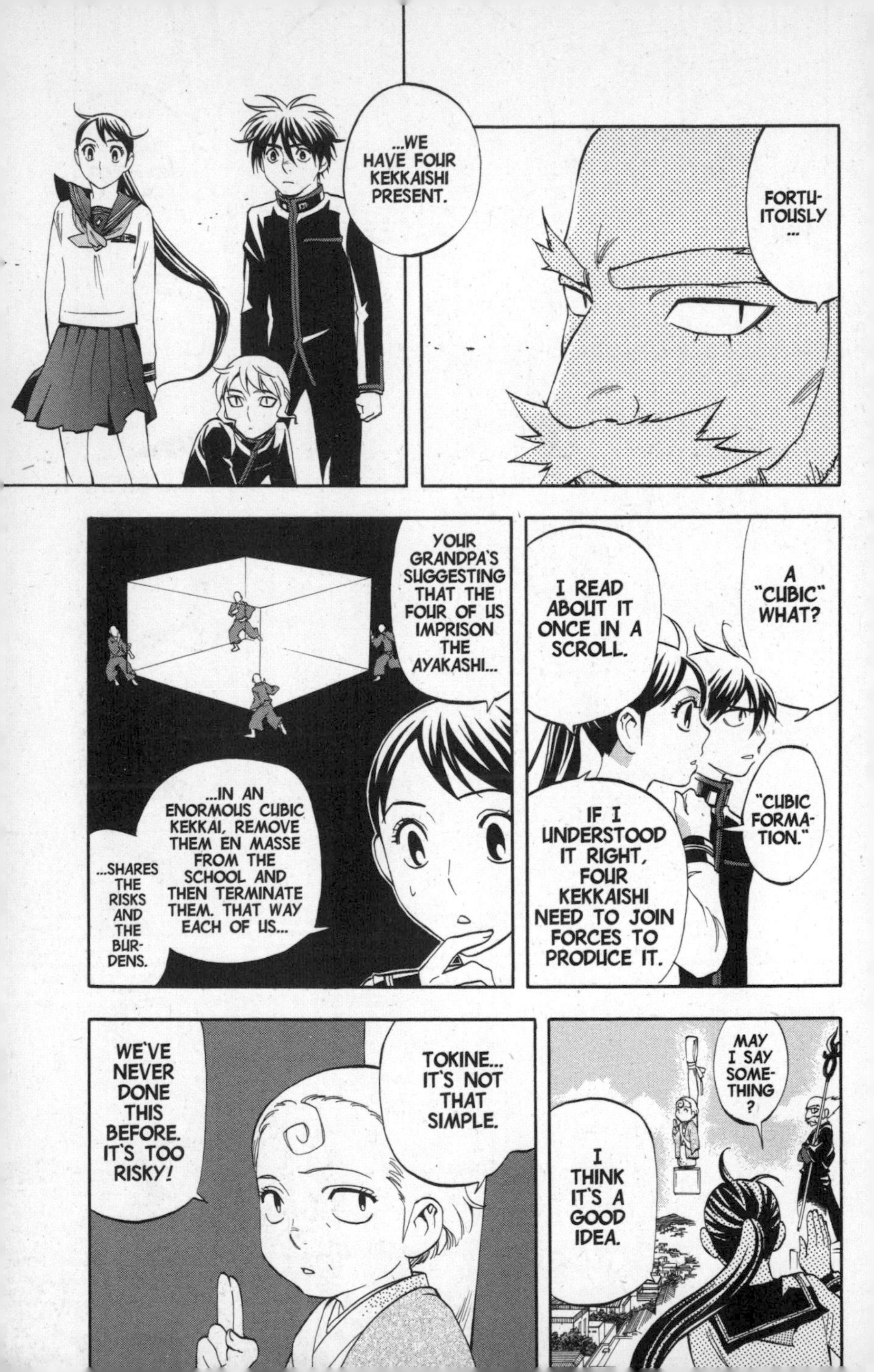
FORTUITOUSLY...
...WE HAVE FOUR KEKKAISHI PRESENT.
A "CUBIC" WHAT?
I READ ABOUT IT ONCE IN A SCROLL.
"CUBIC FORMATION."
IF I UNDERSTOOD IT RIGHT, FOUR KEKKAISHI NEED TO JOIN FORCES TO PRODUCE IT.
YOUR GRANDPA'S SUGGESTING THAT THE FOUR OF US IMPRISON THE AYAKASHI...
...IN AN ENORMOUS CUBIC KEKKAI, REMOVE THEM EN MASSE FROM THE SCHOOL AND THEN TERMINATE THEM. THAT WAY EACH OF US...
...SHARES THE RISKS AND THE BURDENS.
MAY I SAY SOMETHING?
I THINK IT'S A GOOD IDEA.
TOKINE... IT'S NOT THAT SIMPLE.
WE'VE NEVER DONE THIS BEFORE. IT'S TOO RISKY!

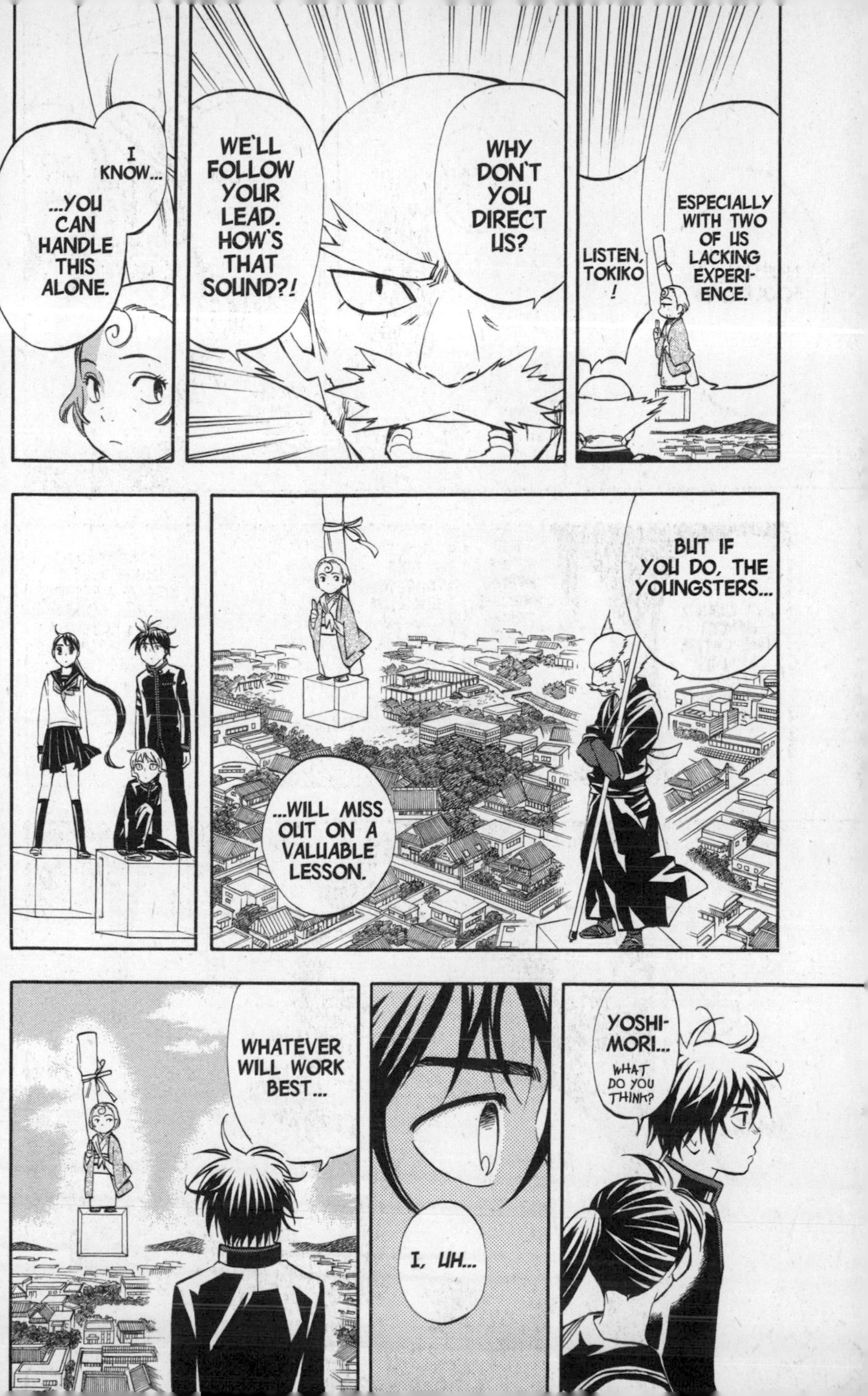
ESPECIALLY WITH TWO OF US LACKING EXPERI-ENCE.
LISTEN, TOKIKO!
WHY DON'T YOU DIRECT US?
WE'LL FOLLOW YOUR LEAD. HOW'S THAT SOUND?!
I KNOW...
...YOU CAN HANDLE THIS ALONE.
BUT IF YOU DO, THE YOUNGSTERS...
...WILL MISS OUT ON A VALUABLE LESSON.
YOSHI-MORI...
WHAT DO YOU THINK?
I, UH...
WHATEVER WILL WORK BEST...

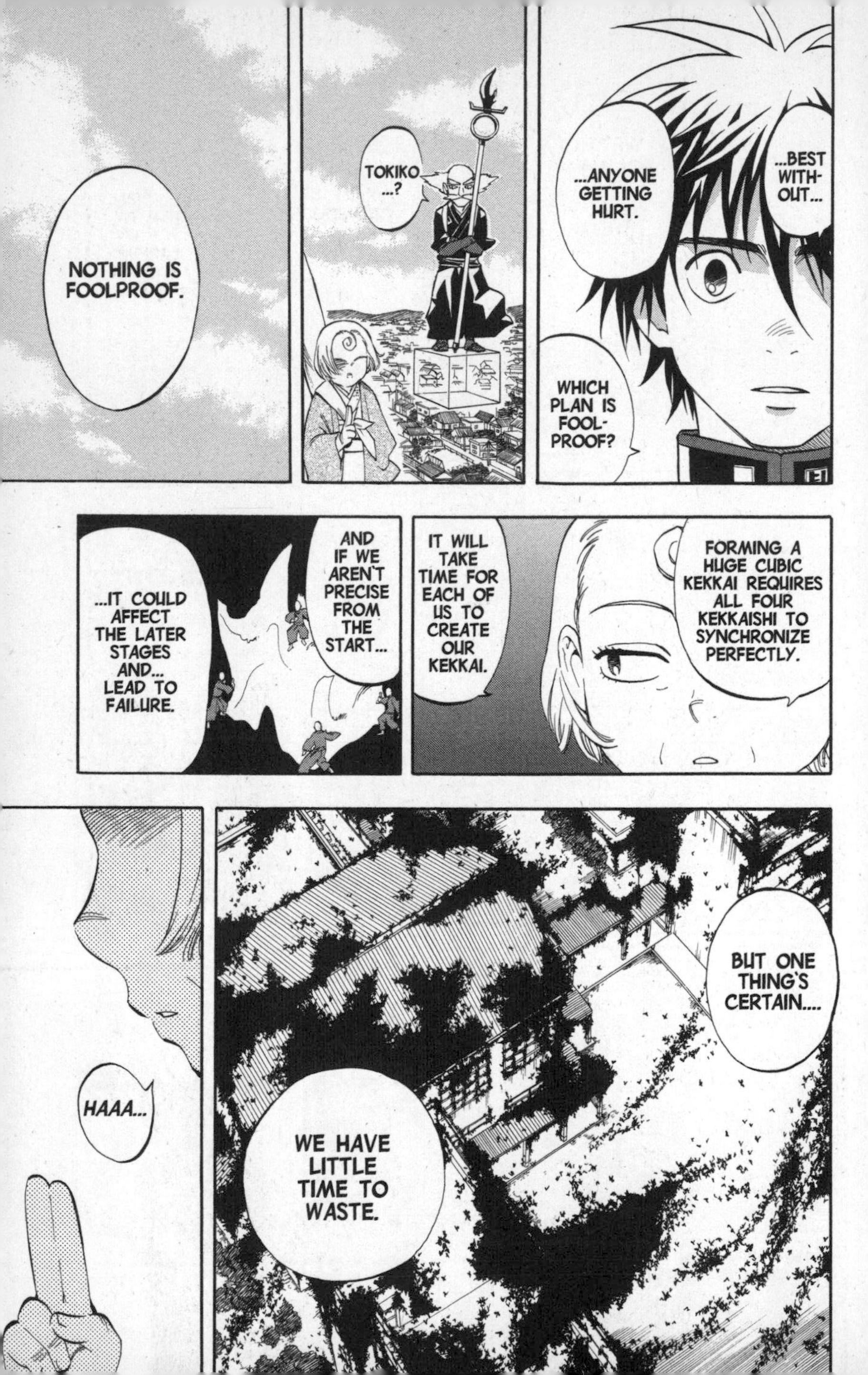
...BEST WITHOUT...
...ANYONE GETTING HURT.
WHICH PLAN IS FOOLPROOF?
TOKIKO ...?
NOTHING IS FOOLPROOF.
FORMING A HUGE CUBIC KEKKAI REQUIRES ALL FOUR KEKKAISHI TO SYNCHRONIZE PERFECTLY.
IT WILL TAKE TIME FOR EACH OF US TO CREATE OUR KEKKAI.
AND IF WE AREN'T PRECISE FROM THE START...
...IT COULD AFFECT THE LATER STAGES AND... LEAD TO FAILURE.
BUT ONE THING'S CERTAIN....
WE HAVE LITTLE TIME TO WASTE.
HAAA...

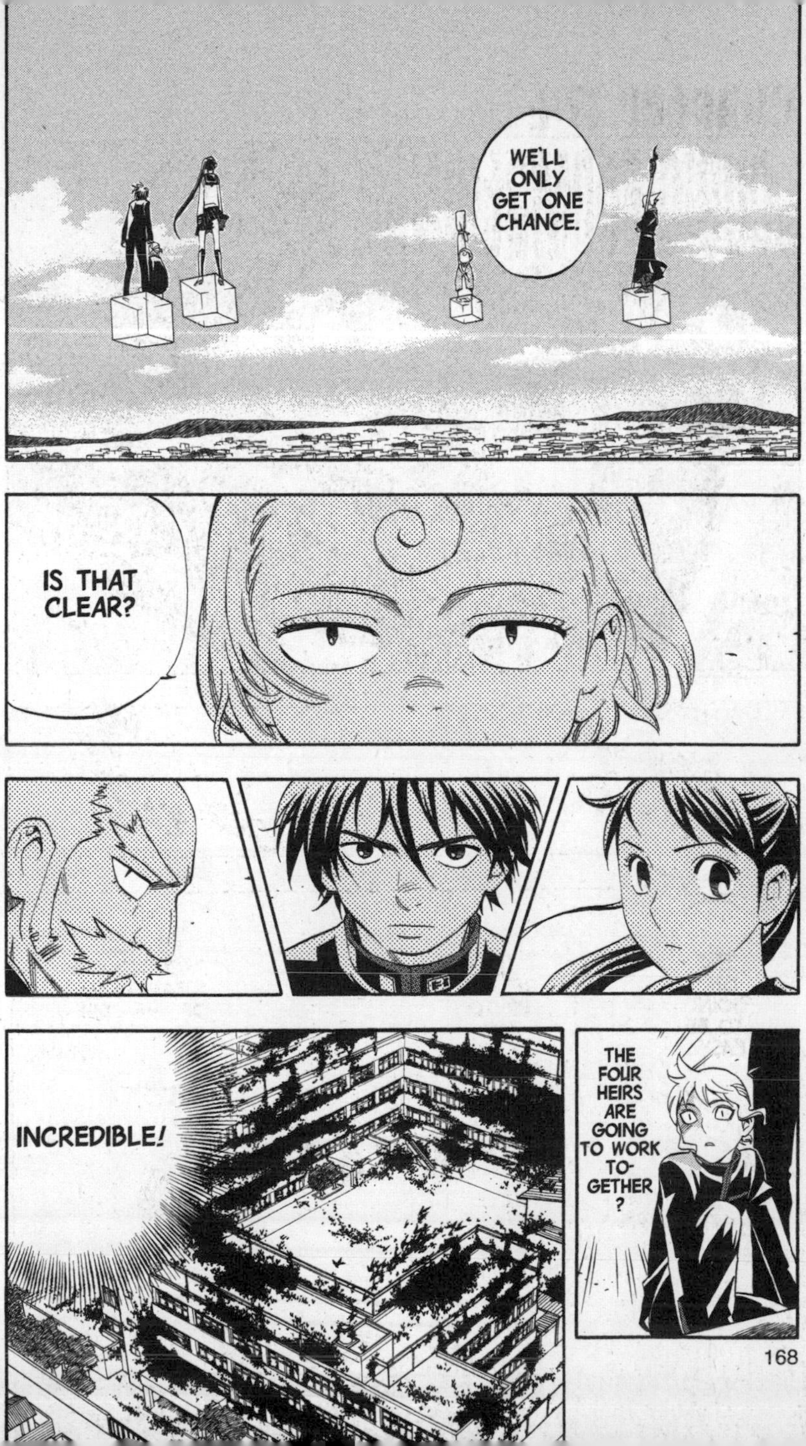
WE'LL ONLY GET ONE CHANCE.
IS THAT CLEAR?
THE FOUR HEIRS ARE GOING TO WORK TO-GETHER?
INCREDIBLE!

Chapter 174: Cubic Formation

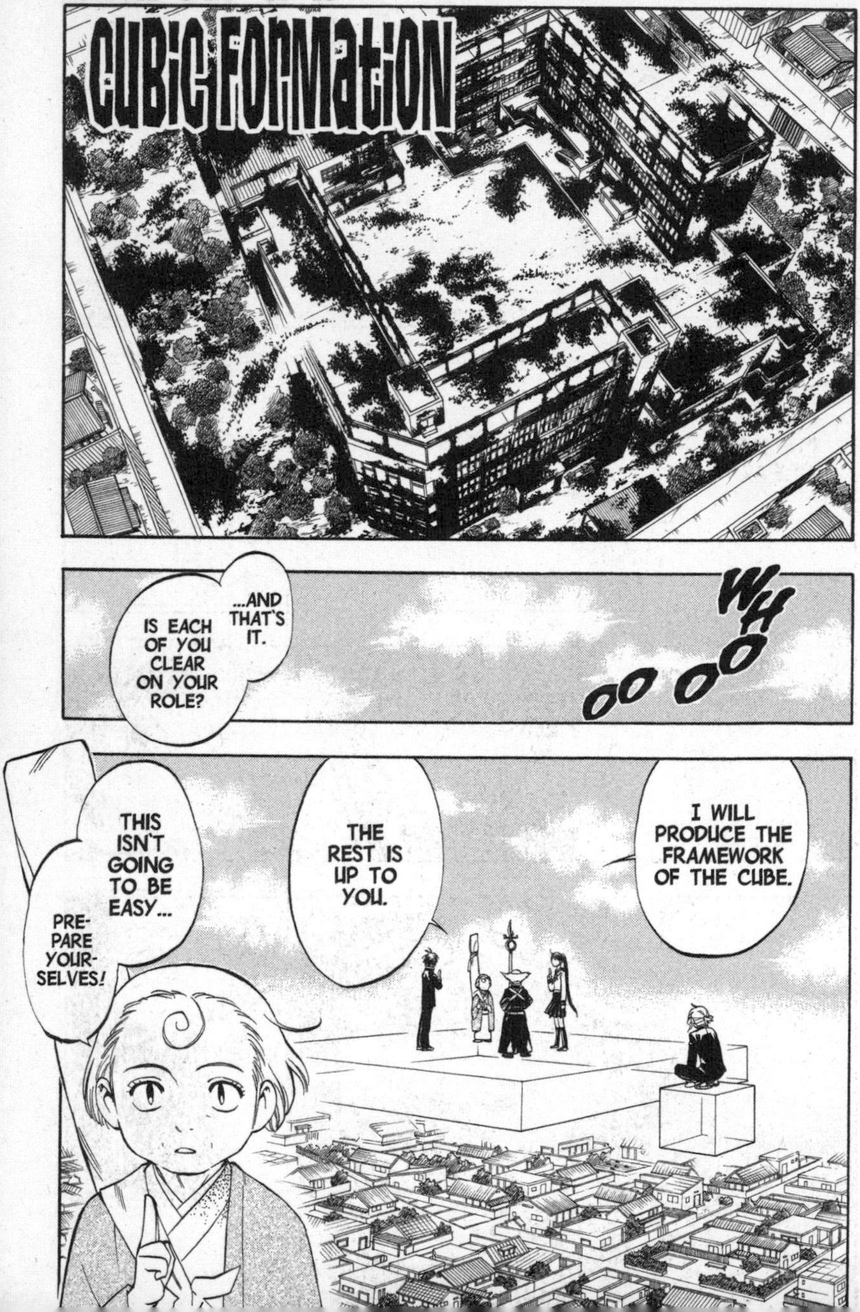
WHOOOOO
...AND THAT'S IT.
IS EACH OF YOU CLEAR ON YOUR ROLE?
I WILL PRODUCE THE FRAMEWORK OF THE CUBE.
THE REST IS UP TO YOU.
THIS ISN'T GOING TO BE EASY...
PREPARE YOURSELVES!

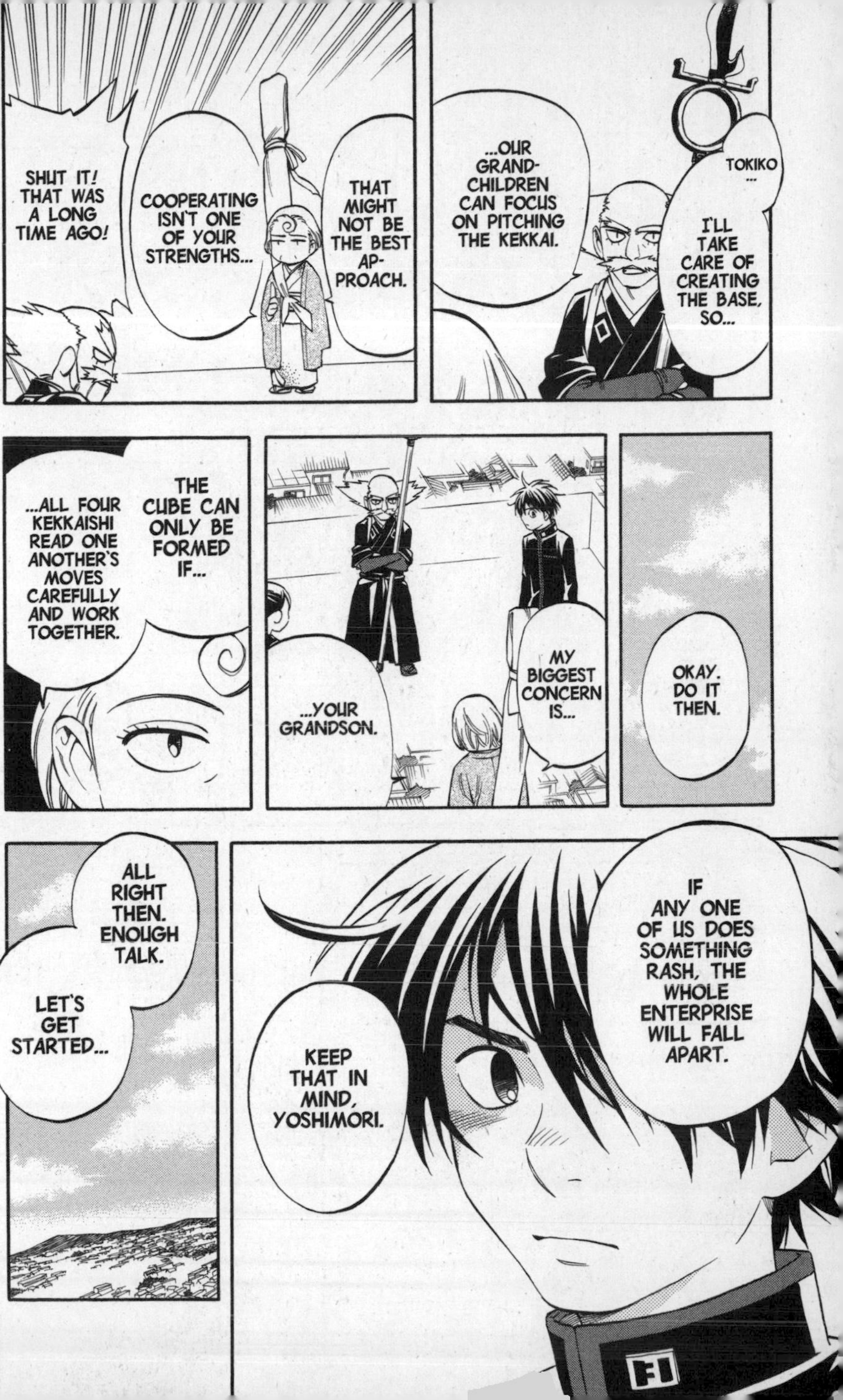
TOKIKO...
I'LL TAKE CARE OF CREATING THE BASE, SO...
...OUR GRAND-CHILDREN CAN FOCUS ON PITCHING THE KEKKAI.
THAT MIGHT NOT BE THE BEST AP-PROACH.
COOPERATING ISN'T ONE OF YOUR STRENGTHS...
SHUT IT! THAT WAS A LONG TIME AGO!
OKAY. DO IT THEN.
MY BIGGEST CONCERN IS...
...YOUR GRANDSON.
THE CUBE CAN ONLY BE FORMED IF...
...ALL FOUR KEKKAISHI READ ONE ANOTHER'S MOVES CAREFULLY AND WORK TOGETHER.
IF ANY ONE OF US DOES SOMETHING RASH, THE WHOLE ENTERPRISE WILL FALL APART.
KEEP THAT IN MIND, YOSHIMORI.
ALL RIGHT THEN. ENOUGH TALK.
LET'S GET STARTED...

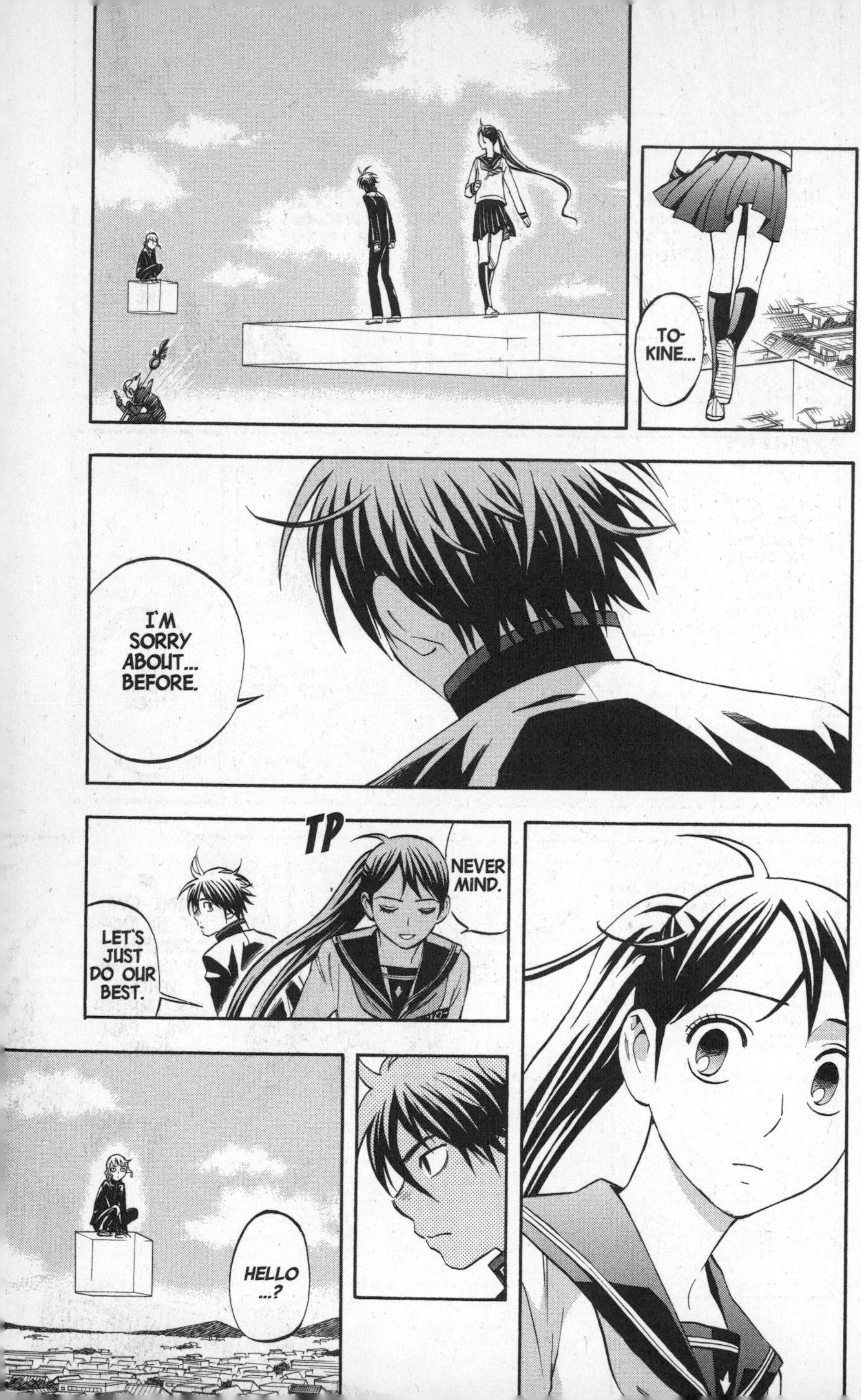
TO-KINE...
I'M SORRY ABOUT... BEFORE.
TP
NEVER MIND.
LET'S JUST DO OUR BEST.
HELLO ...?

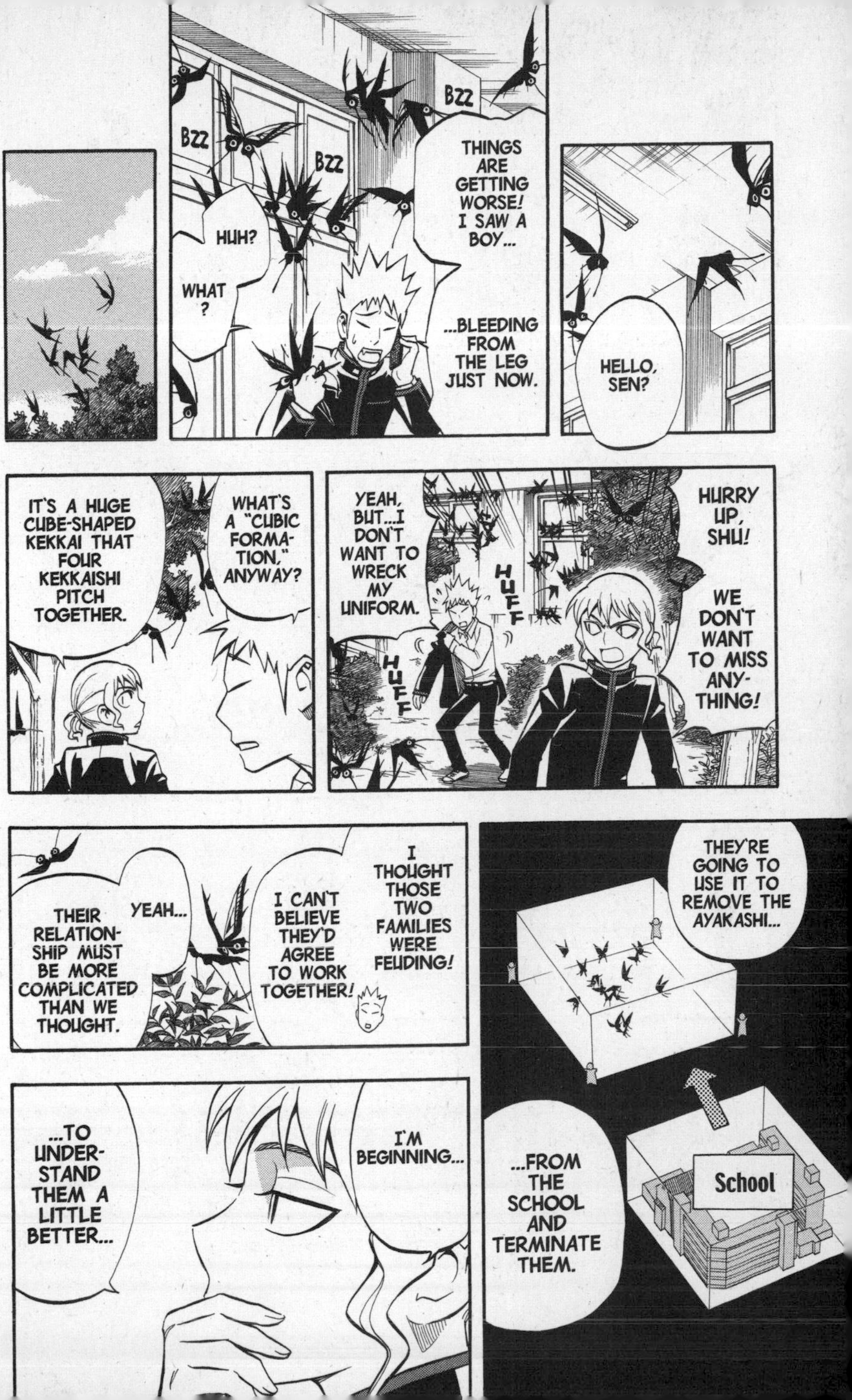
HELLO, SEN?
BZZ
THINGS ARE GETTING WORSE! I SAW A BOY...
BZZ
BZZ
HUH?
...BLEEDING FROM THE LEG JUST NOW.
WHAT?
HURRY UP, SHU!
WE DON'T WANT TO MISS ANYTHING!
YEAH, BUT...I DON'T WANT TO WRECK MY UNIFORM.
HUFF
HUFF
WHAT'S A "CUBIC FORMATION," ANYWAY?
IT'S A HUGE CUBE-SHAPED KEKKAI THAT FOUR KEKKAISHI PITCH TOGETHER.
THEY'RE GOING TO USE IT TO REMOVE THE AYAKASHI...
...FROM THE SCHOOL AND TERMINATE THEM.
School
I THOUGHT THOSE TWO FAMILIES WERE FEUDING!
I CAN'T BELIEVE THEY'D AGREE TO WORK TOGETHER!
YEAH...
THEIR RELATIONSHIP MUST BE MORE COMPLICATED THAN WE THOUGHT.
I'M BEGINNING...
...TO UNDERSTAND THEM A LITTLE BETTER...

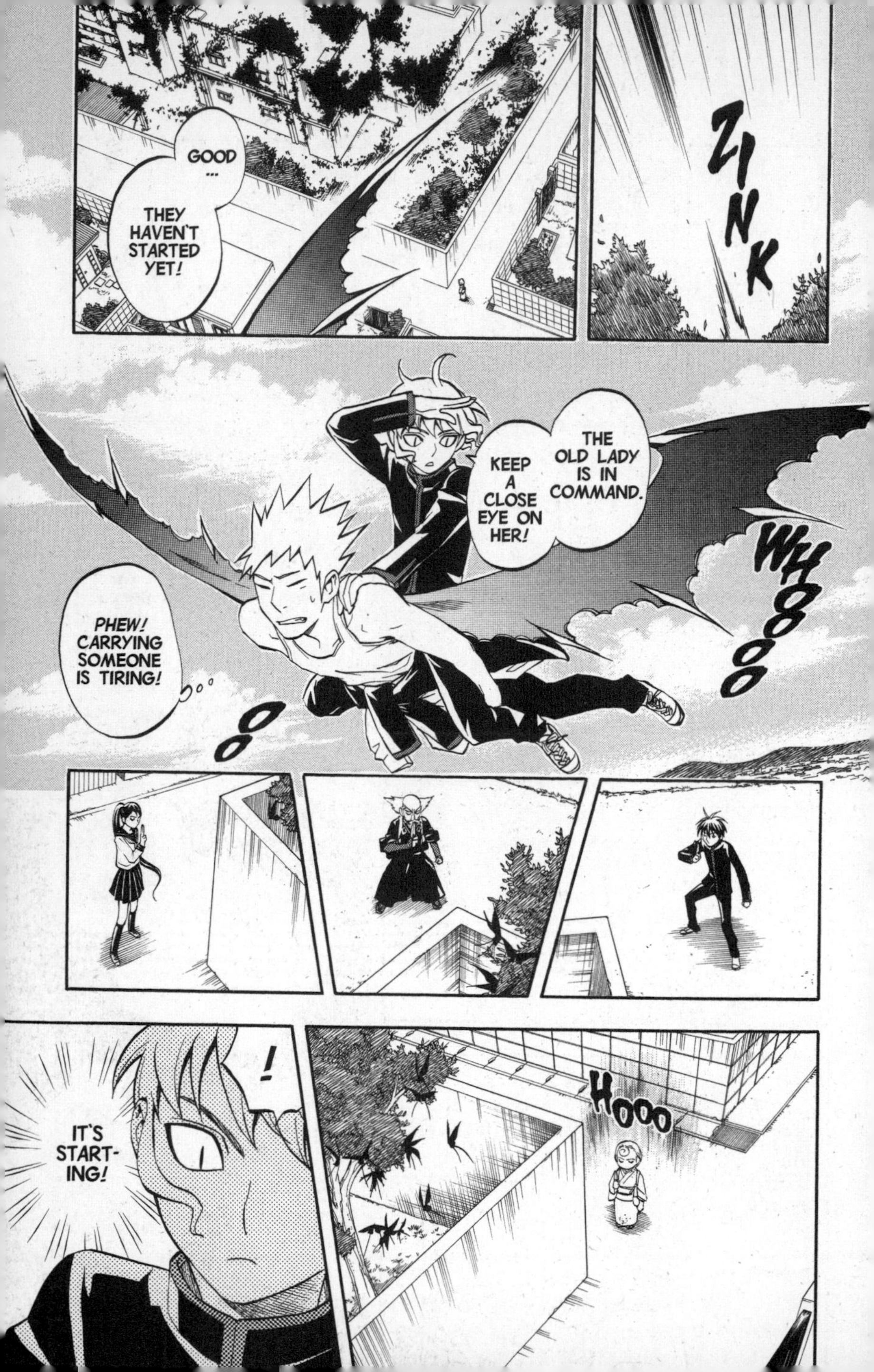
ZINK
GOOD ... THEY HAVEN'T STARTED YET!
THE OLD LADY IS IN COMMAND.
KEEP A CLOSE EYE ON HER!
WHOOOOO
PHEW! CARRYING SOMEONE IS TIRING!
OO
HOOO
!
IT'S START-ING!

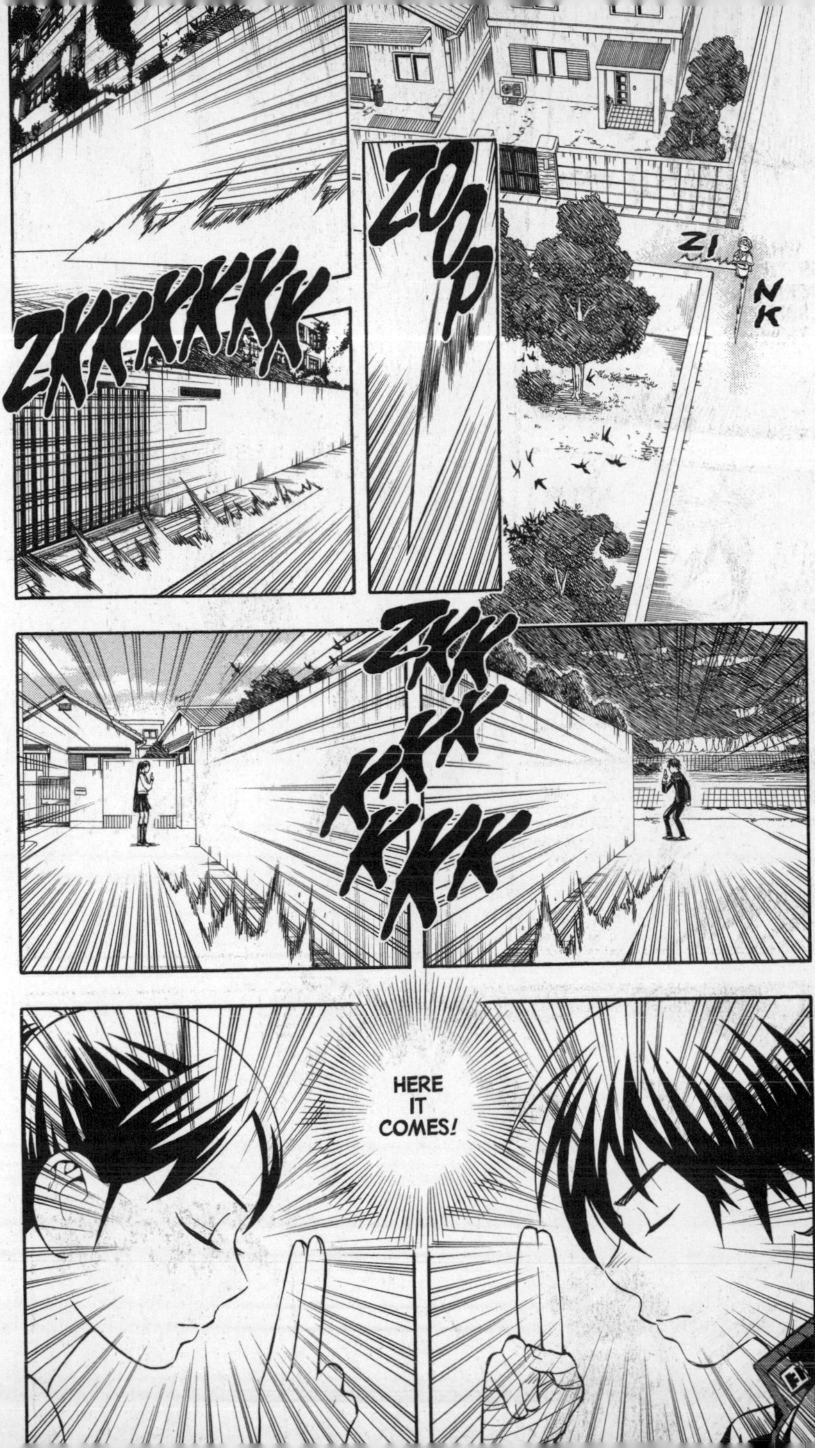
ZINK
ZOOOP
ZKKKKKK
ZKKKKKKKK
HERE IT COMES!

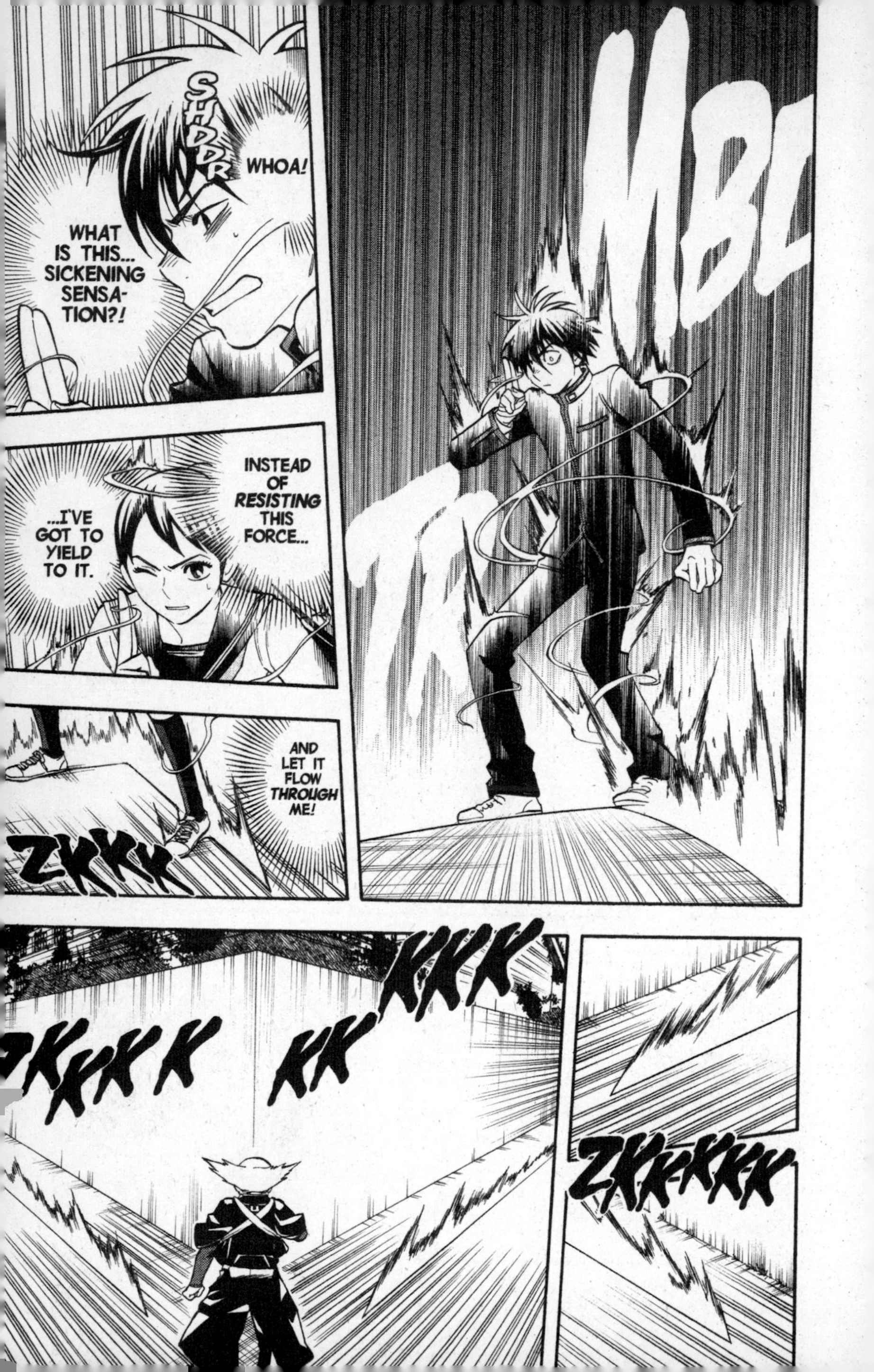
SHDDR
WHOA!
WHAT IS THIS... SICKENING SENSATION?!
INSTEAD OF *RESISTING* THIS FORCE...
...I'VE GOT TO YIELD TO IT.
AND LET IT FLOW *THROUGH* ME!
ZKKK
ZKK-KKK
ZKKKK K
KK
KKKK

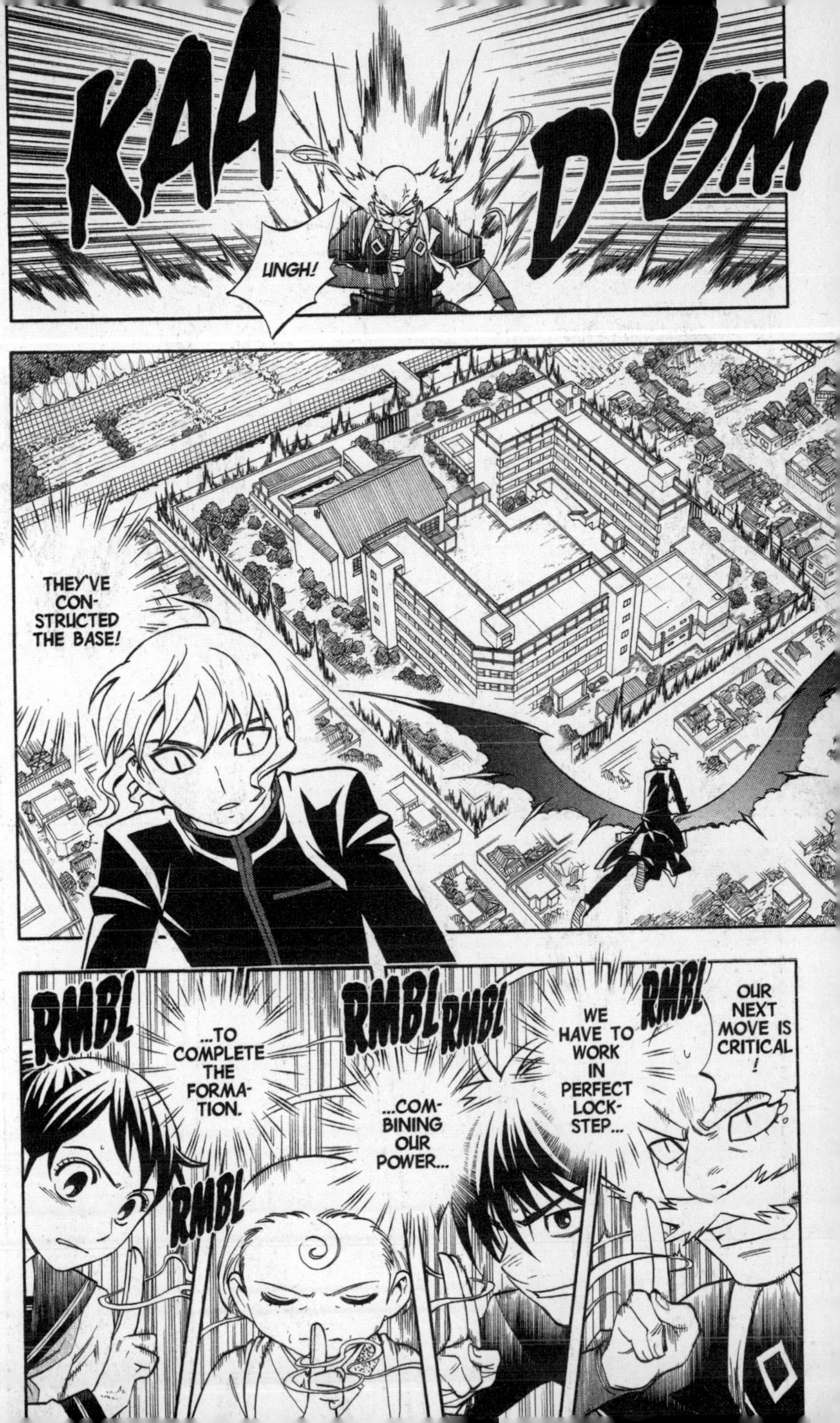
KAA DOOM
UNGH!
THEY'VE CON-STRUCTED THE BASE!
RMBL
OUR NEXT MOVE IS CRITICAL!
WE HAVE TO WORK IN PERFECT LOCK-STEP...
RMBL RMBL
...COM-BINING OUR POWER...
...TO COMPLETE THE FORMA-TION.
RMBL
RMBL

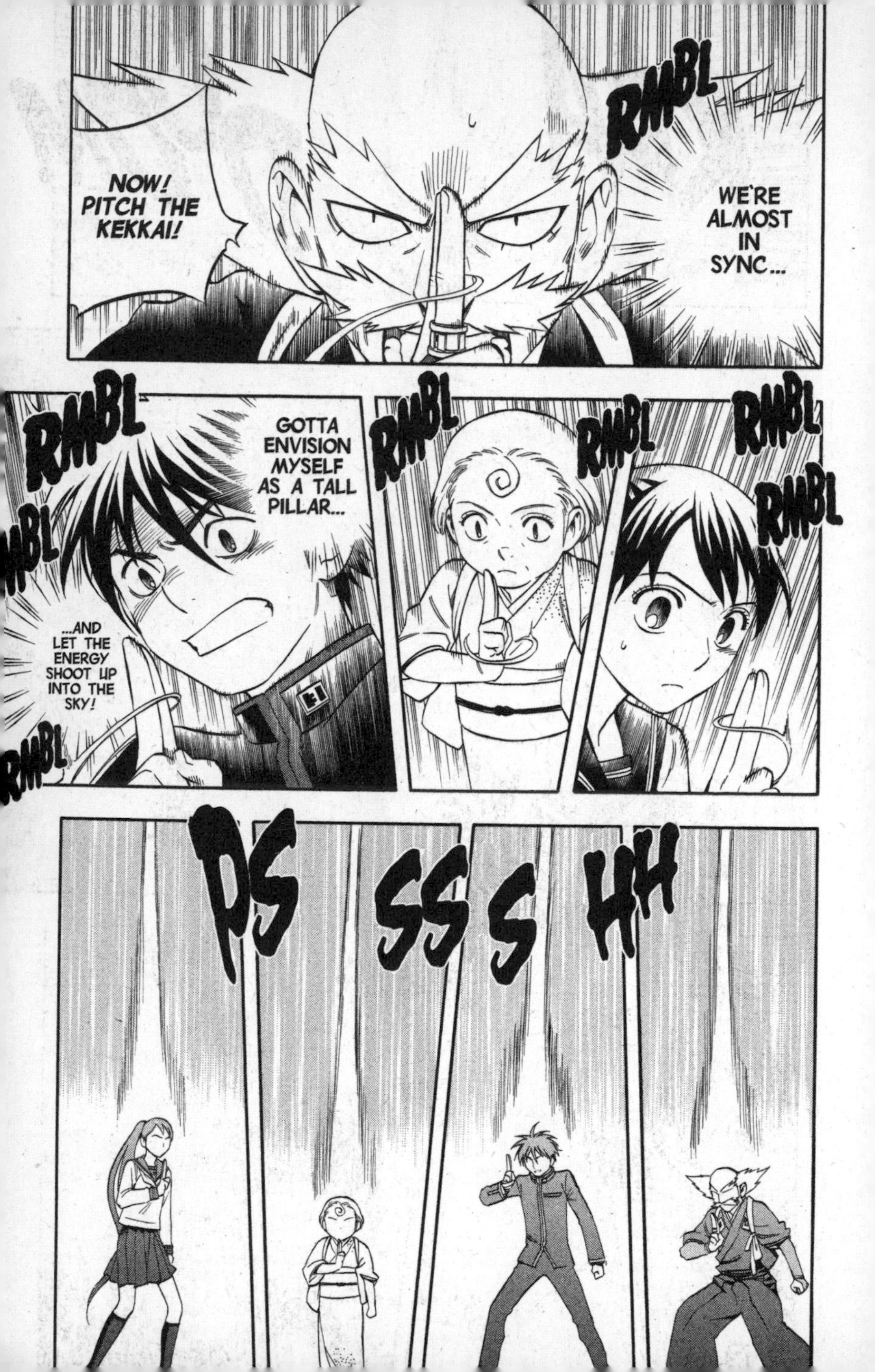
RMBL
WE'RE ALMOST IN SYNC...
NOW! PITCH THE KEKKAI!
RMBL
RMBL
RMBL
RMBL
RMBL
GOTTA ENVISION MYSELF AS A TALL PILLAR...
MBL
...AND LET THE ENERGY SHOOT UP INTO THE SKY!
RMBL
PSSSSHH

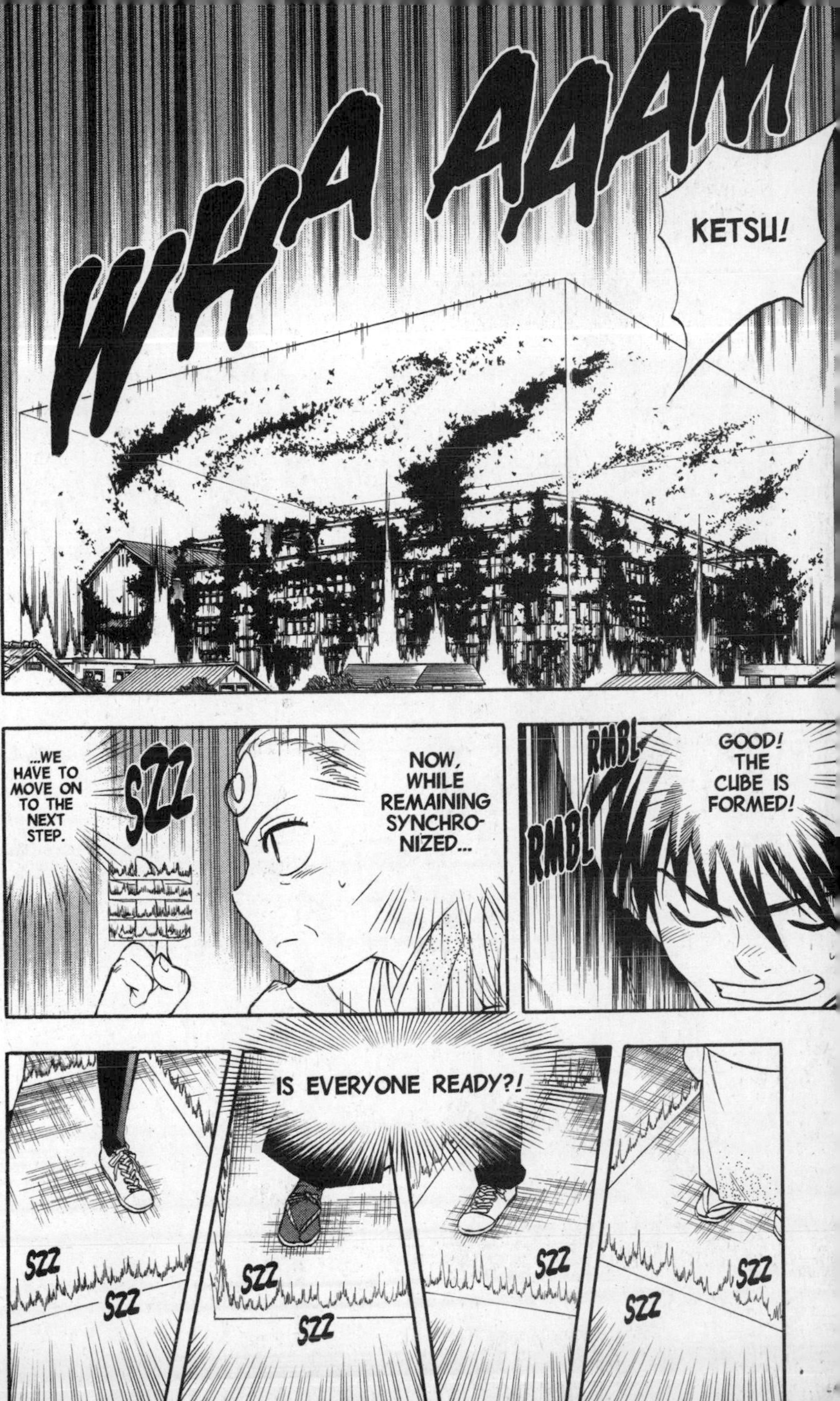
KETSU!
WHAAAAM
GOOD! THE CUBE IS FORMED!
RMBL
RMBL
NOW, WHILE REMAINING SYNCHRO-NIZED...
...WE HAVE TO MOVE ON TO THE NEXT STEP.
SZZ
IS EVERYONE READY?!
SZZ
SZZ
SZZ
SZZ
SZZ
SZZ
SZZ

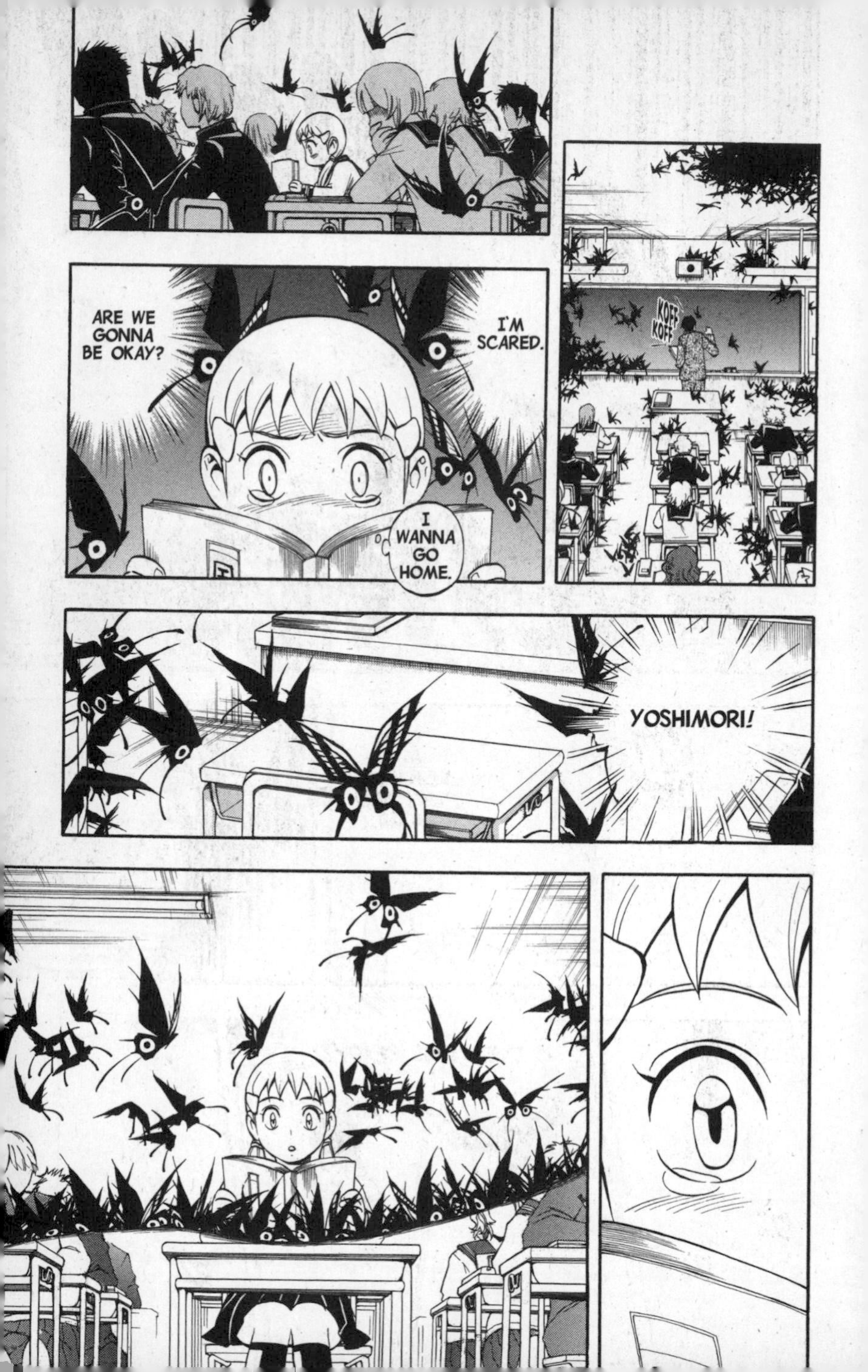
KOFF KOFF
I'M SCARED.
ARE WE GONNA BE OKAY?
I WANNA GO HOME.
YOSHIMORI!

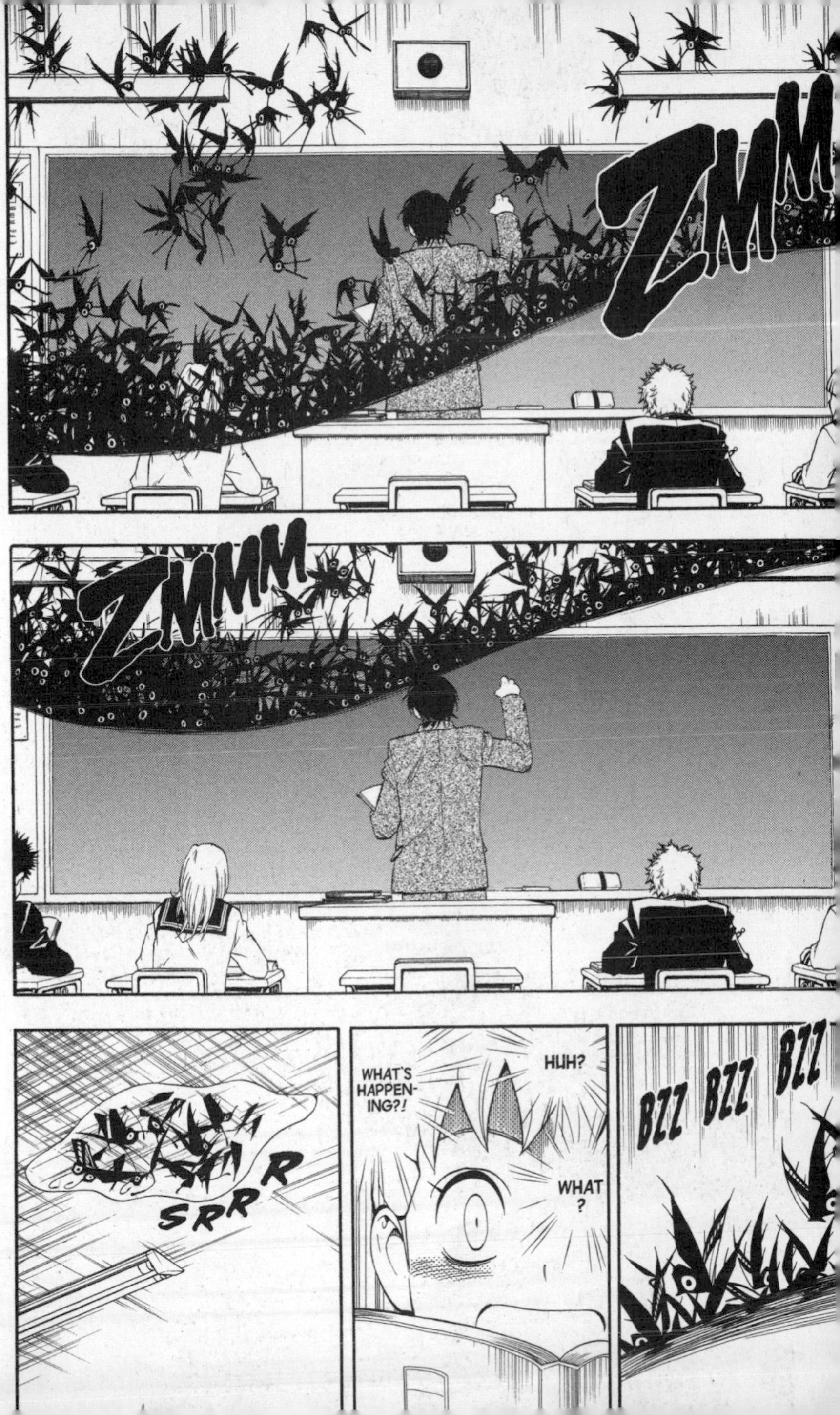
ZMMM
ZMMM
BZZ BZZ BZZ
HUH?
WHAT'S HAPPEN-ING?!
WHAT?
SRRR

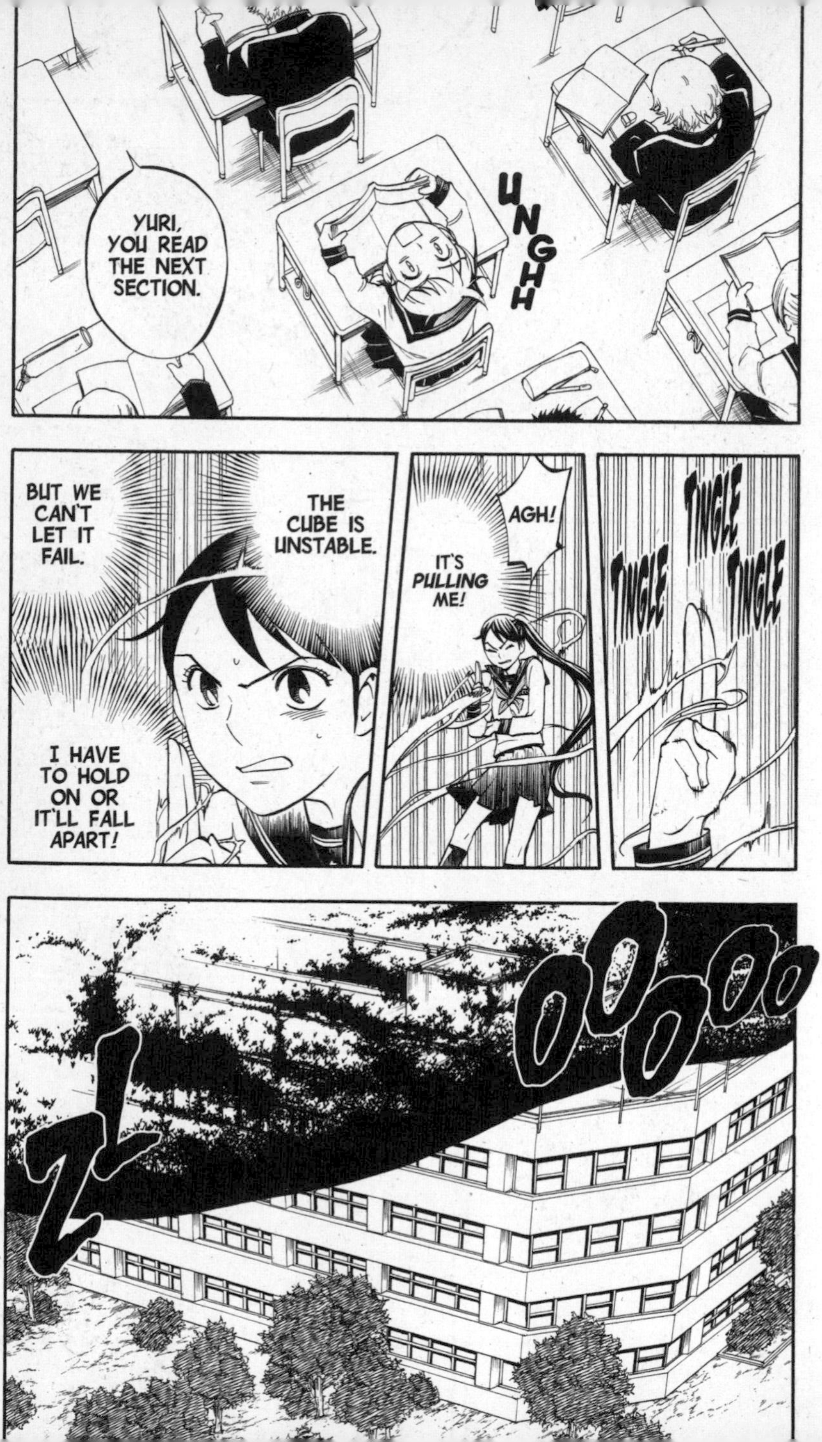
UNGHH
YURI, YOU READ THE NEXT SECTION.
TINGLE TINGLE TINGLE TINGLE
AGH!
IT'S PULLING ME!
THE CUBE IS UNSTABLE.
BUT WE CAN'T LET IT FAIL.
I HAVE TO HOLD ON OR IT'LL FALL APART!
ZZOOOOOO

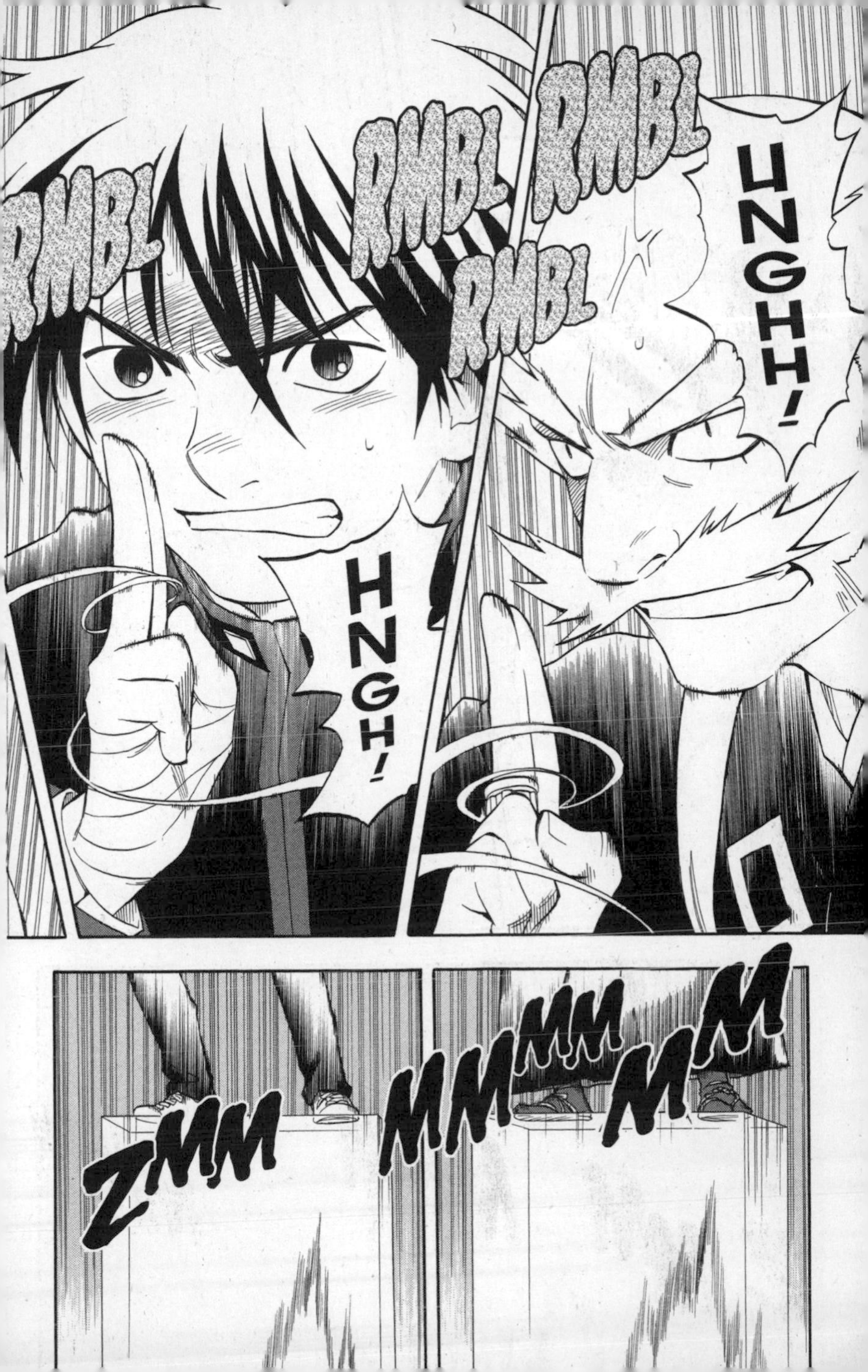
RMBL
RMBL
UNGH!
RMBL
RMBL
HNGH!
ZMM MMMMM MMM

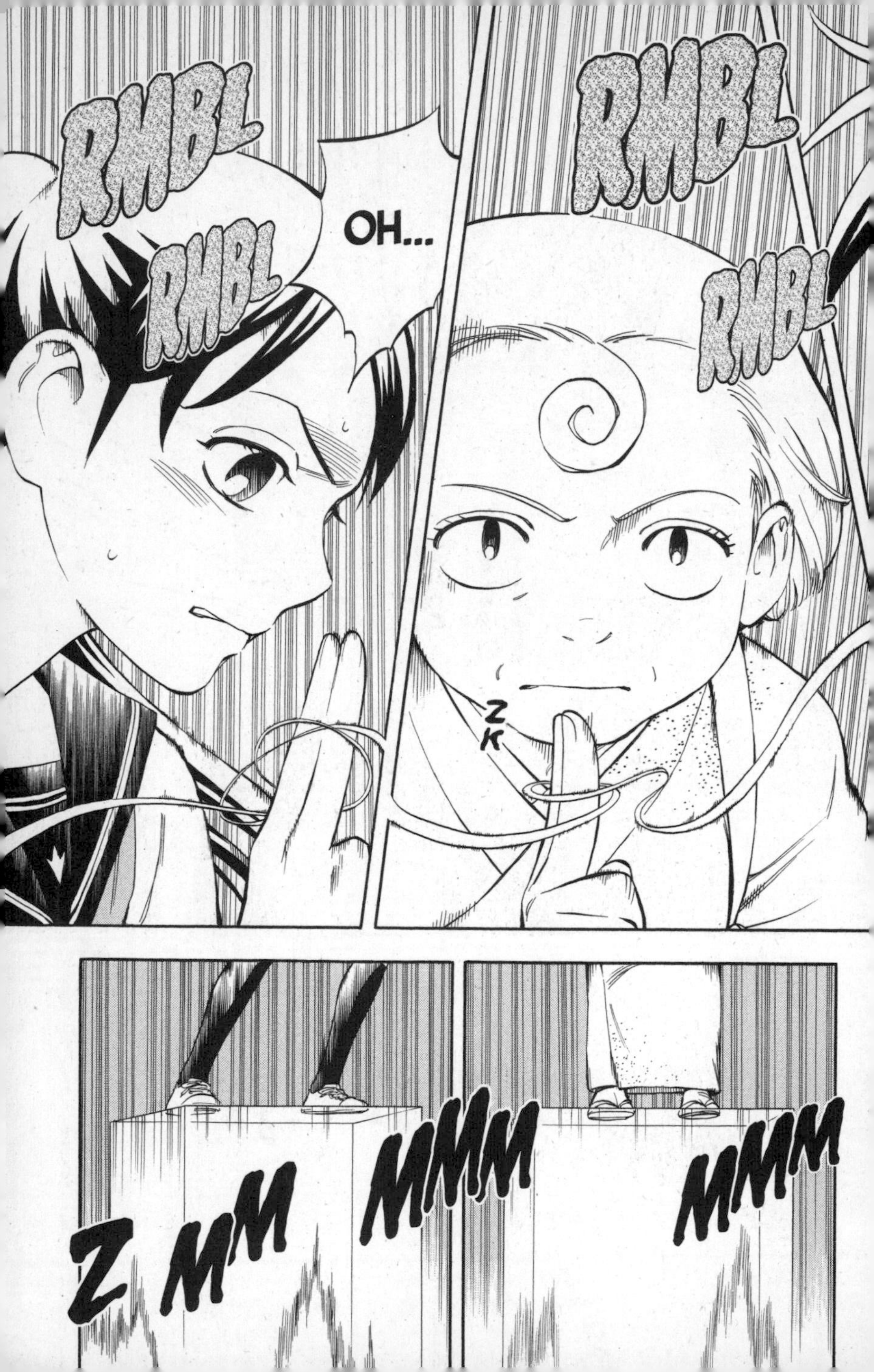
RMBL
RMBL
ZK
OH...
RMBL
RMBL
MMM
MMM
Z MM

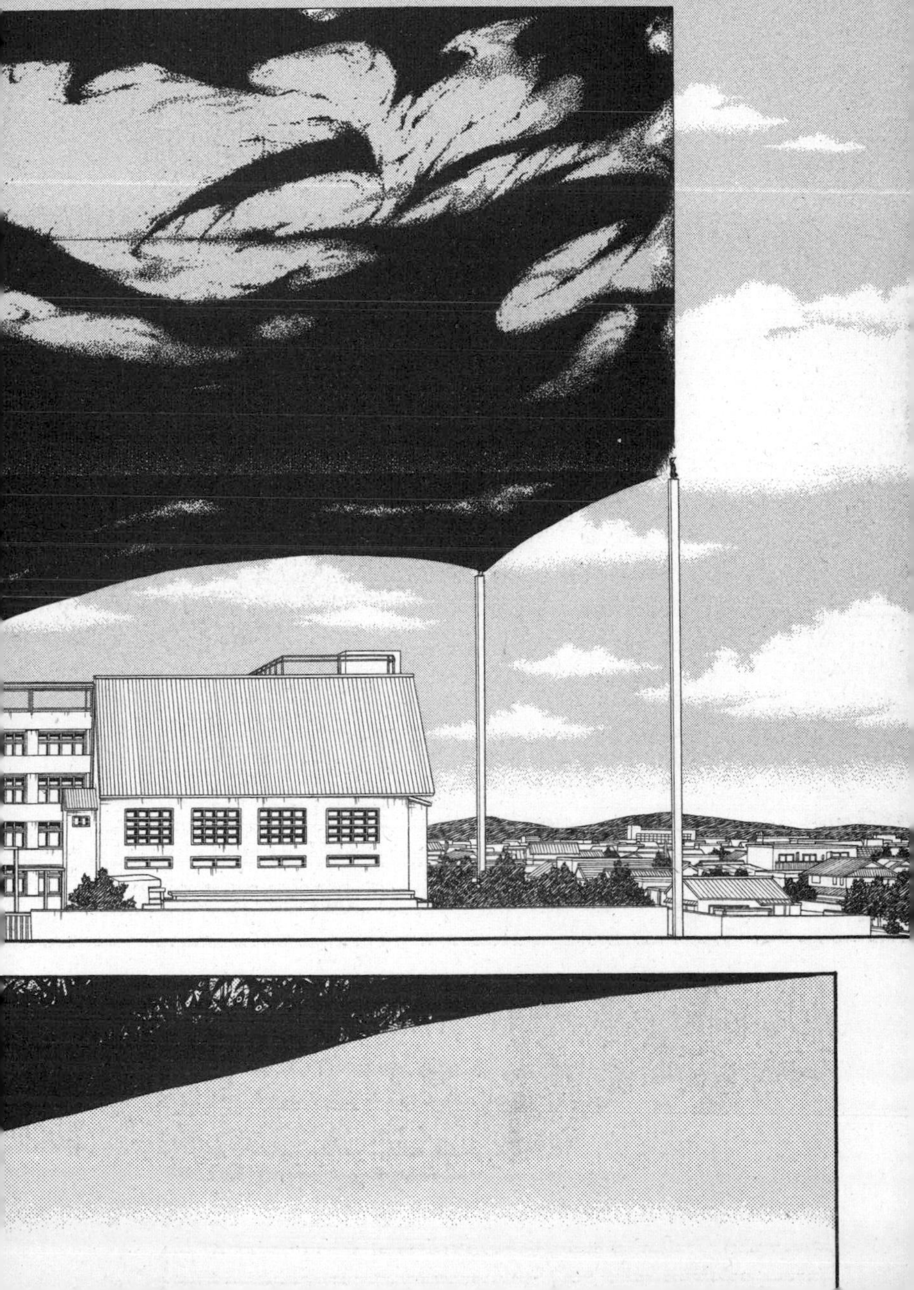

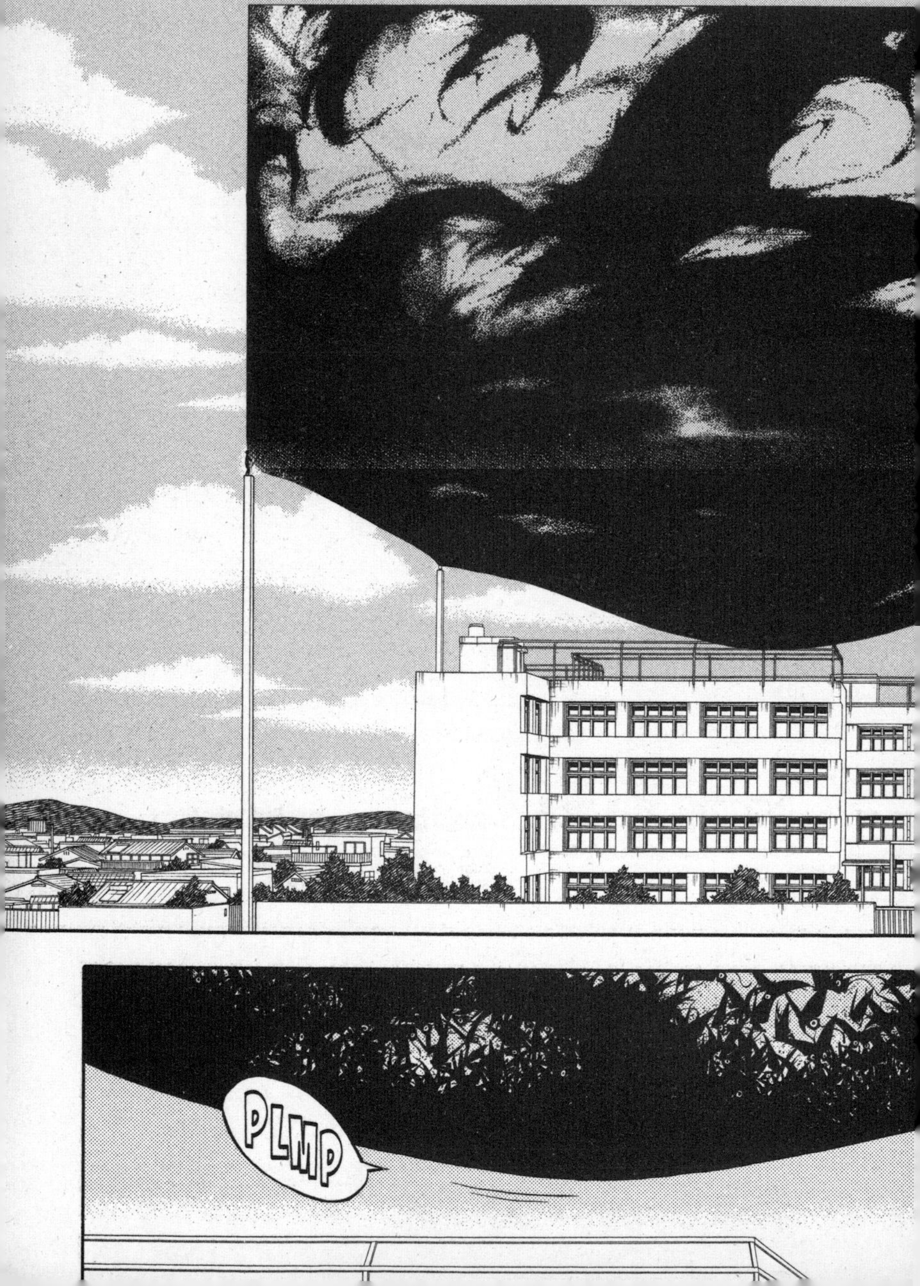
PLMP

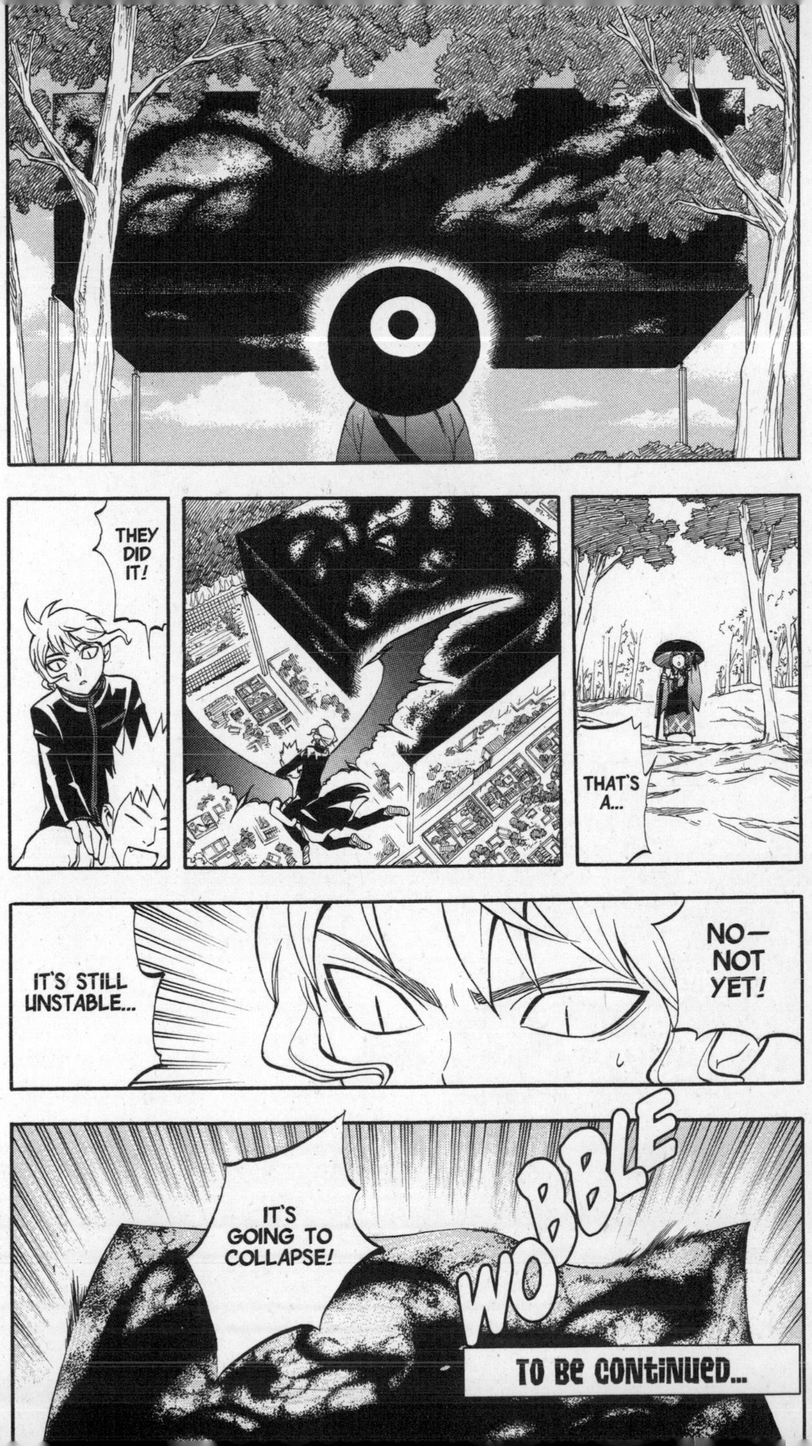
THAT'S A...
THEY DID IT!
NO— NOT YET!
IT'S STILL UNSTABLE...
WOBBLE
IT'S GOING TO COLLAPSE!
TO BE CONTINUED...

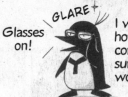

Glasses on!

GLARE

I wonder how myopia correction surgery works.

I normally wear contact lenses.

MESSAGE FROM YELLOW TANABE

I am nearsighted. I can't live without eyeglasses or contact lenses. My nearsightedness didn't come from too much reading of novels and manga. I think I was already myopic when I was a first-grader. Tokyo is an earthquake-prone area. Should anything happen, I must not forget my eyeglasses when I evacuate.

KEKKAISHI

VOLUME 18
SHONEN SUNDAY EDITION
STORY AND ART BY YELLOW TANABE

Translation/Yuko Sawada
Touch-up Art & Lettering/Stephen Dutro
Cover Design & Graphic Layout/Julie Behn
Editors/Ian Robertson & Annette Roman

VP, Production/Alvin Lu
VP, Publishing Licensing/Rika Inouye
VP, Sales & Product Marketing/Gonzalo Ferreyra
VP, Creative/Linda Espinosa
Publisher/Hyoe Narita

KEKKAISHI 18 by Yellow TANABE © 2007 Yellow TANABE
All rights reserved.
Original Japanese edition published in 2007 by Shogakukan Inc., Tokyo.
The stories, characters and incidents mentioned in this publication are
entirely fictional.

The rights of the author(s) of the work(s) in this publication to be
so identified have been asserted in accordance with the Copyright,
Designs and Patents Act 1988. A CIP catalogue record for this book is
available from the British Library.

Printed in the U.S.A.

Published by VIZ Media, LLC
P.O. Box 77010
San Francisco, CA 94107

10 9 8 7 6 5 4 3 2 1
First printing, August 2009

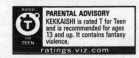

PARENTAL ADVISORY
KEKKAISHI is rated T for Teen
and is recommended for ages
13 and up. It contains fantasy
violence.
ratings.viz.com

www.viz.com

WWW.SHONENSUNDAY.COM

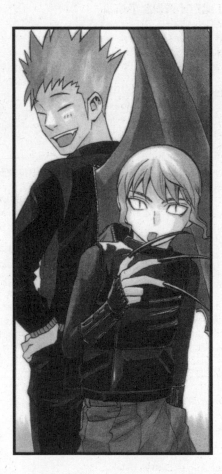

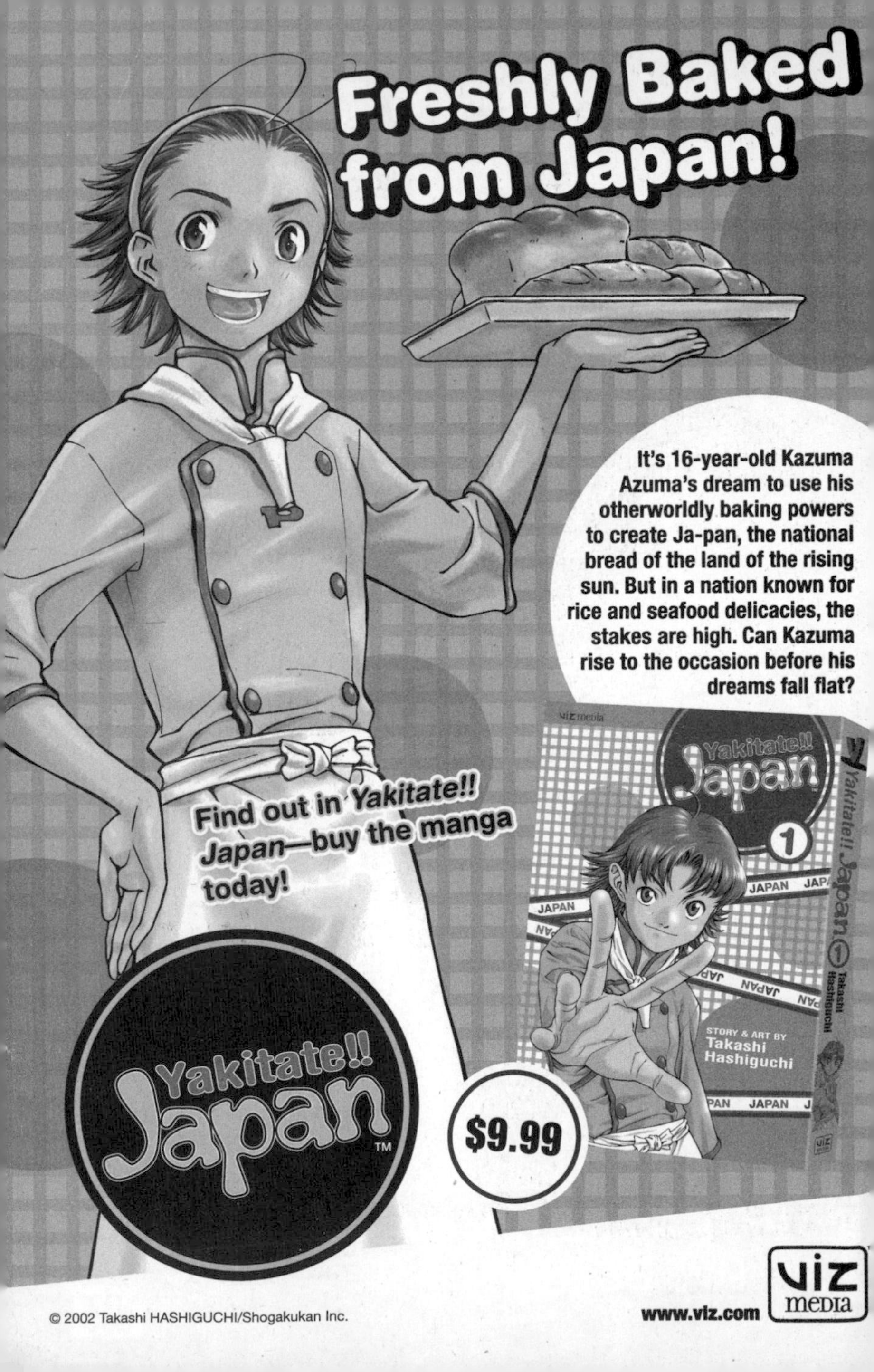

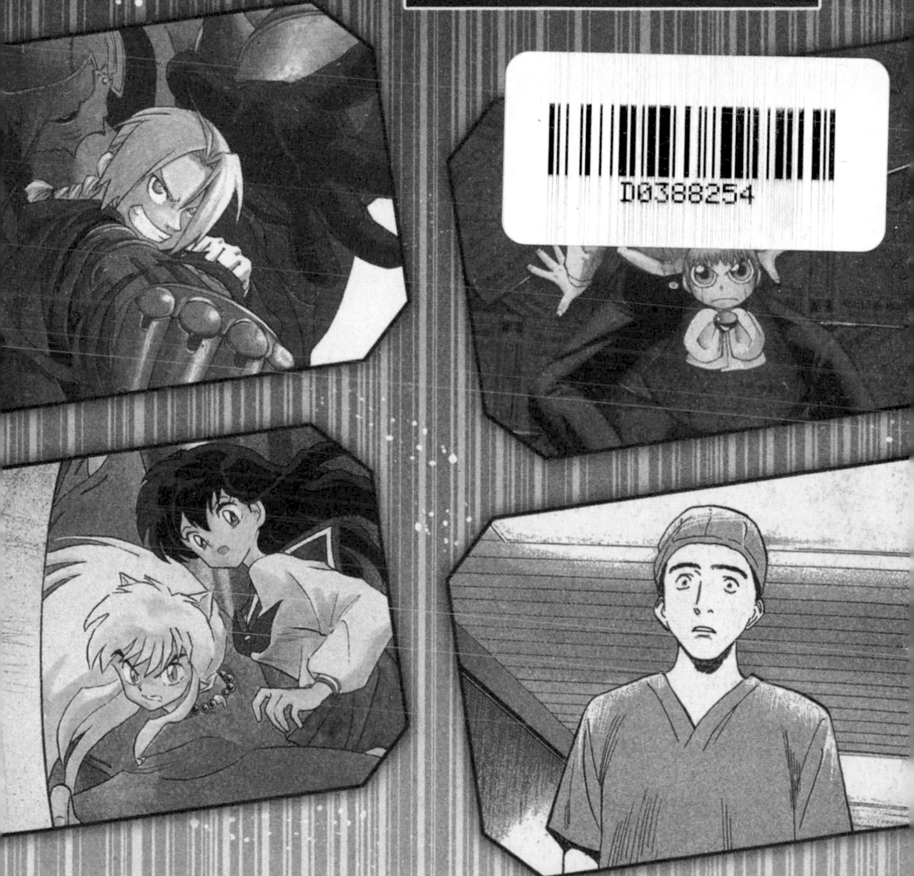